D0167325

Two Nuts in Italy

Sue Ellen Haning

iUniverse, Inc.
Bloomington

iUniverse Star
an iUniverse, Inc. imprint

iUniverse books may be ordered through booksellers or by contacting:

iUniverse
1663 Liberty Drive
Bloomington, IN 47403
www.iuniverse.com
1-800-Authors (1-800-288-4677)

ISBN: 978-1-936236-69-5 (sc)
ISBN: 978-1-936236-70-1 (ebook)

Library of Congress Control Number: 2011906672

Printed in the United States of America

iUniverse rev. date: 6/14/2011

This book is dedicated to Jarrod, Jake, and Jenny. Thank you for your brilliant inspiration.

I love you.

Acknowledgments

Thank you to my readers Betsey Hale, Jean Lewis Koch, and Kathy Lee for your faithful friendship and work on this book.

Thank you to friends who offered suggestions and daily encouraged me, to the Italian people who unselfishly shared themselves, to the Starbucks at Eighth and University Avenue in Lubbock, Texas, where I wrote this entire book, to Debbie Burk, Lydia Eubank, Margaret Nagy Dobbs, Janie Harms, Jean Lewis Koch, Susanne Wiley, and Natalie Goldberg, to Chip Polk for the art cover, and to Jenny for inviting me on the trip of a lifetime.

Table of Contents

Chapter One	You're Nuts	1
Chapter Two	We're Off!	14
Chapter Three	Thirty-five Thousand Feet	25
Chapter Four	Venice	36
Chapter Five	Testing the Plan	49
Chapter Six	Tattoos and Implants	62
Chapter Seven	Beauty and the Priest	78
Chapter Eight	Dong Juans and Beached Whales	90
Chapter Nine	Fascism and Sea Tomatoes	104
Chapter Ten	Buff Grandmas	119
Chapter Eleven	Lunar Landing Module	136
Chapter Twelve	American Women Escape Italian Asylum	149
Chapter Thirteen	The Answer Is No	166
Chapter Fourteen	Thieves	186
Chapter Fifteen	A Scare	201
Chapter Sixteen	Sleeping With An Italian	218
Chapter Seventeen	Has Anyone Seen George Clooney?	231

Chapter Eighteen	On My Own	245
Chapter Nineteen	Died and Gone to Heaven	257
Chapter Twenty	Two More Weeks	272
Chapter Twenty-one	A New Travel Partner	290
Chapter Twenty-two	Italy Again	309
Chapter Twenty-three	Bolgheri	325
Chapter Twenty-four	A New Friend	344
Chapter Twenty-five	Reality	357
Epilogue		365

Chapter One

You're Nuts

"You want to do what? Are you nuts? Don't the Europeans hate us? What about terrorists? Oh, no, I'll be worried sick about you," exclaimed an incredulous friend. I felt the need to discuss this sudden opportunity with my peers, but maybe I could just send them an e-mail after the fact. I hung up the phone, took a deep breath, and called another friend and another and another, to be met with, "Remember, it is Jenny who is twenty-one, not you!" Howls of laughter followed, "You are going to carry a pack on your back all summer? A reality check is in order here." Then I heard a reassuring comment from my friend Robin when I explained the invitation extended me by my daughter Jenny to join her backpacking through Italy for the three summer months. "Why not? I'd do it," she assured.

"Really?" I asked. Then Lydia and Janie, concerned about my eighty-eight-year-old mother I had been caring for the past two years, sent me soaring back to reality with, "But who will care for your mother?" Others were not so encouraging, and the word "nuts" kept coming up in conversations in reference to the idea or to me. The idea thrilled me, and that thrill surprised me, since foolishness and frivolity are not normally a part of my nature, as evidenced by the term of endearment Jenny bestowed on me when she was fifteen. During her farewell speech the night she relinquished her

1

crown at the local beauty pageant, she fondly referred to me as, "my mother, the Terminator." I looked around to see confused faces, both male and female. After all, what loving daughter labels her mother "The Terminator?" Thank God, she gave a brief explanation to the perplexed crowd. "My mother is an expert at removing all "social" blocks to my accomplishing the goals set for me during my reign," she said, then continuing with her beauty queen smile, "She is unequaled in making sure all daily tasks are completed, taking care of business, and forging ahead, conquering all that needs vanquishing." I was sure that every person in the room who looked at me saw Arnold Schwarzenegger. Suddenly my five-foot-four-inch formerly solid frame spilled into a puddle beneath my chair. While today we laugh at this, Jenny still introduces me occasionally as "my mom, the Terminator." It works well with any guys she's not too interested in.

My twenty-one-year-old daughter wants me to spend the summer with her. The thought still thrills me, and I take it as a great compliment. Each time I think about the possibilities of such a trip, I smile. I've been a teacher for thirty-five years and always sought knowledge. Now I can lose myself across the ocean. I can learn things by accident. I want adventure to find me. I want to be surrounded by things I don't understand and maybe even experience hardship. I want to relinquish control and surrender serendipitously. I want to live for three months with only what I can carry on my back.

Ahhhh, the pleasures of midlife! Usually with midlife comes empty nest syndrome. I have it. "Empty nest" is a phenomenon. It's scary, sad, and shocking, while also enlightening and challenging. It forces stay-at-home moms to re-invent themselves. For me, it is hard to shake the feelings of loneliness and uselessness I experience with children no longer needing me on a daily basis. At times, I feel obsolete, like my worth is challenged. My children have all moved away, and it's painful to love someone who is away—you can no longer share in their daily lives. With no children in the house, my thoughts turn inward, and realities I never before considered emerge, like *I'm free, I'm going to die, What do I do with my hands, Break this painful silence,* and then *No, I like the silence, no one notices me,* and other irrational imaginings. I have a chance to have another career. The challenge is going from full-time mom and teacher to whatever I want to become—artist, politician, bartender, landscaper, travel guru, writer, or welder. I have thoughts I didn't know I was capable of having because of this new position, but the mom-mode hangs on me. I can't shake it because I don't want to. If Jenny asks me to go with her, maybe she still needs me. Mom is the career that wins. I remember in my youth, the clock's hands seemed to drag along or not move at all, but once I hit my 50s, those same hands spin recklessly out of control, counting down the minutes until it is "my time." Would a three-month, devil-may-care trip abroad slow the hands?

In 1998, Jenny, her voice teacher, and I spent four days in Italy as part of a two-week, whirlwind trip through four European countries. Before this trip, we joined a world-wide organization for travelers called Servas. A list of available members, phone numbers, and personal information, was sent to us from the countries we planned to visit. Servas's members offered their homes to travelers who made prior arrangements with them. The stays were limited to one night unless the host extended it. We stayed in homes in Germany and Austria, and Jenny realized how much more she enjoyed these two countries because of the personal time we had with our host families. Jenny was fourteen and fell in love with romantic, slower-paced Italy. Curiosity had pinched her, and she wanted to experience Italy on a deeper level, to learn its culture. She vowed she would return to Italy one day and spend several months there. Now, at twenty-one, nothing could hold her back. Her plan was for us to take a backpack, little cash, no credit cards, stay in homes of Italians we did not know (or sleep on park benches if necessary), have no itinerary, keep to the small towns and countryside for the full cultural experience, take the opportunities given us to make things happen, and experience a summer of learning, adventures, and wonderful memories while just drifting with the wind. This was the idea that created disbelief in the minds of my friends, because once you reach the age of fifty-six, the world expects you to demonstrate reason, not reckless insanity, and staying with strangers in a country whose language we did not speak in the year 2005 screamed "Nuts-o."

I was going to be a hippie, a gypsy—or a nut. I passed up my first opportunity in the 1960s. I was too "good" or maybe too scared to spread my wings too far. I never smoked weed, dropped acid, or took part in the mind-altering excursions. I guess the issue was control. I could stop drinking, but I didn't know how far the "trip" might take me, which made "tripping" prospects scary. Now at my age, tapes ran through my mind daily. I was hearing "life is short, enjoy the moment," and it kept squeezing through every crack in my Terminator guard. My clock continued ticking, and my daughter was giving me the opportunity to test the limits of my comfort zone. Suddenly I couldn't get enough of the idea. The old songs ran continuously through my head. "It's been a long time since I rock and rolled," "Where have all the flowers gone," "There is a house in New Orleans," "Come on baby, light my fire." My thoughts were in a never-before-visited realm. The thought of wreckless adventures was lighting my fire. I must admit that traipsing through a foreign country with nothing but my faith, a backpack, and an overly confident twenty-one-year-old had never been a dream of mine, but just thinking about the possibilities made it a dream. People do this all the time, right? "Go for it," I screamed. One last adventure before the ole body wears out. My knees, which had given me trouble for fifteen years, had been behaving lately. My thoughts scared me. I even dreamed of swimming nude in the Mediterranean Sea. I'm the person who was always afraid to put the kids in the car and go without another adult on board. As a child, my father took us on well-planned, two-week sightseeing vacations, but this time there would be no plan. Nothing was out of the question. I embraced the thought that I could see everything with different eyes and leave all my beliefs and securities at home. *I want to risk! I want to be a young, or old, fool.* Of course, every time I saw my friends, the reasonable thoughts returned. "What if this" and "What if that," they quizzed. "What if you get hit by a car? What if they treat you badly because you're an American? What if you get sick? What if the two of you are separated and can't find each other? What if your passport is stolen?" "What ifs …" can warp you, and I couldn't deal with the word "if" any longer, so I beat "if" mercilessly until it was pummeled into oblivion. No more "ifs" in my vocabulary. Now I could get on with my plans. In my imagination, I could see the emerald, silver, and forest greens I remembered from our brief trip to Italy in '98. The fields of sunflowers waltzing in the Tuscan breeze tickled my thoughts. The juicy, red explosion of the world's finest tomatoes filled my mouth, as did the tough bread and tempting wines I remember as part of my experience long ago. "Yeah, why not," I told myself. So, one day during a daydream, I grabbed a date out of the air, May 25, chose Venice as our entry and departure city, and picked August 31 as our return flight, and bought plane tickets online for $835.98 each. We'd be sleeping three months and six days with no reservations. Next, I created an e-mail address to communicate our adventures and to send evidence of our continuing life to the worriers back home: twonutsinitaly@yahoo.com.

Beginning in February, Jenny spent day and night on the computer learning what she could about Italy, our summer home where we hope to be temporary locals. She found websites for travelers and created profiles for us. "We'll find places to stay with the members of these groups," she assured me. One was hospitalityclub.org and the other was couchsurfing.com. These are worldwide organizations of travel lovers and people wanting to make friends around the globe with the incentive to volunteer being cultural understanding. Jenny was more computer savvy than I and wasn't frustrated by the glitches that plagued me whenever I was in cyberspace, so I kept telling that monster in the back of my mind to shut up and trust Jenny to find beds to sleep in. Of course, when you're twenty-one everything is easy, including sleeping on park benches. "Are you nuts?" rang intermittently in my ears. I was trusting in something that wasn't logical—a three-month trip with no plan. One day, Jenny announced she had found us a place to stay in Cecina, a coastal town in Tuscany on the Tyrrenhian Sea. She had met a guy in an Italian chat room. He told her if we got to Cecina, he'd give us a place to stay. Something gripped the pit of my stomach. It is only March, and our tickets are for May 25. Anything can happen in two months, right? I could break my toe and not be able to walk, the world could end, I could come to my senses, or any number of other possibilities. While Jenny spent hours and hours on the computer, I busied myself with making lists of necessities to take, shopping for backpacks, and reading about "how to fly by the seat of my pants." My knowledge of this type of living was akin to my acquaintance to life on Pluto.

A greeting from God jumped off the page of a book I was reading by Wayne Dyer. I handwrote it on bright yellow paper and made one for each of us to carry. It said:

Good morning!
This is God.
I will be handling all of your problems today.
I will not need your help, so
Have a miraculous day!

I had the three-by-three-inch pieces laminated and told Jenny we would read these every morning and be relieved of any worry. She replied, "Okay, Mom, whatever you say." She evidently already had this faith. I was doing this for myself, and we both knew it.

Every day I felt younger and younger. I got the twenty-one-year-old spring back in my step. I laughed more. Every time someone said, "You're nuts!" I responded amidst my own laughter, "You're right!" I dreamed in Technicolor. I listened to tapes on learning Italian. I checked the days off the calendar, but the most difficult task was finding the perfect assisted-living facility for my mother. Her funds were limited, and she has always promised she would live to be a hundred and ten. I've tried to help stretch her money by caring for her in my home as often as possible. Having dementia means she experiences daily confusion and insecurity. A smaller, homey place would be better than one of the grand, fancy, Taj Mahalish facilities that house hundreds, display fresh cut flowers daily, offer choice menus, have gold-plated door handles, chandeliers, lush carpets, high ceilings, entertainment and activities managers, in-house nurses, and a never ending list of amenities attempting to assure the residents they are "going out in style." I began visiting places, and the more I visited, the more impossible became the task of finding someone to replace me in my mother's life. Being an only child continues presenting challenges I despise. I visited facility after facility, but they were too big, too expensive, too dark and dreary, or they contained someone who screamed mindlessly all day, or something equally disheartening. This is my mother, and I can't ask her to stay anywhere I wouldn't want to be, so the search continued and continued and continued. Finally, I found the perfect place. It was small, clean, homey, room for only five and supplied the perfect new friend, a cheery Alice, to room with and to remind Mother all is well. There is nothing easy about dropping your mother off for someone else to care for, no matter how crazy you think she is driving you. My mother is sweet, not demanding or crabby as so many become in later years. I guess you could say she has happy dementia. But, after listening to her repeat the same questions I answered for what seemed like hundreds of times a day, I thought I was losing my mind. Once I kept a tally on her favorite question, "When can I go home?"—seventy-five times in one day! Yes, she varied it, and sometimes the question became, "Don't I have a home? Who's paying my rent? How did I get here? Can you take me home tomorrow? Take me home." How could she still be asking these questions after living here for five years? I was about to tear my hair out, but why did I feel like I was disposing of her? She cried when I took her to her new home on May 15 because she had no idea what was in store for her or why I didn't want to take her to Italy with me. "I can walk as far as you any day," she reminded me, and while this was not true, in her feeble mind, it was very true, and she was more aware than anyone that I am all she has in this world. I thought if I didn't get away soon, I would be committed to an institution for the criminally insane. At the time, it all sounded like excuses. Oh, the guilt we inflict on ourselves!

Back in January, when Jenny's plan to traipse across Italy itinerary-less was in the embryonic stage, we invited both of my sons to go with us. Jarrod, thirty-one, a blossoming real estate mogul in South Carolina, didn't have time. Jake, twenty-four, a ballroom dance teacher in Austin, also declined. I must admit I was relieved since three (or four) can be awkward, demanding, or at least drastically change the dynamics. By May 1, after intellectualizing and analyzing the idea for a few months, Jake wanted to go with us. My imagination went wild, and I envisioned the same people who might have offered hospitality to two females just scoffing at us and thinking, "They've got a man with them. He can provide a place for them." (Is this one of those southern ideals?) My mind was drowning in negative thoughts about Jake going with us. Sure, I wanted him to go for his own experience. He was the perfect age to take one last fling before he settled into the realities of life for sixty or seventy years, but his interests were different. Jenny and I were good travel partners and had taken spring break and weekend trips many times in the past few years. Jake's ideas about a good time were different. His sister, on the other hand, thought his decision to go was great. She handed me the yellow three-by-three-inch card and said, "Here, Mom, read this."

Shopping for backpacks took five full days. After visiting four stores and trying on at least fifty packs of varying sizes, shapes, and features, we settled on a simple school-sized pack with waist belt and padded shoulder straps. I refused the helpful suggestions of the store clerk concerning loops for my sleeping bag, blanket, and pillow. Had I overlooked something? Sleeping bag, blanket, and pillow were not on my necessity list. Maybe I should reconsider since I had no hotel reservations? After mulling over this thought and visualizing myself loaded down with sleeping gear, I decided I could take a small pillow—the kind filled with thousands of tiny pellets that won't fold or change shape. We bought two of these, which were round, eight-inch diameter, perfect fits for our little heads. Our choice of backpacks hung on the wall before us. I chose the red one (my favorite color) with black zippers on all the hidden pouches and compartments. My thoughts were light as air as I visualized us packing through Italy with ease. "Mom, let's go," jerked me back to reality. Suddenly, in that split second of daydreaming, I was renewed. I understood why children engaged in it regularly and vowed to try it more often. Jenny took the solid black pack just like mine. Now we were ready to attempt stuffing the seemingly endless list of necessities into our new three-cubic-foot packs, which would become extensions of our backs, and possibly our summer homes. We chatted incessantly on the drive home from Academy Sports comparing lists of necessities. As Jenny read her list, I gave thanks that I wouldn't be burdened with eye shadows of every shade, ten lip liners, and twenty lipsticks. "Do you think you need to take that much makeup?" I asked.

"Mom, we'll be gone for three months, and I don't know what kind of makeup they sell in Italy," came the reply. I reminded myself that Jenny would have to negotiate with the backpack for space, not me. She continued reading her list, "six pair undies ..." (that's where she'll negotiate the room, I thought). What she calls underwear is a contradiction of the term. I was only taking three pair. Mine weren't thongs; I couldn't afford the space for more. As Jenny continued reading her list, my mind wandered. Visions of my children in awe of my strength and endurance flashed before me.

"Three pair high heels," she continued.

"What?" I asked. "High heels? Are you nuts? What could you possibly need high heels for? We will be walking with packs on our backs for three months!" I took a deep breath, calmed myself, and remembered I would not be carrying the high heels. Why was I surprised? Why would these three months be any different to Jenny than any other day in her life? This is the girl who began dressing "to the nines" when she was three years old and acquired her first pair of high heels, red ones, size eight, from a garage sale. Over the top is as much a part of Jenny as her red hair, brown eyes, and five-foot-nine-inch frame. "Mom, we might have the opportunity to go somewhere nice," she answered, just as sure of herself as ever. I'm thinking, *What difference does wearing high heels make if you are covered in dirt and sweat with rips in your clothes?* I constantly fought the controlling Terminator thoughts. Knowing that my thinking had to change if I were to enjoy this summer, at that moment I began thinking of everything as a possible adventure. I imagined the heels poking holes in her backpack and spilling the lip liners. I had never experienced standing in the middle of a busy street in a foreign country retrieving the contents of a backpack, nor had I reached under a train to reclaim underwear, lip liners, tampons, or high heels. I had worked myself into shallow breathing, much like I remembered doing while giving birth. *Okay,* I assured myself, *you can do this.*

The last few days I spent negotiating with my back's new extension, the red and black pack. I sacrificed makeup space and smell-good personal hygiene products to carry security, my personal version of a medicine cabinet, which included vitamins, supplements, herbs, and the inhaler that I seem to need when I'm under more stress than usual. *Hmmmm, maybe you should take an extra one, or two, or three inhalers,* I thought. *No,* I reminded myself. *This is going to be fun, an adventure, no stress. You are going to be impulsive. Remember, you want to risk and experience not being in control.* This is ideal thinking, but is it in the realm of possibility for me, a mother of three who has always been organized, goal-oriented, in control, and security-based, to just let it all go? Yes, yes, yes! It is possible. I had to pat myself on the back, for a few months ago, my perception of reality would have prevailed, and I wouldn't have been able to bring myself back to the positive thoughts.

Surprised at myself, I knew I was ready to go with this young, naïve, carefree thought. The daydreams were changing my thinking. This was a good sign, for to preserve my sanity, it was necessary that I know how to break from reality. I had never experienced the type of education that was facing me for the next three months. The hardest part for me was letting go of my own cultural assumptions about how people would respond. I know how people in my hometown would react to seeing a fifty-six-year-old woman with a loaded backpack looking to go home with someone on the street. It isn't a pretty thought! Would the Italians respond the same way? Jenny kept assuring me we would be safe. I'm not sure we both understand the definition of the word safe. Webster's definition is: secure from danger, harm, or evil; free from danger or injury, unhurt; free from risk; affording protection. The word *safe* was taking on a new meaning for me. During the months prior to leaving, I constantly battled thoughts of safety, security, protection. The mother in me is not something that turns off, but I can muffle it at times sort of like stuffing the Jack-In-The-Box down under the lid, knowing it will pop up again. Deep down in the core of my being a fire was burning. I wanted to have this experience and stretch myself far beyond my comfort zone. It was three days from take-off, and I had a zillion things to do.

Have you ever known a totally selfless person? You know, the one who somehow always has time to help even though she has twenty-four hours in her day, too. My friend, Rachel, who is barely five feet tall but can work like a horse all the while maintaining the cheeriest attitude, is one such person. Rachel has a special gift for loving people. I think she gains physical pleasure from others' good fortune. In spite of having a full time job, she has often helped me with my mother when I leave town for a few days at a time. She would also look in on Tobey, my feline companion, and take care of weeding and watering my flowerbeds. I knew I risked putting a strain on our relationship if I asked her to help me for three months. Weeding in the west Texas sun is a challenge, and daily watering is often necessary. Luckily, Rachel lives only five blocks from me, which makes stopping by convenient. I offered her what I considered a generous payment for three months of weeding, watering, and checking on Tobey. "Don't you worry about a thing," she said, waving her hand in a downward stroke, "just go have fun. I'll take care of everything." Once Rachel said she would take care of things, I knew they would be taken care of and better than I could do them myself.

It was time to get serious with what I could and couldn't live without for the next three months. No amount of negotiating with my backpack allowed the one hundred and two items in. I thought about the only other backpacking trip I had made. Years ago, while living in Pocatello, Idaho, I took a three-day hike, sponsored by the park and recreation department, with ten other people. I was twenty-eight years old at the time, and we were given a list of exactly what we would need. It was easy not having to think about everything to take. What personal items could I purchase in a small town in Italy? I began marking items off my list thinking I would not need them but soon returned them after I realized most came from my favorite health food store. Yes, I would take the Stone Free for kidney stones, cranberry pills for bladder health, oils, herbs, and supplements that could all be life-preserving. Maybe I could trade clothes for space. I began bargaining with my clothes. I ended up settling for one long skirt, one pair of black capris with matching zippered jacket, a black t-shirt, a white t-shirt (a dumb choice), a capri set that was black with a pink stripe down the side, my summer pajamas, three pair of underwear, my navy Birkenstock sandals, red Keen sandals, my favorite Sketcher slip-ons, and one pair of thongs. Yes, thongs. When I was Jenny's age, we called them thongs since the rubber piece went between our toes. Even today, Webster's definition for thong is "a sandal held on the foot by a thong between the toes." I still call them thongs, much to Jenny's embarrassment, but heck, someone stole this term and applied it to underwear forty years after I had been using it in reference to shoes.

Jenny became a bit edgy when she had to face the fact she could not have a hair dryer or curling iron for three months. There are certain things twenty-one-year-old females cannot sacrifice, so we bought a five-inch, foldable, butane curling iron that fit perfectly in her pack. Backpack wrestling continued. I couldn't get my pillow in, and Jenny hadn't negotiated a spot for her high heels. One day from take-off, Jake drove in from Austin with an oversized pack he had borrowed. Jenny tried to talk him into carrying her heels. Anyone with a brother can just imagine what he said, so we made a midnight trip to Wal-Mart for some bungee cords to strap the heels on the outside of Jenny's pack, and my pillow to the top of mine. The innocent, red and black pack that hung limply on the wall at Academy Sports now bulged at the seams, so pregnant that it kept falling over. There would be no way I could quickly reach anything inside the mathematically stuffed pack. Oops.

Jake was already asleep, so I called good night to Jenny, who was introducing the bungee cords to her high heels. Six hours remained until we had to be at the airport. My body was tired, but my mind was squirming. It appeared I was going along with this hare-brained idea to walk around Italy with a pack so heavy I could not hoist it onto my back by myself. "Mom, you need to be able to handle your own pack," Jenny said. I reminded her she had promised to help me if I needed help. Jenny reminded me of years ago, when we'd make our weekly trek to the library, and both she and Jake wanted to bring home fifty or so books. I told them they could each take a backpack and bring home only the books they could carry. Now I was on the receiving end of those words.

Chapter Two

We're Off!

It arrives. Dawn. May 25, 2005. It is 7:00 a.m. and I haven't broken a toe. The world is still spinning, and I evidently haven't come to my senses. Last night's sleep consisted of mulling over in my mind things that someone else would have to do while I was gone. I did sleep long enough to dream that I was standing with my backpack on, smiling, while conversing with a group of Italians—in Italian! *Ha, ha, oh yeah, that's why we call them dreams,* I think and grin at myself in the bathroom mirror. *You hippie, you.* My mind was hopping, but my chest and gut were troubled. My chest felt exactly as it did when I was five years old and had to jump off the diving board on the last day of swimming lessons. My own breath had betrayed me. A boulder inside me was crushing and I would surely sink to the bottom if I jumped. I was afraid of heights and from that board, four feet off the water looked like four miles. My stomach churned as I stood on the end of the diving board and peered into the turquoise abyss. I jumped. The water held my little round body as I paddled to the side. Rather than being exhilarated, my success was exhausting. Now, unlike that little five-year-old standing on the end of the diving board listening to the adult shout, "Trust me, jump. You'll be fine," I was the adult listening to my daughter say, "Trust me, and jump into this abysmal machination!" My fear of heights had never left me, and I was getting ready to board an airplane that would carry me across the Atlantic Ocean. We had no plans other than a few e-mails Jenny had sent to Hospitality Club and Couch Surfing members, and a few suggestions read in travel guides. My imagination worked overtime conjuring up images of situations we could be in that required money. Being the mom, I thought I needed to make it clear to Jake and Jenny that I did not have the money to bail us out. "We are each on our own for food," I had told them. I'm sure both of them trusted that I would come to the rescue if necessary. After all, that's what mothers do, right? I don't think they heard me, understood me, or took me seriously, because when Jake arrived ready for the three months abroad, he had six hundred dollars! Jenny had twice that much and I had around three thousand dollars. Even if we pooled our money, that would give us each less than twenty dollars per day. Who were we kidding? Evidently ourselves. We were about to become creative financiers—or beggars! *Where is that yellow card?* I thought. *Now would be a good time to read it.*

At 9:05 a.m., we threw our packs into the car and headed for Lubbock Preston Smith International Airport, seven miles from my house. Robin, the first to encourage me to go on this adventure so many months ago, would meet us at the airport to take my car to her house. She had promised to drive it every week to keep the computer active and the tires inflated. We parked in the loading and unloading zone and went inside to the check-in counter. There stood Robin and her husband, Chip, with concerned looks on their faces. I had been battling a kidney stone for several days and they knew it.

"How are you feeling?" Robin asks.

"Full of faith," I answer, surprised at my reply, but realizing it had come from the depths of me.

"You'll be okay," Chip says, his sky blue eyes smiling in stark contrast to his white beard. "I hear kidney stones explode at thirty thousand feet!"

"Really?" I half-laugh.

"Yeah, you'll be okay," he assures. As excruciating as an

exploding kidney stone sounded, I had been reassured and that's exactly what I needed at that moment. Chip had just shortened the words on the yellow card and shared them with me. 'You'll be okay.'

While I talk with Chip and Robin, Jenny and Jake check in and deal with luggage security. "Mom!" Jenny calls with panic in her voice. "I can't take my curling iron! Mom, I have to have it!" The two-inch cartridge that hooks to the curling iron looks harmless, but it is butane. At this very moment, when everything could turn sour—at least for Jenny who tragically had not been able to mate the bungee cords with the high heels—the robust, dark-haired, uniformed man behind the counter says in an optimistic voice, "We'll put it in a small box, tape it shut, and you can check it." *He must have a young daughter,* I thought. It's unthinkable that a beautiful, young girl should have to face both ends of her body ugly at the same time—no high heels and bad hair days for three months! This guy obliterates all stories about security check personnel being heartless—or maybe he just wants to spend more time with this pretty redhead whose thongs he is about to go through! *Oh, shit,* I thought. *This nice man is going to empty my pack and I won't have time to restuff it before takeoff.* I spent three days of rigorous packing, thinking, and rethinking necessary and unnecessary items just to get to this point. By now, Chip is carrying my pack to the scales. It weighs twenty-five pounds and bulges at the seams. I follow him, check in, and then move over to the security counter. Sure enough, they empty my two pair of granny panties in their search for unsafe items. I guess the laceless, beige panties can be considered dangerous. I could probably choke someone with them. The security personnel decide I cannot take my *iron hooks* on the plane. These are the same tools the hygienist uses to clean my teeth. These hooks are important to me since I have no idea how often I will get to brush my teeth or under what conditions. With the hooks, I can at least scrape the crud off my teeth. The guys stuff as much as they can back into my pack and then slide the rest down to the edge of the counter with a cheery, "Good luck." I lift my pack off the counter and lower it to the floor to repack it. In the next few minutes, sweat drips into my eyes as I work to replace the pack's contents—I am in big trouble facing a European summer when I'm breaking a sweat in an air-conditioned airport!

At this moment, reality splits me in two. During the previous months of busy preparations topped with excitement, daydreams, and too much to think about, reality had been hiding somewhere in the background. Simultaneously, I feel my throat closing with tears, while bursts of laughter escape my mouth. "Need any help?" Robin asks. I manage to stuff everything except a roll of packing tape back into the pack even though the zippers won't close. We need the tape in case one of our packs splits. When I come up from the floor, hair wet with sweat, Robin notices my cracking expression and decides this is the perfect time to give me a present. "Here," she says, handing me something wrapped in earthy, brown paper with tan flowers. "Hopefully you can find a place in your pack for this." My pack is dripping its contents, and Robin is giving me something to add to it. The paper is beautiful and I tear through it like a child on Christmas morning. Inside is a dark brown, leather journal with tan stitching. In the corners and center of the cover, swirls of stitching tease of leaves and flowers. The journal closes with a braided string of green, red, and tan threads that I unwrap to reveal beautiful earth-friendly pages within. It is the perfect gift for recording my adventures. It's flexible—about five-by-seven inches, a great size to hold. With the giving of this gift, Robin manages to interrupt my mental breakdown, but how will I carry it? The roll of tape, now sitting on the counter, will go in the box with the butane curling iron. I add my little red Swiss Army knife, an opened package of neon colored plastic ties (reflectors for walking at night), and my iron hooks. We tape and label the box and check it so it can ride in the luggage compartment. Now, instead of walking through the airport in Venice, we will have to join the other three hundred or so passengers in baggage claim to pick up the little box when we arrive at Marco Polo Airport tomorrow, May 26. Oh well, it'll be worth it.

Checked in, with boarding passes and packs in tow, we are accompanied by Robin and Chip to the final security check, the metal detectors. We say our good-byes and thank-yous, and they leave. After showing my photo ID and boarding pass, I heave my pack up on the conveyor belt, take off my fanny pack and shoes, lay them next to the backpack, and walk through the metal detectors. Having successfully arrived at the other side, I reached for my fanny pack. The agent behind the conveyor belt puts her hand out to stop me as she says, "Wait. What is this?" She points to the picture of my fanny pack on her screen. "I don't know," I answer, not remembering anything I had put in my fanny pack other than money, driver's license, and passport. By now, all security personnel have stopped, and all eyes focus on the picture of my fanny pack. The guard carefully pulls my pack along the conveyor belt and says, "Open this slowly, please." As soon as I unzip it, I recognize the familiar white plastic of my Albuterol inhaler. I grab it and in a gesture of fun, aim it (the long end) at her, wink, and say, "Gotcha." Her eyes pop out of her head as she says, "Don't ever do that again!" Shakily, I put my shoes and fanny pack back on. The security person at the end of the line hands over my backpack and whispers, "You could have been arrested for that gesture. Be careful."

"Yes, sir," I squeak. Had I been arrested, I wouldn't have gone on the trip, so I take my freedom as the ultimate sign I am to go.

At Gate Four we talk with the others who will be riding this Continental flight 2812 from Lubbock to Houston. In Houston, we will board British Airways flight 2024 to London for the next leg of our trip. Even though we are speaking with total strangers, the response to our three-month plan is uncannily familiar to my friends' comments. People younger than I look at me as if I have three eyes, am made of plastic, or something equally unreal. Eyebrows rise in disbelief as questions come my way. "No reservations? Well, good luck. I couldn't do that. Where are you going to sleep?" *Despite my nervousness, I have embraced this upcoming adventure*, I think. With the attention I am receiving, for a second or two I want to run home while I still have the chance. I ask a man to take our picture. We all have our packs on and line up sideways so the packs show in the picture. He aims the camera at us and says, "Stand up straight." I look at Jake and Jenny who are straight as arrows. I have to lean a little forward or I'll fall backward. Hanging over my left arm is a small bag of yarn and number fifteen AddiTurbo circular knitting needles. My mother's saying, "idle hands are the devil's workshop," is still with me. The announcement is made for us to board. A wave of gratitude warms me. I give an audible thank you and head through the gate to find seat 12B.

Waiting our turn in line to find our seats, Jenny notices the sweat dripping down my face and asks, "Are you okay, Mom?" She knows I never completely settle in until I feel the wheels touch the ground during landing.

"No," I answer. I can't be still, and after we sit down, my legs involuntarily bounce up and down. Inside me, a volcano is about to erupt. The swells of energy that fear, excitement, and anticipation create intensify. I want to run screaming through the plane just to release some energy. I probably glow or send off sparks from the imprisoned force. If I'd been practicing Reiki, I could heal everyone on the plane at once. How I wish I could bottle it. I'm sure I'll need an energy shot here and there throughout the summer.

"Mom," Jenny abruptly grabs my knee. "What's wrong with you?"

"I think I have to pee!"

"Mom, get a grip."

"I'm going to jump out of my skin."

"Okay, take some slow deep breaths."

I lean back in my chair and take the deepest breath I can with the muscles surrounding my diaphragm freaking out. Slowly I release it and feel a softening; I close my eyes and breathe deeply as the plane leaves the ground and begins its power assent through the west Texas air, higher and higher and farther and farther away from home.

"Better?" Jenny asks.

"Yeah, I think I'll take a nap."

"Right," she laughs, knowing that's an impossibility for me.

I look across the aisle. Jake is already snoring. How does he do that?

Jake, my middle child, is tall, dark, and handsome. Jenny says he looks 'ethnic' with his olive skin and black curls. The librarian in the children's section of the library has known him since he was three. "He grew into a Greek god," she said one day when she saw him at age fifteen. His jet-black hair is almost to his shoulders, and if he combs it, it becomes a huge afro, so he washes it, pats it to his head, and lets the curls hang. He twiddles these curls when he is drifting off into his own "Jake world" and at times, they stick straight out from his head like corkscrews and you can count them. His chocolate brown eyes, rich as Columbian coffee, reach through my shirt and melt my heart. This was particularly true when he was a child and his face hadn't quite grown into his big, round eyes. As a seven year old, Jake was very interested in science. He'd been reading since he was five and had figured how to take a wire, a bulb, and a battery, and create a homemade flashlight that he would use when he hid under the covers late at night and read. I got mad and punished him when I caught him numerous times still reading at 3:00 a.m. When you're seven and pull an all-nighter reading, it's hard to function the next day. Jake's zest for life was always contagious. His interests knew no boundaries. When he was eight years old, he wanted to study "our insides," so I told him we'd have to find a cow's eyeball or maybe we could dissect a rat or something. One day, while I was washing dishes, he was on the phone at the opposite end of the house. He came running down the hall calling in his happy-go-lucky voice, "Mom, the man at the Slaton packing plant says we can have a baby pig to dissect. We just have to go get it. Can we, Mom?" Those brown eyes snared me every time. He said he called three meat packers before someone could give us something to dissect. This fetal pig dissection is one of my favorite videos to watch. Jenny, age five, is seated on one side of the kitchen table keeping her distance from the pig. Jake is directly across from her, with the dead pig cut straight down the middle in front of him. He is holding a scalpel in his right hand. Jenny's face is scrunched up as if she has just sucked a lemon and Jake is gleefully pointing out the parts. "Look at the tiny heart. Here's the stomach. Jenny, look at the two kidneys. Wow, this is cool. Mom, can we measure the intestines?" On Christmas day, it was Jake who was most excited—not just about his gifts, but the gifts of others too. He has always been brilliant, creative, and talented. Everything he touches turns to something beautiful. Now, there he is, across this small plane's narrow aisle with not a care in the world, sound asleep.

An hour later, we land at George Bush International in Houston and pick up our packs from the front of the cabin as we leave the plane. The kids throw them on their backs as if they are putting on jackets and begin walking through the tunnel. "Whoa," I yell. "I need help." Jenny returns and lifts my pack to the level of my back so I can slip my arms through the straps. "Oh my god, it's heavy." I carefully walk humped-over toward the terminal.

"Mom, straighten up. You'll never make it all summer bent over like that."

"Until I get used to this thing, please don't walk so fast," I beg.

Where is Jake? He's twenty-four and can still disappear in an instant just like he did when he was two. He can be standing next to you one minute, and in the time it takes to turn your head to speak to him, he's out of sight. No sound accompanies his swift departure, not even a *poof*. He's just gone.

Walking through the terminal toward the British Airways counter is challenging. With each step, I propel myself straight ahead. *Just one step at a time*, I remind myself. There are hundreds of hazards before me in the form of human beings. Each time I have to change directions to avoid colliding with someone, I lose my balance. It was the same when I was six years old in dance class.

Each time I "twirled," my unbalanced body began to fall, setting off a domino effect on the other girls in line. After a few weeks, when my twirl was not advancing, the teacher took me from the line, brought me forward so I was in front of the others, and helped me twirl by holding my hands above my head as I turned. During the recital, I didn't get to twirl. I was a bride dressed in a short, white, lace dress with a veil on my head and black patent tap shoes. A boy dressed in a suit stood beside me holding my hand while the old song "Tea for Two" played. We sang and did a few easy steps. This pack puts my body in that same precarious situation that the twirl did each time I try to dodge someone. If these people only knew the danger they were in, they would all go running to clear a path for me. In spite of my youthful thinking these past few months, I am neither as strong as I thought I was, nor as young.

The British Airways counter is in sight with hundreds of people crawling around it like a wolf pack near its prey. There is Jake. We join him and wait our turn to check in for the nine-hour flight across the ocean. I cringe, thinking about it. I hear prim British accents coming from behind the counter. The BA personnel look at our passports and check their computer screens. Confusion arises among these three people, and they mumble behind the desk. They ask us to step aside and wait. Passenger after passenger walks past us and boards. I walk to the counter and say, "Excuse me. Did you forget us?"

"What's the name?"

"Haning, three of us." All of a sudden, three sounds like too many. The agent behind the counter proceeds to discuss something pertaining to boarding with the other two personnel. "Passports, please." We produce the passports again. By now, we are the only passengers with tickets for this flight who haven't boarded. They talk among themselves each pointing to the others' screens. They've overbooked, and we are the ones who get the ax. I just know it. Two women come running breathlessly to the counter, produce their passports, are given boarding passes, and away they go to the plane. With each question I ask, the BA personnel give the least response possible. Usually, "Just wait" or "hmmm" accompanied by mumbles, or they just talk among themselves seemingly not interested in us. A young man, probably in his twenties sporting what a month ago would have been dreadlocks and wearing a black pack that has seen better days, comes running toward the counter yelling, "Wait, wait." He produces the passport and is given a boarding pass. He walks through the gate, a gray sock dangling from a hole in the bottom of his pack. We stand waiting. Jake doesn't waste time to practice a dance step, and right now he and Jenny practice twirls around their resting packs as if nothing is wrong. The clock on the wall behind the counter reads 3:50 p.m.—five minutes until take-off. "We are getting the ax. I know it," I whisper to myself. "Passenger profiling, probably. I bet they're thinking backpackers are used to sleeping in chairs, on the floor, or standing up and can wait until the next plane. They're probably exactly three seats short." At this moment, I decide that if I do not get on this plane, it will be a definite sign that I am not supposed to go, and I will hop the next plane back to Lubbock, settle into my uneventful life and be happy. A bright British accent interrupts my dismal musings, "Okay, Hanings, we have upgraded you three to first class. Have a wonderful flight," she says, handing us boarding passes. Jake is first to speak. "Well, thank you very much," he says with a smile that the orthodontist would be proud of.

"Are you kidding?" I ask incredulously.

"I'm sorry you won't all be together. We have two seats together, and one of you will have to sit alone on the opposite side of the plane. We are sorry for this inconvenience." A smile smears across Jake's face. He thinks he's died and gone to heaven. Now he won't have to listen to Jenny and me chatter for nine hours, trying to engage him in conversation with our questions. He turns and shoots through the tunnel. This angel dressed in navy blue and white has just upgraded us to first class and is apologizing because we can't all sit together. Jenny and I look at the person behind this cheery voice and chime simultaneously, "Thank you." I'm sure our faces tell it all. We begin giggling as Jenny helps me loop my pack over one shoulder. I walk through the tunnel as quickly as I can, giggling all the way. We are escorted to our seats and immediately treated like royalty. "May I get you anything, ma'am? Champagne? Orange juice? Here, I'll place your pack in the overhead for you, ma'am." We haven't even sat down yet, and they want to serve us. This is going to be fun!

Chapter Three
Thirty-five Thousand Feet

My usual horrors at take-off are diminished by the attention the attendants in first class give us from the moment we step into the plane. We have never experienced first class on any airline, and it will prove to be an adventure. Everything emerges in British Airways's theme colors, navy blue and white. The ear buds and fleecy blanket are waiting in the pouch next to the seat. Our reclinable chairs face each other in a love seat configuration with a gray accordion screen resembling a giant fan between them for privacy. Jenny instantly folds the fan out of sight. "This is going to be fun, Mom, can you believe it?" This is the first day of our three-month adventure and pleasant surprises are rolling in. The yellow card is coming alive. As soon as the pilot gives the cue, the navy/white clad attendants scatter through the aisles. Our blue-eyed, strawberry-blond attendant with a spray of freckles across his nose appears in his starched uniform with gold wings on his shoulders. "May I get you a drink now?" he offers in his proper British English and when we decline, the poor guy looks dejected. "My name is Tim. Please call when you want something." I refer to his language as British English because the differences in British English and American English are vast in vocabulary as well as pronunciation. It's all very interesting to me since I'm a phonics teacher. For example, the loo is the bathroom, cue means to line up, and the lift is the elevator. The spellings are different enough to cause the American brain to space out momentarily when it tries to register *memorise* (British) as *memorize*, or *favourite* (British) as *favorite*, or *cheque* for *check*, and *encyclopaedia* is the British spelling of *encyclopedia*.

Jenny and I sit familiarizing ourselves with the buttons and gadgets around our seats. Our attendant notices our fiddling and stops to show us how the seats fully recline, and how a detached footrest combines with the seat to make a six-foot bed that lies completely flat. He makes sure we know which button to push if we need anything and assures us he will come running each time we push this button. *It just gets better,* I think. I have heard that the British are stuffy or a bit aloof, but this is not the case with these attendants. I do my best to take it all in and enjoy each moment. In coach class, the high-backed seats that fill the cabin obstruct one's view and give a claustrophobic discomfort. Here my vision drifts around the cabin unrestrained. Next, a menu arrives—three courses with three or four choices in each. We are instructed to give our order to the attendant in ten minutes. Do I want chicken or fish with white wine, or beef and red wine, or lasagna with steamed vegetables? An attendant carrying white, moist, steaming, cloth hand towels delicately lifts a towel with silver tongs from their silver tray and offers it to me. The steam rises in swirls and the towel is almost too hot to hold. We are given just enough time to bathe our hands in the steamy warmth, when another attendant quickly retrieves the used towels.

Spicy, sweet aromas fill the cabin. *Mmmmm,* I take a deep breath to enjoy them. In coach class, I have rarely smelled food (at least no appetizing aromas). Instead, a large, rolling, stainless cart suddenly blocks the aisle and slowly creeps along as an attendant plops a tin foil or plastic container on each tray. This food is accompanied by a small plastic bag. In the bag are a plastic fork, knife, a paper-thin napkin, a small helping of salt and pepper, and a pre-packaged moist towelette that smells like a doctor's office. But we are in first class, and a couple of minutes before our meals are served on white porcelain plates, we are given white cloth napkins complete with stainless steel flatware neatly hidden inside. Each dinner is hand delivered, no rolling carts here.

"Presentation is everything," the sorority housemother instructed me in a 1967 pledge class orientation and training. "Blah, blah, blah," she continued as I thought about hitting a homerun in the softball game I'd be playing in an hour. "Your guests' taste buds will be aroused as their eyes meet a beautifully set table." The word *aroused* snapped my eighteen-year-old ears back to the moment. I had not associated the word aroused with taste buds, but the thought painted an interesting picture in my mind. All members and pledges ate the evening meal together in the sorority house. Each night we ate on white china, drank from crystal stemware, and lifted food to our mouths on sterling silver flatware. I relished the clear *ting* that came from water glasses as they were lightly tapped, signaling quiet in the room so an announcement could be made. Only an officer or the housemother was allowed this privilege. Once, during my freshman year when no one was in the kitchen, I took a glass, half-filled it with water and with a dinner knife, "tinged" it a little too hard. The glass cracked. Oops, maybe I'm not ready to make announcements.

My favorite herb, rosemary, sits atop my dinner that Tim carefully presents. "May I bring you anything else?"

"No, this is wonderful. Thank you," I say, enjoying every minute of being served.

"Just push this button," he reminds me and points to the button that calls him to my side. The sprig of rosemary on the potatoes tickles my nose. "Mmm," I moan. The spicy smells of curry chicken drift toward me, wetting my mouth. The housemother was right. Presentation is arousing. My eyes promptly inform my senses (of smell, taste, and general well-being) that this is going to be a satisfying experience.

"Where is Jake? I wonder what he is enjoying for dinner." Food is more than nourishment to Jake who is the family's culinary virtuoso. More offers of wine, champagne, drinks of all kind continue. Our fair-haired attendant, with his prim accent says, "I want to present you with a gift from British Airways thanking you for flying with us today." In a navy blue, square, zippered pouch are a pair of fuzzy, soft socks, travel toothbrush and toothpaste, floss, mouthwash, eye mask, lip balm, body lotion, and several other niceties. "Jenny, gifts! Are you kidding me? Wow! Thank you."

My eyes are magnetically drawn to the huge screen in front of the cabin with its nonstop picture of the eastern part of the U.S., the Atlantic Ocean, and western Europe. A plane moves across the map, advancing along our route to London. Flashing across the screen is our altitude above the Atlantic Ocean, how far we've flown in kilometers and miles, the estimated remaining time of the flight, and the temperature outside the window at thirty-five thousand feet. It is a negative fifty degrees Fahrenheit!

One by one, lights click off and chairs recline as travelers attempt to keep their normal sleep schedules. The cabin is dim and quiet. Most are sleeping. I walk around, releasing nervous energy. I wander into the pantry that holds anything I might want to eat in the middle of the night or whatever time it is. Somewhere over the ocean, our time rushes forward six hours as we cross time zones. Did I want a cookie, candy bar, chips, sandwich, ice cream, fruit, something hot, or an adult beverage? I'm not hungry, just unable to sleep. I walk through the cabin of the comatose and finally make my way back to my seat where I wrap myself in my soft, snuggly blanket, load my CD player with my favorite relaxation tape (yoga nidra), recline my chair, and attempt sleep.

It's amazing what the responsibility of children can do to one's sleep. When I was in college, I used to sleepwalk, which can be entertaining for others or scare the liver out of them if the sleepwalker comes to their bedside. My mother told me, when I was a child she would hear me talking in the middle of the night and would come to my room to see me sitting up in bed pretending I was talking on the phone. While still in high school, a friend and I spent the weekend with a college friend of ours. While I slept, the two of them drew on my face with a black magic marker. They couldn't believe the piercing odor didn't wake me. I never knew a thing until the next morning as they ruptured in laughter when I awoke. Since children entered my life, I can hear a pin drop on carpet.

My yoga nidra CD is taking me away to the land of relaxation, when I hear a child screaming in the background. He must be near the front of coach section. The dark curtains that hang between the sections protect us from general noise, but do little to muffle this shrill squalling. Jake and Jenny seem unaffected by the ear-piercing noise—neither are many others. How do they sleep when a child is distraught? I crank up the volume on my CD player. What seems like an eternity in hell is four hours. Then, there is breakfast. The child screams from the time I attempt to go to sleep until we are served breakfast, when he promptly falls asleep and never makes another sound. My heart goes out to his poor mother who vainly spends her night trying to keep him quiet.

The concept of the curtains separating the cabins interests me. Anyone can move them and walk into a different cabin. I guess I've never paid much attention to them. Are they kept pulled so first class passengers don't experience the masses? Are they there so the masses can't see the luxuries of first class that they are denied? If the masses know how great life is in the front, British Airways risks rioting. Yes, the curtains are for the masses. The haves versus the have-nots. There's no escaping it, even at thirty-five thousand feet.

Finally, the big screen before me shows the plane is once again over a green section of the map. Land! My chest feels lighter already. Jake, on the opposite side of the cabin, has evidently awakened just long enough to eat his fabulous hot breakfast and is again fast asleep. I am traveling with two people who can sleep on anything, at anytime, in any place, surrounded by tornadoes, hurricanes, earthquakes, and screaming children. I'm traveling with the young and eager. I can claim the 'eager,' but I'm not sure the 'young' fits me anymore. The sleepy sun rises to peek around the drawn shades. The cabin erupts in whispers, mumbles, and signs of life. Jenny is repairing the makeup that smeared in her overnight drools. She makes adjustments to her face with a brush sporting no more than three hairs, while peering out the window excited to see London beginning its day. We discuss the upgrade we've been given. "Mom, there's a lot to this," Jenny says, waving the yellow card. "Out of everyone on this plane, they chose us to upgrade. We need to read this every morning."

"Yeah," I whisper. At this moment, gratitude swells in us both. "We will be grateful for everything that comes our way even if it is nothing." With no plans, we have no idea what is ahead of us. I laugh at myself as I succumb to one last doubt. *Can I really pull this off?* I want to get away from the ordinary. I want to see the world is different than I think it is, and most of all I want to experience the world outside my comfort zone. *I'll give it my best try.* "I wonder where we'll stay tonight," Jenny says. "Do you know if Jake contacted that guy in Hospitality Club in Venice?"

"I don't know," I answer, biting my lip so I won't smile. I know exactly where we will be staying. I had to know that on our first night in a strange land, after a long flight, I would have a place to rest. I took the name of a little *albergo* from Rick Steves' *Italy 2004* book. While full of valuable information, the book weighs over a pound. I never thought a pound was much, but when every ounce counts, it is. We brought it with us and promised to take turns carrying it. This book has instructions on how to call Italy from the USA. Just dial 011-39 and then the number. Two weeks before our departure, I tried this dialing sequence and it worked. The rings sounded exactly like my grandmother's phone in the 1950s. Someone on the other end jerked me into her culture with, "*Pronto.*"

"Uh,um, English?" I enunciated, raising my voice as high as a question mark can take it.

"*Si, si, si,*" came the response.

"English?" I tried again. (Rick Steves' book said that someone at this number spoke English.) With the same lift in my voice, I asked, "Andrea?" This was the name listed in the book.

"*Si*, yes, I am Andrea."

Deliberately and loudly, I said, "I ... want ... to ... make ... a ... res ... er ... va ... tion." I'm not sure why speaking with more volume helps the other person understand, but it is a natural action to take when talking to someone who speaks little English. I guess it comes from the training my kids gave me. Turn up the volume and they understand.

"*Si, si.* The day?"

"May 25."

"*Venti cinque di maggio.*"

She spoke quietly, and I imagined she was talking to herself as she looked over her reservations.

"Yes." 25 May. How many persons?

"Three."

"Nights?"

"Yes," I answered, barely keeping my grip on the conversation between Italian words and her accent when she spoke in English.

"One, two, three nights?" she asked.

"Oh, yes, one night."

"Okay, name?"

"Haning," and I began to spell, "H – A - N

"No, please, first name?"

"Sue Ellen" and before I could spell it she shouted, "Ah, Sue Ellen, J.R., *Dallas*! The *Dallas* on TV. I like it." I'm wondering if the Italians are just now watching the 1970s nighttime soap opera.

"Okay. 25 May. Three persons, one night. Credit card?" I gave her the information.

"When arrive?"

"I don't know. Our plane lands at 4:10 p.m., but I don't know how long it will take us to get to you."

"Okay, bye-bye, Sue Ellen. I see you 25 May. *Ciao, ciao.*" Andrea spoke to me as if she had never anticipated anything so exciting as meeting us.

"Good-bye." I had a reservation for May 25. A bolt of lightning hit me. Oh my god, that's the day we leave. We arrive May 26.

011-39-041-521-0629

"*Pronto.*"

"Andrea?"

"*Si.si.*"

"This is Sue Ellen. I made a mistake. We ... need ... the ... room ... for ... May 26."

"Okay two nights?"

"No, just one night. May 26. Not the 25. And do you have directions?" Andrea proceeded with her directions. I could not follow them. As the summer passed, we learned about Italian directions. They are reliable ... always confusing.

"Okay, thank you." Then very slowly I add, "See ... you ... May 26."

"*Ciao*, Sue Ellen. *Ciao, ciao.* Tell J. R., *hi*," she laughed. When I hung the phone up, I crossed my fingers that she understood and we would indeed have a room for May 26.

The pilot announces our approach to London's Gatwick Airport and we are all upright with seatbelts fastened. As soon as the rear tires touch the runway, my body relaxes. Our six-hour layover will give us enough time to see Gatwick Airport. My head feels like a bowling ball and my neck is having trouble holding it. My body keeps going with little shots of adrenaline, thanks to my tired adrenal glands. Jake sees what he needs to see to remember Gatwick, then stretches his six-foot frame across a blue tub chair and dozes off. This rounded chair has downward sloping sides, and how Jake manages to sleep with his head resting on one sloped arm and his legs dangling off the other is magic. Tingles of envy float across my sleep-deprived brain. Jenny and I drop our packs next to

Jake's and ask him to watch them for us. We trust a dead man to guard our backpacks while we gallivant around the airport.

At 12:45 p.m., we board British Airways flight 2384 for Venice. This two-hour-and-ten-minute flight gives us breathtaking views of the French Alps' grandeur that taps directly into the core of my energy. Snow and mountains in their geometric wonder never cease to fill me with awe. I breathe God when I'm in the mountains. There's no place I'd rather be. "Mmmm, something smells good," I comment to the kids. No sooner said, than the cart full of piping hot personal pizzas rolls down the aisle. "Welcome to Italy," the attendant says in her British accent as she puts the rectangular-shaped cardboard box before me. The bubbling cheese slides down my throat as I savor every bite. Who knows when we will eat again? The pizza's piping hot, familiar smell grabs Jake's attention, and he awakes fully for the first time all day. Before I know it, my ears fill with the roar of the engines reversing and we safely land in Venice. Venice time is announced as 4:10 p.m. We have lost another hour between London and Venice.

Venice's Marco Polo Airport is a modern, glassy terminal, spacious and stark in appearance. We follow the masses to luggage to retrieve our little box that holds Jenny's butane curling iron. Forty-five minutes pass as we watch luggage jumping around on the carousel. No box. "I'm not leaving without it," Jenny informs us. We ask for help at three different windows. This is our first attempt at communicating with Italians. I have no idea what anyone said, but the verdict was given. "Return tomorrow and it (the box) will be here." If my dental tools hadn't been in this box, I probably would not have accepted this information gracefully. We stop by the ATM and watch our U.S. dollars shrink to euros. On this day, it takes $1.29 to make one euro.

"*Autobus per Venezia?*"

"*Numero uno,*" we hear as our eyes follow a finger pointing out the front door.

"I wonder how long we will have to wait."

"Look, there's number one." Jake and Jenny head for the front

door with their backpacks jumping on their backs. We've all worn
our packs since leaving the plane. I am hanging between exhausted
and dead. I should have spent the past three months walking ten
miles every day with twenty-five pounds on my back. I'm walking
as fast as I can and swaying like a drunken hoot owl. I'm glad I
wasn't in the bus watching me wobbling back and forth. It was
probably both hysterical and frightening. "Wait for me." I could
never say with assurance that my darling adult children wouldn't
leave me. Oh, I know they wouldn't do it forever, but just for fun
maybe once. "Come on, Mom, you can make it," Jenny yells from
the steps of the bus. My dominant thought is, "I can't wait to lay
my head on a pillow."

The bus ride from Marco Polo to Venice is a relief. I have a
chance to catch my breath as I watch Italy whiz by. We ride as
far as we can. The road ends at the canal. Now what? We stand,
looking around, totally lost. "Who's got the Rick Steves' book? It
should tell us which way to go."

"You do, Mom."

"Well, I guess we better look for directions on which water
taxi we take."

"Jake, did you e-mail that guy in Hospitality Club who lives
here?"

"Yeah, he can't keep us tonight." Jake does not stress about
anything. He deals with stress by talking, almost inaudibly, to
himself while walking around. The more intense the situation, the
more walking turns to pacing, and talking gets faster and higher
pitched. He never raises his voice to anyone and works everything
out with imaginary people. When he was a little boy, we would
say, "Jake, who are you talking to?" His reply was always, "Nobody."
When we asked this question during his teen years, his reply was
always, "None of your business." Jake keeps his cool in all situations
thanks to his invisible friends who carry out lengthy discourses
with him.

"Well, we need to find a computer so we can access Hospitality Club or Couch Surfing," Jenny adds.

"No need," I say smiling. I couldn't wait any longer to tell them. "I made a reservation for tonight."

"Mom, you didn't. We don't have the money, and staying in people's homes, not hotels, is our plan."

"It's my treat," I reassure Jenny.

"We have three months to live on what we brought and we don't know when we'll need it. We can't start spending the first day," she adds in disbelief. At this point, I seriously question that she and I live in the same world.

"I had to know after that long plane ride I'd have a bed to sleep in."

"Mom, we can find a free place. I know we can," Jenny insists. She is ready to sink her teeth into her plan and wants the first adventure to be tonight. I want to tell her to shut-up, that she is crazy, but instead I say, "We don't know the language. We can't even read the dumb signs, and you want us to find a free place to stay?"

"Mom!"

"Just let me be old this one last time," I plead. By nature, Jake is placid, but at this moment, I can tell by the look on his face that he's questioning his sanity in plunging into a three-month venture with two disagreeing females.

Chapter Four

Venice

"Andrea?" I call, peering into the doorway of what I hope is our reservation for the night. This *albergo* hid from us for two hours as we exhausted all directions given us. We found the landmarks near the building that held our one night reservation, but never went quite far enough into the shadows to find *Allogi alla Scala*. My body and mind are clinging to each other trying to stay alive. The space between my ears feels like any moment it could provide hallucinations for my enjoyment. I am numb. The water taxi ride, for me, had been surreal—something, somewhere else in a dreamland—but I am here with my children, and all around me is evidence that we are seeing Venice. After anticipating this moment for months, I am now too tired to experience it fully. I wish I had splurged and reserved two nights. My memory is a blur from the time the water taxi dropped us at the pier in Venice until we arrived at Andrea's around 9:30 p.m. All I remember is wandering around and around and around narrow streets that are really just sidewalks. "I thought we were going to stay in the countryside and small towns," I moan.

"Mom, it was your idea to land in Venice, remember?"

"Oh, yeah."

"Sue Ellen?" Andrea responds with a broad smile as she opens the door wide.

"Yes, I am Sue Ellen, and this is my son, Jake, and my daughter, Jenny."

"And J.R.?" she laughs as she again tells me, in broken English, how much she enjoys the weekly showing of *Dallas*. "Ah, *buono*," she says as she brings her hands together in front of her chest as if to pray. "You are tired," she says, stating the obvious. "Come," she says, leading us to our room, which is the first of the seven rooms she rents in this large, antique building. The twenty-foot ceilings match the furniture, windows, walls, and floors. Old. A double bed for Jenny and me and a twin bed for Jake stare out the door at us. I hear the double bed calling my name. *Sue Ellen, come here*, it seduces. I drop my pack on the floor and fall on the bed. "Oh my god, it's a bed, a real bed," I say, burying my face in the heavy bedspread. "Mom!" Jenny says in the tone that carries both attitude and embarrassment, which only one's children can convey in a single word. "I can hardly wait to go to bed," I respond.

"This is Venice! We can sleep some other time," Jenny reminds me. Jake is inspecting the books that fill the bookshelves behind an old desk.

"*E il bano*," Andrea says as she heads down the hall. We *ooh* and *aah* and comment on the furnishings and pictures in the hall, to which she obliges with little glimpses of her past. Tonight Andrea is all smiles, but no one in the pictures is smiling. One man with dark, earnest eyes shouldered a burden. I saw nothing else in those eyes. Life was difficult in Italy. "*Il bano*," Andrea announces, opening the door to a modest, clean, white-tiled room complete with bidet, toilet, shower, and sink. I'm wondering how many share this bathroom since there are three of us and only two tea towels hang on the wall just inside the door, but I am too tired to ask.

"Thank you," I say, walking back to our room. All I want to do is jump in the bed and cover my head. Outside our windows are singing gondoliers and laughing tourists. How fascinating to learn that all of Venice is built on a support of pilings made with alder wood! Dark wallpaper with large maroon stripes adds to the dimness of our room. One small wall sconce to the right of the door emits light equivalent to a nightlight I had in the bathroom when the kids were little so they could find their way, although this lighted sconce shines its light up not down. This dim room is for sleeping—ah, sleep.

I take my first Italian shower, hoping Italy's water can energize me. Italians discourage weight gain, or showering, or both, by constructing showers exactly two inches too small. Contorting my body so I could shave my legs became a challenge similar to mastering the vertical splits. Shaving legs must not be important to Italian women. I managed the challenge only to meet the next one—drying my supple body with a tea towel. The towels furnished look like three-foot long tea towels. No thirsty, terrycloth towels here. I emerge feeling like a new person, after shedding the air travel of the past twenty-four hours. The bathroom is next to Andrea's kitchen, whose door is open. I peek in as I leave the bathroom to see a Formica table and chairs and an old, wooden radio on the counter. These items were a part of my childhood in the 1950s, except our table was sunny yellow and Andrea's is green. A small, wooden table holding a telephone leans against the wall outside our door. Andrea talks to someone in Italian. She speaks with the same cheerfulness she had when I called to reserve the room. I want to sit and listen to her Italian all night. I love the language and remember what Lord Byron wrote in 1818 in his Venetian story, *Beppo*:

> I love language, that soft bastard Latin
> Which melts like kisses from a female mouth
> And sounds as if it had been writ on satin
> With syllables which breathe of the sweet South
> And gentle liquids gliding all so par in
> That not a single accent seems uncouth.

Andrea is patient when we quiz her, seeking help with a few Italian phrases before we go into the Venice night. She is practiced in speaking slowly to foreigners.

"*Ciao*," I call as we exit the front door at 11:00 p.m. *This is going to be a long summer.*

Venice does not present itself well to us. It's probably not Venice's fault. The first day of our trip, our tired, hungry bodies are the problem I'm sure. Rick Steves describes Venice as "elegant decay." It smells, is muggy and dirty, and the narrow streets are shadowed by a maze of buildings. Maneuvering cramped streets packed with people is not my idea of getting to know a new place. I would rather sit and watch people walking past as I did as a child in the 50s. My mother drove us downtown and parked on Broad Street in Texarkana, a small east Texas town famous for the Texas/Arkansas state line that splits it. We would sit in the car watching the people walking by. She brought my attention to how they were dressed, their body language, and how they walked—and told me all that we could infer from what we saw. People-watching was our entertainment. I always thought it would be more fun if we could have a banana split, a bag of popcorn, or a Snicker bar while we sat and watched. If what Mother said was true, I thought I knew everything about those strangers I observed. Sometimes we would just comment on the clothes. Mother made everything we both wore, and she loved looking at clothes.

I labor walking through the streets. The language invades my ears; the cobblestones rape my feet, legs, and back; the stench offends my nose, but my eyes bathe in history, art, architecture, beautiful Italians, and high fashion. I see no one with rubber soles on their shoes except obvious tourists. Italian women of all ages glide across the uneven, cobbled streets in stilettos. Jenny is impressed with this talent. I am blown away since my broad-soled Sketchers are having trouble keeping me upright on this challenging walk. We pass window after window as Italy introduces us to its *panino*—two pieces of white bread, either round or rectangular, with a piece of thinly sliced meat (usually *prosciuto crudo*, raw meat), one thin slice of tomato, and sometimes a bit of cheese. Not ready for these dinner options, we forge ahead. "Maybe we're not in the right part of town," Jenny offers. Now I understand why the Italians we've seen are thin. They eat three-inch diameter sandwiches and walk athletically challenging streets.

"Jake, please call that Hospitality Club guy and see if we can stay with him tomorrow night."

"I don't have his number. If we can find an Internet Point, I'll e-mail him," Jake offers. The simple idea of staying in Hospitality Club members' homes suddenly becomes difficult. We have no cell phone and no Internet access without the Internet Point as they call it here. Every day we will have to find a computer and possibly a phone.

"Okay, let's do this computer thing quickly. I paid for a bed and I want to be in it."

"Mom, you can go back to Andrea's and go to bed. Jake and I'll be fine."

"I have no idea where it is. Besides I can't leave you guys alone."

"Why not? I'll even take you back to the room," she offers.

I can't think about leaving my twenty-one and twenty-four year olds alone on the streets of Venice on our first night. A quick self-search reveals I need to let go, but a conflict called *hold on* wins out and I push ahead, staying with them. At some point around midnight, I sit down in St. Mark's Square, unable to walk any farther. Jake and Jenny continue ahead, looking for an Internet Point. I have to be in a dream. St. Mark's cathedral stands before me in the moonlight in all its golden glory—so beautiful at midnight in the moonlight. Bands set up around this huge square offer any type of music I want. I choose the familiar Big Band era music to listen to while Jake and Jenny are gone. As we walk back toward our little hotel it is 1:30 a.m. and the streets are still swarming with people. I need sleep or I won't be able to "keep it together."

Our heads hit the pillows at 2:00 a.m., and Jake and Jenny promptly leave the planet to some other consciousness. I swat mosquitoes all night. It is too hot to close the ten-foot tall, screenless windows. Jake and Jenny snore, in harmony with my swearing at the buzzing proboscises. At some point, I fall asleep and wake myself slapping the nuisances.

Day breaks early in Italy, and the sun, accompanied by voices, crashes the mosquitoes' sultry party. *It is too early for gondoliers to be serenading their passengers!* I lean out the window to hear, "When the moon hits your eye like a big pizza pie, that's *amore*. When the world seems to shine like you've had too much wine, that's *amore*."

"Okay, time to get up." The two dead people sharing my room never hear the belting gondolier or the laughing, singing tourists. I take the yellow card out of my backpack, stand in front of both beds, and begin to read aloud to nobody:

"Good morning!
This is God.
I will be handling all of your problems today.
I will not need your help,
So have a miraculous day!"

My thoughts wander positively to where I might be sleeping tonight. Maybe someone's home will have screens on the windows. *First thing in the morning and I'm thinking about sleep.* "Let's go find the computer and see if that guy answered Jake's e-mail," I announce. Jake and Jenny barely arouse, informing me we have all day. "No," I say, clapping my hands together as loudly as I can. (I'm in mom mode now, and probably sound like a drill sergeant.) "Get up. You've been asleep for six hours. Get up, sleep hogs." It isn't easy peeling them off the beds.

"What's the hurry?" Jenny asks.

"The hurry is it will take you an hour to get ready. Remember, you don't have the curling iron. It'll be a bad hair day. I'm sure you'll need to compensate by spending more time painting your face. Now get up." Luckily, I can go without breakfast, but for the first time in my life, I wish I drank coffee or took amphetamines.

We leave the building at 10:00 a.m. Andrea is happy to let us leave our packs on a pile of others whose owners have gotten an earlier start. Our day will include another trip to Marco Polo Airport in hope that the butane curling iron has arrived. My head feels thick, dull, adulterated. I spend most of my energy trying to smile and be happy. We Southerners are known for our smiles, which often hide our true feelings. Smiling and a happy nature are a part of the famous southern hospitality. We aren't about to add to your woes by sharing ours, so we just smile. It does get in the way of being grumpy. We walk around in circles for a couple hours looking for the Internet Point. The most fascinating thing I see all day are construction workers working out of a small boat with an outboard motor. Hammers, trowels, shovels, boards are all piled in the boat, leaving just enough room for a small cement mixer at one end, and two men stand balancing in the rocking boat as they work to repair the outside of a building. They are floating on the sludgy filth of Venice's famous canal. I'd like to see the spasms OSHA would have trying to regulate this site. Wow, the unions back home would have a heyday with these work conditions.

We finally find a computer. Nic, our host for tonight, has e-mailed his cell phone number to Jake. He said in the e-mail that we could stay only one night because he and his wife, Christina, are leaving for vacation the next day. Would I be willing to host three foreigners the night before I left for vacation? No. Jake phones him and through Nic's lack of English and Jake's lack of Italian, Jake understands that Nic will pick us up at the corner nearest the canal at 5:00 p.m.

Jake and Jenny are determined to find cheap sandwiches, or at least one with some size to it. Our "Whopper" mentality keeps us wandering around, looking for something larger. Suddenly it happens. We round a corner to feast our eyes on a kaleidoscope of rich, ripe colors. Our vision floats past table after table of fresh produce and homemade breads. The colors and textures drench my senses. All desire for sandwiches vanishes in favor of real food. We have stumbled on the street market. "Let's each buy something and then share," Jenny suggests. "It'll be fun. Mom, just do the best you can," she says, referring to my sad attempts at communicating in Italian. She walks away to a table that is calling to her taste buds. The next few minutes I spend staring at the plump, red tomatoes. I have no idea how to ask in Italian, so I point to a stem of cherry tomatoes. There are at least fifteen swollen, ripe, red jewels on this one stem. A man in a dirty white apron, with stains from top to bottom, smiles at me and says, "*Due?*"

"*Sì.*"

"*Due euro.*" He carefully lowers the juicy, red prizes into a plastic sack. I hand him the blue five-euro bill that is like small play money. He drops two coins into my hand with a cheery, "*Grazie.*" I smile back at him and attempt a "*grazie,*" which I'm sure hurt his ears. It takes me two more weeks to learn how to properly say, "*grazie.*" At the table next to me, two women are scrutinizing each item before them, nodding seriously to one another while directing verbiage toward the vendor. So pensive are they that I think they must be judging for a produce competition. Buying fresh foods, at least to them, is an intense experience. I didn't understand such scrutiny when everything looks delectable. I move away from the table to the jingles and jangles of euros dropping into apron pockets and makeshift cash boxes.

Purchases made, we meet at a brick water fountain in the center of the courtyard behind the tables. Jake bought luscious red grapes and a hunk of bread. Jenny bought two pieces of cheese, and I presented the tomatoes. I wonder where the water originates that trickles from this tarnished brass spout. Others are leaning over to wash their food in the water and no one is keeling over dead, so we join in the fun. We look around for a place to sit, met with thousand-year-old steps spotted in pigeon pooh. Our hungry minds convince us we can stay away from the filth if we sit on our plastic sacks. No utensils available, we use our hands to break the bread and cheese. Of all the varied and extraordinary Italian cuisine I will eat for the next three months, this simple picnic is unparalleled—a visceral tsunami. Children chase each other around the bricked square that holds the water faucet. In this ancient, dirty, simple setting with my children, I soak in the moment and experience the gift of life. In this *aah* moment, in spite of the filth and heat, I wonder, *How can one possibly moan about anything?*

Jenny chats with a group of gondoliers during a mid-afternoon slump and talks one of them down from thirty-five euros per person to twelve euros per person. That's profitable flirting, I'd say. How could we miss a ride in an authentic Venetian gondola? Our gondolier, Giorgio, is dressed in a red and white striped shirt with a red bandana around his neck and a straw hat with a flat brim that sports two ribbon tails that hang in the back and flap in the breeze. He wears black slacks and black sunglasses. He serenades us with Buddy Holly's "Peggy Sue" (in broken English) when he learns we are from Buddy Holly's hometown, Lubbock, Texas. This gondolier, living in Venice, Italy, knows Buddy Holly is from Lubbock. The ride through the green canal is great fun, as long as I don't look at the yuck on the water's surface. Giorgio is an entertainer and has us hooting and hollering.

Nic arrives twenty minutes late. His tall, thin frame bounces out of a dark blue Subaru and runs around to greet us. His blue eyes and blond hair match his pale skin. He peers through silver, wire-framed glasses, and his pride in the English he knows bursts forth with energy and personality. He puts us all at ease when we know he wants to communicate in English. Fortunately for Jenny, he is willing to stop by the airport on the way home to pick up the little box. Jake and Jenny work on their Italian with Nic, and Nic and I work on English. It's incredible that total strangers, who can't speak each other's language, can have so much to talk about. Every so often, the car sinks in silence while thought and processing take over, then Nic breaks the silence with another question in his fractured English. "Sue Ellen, you comfortable?" or "When arrive?"

We pull up in front of Marco Polo Airport and Jenny goes in

alone. She returns fifteen minutes later, empty-handed, with that look of despair only a drama queen illuminates.

"They said maybe tomorrow."

"Jenny, just wear a ponytail," I suggest.

"I can't pull my hair back for three months!" Her hair shines like new copper pennies and to the world is beautiful no matter how she has combed it. The copper color frames her peaches-and-cream skin and brown eyes. She doesn't need a curling iron.

"Third time's a charm. I'll just come back tomorrow," she informs me.

Nic lives in a large two-story apartment in Maestre. His animated, outgoing personality isn't that of any accountant I've ever met, but his apartment fits—it is organized, has few things, and is very clean. Nic shows us everything in every room of the downstairs. We will learn through the summer that giving a home tour for guests is the Italian way. It is actually more than a home tour. They want their guests to feel comfortable with every item in their homes. He does not take us upstairs, but promptly seats us at the large wooden dining table and offers us some potato chips and glasses of water. The glass size is modest, four ounces. The pitcher isn't much larger. Four ounces doesn't cut through my thirst, and I want to turn the pitcher up and guzzle its contents. We are being introduced, bit-by-bit, to the Italian way—small showers, mini cars, dainty sandwiches, and miniscule water glasses. Then, Nic brings in a bottle of white wine that is three feet tall and twenty-five inches around. "This is Italy," he proudly announces. He stands hugging the bottle and resting it on his right leg as he pours us each a glass of wine and offers a toast. "To the English words," he says with his glass held high. "Excuse me, *uno momento*," Nic says as he leaves the dining room. He returns with a dictionary, a pencil, and some paper. With our help, he wants to write some English sentences, so he can study them later. He has three English-speaking tutors, two of whom want to pick his Italian brain for Italian words. I just want to rest my English brain and re-hydrate. Nic confidently pronounces the English word as he lifts each item, "Pen-chl," he says as he holds the number two yellow pencil in the air. "Deek-show-nar-i," and he raises the Italian/English dictionary. "Shit of pa-per," as he holds the white paper. We burst into laughter, and Nic looks surprised. "Shit of pa-per?" he asks, enunciating precisely.

"It's sheeeet," Jenny emphasizes. "Sheeeet." Nic, pleased with the English he knows, opens the dictionary, finds the word, and proudly announces, "Here," as he points to the corresponding Italian word. "In English, shit." He once again holds up the piece of paper and says, "One shit of paper." He returns to the dictionary and attempts to spell *sheet* in English, which reveals his limited knowledge of the English phonics. Jake's body is laughing. No noise leaves his mouth, but his entire body is engaged in sidesplitting laughter. He alternates bending at the waist, pumping up and down, stretching his legs out in spasms, grabbing his chest, and generally shaking hysterically. So entertained is Jake that he can no longer participate in the conversation that has now become a serious lesson in proper English pronunciation.

"Nic, look," Jenny says as she points to her mouth. She draws out the sound of *ee* as far as she can. Nic flattens his mouth and says successfully, "*eeeeee.*" We all clap in praise, but "shit" is programmed into his Italian brain as the correct English pronunciation of the word *sheet.* "*Eeeee,*" Nic practices, then again he raises the paper and says, "One shit of paper." It is hopeless and even more hysterical as he raises two sheets of paper and emphatically says, "One, two shit of paper." Who am I to laugh? I am still working on pronouncing "*buon giorno*" without drawling it out to "*bone jor-no.*" The Italian word for *hello* (*ciao*) is one syllable, but when a phonics teacher sees three vowels in a row, she feels an obligation to them all.

Through our laughter, Nic hears his wife, Christina, arrive. He jumps up and runs to greet her, grabs her hand, and pulls her toward us. "Christina, my good wife," he introduces. I wonder if he always met Christina with his smile that could melt a glacier. Good wife is another English term he knows well. Christina is quite shy, with a pretty smile and friendly blue eyes. She is not confident enough to try her English with us, so she looks longingly at Nic for help. When Christina excuses herself and goes upstairs, Nic says, "She make a meal." I immediately get up and start for the stairs. "I want to help Christina." Nic comes for me and leads me back to my chair. "No, Christina make meal." I'm thinking, *Typical male, let the woman who has worked all day prepare the meal.* In my world, the women help each other in the kitchen. I can hardly sit knowing she is preparing a meal, for five of us, with no help. Once again, I head toward the stairs. Nic shouts in an urgent tone, "*Non e possibile.*"

"Please," I plead. Nic escorts me up the stairs and says something to Christina. With a cutting tone in her sweet voice, she answers him, which brings a look of sudden disaster to his expressive face. I don't know if she is just painfully shy or if she is afraid of the language barrier, so in my kindest voice, I say, "*Por favor*" in my Texas accent. They look at each other and giggle and smile. "*Ah, capisce espanol,*" Nic informs me. As the summer progresses, I will be guilty of throwing in Spanish words regularly. I must have retained some of the four years I studied Spanish in high school. Christina points downstairs, and Nic and I obediently go back and sit, awaiting our meal.

Satisfaction beams on Christina's face when she presents our meal. In one bowl is a salad of lettuce, tomato, and buffalo mozzarella balls. Vinegar and oil is the only dressing option. Hot spaghetti steams from another bowl, and marinara sauce with tuna fish sits near. We watch to see what we are to do, and learn that here the salad is not eaten first. Nic smiles at Christina and says, "Good wife, good wife."

Our contrasting cultures are evident to me as I think about the exchange concerning my helping Christina in the kitchen. In American culture, the guest offers, and can even insist, on helping the hostess in the kitchen with positive response. At least, it is considered polite to offer help. Christina's response was heavy, as if she would feel violated or be in trouble with the Italian sisterhood if I helped in the kitchen. We were to learn after many attempts to help in kitchens all over Italy that nothing makes an Italian, male or female, happier than to provide fine hospitality, treating guests as they would nuggets of gold or priceless gems.

Chapter Five
Testing the Plan

Marco is a thirty-three-year-old, Italian businessman we met on the street in Venice. His eyes met Jenny's eyes and locked. I saw it and felt like I was in a movie, a love story. His muscular build, *ripped* as the kids say, complimented his coal black hair, which was slicked back with just a hint of a curl hanging in front, reminiscent of Elvis Presley's hair. Marco had the straightest back I've ever seen, but in spite of his erect posture, he was barely Jenny's height. Marco has two out of the three sought after attributes. He is definitely dark and handsome. He sells fine art by appointment only and often must communicate in English. He understood enough of what Jenny told him to realize that tonight we were staying with Nic, a total stranger. In their brief exchange on the street in Venice, Marco left Jenny with his cell phone number and told her if she wanted to go to the movies tonight, she could call him. I never gave it another thought. My twenty-one year old wouldn't call a stranger in a foreign country and go out with him, would she? No, she has more sense. After all, this is our first day here. We don't know much about Italians except what we've seen in movies. Later, we learned that Marco was as concerned about our staying with Nic, as Nic was about Jenny's going out with Marco. After Christina's delicious dinner, Jenny asked to use a phone so she could call Marco and go to the movies. Nic suggested she invite him to come in and visit for a while so we could all meet him.

Marco arrives, biceps bulging from his white t-shirt and quads stretching his white jeans that are a size too small. I begin planning how I will talk him into staying and visiting instead of taking Jenny out. He sits and visits for an hour. Mostly he and Nic converse in Italian. I keep eyeing him, trying to size him up. Unlike happy Nic, Marco is serious and guarded and is the first Italian I have seen in my two days in Italy who looks like he is a Mafioso. My body feels weak, as uneasiness engulfs it. Putting it mildly, I am freaking out as Jenny and Marco leave the house at 11:00 p.m. Flashes of life without Jenny occupy my mind. Will she return? Will he mistreat her? Will we find her dead in a ditch somewhere? Will the Italian officials care to look for an American? I ache. It is torture. Under normal circumstances, I would not sleep, but my exhausted body falls unconscious across the hard cot and I don't wake until 2:00 a.m. Jenny hasn't returned. Adrenaline shoots through my body, preparing it for the Terminator mode. Marco had given me his cell phone number, so I call it. Jenny answers, "Mom, we're sitting out front." I hang up the phone and, in my pajamas, go directly out to the car. If the sight of me in my pajamas at 2:00 a.m. doesn't scare Marco away, nothing will. Greatly relieved and energized by my two and a half hours of sleep and the adrenaline cocktail, I say, "It's 2:00 a.m. We have to get up in five hours!" Suddenly, five hours sounds like an eternity. I'm going to enjoy five hours sleep tonight.

"Okay, Mom, I'll be there in a minute."

The next time I volunteer, it is going to be in the labor rooms of a hospital. I will assure the young mothers who are agonizing in labor how blessed they are to be experiencing this grand physical pain and assure them they should enjoy every gripping contraction that hardens their abdominal roundness. The mental anguish, emotional pain, sleepless nights, exhausting days, and heartbreaking decisions they will face over the lifetime of this new addition make these few laboring hours the last hours of their freedom, rest, and sanity. I will assure these vulnerable moms-to-be that as a mother of three adults, it doesn't get easier. The anxieties are just different. Another thirty minutes and Jenny comes in. Of course, she has to recount her past four hours with Marco, in her dramatic, exaggerated way. She is incapable of being half-hearted about anything; it's one of her endearing qualities. Marco had said to her, "You can't be asking people to take you home," to which she replied, "Why not?" I hope Marco didn't think our bold nuttiness could somehow dissolve Italian/American relations, start a war, or something equally earth-shattering. "He thinks we're nuts, Mom. He's very concerned. He said, '*voi state pazzi*,' which means, 'You are nuts.' He said we needed to stay in hostels with other backpackers and travel in groups for safety. I told him that we want to be with Italians, not Americans." Marco had things on his mind concerning Jenny. I'm sure of it, but even considering this, it seemed unlikely that he would be so concerned about us. My tiredness wins over my ruminations, and I doze off at 4:00 a.m.

Nick and Christina take us to the airport on their way out of town. It's fascinating how Italian cars drive themselves. I count, and Nic touches the steering wheel six times. These are times someone else is talking, and he doesn't need his hands. Amazing. After finding the appropriate service window inside Marco Polo Airport, we are given the box that we have longed for these past two days. The curling iron has arrived. There is a God. No more bad hair days. We aren't sure where we are going today, but we will leave with the butane cartridges and a three-inch-long curling iron. We each retrieve our things from the box, and I find a place in my pack for my dental pics, plastic ties, and miniature Swiss Army knife. Once again, we board Bus Number One from the airport back to the canal. We are on our way out of Venice.

Jake and Jenny are linguistically emboldened after their conversations with Nic. Armed with new Italian vocabulary, they are willing to at least attempt speaking in Italian. Language is deep for me and will take me longer to be free with it. I am the one who listened to the *Speak Italian* tapes before we left, and now I realize they didn't help. Hearing the natives speak in their different dialects varies from the study-at-home language courses.

Jake has created some beautiful blown-glass items from his glassblowing classes back home. My favorite is a fourteen-inch-tall vase I call "the inebriate." It is made with a slight lean at the top and Jake wove colors of blue, rose, and yellow in with the clear glass as undefined flurries and flecks. The slight lean finishes it in artsy flair. We all want to see the world famous glass, so we hop a water taxi and spend the next few hours gazing in windows at beautiful handblown objects on the island of Murano. To our disappointment, the glassblowing masters are off for the afternoon, a common Italian habit. Murano is basically a pier, and some men are selling produce out of their boats, so we buy some juicy peaches and plums for our lunch. The fruit weighs grams and kilograms, instead of ounces and pounds. The metric system is supposed to be easier. It's not. The only thing I ever mastered metrically was changing kilometers to miles. Since we are walking, this calculation is important. Although it is 1.6 kilometers to a mile, I just round it to 1.5 when I convert. It works for me.

The afternoon's heat wilts us, and we find a shaded corner to sit and rest. If my friends could see me now! Here I sit on the dirty ground, leaning up against an ancient wall of broken brick, deteriorating plaster, and patches of stone, while eating a peach. A few peaches will not fill a backpacker no matter his age, so we break down and buy *panini*. We exhaust window-shopping in Murano and follow a rumor that the island of Jesolo offers jobs for travelers and places to stay. Rumors are interesting creatures. They presumptuously jump in your lap, wearing a mask, and once unmasked, they quickly turn into rumors, but we head to Jesolo anyway and arrive at 7:00 p.m. to find that Jesolo is made with the tourist in mind. The bus station is central, with an Internet Point directly across the street. A quick search and Jake learns there are no Hospitality Club or Couch Surfing members in or around Jesolo. We have our first opportunity to test the plan of going home with someone on the street, but first, Jenny calls Marco and asks if he knows anyone in the area who houses travelers. "No," he says, "but I will call you later." I am rested enough to think I can sleep on the beach if necessary. Jesolo is small and much more inviting than Venice. The atmosphere shouts, *Relax, this is seaside Italy*, so at dusk we walk the empty beach. The misty air teases the day's last light, and the setting sun puffs pink through the haze over the sea. My backpack pulls on my back, but the cool sand against my bare feet carries me along step by step. We come to a dock where four happy college-age Italians are enjoying the setting sun. Jake and Jenny introduce themselves and attempt conversing in Italian. One of the four, a girl with long black hair and dark eyes, dressed in an airy, white skirt and blouse, speaks broken English and attempts translating for the others. I sit in the cool, moist sand, leaning against my burden, watching and listening to this international conversation. I am slowly sliding into my role as Bohemian. I have no idea when my next bath will appear, and when I get up, sand will be stuck to my backside, feet, and legs.

The young Italians are open and eager to attempt conversing with these two bold Americans. Soon they are all laughing, singing, and even dancing on the pier. Jake's international language is dance, and he's good at it. One of the girls is willing to attempt swing dancing with him. In twenty minutes, this group interacts as if they have known each other for years. What is it about age that restricts this free interaction? If these six youth were fifty years old, would this be taking place? Wisdom and experience put up barriers, and those barriers prevent us from sharing with each other. Is it the day-to-day, year-to-year, routine of life that stiffens our minds?

Jenny hoists my pack and holds it until I strap myself in. We all leave the pier together and stroll toward the bus station in a chorus of laughter and slaughtered languages. My attempts at speaking Italian are disasters. I'm still trying to process the unusual names I'm hearing, Gianni, Silvio, Giusseppe, Alessio, Graziella, Niccolo, much less form phrases. I can only hope that listening to this constant unfamiliarity is working my brain, loosening it, and sweeping out the cobwebs. The air is thick and quiet. I wobble and weave with the pack on and hope no one bumps me because I'll taste the dirt. We have no place to stay and the time is 10:30 p.m., but whatever happens, happens. Each day that I survive in a foreign country with no disaster gives me strength. The English-speaking girl tells us about a club that opens at 1:30 a.m. and is a popular dancing spot. With Jake along, we have to check it out, so I guess we'll sit around until 1:30 a.m. *What have I gotten myself into?* We part, never to see these delightful young Italians again.

On the way to the bus station, we encounter a young man sitting alone on a bench just enjoying the cool ocean breezes. We stop as he speaks. "Hello, you are Americans?"

"Yes, from Texas," Jenny announces.

"Hello, my name is Carlo." We introduce ourselves and ask how he knows we are Americans. "You don't look Italian. I just guess," he says. A charming and gentle young man, Carlo was born and raised in France. His grandfather married an Italian and has a home in Cornuda, sixty-two miles from Jesolo. After his grandmother's death, his grandfather moved back to France. Currently Carlo is living in his grandfather's house and attending the university nearby. As would become our way, at some point we turn the conversation into a request for a bed(s). This is a very humbling experience. Our unique way of travel intrigues Carlo, and he asks many questions, mostly on the idea of no plan or money. His English is the best we have heard thus far. His black curly hair and dark eyes are definitely Italian, but his six-foot-two-inch frame and gentle manner must be French. The air is heavy and smells of salt and seaweed, and we stand conversing with the salty breezes against our faces. At age twenty-four, Carlo is fluent in French, Italian, and English. His happy smile and boyish look are inviting. I wish I could sit on the bench and talk with him all night. "I do not know of any beds for you," he says, "but I wish you good luck." We continue on our way toward the bus station. The sidewalk outside the station swarms with young people. I am the only older person

I see. I sit happily on a bench under a sprawling tree, not knowing where to go or what to do, just watching in amazement the bold attempts at communicating in Italian that my two children display. Watching them enjoy themselves in these attempts is eye opening. We are in a foreign country. No one knows us. It is okay to make fools of ourselves, right? Mentally, I am working on Italian syntax. The word order is twisted compared to English. I have allowed my not knowing the conjugations of the Italian verbs to stifle my attempts at communicating. After all, I'm an English teacher, and subject/verb agreement is important to me! I envy Jake and Jenny's comfort with all this strangeness.

So, here we are, just hanging out at the bus station with some locals, some travelers, and my hopes of a place to sleep. At fifty-six years old, I never thought I'd be 'hanging' at a bus station. Sweat is once again dripping down my face. Marco has not called, so Jenny decides to call him again. At this very moment, I see Carlo wandering through the crowd. Jenny is easy to spot in a crowd with her flaming red hair, and he walks up to her and says, "If you don't mind traveling sixty-two miles to get to my house, you can stay with me."

"My mom and brother, too?"

"Yes," he replies. Jenny shouts, "Mom, Carlo said we can stay with him." I instantly love him. He has spent an hour and a half thinking about this. Taking home three strangers is new to him. I think my presence as a mother eased his concerns about embarking on this new experience. In fact, I'm sure of it. I have an honest face, and I look like a teacher, which may not always be a positive, but it has served me well. Back home at the corner of 26 Street and Avenue X is a stop sign. Eighteen years ago, on a warm spring day early enough that the buds on the elms were just opening, the kids and I were returning from a neighborhood grocery store. This was before cell phones and markets that sprawl over acres of land and offer everything from motor oil to false fingernails. I approached the stop sign as if it were an old friend, then touched the brake pedal just enough to slow down so I could look both ways. The stop sign had not been at this corner for long. For years, I had floated around the corner, slowing just enough to look both ways. I did the same today, and suddenly adrenaline spiked through my body as it always does when I see flashing red lights signaling my brain that I need to pull over. I pull to the curb, announcing to my children that I have just broken the law. The officer saunters to my door as I'm rolling down the window and says in a slow drawl, "Ma'am, you didn't stop back there. Did ya know that?" He looks in at Jake, age six, and Jenny, age three, who are staring at him in awe and hanging on his every word. "That sign hasn't always been there. I guess I was careless," I answered. I'm reaching for my license and insurance card when he says with a lighter tone, "Ma'am, did you teach school in El Paso?"

"No," I answered looking at a row of the whitest teeth I've ever seen. They looked like someone had taken all the stars in the sky and arranged them in his mouth. They sparkled and glistened against his black skin. His smile grew wider and his eyes brightened. "Are you sure you never taught second grade in El Paso?"

"No, sir, not in El Paso. I did teach second grade though." He held his gaze on me as he grinned and shook his head. "I can't believe it. You look just like my favorite teacher." He took my license and just held it. He was more interested in talking about his old school days than anything. "I can't remember her name," he continued, "but you look just like her. She was the best teacher I ever had." He handed me my license and insurance card and said, "This stop sign is always here, so you stop next time, okay?"

"Yes, sir," I promised. He looked in at the kids. "You kids take good care of your mother, ya hear?"

"Yes sir," they replied, wide eyed. He turned and left, and I sat in disbelief that my face had just saved me from a ticket.

Jenny relays the message to Marco that we have a place to stay. "Is not safe," he tells her.

"Marco, why don't you come dancing with us?" she asks.

"Wait at the station. I come there." He says he wants to meet and talk to Carlo before we drive off into the darkness with him. Marco's concern for our safety supersedes our own. We aren't operating on reason, just on our faith and good looks. Jake, Jenny, Marco, and Carlo dance until 3:00 a.m. I sit outside, on a bench in the night air, watching people. The fine clothes and shoes that parade before me could rival fashion week in Paris. Italians wear their clothes well. Every male has on a button-up shirt. Many are open three-fourths of the way down, exposing gold chains and hairy chests. Shiny leather shoes, mostly loafers, dress their feet. The women, all in stilettos, look like they are either on their way to or have just returned from a fashion runway. I gaze at my red Keens with thick rubber soles and canvas straps. *Yeah, you can't hide your Americanism.* The more time we spend in Italy, the more evident it becomes that average Italians may not have much, but they have some fine clothes.

Carlo takes a break from dancing at 2:00 a.m. to sit and talk with me. He begins the conversation by asking me about politics. Quick enemies or fast friends materialize over these talks. He surely feels comfortable with me as he directs the conversation. I've never talked about more controversial ideas in one sitting, than I did on the bench outside the disco in Jesolo. Carlo is interested in America beyond what he reads in the paper or hears on Italian TV. He has the undivided attention of a real American. We disagree on many things we discuss; he respects my views and never interrupts me; he listens intently and expresses his appreciation to me for helping him understand a different point of view. *Wow*, I think. *He's twenty-four.* I leave very impressed with Carlo's ability to express himself in English and converse intelligently with insight into the differences in cultures and politics.

After meeting sweet, gentle Carlo, Marco is still not convinced we will be safe—or maybe his concern comes from wanting to spend more time with this beautiful American redhead. Jenny rides in Marco's car, while Jake and I ride with Carlo in his little blue Renault Twingo, for the sixty-two miles to Carlo's house. At 4:30 a.m., darkness hides the setting, but once in Cornuda, we drive down a dirt road where Carlo stops at a locked gate. He opens the gate, drives down a narrow drive past a palm tree, and stops at a two-story structure. Carlo lives upstairs, and the entire downstairs stands empty. We enter downstairs to a large living area; on our left, leaning against the wall, is one dark green couch, frayed and flat. A wood, dining table and two rickety, wood chairs stand alone in the middle of this large room. The walls are a dingy white, and bare. A musty coldness permeates the air. The pale, gray, linoleum-tiled floor is even colder. Dust blankets everything. The living room opens into a small kitchen that is bare except for a dirty, freestanding gas stove, which holds an aluminum tea strainer, a black teacup, a cracked white teacup, and a small pot. A straw broom with a yellow splintered handle leans against the wall next to the stove. Carlo points toward the opposite wall where two beds hide in a bedroom. A large, old wardrobe and a dresser with a foggy mirror squeeze into the remaining space in the bedroom. A gold-framed picture of Christ, palms-up, exposing his nail-pierced hands, hangs above the double bed. The beige, chenille bedspread looks more dusty than beige. A plastic cross with Christ hangs over the twin bed that is covered by a multicolored crocheted throw that Carlo says his grandmother made. Carlo introduces us to everything downstairs, reminding us that no one lives here, so it may not be clean. We all three tell him dirty doesn't matter to us. We are grateful for a bed and a shower. Jake, Jenny, and I sleep in the bedroom. Marco sleeps on the couch in the living room. Carlo doesn't seem offended that Marco has followed us and is sleeping on his couch. It is near 5:00 a.m. when we all crash, and I hear Marco leave at 7:30 a.m. to get to work in Venice. I am amazed that he spent his evening following us.

We have the good fortune of sleeping as long as we want. I rise at 9:00 a.m. to the hum of tractors outside. I can hardly wait to see the countryside. As soon as Carlo sees I am up, he offers me coffee or tea and cookies. I have my breakfast upstairs in his sunny kitchen, where small cactus plants smile from the windowsill. The view is spectacular with *il monte grappa* in the background. We finish our tea and cookies, and Carlo takes me on an outdoor tour. For 360 degrees around this four-home complex, the countryside is complete with cornfields, flower gardens, vegetable gardens, and farmers driving small, old Lamborghini tractors. "Would you like see my garden?" Carlo asks.

"I would love to see your garden. I have several gardens at my house and someone else is weeding them for me," I say, thinking about poor Rachel in the blazing west Texas sun. He leads me to his vegetable patch where I help him water. There isn't a weed in the garden, only healthy plants in perfectly straight rows of melons, cucumber, lettuce, spinach, pepper, onion, beans, and of course, tomatoes. I dig my fingers into the ground. The soft, brown earth crumbles around them—heavenly. Gardening feeds every cell in my body. For me, it's a spiritual experience akin to an awakening. I tell Carlo of my forty-one rose bushes, yellow daffodils, Shasta daisies, red dianthus, purple larkspur and asters, red Oriental poppies, and golden lilies. He smiles, "Weeds take my flowers. My time is in vegetables."

"May I weed for you?" I ask.

"No, no, not necessary."

"I would like to since you are offering this wonderful hospitality to us." Reluctantly, he takes me to the flowerbed, offers some garden gloves, a wheelbarrow, and an old, rusty shovel. As I weed, I drift into my own world, become distracted, and touch the stinging nettle vines. A burning sting creeps up my arms like snakes up a tree. Instantly, huge welts break out over both arms. I've never experienced anything like it. I look for thorns on my arms, because a constant feeling of needles piercing my skin with a burning sensation persists. Carlo had returned to his vegetables.

"Carlo," I shout to him, motioning him my way. As soon as he sees, he says, "Oh, no. The nettles."

"I've never seen nettles."

"My remedy," he says, "is rub seven different leaves on the skin."

"What?"

59

"It heals," he assures me. "I gather seven leaves for you."

"Sure," I say, thinking I really just want some cold water. He brings leaves from the linden tree, geranium, peach, elm, angelica, basil, and laurel. We apply the leaves. My mind stretches pretty far concerning alternative healing, but this was a little too far.

"Have you seen this work?"

"If you believe it, it works," he replies with a smile.

"Of course," I answer, winking at him. We are applying this same belief in the words on the yellow card. After a few hours, the stinging subsides, but the skin irritation and some raised spots remain another day.

My 9:00 a.m. cookies and tea run out by noon, but I can't impose. Surely, Carlo will get hungry. I hint, offering to buy some groceries if he can take me to the store. He says, "Not necessary." I remain outside all day, drinking in the Italian countryside, watching the farmers on their small, open-air tractors and enjoying the opportunity to just be. It is 3:00 p.m. when Carlo calls us to the kitchen. I bolt upstairs. As Carlo stirs the meat sauce, he says, "The meat is 50 percent cow."

"50 percent beef?" Jake asks a bit skeptically.

"Yes, beef," Carlo corrects himself.

"What is the other 50 percent?" Jenny is intently watching Carlo for his response. "I don't know," he answers. We never learn what the other meat was. We all look at each other, but our hunger welcomes the 50/50 mix. Carlo picks up the pot of spaghetti, rinses it in a colander and turns to begin serving when I, curious about the pronunciation of the vowel *i*, ask him about it. With Carlo's knowledge of three languages, I eagerly anticipate his answer. Jake and Jenny sit poised over their plates licking their lips, their eyes glazed and fixed on the spaghetti. When I voice the question, Carlo stops short of delivering the steaming strings, and gives me an incredibly interesting lesson on the letter *i* while he stands holding the colander. The lesson covers the little *i*'s pronunciation and contribution to both Italian and French. I am fascinated with this young man's linguistic knowledge. Jake and

Jenny are drooling into their plates when Carlo finally serves them. Our next meal with Carlo is rice with spinach from his garden. How can I escape losing weight with this kind of diet? Answer: I discover gelato. That luscious, icy, tantalizing, creamy Italian gelato is made available in Italy as Starbucks makes coffee available to Americans—it is everywhere. Gelato is the most satisfying gift on hot Italian summer days.

Jenny and I spend the late afternoon strolling around this quiet town of vacation homes and large, single-family dwellings. Cornuda is impressionistic, complete with dirt roads and porches splashed with red geraniums. While Jenny and I are strolling, Jake is e-mailing Hospitality Club (HC) members in Padova. (Padua in English. The Padua of Romeo and Juliet). Tomorrow, when Carlo takes the train to school, we will go to Padova. Everything slows these two days in Cornuda. My senses open. I have time to breathe and think about how, at home, the days are a blur, sliding by in a steady stream of routines. Carlo, a Frenchman, is introducing me to the casual, laid-back Italian culture that he loves. This strangeness requires me to concentrate, focus, and listen. Trying to read a road sign or listen to a conversation has slowed me.

I give Carlo twenty euros when we leave and wish it could have been more. So little, for so much. I hope it will pay for the rice and spaghetti. He was instrumental in opening my heart and mind to a new way. This was his first experience hosting total strangers and I hope he enjoyed it. In his gentle voice, he wishes us well in our unconventional way of travel. We take pictures and exchange e-mail addresses. Our three packs won't fit in the backspace of his tiny Renault, so Jake, who sits in the front, has to hold one on his lap. I leave, hoping Carlo will someday come visit Texas and stay at my house.

Chapter Six

Tattoos and Implants

The train's windows are down and its passengers are hoping for any breeze to cool them. We pull away from the station in Cornuda, and make our way along the tracks through Montebelluna, Castelfranco Veneto, Camposampiero, S. Giorgio Delle Pertiche, Campodarsego, Vigodarzere, and finally Padova. I look to the right and see mountains, not so grand as the Rockies, but mountains just the same. Miles of wire support vines covering the foothills whose vineyards burst with hope for the future. I look left and see areas of unkept countryside, shacks, and clothes hanging on lines so near the rails they must surely dry with train tracks across them. I wonder how anyone can live this near a train track, with only a flimsy fence of wire separating the house from the tracks. With each passing train, surely the house shakes and the bodies within vibrate. At each stop, one or two get off, and one or two get on for a ride down the tracks. Our trip to Padova is scheduled to be fifty-nine minutes. When we arrive in Padova, Jenny uses a payphone at the station to call her Hospitality Club contact. Using Italian phones is an adventure in itself. Sometimes they connect and sometimes they don't. Sometimes all you need to do is dial slower. Sometimes you need to let three seconds lapse before pushing the next number. Sometimes they don't work in the afternoon, during rest time. Sometimes they don't work if we are talking while dialing, as if the phone doesn't understand English. Often we try several times and leave the phone in frustration to see an Italian have success dialing on the same phone. We are beginning to have respect for the Italian version of the payphone. In fact, we talk about them as if they were people. "I wonder if this one is on break," or, "Let's see if this one speaks English."

In Italy, businesses close from 1:00 to 4:00 p.m. for a rest. I think about how proud Americans are of our productivity, and we eagerly listen to the news for the announcement that American productivity is up. In Italy, business hours are 10:00 to 1:00 and 4:00 to 7:00—sometimes. If they don't want to reopen in the afternoon, they don't, and no sign is placed on the door for the potential customer who may stand outside waiting for the opening. In Italy, the goal is not to produce as much as possible, nor is the goal to fix the problem as soon as possible. The goal is to have a relationship. If the problem is remedied right away, the opportunity to talk and talk, and meet over a shot of espresso to talk some more about the problem, is denied to the parties involved. A single relationship is much more important to Italians than productivity.

"You late," he tells her, "I give boys sofa. They are now." Jenny hangs up the phone and says, "Well, let's look for a computer. He didn't wait for us. Some boys got here before we did, so we lost our couch." *Oh, not again, not the computer search.* My experiences looking for a computer in Italy this past week could last me a lifetime. "*Dove computer?*" becomes our mantra. Later we learn our question is not grammatically correct. Literally we were asking, "Where computer?" We then add the *e* and *il* to complete the sentence with "*Dove e il computer?*" Many Italians have never seen a computer, let alone know where one is available. Italy is about twenty years behind America technologically, and this is one reason Italian culture is so appealing. Italy takes us back to a slower time, a less demanding time, a simpler time. It seems we ask every other person on the street in Padova where the Internet Point is or where a computer can be found. Each person sends us in a different direction or just shrugs his shoulders. Maybe this will be our first night to sleep on a park bench. I keep anticipating this experience because it will be a turning point for me. I will no longer mind being sweaty and dirty; I won't fear the unknown; a shift in my thinking will have to occur once I've experienced a night with no shelter.

We literally stumble on a street market just before we all collapse into hungry, tired nothingness. I stub my toe going over the curb and fall just missing the nectarines. I can see myself under a pile of fresh produce and Italian breads, but not this time. "Are you okay, Mom?" Jenny asks.

"Yeah, that was close," I reply as she helps me up. The juicy, red tomatoes, white cheese, leafy lettuce, and tough bread we eat at just the right time provide us a heavenly experience and much-needed rest. I could live here permanently, just to eat the tomatoes every day. The gastronomic pleasures of Italian produce minimize my ability to create worthy verbal descriptions. The red tomatoes in supermarkets back home are deceiving—there is never perfection inside. Even my homegrown tomatoes, though ripe and juicy, do not have the depth of flavor Italian tomatoes have. Italy's tomatoes are ineffable and defy description, so I stop trying to abridge their glory. We sit, slurping our tomatoes and watching people in the piazza. Before us sits a group of nine American students. Hot and tired, they sit on the sidewalk in the shade of a building. It is easy to talk to one's own kind when they are discovered in a sea of foreigners, so I jump up and greet them. What a small world it is! They are from Texas Tech University in Lubbock. We chat and take pictures, then they, knowing exactly where we can find a computer, give us directions to the University of Padova. Hearing directions in English is music. After walking the streets of Padova for hours, asking directions to the nearest computer, this group of college kids from our hometown saves us.

With sweat pouring from my head and my pack discouraging

every step, my only driving force is the hope of finding that technologically advanced piece of equipment on which students worldwide depend—and then suddenly before us stand the great white pillars of the university. As we enter the building, the first thing to catch our attention is a sign with "Labs" printed on it and an arrow pointing up the stairs. "Maybe they're computer labs," Jake says.

"Let's find out," Jenny adds, dropping her pack at my feet as my hot, tired body sinks onto a brown, wooden bench leaning against a wall. They bound up the stairs to find the labs.

Adjacent to the bench and through a glass window is a room large enough for two people. The wall behind the counter holds brown, green, blue, and clear bottles of liquor and beer. Shoved against another wall is a portable ice cooler with "Gelato" written across the front. The clerk is dwarfed by the racks of cigarettes, chewing gum, and candy that rest on the counter around him. A sign hangs on the wall behind him listing the drinks. I quickly practice what I will say to get my hands on a cold, green bottle of beer. I remember in 1998 when we made our first trip to Europe, no one served cold beer. It was always room temperature, but now cold beer is everywhere in Italy.

"You can do this," I encourage myself. "*Una birra per favore,*" I practice audibly as I look at the cashier on the other side of the glass window. "*Una birra, per favore. Una birra, per favore.*" I enter and look straight into the cashier's eyes and say, "*Una beer, por favor.*" Question marks cover his eyes. I smile my Texas smile. "*Birra?*" he queries.

"*Si,*" I answer and begin to apologize. "*Non parlo italiano.*"

"*Ah, bene,*" he responds with a smile. "*Americana?*"

"*Si, da Texas.*" The word Texas is an icebreaker everywhere. Those who have not visited Texas believe we still ride horses to work and carry guns. Well, half of that is still right. Some things don't change. The world knows President Bush is from Texas, which adds conversation beyond horses and guns. Thank God, this man doesn't dive into a political verse. All I can think of is a cold beer. He looks at the sign above his head and asks me something else. Not understanding, but taking his body language to mean I am to choose which beer I want, I say, *"Peretti."* He produces a green bottle and pours its cold, foamy contents into a plastic cup. *"Quanto?"* I ask.

"Due euro." I pay him and say, "Thank you. I mean, *Grazie."* He smiles and motions me out so someone else can come in.

Sitting, I heave a sigh. My insides are cooled as I pour this cold, golden liquid down my throat. A break from the heat, one beer, and it's time to rest my eyes. The kids' packs are at my feet and mine is on the bench. I lean against my pack and evidently doze off because a man standing over me, scowling and shaking his finger, awakens me. I surely look a sight with my sweaty hair stuck together; my long, dirtied skirt; wet, black t-shirt; and red Keen sandals hardly hiding my grimy feet. He probably thinks I am a vagrant sleeping on the bench of this great institution of higher education founded in 1222— the very institution where Copernicus, Petrarch, Dante, and Galileo taught or studied. I manage a smile that must have scared him. He steps back, looking indignant but continuing to shake his finger. I interpret his scolding to mean I can sit but not sleep. I sit up and put my pack on the floor. He returns a few minutes later to check on me. This time he looks at me, shakes his head, and walks away. If my friends could see me now, making a debauchery of history and higher education.

Jake and Jenny return, saying we will meet Robby at 6:00 p.m. at the fountain near a big building. *Great,* I think, looking at my watch, *we have four hours to find a fountain by a big building.* My afternoon has just been planned. We begin by looking around the university. In this setting, it is easy to imagine great thinkers strolling among the buildings, talking and teaching. I wish I could have been here when Copernicus introduced his theory of the sun being the center of the universe. That blew some wigs off!

We find the fountain around 5:45 p.m., just in time to sit a minute on its edge. This fountain splits the busy street, and cars, Vespas, dirt bikes, and busses zoom by on both sides, keeping the hot air swirling. We sit on the brick wall that surrounds the fountain and enjoy the spray that rides on the breeze toward us. The new building across from the fountain is where Robby works—we hope. We sit gazing up at the building, one of the taller buildings we've seen in Italy. "How old is Robby, Jake?" Jenny asks.

"I don't know. I guess around thirty."

"What's he do for this company?"

"I don't know. Something with computers I think. I hope he has a computer at his house."

"My feet are black," Jenny says as she dips them in the fountain's cool water. She has walked all day in her flip-flops, exposing her feet to the soot, dirt, and grime of this thousand-year-old city. She stands up and walks around in the fountain, her red hair tousled by the breeze. Cars honk and shouts of, "*Ciao bella*" and "*Bellissima*," accompany a few wolf whistles that come her way. She sits down and tries to rub the black from her feet. Her long, turquoise broomstick skirt with silver threads running through it is now wet around the bottom.

Jake retreats into his Jake world, conversing with someone we can't see.

"Who are you talking to, Jake?" I love asking him this.

"No one. Why do you think I'm talking to someone?"

"Because your mouth is moving but no sound is coming out."

"I guess I'm just practicing a conversation I might have later."

"Okay. You mean you are practicing? Why didn't you tell me this twenty years ago? All these years I've been worried about you, and you are just … practicing?"

A young man with coal black hair and beard appears and says, "Hello, I am Robby, and you are to go home with me." His English is good, and his friendly, silver rectangular glasses sitting crookedly on his nose frame black eyes. His long black beard is of the Amish persuasion, and his bushy, black hair is an art piece in itself. "I am Padova's Hospitality Club chairman," he adds, "and one of you will be the three-hundredth person I have in my house in eighteen months."

"Wow," I respond, "you must love strangers." Robby is wearing a pale blue dress shirt, black slacks, and black leather shoes that have seen better days. He carries a brown leather briefcase that looks as if it has been dragged behind a car the entire length of Italy. "I walk to work, so we walk home," he says as he walks the length of the fountain, then stops and adds, "Oh, yes, and do you need groceries? The store is there," he says, pointing across the street.

"Yes, we need groceries. None of us is willing to carry food. We've just been stopping at vegetable stands," Jenny says. Jake and I wait while Robby and Jenny shoot across the street for groceries. We both turn, facing the wind, hoping for another spray across our sweaty faces. When Robby and Jenny return, he says, "Okay, we go." Jenny is carrying a brown paper sack with a package of spaghetti in it. Man, if I don't lose weight on this trip, I never will. We've been walking and sweating all day, and we're going to have dry spaghetti for dinner.

"Mom, Robby told me why tax is never added when you buy something. It's included in the price, and guess what? It's a 20 percent tax!"

"Their sales tax is 20 percent?" I asked incredulously. "Wow, food would be nearly free without the tax." I set my pack on the fountain's wall and put one arm in a strap making my best effort at putting it on alone.

"Jenny, help me."

"Mom, you can do it."

"Jenny, just help me. We're going to get separated from Robby and Jake."

"They'll wait."

"Jenny!"

"Oh, Mom," she says, as she lifts my pack to enable me to slip my other arm in. "At least you got one arm in alone."

"Yeah, I'm getting better, huh," I say, grinning. Jake and Robby, lost in their own conversation, get far ahead of us. Robby realizes this, and they turn around and wait. The walk to Robby's house is a challenge for me. I'm hot. I'm tired, I'm feeling old, and Robby says it is four and a half kilometers (almost three miles). Robby, who is backpackless, young, and strong, walks much too fast for me. Twice I ask him to slow down. The second time he stops, takes my pack, and puts it on. "This is heavy," he says. "You are a strong mother."

"Thank you," I say, adjusting my head on my neck. We continue walking and weaving in and out of miniature cars parked along and on the sidewalk. I am grateful I don't have to squeeze into these tiny cars everyday.

"Not much more," he says.

"Can we slow down a little and enjoy the scenery?" They all oblige without a comment. During this trek, we learn about Robby's computer work; that he is twenty-eight years old; that he is going to visit his family in Sicily in two days; and that we are lucky because his roommate is leaving tonight, which means we can stay two nights if we want. As we continue deeper into a housing district, Jenny whispers, "He lives in the ghetto." All around us are apartments piled on top of each other in varied colors and stages of decay. Open windows are decorated with lines of drying laundry stretched across them. Dingy whites are sprinkled among colors. Below the hanging lines, the ground is littered with glass, trash, and dirty children playing.

"I live in the ghetto," Robby announces, "but it's not too bad."

"This is my car," he says as he points to an old white, Fiat Panda with a dent that caves in the right door. Rust, dents, and dings make it more a metal sculpture than a vehicle. It begged to be buried. We could plant vines and red geraniums to grow out its windows, which would go a long way to beautifying the neighborhood. "Here, this building," Robby announces as we follow him through an open gate. Two children are playing with a soccer ball. They take turns throwing it up to a boy leaning out an open window. He catches it and tosses it back to them. The girl on the ground misses the ball as she watches us. Her friend yells something to her and runs into the street to get the missed ball. "I can't believe I made it," I sigh. They all ignore me as we enter a brick building and pass a toddler sitting on some steps playing with two small rocks. His only clothing is a filthy cloth diaper. We make a right turn and go up four steps, turn left, and go up four more. Robby opens the door and immediately unloads my backpack just inside.

Padova's Hospitality Club chairman? I think, as the hairs in my nostrils stand on end. Loud techno music greets us. It is so loud we can't hear each other. Robby motions us to come in as he disappears and turns the music down. He returns and reminds us his roommate will be leaving soon. As soon as he says this, the music blares again, and the roommate appears, paying us no attention as he yells something at Robby. The air is a thick soup of pot and patchouli. My lungs tighten and send me signals, in the form of wheezes, to reconsider sinking further into this air. Robby attempts to introduce us to his roommate. I never hear his name. All I hear is Jake saying, "Cool." My first thought is that he ate his grandfather's tackle box. His face is covered in metal. I don't know which silver ring, hoop, or stud to look at first. I'm sure my eyes express fear, incredulity, or disbelief. The roommate wears only a dingy pair of canvas pants, torn and frayed. His right knee is totally exposed. Tattoos cover his back, chest, neck, and arms that both have raised rings under the skin. "They're called implants, Mom," Jenny informs me, as she shuts my gaping mouth. "Keep your mouth shut," she whispers. The implants resembled doughnuts under his skin, and just looking at them made my arms hurt. His dark dreadlocks meet his shoulders and desperately need attention. I step back. I can't believe what I'm seeing. I am overwhelmed and a little frightened. To see one so young altering his body to this degree is disheartening. I'd like to see him in thirty years, when gravity heaps lasting and permanent changes as his tattoos sag and the metal on his face takes a different slant. When he left, Robby turned the music off and it was off for the remainder of our stay.

As with Nic and Carlo, Robby treats us to a tour of his

apartment. We are standing in the living room, a large room with two covered twin beds shoved against two adjacent walls. Their covers are floral throws in sullied browns and faded blues. They resemble old, rugged bedspreads. Next to one couch is a table with a computer on it. Robby designates this as his computer. A broken recliner completes the furniture in the living room. The wall next to the recliner has three shelves made from cinder blocks and raw boards. Various books and computer parts lie on the shelves. At the opposite end of the room, next to the open, curtainless windows, is a large, wooden table with four chairs, two of which would actually remain standing if I sat in them. The chair nearest the open windows leans disjointed against the wall with its fallen cushion resting on the floor. The table is shoved up against this chair pinning it to the wall. A weak ceiling light offers little to brighten the dingy walls. For some reason Robby did not show us the kitchen; instead he turned and took us to the bathroom across the hall from the living room. It is a large rectangular room with a sunny window at the far end, lighting the bare, off-white walls and dingy sink and toilet. On the back of the door hangs an olive green sweatshirt. The tub hides in the corner behind the door, embarrassed. A pitiful, white curtain hangs from an aluminum pipe and makes a half circle around the tub. Near the drain is rust, which blends with the general scum of the tub. There is no towel in the entire room. Jake is not the least bit concerned about any of this. Jenny and I stand in the bathroom's entrance covering our mouths trying not to laugh. Why we think this is funny, I don't know. Not sure I want to see the bedrooms; I hesitate to follow Robby as he announces, "The sleeping rooms next."

"Jake sleeps here," Robby says as we peer into the roommate's abode. *I hope the monsters on the wall don't get Jake while he is asleep, and no telling what might crawl out of that bed.* I am grateful I get to sleep in the living room. Robby's room is—well, I'll just say—is Robby's room.

Back in the living room, Robby points, "Here is my computer. Here is your computer. All guests have unlimited use of this computer, not my computer," he says as we follow him to a narrow room that looks like an afterthought. "Please help yourself to tea, coffee, anything," he says. I wonder if his mother ever comes to visit. The bathroom is cleaner than the kitchen. The kitchen is maybe five feet wide and ten feet long with a single, stainless steel sink. Cracked and torn tan-colored linoleum covers three feet of counter space. Next is a small gas stove whose burner guards are distorted by baked on food. On the opposite wall is a small table with an espresso machine. A refrigerator stands, supporting various cleaning supplies, brooms, vacuum, mop, etc., all in a state of severe depression due to lack of use.

Jenny and I are dying to take a shower, but haven't gathered our courage to actually step in the tub. Our beds are in the living area where Jake and Robby are both enjoying the computers, so the possibility of going to bed at a reasonable hour is slim. We all hang out talking about life in America and Sicily. "Well, I have work tomorrow," Robby announces. "Here is the key. Do what you want, but you must be here when I arrive from work." He gives Jake a map of Padova and says he will see us tomorrow evening when we will all go to a party at the university. "Good night." As he is walking down the hall, Jenny whispers, "Mom, what are we going to do for a towel?"

"I guess we could use my long skirt or yours."

"No, you've had it on for two days."

"Ask him if we can have just one towel."

"You ask him. You're the mom."

"No, I'll just use my skirt." Jenny follows Robby to his room to ask him for a towel. I follow her for moral support.

"You're backpacking with no towel?" he snickers.

"Yeah," she says. "Stupid, huh?" Jenny's eyes widen as he hands her a towel.

"I just have one clean towel," Robby answers. Mentally, I'm questioning his liberal use of the word clean, but it's real terrycloth even though it's a hand towel. Jake, Jenny, and I all use this one towel for the next two days. I'm glad I only have to share with people whose diapers I have changed.

While Robby works the next day, we see the "free" sights in Padova. The Basilica of St. Anthony offers works by the early Italian Renaissance sculptor, Donatello, including the equestrian statue in front of the church, the first life-size, secular, equestrian statue cast in bronze in a thousand years. Aside from the interesting, Romanesque/Gothic architecture of the building, which was begun in 1231, and the frescoes and reliefs we see, St. Anthony's tongue encased in glass is the clincher for me. This man spoke some mighty fine words for his tongue to be enshrined. We spend at least two hours here. As we leave, I look up to see St. Anthony on the outside of the building looking down on us. I thank him for his blessing. I am too hot and tired to walk, so we hop a bus and ride a while. Jake sits across from the cutest little old lady wearing a 1950s shirtwaist dress in browns and blues, black orthopedic shoes, tan knee-high stockings that peek from the hem of her dress, and a blue triangle scarf tied neatly around her hair. She is clutching her black handbag close to her matronly waistline. After glancing at each other for a minute, Jake strikes up a conversation with her and a smile comes to her face that could light the world. Jake does his best to communicate in Italian. It is a sight to see them, two generations apart, from different cultures and continents, attempting to relate. We get off the bus at a park, where we wander looking for the Scrovegni Chapel that houses the famous collection of Giotto's frescoes, but instead run onto a graduation party for several law students. As is tradition, the students must be in the town square in their underwear, covered in white powder, wearing laurel wreaths on their heads with cherries hanging out of their ears. The law graduates stand by a large poster caricature of themselves, on which their friends and families have written funny poems about them. The graduates read aloud the poems while all stand around laughing. These law graduates are publicly mocked, and then they go practice law.

Thanks to Jake, we find our way back to the ghetto. Robby

arrives home from work and announces that Duke Cancun is coming to stay for the night, and he guesses he'll have to sleep on the floor. "Duke Cancun is staying here!" Jenny screams. "I know him. I met him on the Hospitality Club site." Duke is from Cancun, Mexico, and was born Brian McDonald. With this new information, Jenny quickly exits with her make-up to freshen up. Thirty minutes later, in walks Duke. This twenty-seven-year-old is over six feet tall and muscular. He is wearing an enormous backpack, and a guitar case hangs from his left shoulder. "I can't believe we are actually meeting," Duke says, with a broad smile when he sees Jenny. "I was just kidding when I said maybe we'd meet somewhere in Italy."

"You look like Ricky Martin," I say.

"I hear that all the time," he laughs.

"So what's your story?" I ask, trying to be cool.

"I sold all my belongings including my VW. I had to see the world." He tells us he plays his guitar and sings in plazas, which makes him enough money to eat and ride a few trains. He doesn't look like he has missed any meals and was so happy that I think about selling my worldly possessions and joining him. We are all inspired by Duke's story, and the very next day Jake leaves us and spends the remainder of the summer traveling alone in France.

We leave the house for the graduation party around 9:00 p.m., and all five of us squeeze into the tiny Fiat whose right door wouldn't open. Being squished between Jake and Jenny brings back my high school memories of cramming one too many friends into a 1965 orange VW Bug and dragging the drive-ins. Those were the good ole days, when we laughed and laughed with not a care in the world. For me, every minute of the graduation party is better than the one before. Beer is free until it runs dry; no outside liquor is allowed, and the party ends at midnight. We are outside in the humid air under the midnight-blue sky in its splendor of twinkling diamonds. This is supposed to be a graduation party, but I met many who were not associated with the school. My greatest surprise came when all the college-age people I met were genuinely interested in me; in fact, they would just walk up to me and begin talking: what was going on in my life; what brought me to Italy; would I like another beer; I was a cool mom, etc. A young man in a white t-shirt and khaki shorts introduces himself. "Hello, my name is Paul. Are you his mother?" Robby laughs and tells Paul that my kids and I are his guests for a couple days. "How are you in Italy?"

"I am backpacking with my son and daughter."

"Very good," he says, impressed with this information. "Hey, Jon, come meet … Excuse me … your name?"

"Sue Ellen," I reply as his friend joins us. "This is Jon. We are on bicycles."

"Yeah, very old bicycles," Jon adds.

"How old are you?" I asked, thinking they couldn't be over eighteen.

"Twenty-four, twenty-three," they answer together.

"I am from Portugal," Jon says, "and Paul is from Spain. We have biked twenty-five hundred miles to get here and are on our way to the Ukraine."

"Twenty-five hundred?"

"Yes, is long way to Padova," Jon adds, smiling. Twenty-five hundred miles on a bicycle doesn't compute, so I move on.

"Your English is great," I say. They laugh and discount my compliment. "Were you invited by one of the graduates?" I add.

"A friend invite us," he says. They tell me of their nights sleeping on the road trying to stay dry in a downpour, of broken-down bikes, of days they had nothing to eat, and on and on. I hope these aren't the kinds of stories I will be telling when I get home. Robby's dirty bachelor pad begins to look better.

"Do your parents know where you are?" I quiz. They both laugh and say they call home from time to time whenever they can find a phone. They have both graduated from college and are using the money their parents have given them as graduation gifts. "We want to see as much of the world as we can, so we are taking a year off for this." I learn a little about life in Spain and Portugal, their families, and how happy they are. I am most surprised by the sobriety I see at this graduation party. I have attended my share of American college parties in the 60s, as well as others with Jake and Jenny in the past five years. There is always much drunkenness and stupor, and the American kids look at me as an alien to be avoided, not conversed with.

All the performing bands play 1960s music and sing in English with an Italian accent—even "Mustang Sally," which brings back mega memories of my life in the 60s. "Come on, Mom, let's go dance with Duke."

"Jenny, you know I can't dance." My son, the dance instructor, has been patient with me in his attempts to teach me swing dancing. I would love nothing more than to feel comfortable on the dance floor, but my failed attempts as a six-year-old replay in my head every time I think about dancing.

"I'll teach you," Duke offers. How can I turn down that broad smile and his flirty eyes? "Can I do the twist?" I ask, thinking I can pretend I am drying my backside with a towel in rhythm to the music.

"Sure."

"Okay," I sigh as they pull me toward the band. Duke dances with both Jenny and me on the soft grasses that are the dance floor tonight. He even twirls me around once or twice as he holds tight to my hand. It is fun, but I beg off in favor of going back where I am comfortable, talking. On my way back across the lawn, I see a circle of people standing, watching with smiles and applause. I squeeze my head through a couple to see Jake dancing with a girl, showing off his swing dance talents to the delight of those gathered around. The cute blonde, whom he had asked to dance, had no idea they would draw such a crowd, but that is Jake's showmanship. He can draw a crowd without trying, and dancing puts a smile on his face that makes everyone happy. The young people I meet that night are impressed with my braveness. None of them think their moms would attempt a backpacking trip anywhere, much less in a foreign country. "You should ask her. She might go," I encourage. I bet lots of moms would go if they were asked. I enjoy this positive attention from college students. Mostly, it gives me hope. These twenty year olds have a much different outlook on life than American college students. I find myself talking about history, politics, and making observations with students from around the world. I am blown away.

Chapter Seven

Beauty and the Priest

After a fun-filled evening with our Sicilian host, Robby, and fellow Couch Surfer, Duke Cancun, we crash on our couches around 3:00 a.m. This crashing is hard on an old woman, but I never let anyone know it. I'm trying to fit comfortably into the "cool" mom label, something I'd never considered being. In a chivalrous move, Jenny decides to yield her couch to Duke. She sleeps in the broken-down recliner, so Duke, Jenny, and I all sleep in the living room. I sleep snuggled in the stillness my tired body provides and rise reluctantly around 10:00 a.m. We hang around the apartment talking, exchanging cultural stories, and learning Italian most of the day. The three-culture conversation is fascinating, covering such topics as technology, automobiles, motorcycles, walking vs. driving, soccer, American football, economics, Italian vocabulary, politics, and sex. I am informed about sex within the Italian culture. I think the conversation had initially been American dating versus Italian dating. Robby was quite open with his information. He obviously felt comfortable with me when he matter-of-factly announced, "In Italy, if you haven't had sex by third date, you know she's not going to." I can't imagine I would ever hear this from any male in my country. It is more information than I need, but I file it in a corner on the left side of my brain as my children quickly change the subject.

Amid the laughter and chatter, I am thinking, *Shouldn't we be getting to the train station? Wouldn't it be beneficial to arrive at the next stop before dark?* Trying to lean the conversation in this direction, I ask, "Where are we going today, Jenny?"

"Livorno," she answers, not missing a word in her conversation with the guys. I remind myself that I am just along for the ride. I'm here for the experience of stretching myself, learning to loosen up, enjoying things outside my comfort zone. Read the yellow card.

We have cookies and tea for breakfast at 10:00 a.m., and by 2:00 p.m., when Robby serves us a plate of fettuccini and pesto, the aroma alone captures my hunger. I could exist on just the aroma for days. After gazing at the plate of flat pasta with a scoop of green pesto in the middle, I scarf it down and want more, but there are no seconds. If our eating habits continue the way we have started, I will return home svelte. As good females often do, Jenny and I brave the kitchen and do our best to clean the dishes, counter, and oh, my god, the stove. We stay until 4:00 p.m., when Robby has to leave for Sicily to visit his mamma.

On his way to the airport, Robby drops the four of us at the train station. Duke is on his way to Germany, and Jenny and I buy tickets to Livorno, which is well known as the birthplace of communism in Italy. Jake heard there is good dancing in France, and after being assured by Duke that hitchhiking in Europe is no problem, decides to check out the French dance scene. Jake's going alone to France is scary for me, the mom, since he is inexperienced in solo travel and often loses track of time, temperature, and terrain when he visits his 'Jake world,' but today I choose to touch base with the new-found freedom in me and say, "That's cool, Jake, have fun." Before I can stop myself, I grab him in a lockdown bear hug and say with teary eyes and quaking chin, "Please be careful." What I really want is to beg him to stay with us.

The reason Jenny had decided to go to Livorno is that three months ago she began regular visits to an online Italian chat room. When she first logged onto the chat room, she was typing in English, hoping an Italian who knew English would respond. A guy responded with, "This is Italian room. If you want English, go to English room." Jenny wouldn't be put off, and told the guy she was staying because learning Italian was the reason she logged on in the first place. They continued meeting in the chat room regularly during the three months prior to our departure. I'm not sure how much Italian she learned since he was more interested in practicing his English, but the dialogue created a friendship. He told her if we ever got to Livorno, he would drive the distance from his home in Cecina to pick us up. My guess is that he never dreamed we would actually do this—like I know that I will not have a steady stream of visitors pouring into my home in Lubbock just because I invite them. Who wants to visit Lubbock, when they can see the beautiful hill country of Texas, Big Bend National Park, or the coasts of Galveston or Corpus Christi?

After some help from Duke at the train station, Jake heads west toward France, and Jenny and I buy tickets to Livorno for twenty euros (approximately twenty-five dollars) each. We grab two pieces of pizza to eat on the train. At 5:56 p.m., the IC Regional leaves for Livorno. IC is short for *slow train that stops at every village and creeps along the tracks at twenty-five miles per hour between stops.* We have to change trains in the huge station in Firenze (Florence). Thanks to Jenny, we manage the train change. Jenny has never traveled by train either, but it is amazing how quickly youth can read signs and catch on to new things. We will arrive in Livorno at 10:24 p.m., an unlikely hour to find a place to stay.

One of the many stops between Firenze and Livorno is Pisa. As soon as the train stops at Pisa Centrale, an announcement is made. "Oh, great, they just said our train has been delayed twenty minutes," Jenny says.

"How do you know what they said?" I ask.

"I understand some Italian."

"Really? I'm impressed."

"I guess I'll throw this trash in the can outside since we have a wait," she says as she gathers the napkins and sack from our pizza. In a flash, she is on the platform depositing our sack in the trash receptacle. She then stretches and twists to pop her back and sits on a bench with some girls. *The doors of the train close.* My adrenals move into action with a shot of their fight-or-flight cocktail. I first pound on the window, then I jump and run to the doors as the train jerks into motion. Jenny isn't on the train and it's moving. Primal fear—there's no reasoning with it. I begin screaming, "Jenny, Jenny, oh, no, Jenny, Jenny," as if the doors will magically open to the sound of my voice. Adrenaline continues inflating my muscles. My heart pounds. Jenny realizes the train is moving, runs, and jumps onto the step. I have the doors' handles in a death grip and am simultaneously pushing and pulling them while screaming as if I believe they will respond. Being separated from Jenny and alone in a foreign country has been my greatest fear from the birth of this backpacking plan. I did not consent to come on this trip until Jenny promised she would never leave me anywhere unless I agreed to it. I did not agree to ride the train alone to a place I've never been. Another shot of adrenaline spikes through me, and I know I can open the doors of this moving train to let Jenny in safely. It is a miracle that the doors do not fall off their hinges and onto the tracks with the might I exert on them. Jenny is on the outside step yelling at me, but I don't hear her. Panic overcomes me, and all I can think is my baby is outside, and I have to open these doors before she falls on the track and under the moving train. The train's speed increases. Suddenly I am pushed back, breaking my stance. Jenny manages to slide the doors open and is stepping inside. Another miracle—they opened. My heart has jumped out of my body and suddenly I am numb. "Mom, the doors slide open. You were not helping by pushing on them." I grab her and say, "Don't ever do that again. You just took twenty years off my life."

"What's the worst that could happen? I'd just take the next train," she says as I collapse in my seat.

"I have the tickets. I have both backpacks, and I have all the money. You couldn't buy a ticket," I snap. "Oh my god, it could have been a disaster." Why is it only mothers realize danger? Jenny is still in the "I am indestructible" stage of life. What does she know?

A nice Italian man, who has witnessed all this, walks up to me and pats my shoulder. He points up toward the door. A red emergency box with a silver handle sits over the door. He nods and pretends to pull the handle down showing me what I can do in case of an emergency. I muster a smile and say, "*Grazie*," to which he replies, "*Va bene*," which means *it is good*. *Va bene my ass! I'll have nightmares about Jenny falling under a train for months.* My breathing is still rapid, and I want to cry. Coming off an adrenaline high is not easy. Internally, my body is trembling as I try to melt into the royal blue seat.

This is June 1. We've been gone from home seven days. In my tiredness, I feel like I've lived a lifetime in those seven days. The Italians have greeted us with friendliness and helpfulness in every situation. I remember in the planning stages of this trip someone saying, "Don't they hate Americans?" No, they don't hate us. They are as infatuated by our foreignness as we are by theirs. The Italians want to hear about America from Americans. They know their papers are one-sided, leaning toward the communist/ fascist thought. I am resting my eyes and praying really hard for a place to stay tonight when Jenny announces, "This is our stop." She grabs her pack and helps me with mine. We detrain and walk down the platform to the stairs, cross under the tracks, and climb back up the stairs into the station. A synonym for Italy is stairs. A sign hangs from the extended ceiling, announcing that this station has been renovated just for TrenItalia's (national train company) patrons. The station is light and airy with circular wooden benches in the center of a beautifully patterned tile floor. The doors to the outside are open, allowing the night air to nonchalantly float through the room. The feeling is inviting and clean and I relax knowing I could sleep here. For some reason, I keep thinking I will have crossed an unspoken hurdle and be inducted into the Ya Ya Brotherhood of Backpackers if I have to sleep under a tree or on a bench somewhere. There is a stigma attached to need, and I'm loaded with need right now. Thoughts of dependence dominate. I can somewhat relate to my mother. Even in her state of dementia, she knows she does not like being dependent on me. It is a weak and desperate feeling. Dependence is a vulnerable position to be in, and for this summer, I am placing myself at the mercy of foreigners. I put myself in this situation. I agreed to the terms, and it is incredibly humbling trusting strangers for help. Right now, I crave a dependence on guardian angels appearing at just the right time. "Now what?" I ask.

"Let's go outside and just ask those people if they can help us."

"You've got to be kidding."

"Mom, it's too late to find a computer, and we're not paying for a place to stay. Maybe they know about free rooms here. This is what we came to do, remember? Stay with Italians. Come on, maybe one of them can help us." The left and right hemispheres of my brain begin to chitchat.

Left brain: *I can't believe you are doing this.*

Right brain: *Every day is a new adventure. I wonder who we will meet next.*

Left brain: *You're weird. What makes you think those people want to help you?*

Right brain: *It's fun doing things I've never imagined before.*

Left brain: *You're stupid. Those people are probably ax murderers.*

Right brain: *Look at the moon and stars. I want to paint the sky.*

Left brain: *You can't paint. Ha, you don't have sense enough to open the train doors.*

While nice enough, the four adults offer no help. I'm not even sure they understand what Jenny is attempting to say in her broken Italian. They turn and walk away. To our right is a group of teens. Jenny walks toward them, "They'll know where we can stay."

"*Parla inglese?*"

"No," they all answer, shaking their heads. On the train ride to Livorno, I received a lecture about trying to speak Italian and being brave. "If you don't try, how can you ever learn? They don't care if you use the wrong verb tense. Just try," Jenny said. So I try, "*Dove … uh … dove il church … no … vorrei un letto*," I attempt to the amazement of these youth. Jenny gives a try, asking for a free bed. She, too, mentions the word church. I wish I had a picture of the puzzled looks on their faces. Even the Italian youth cannot bear our raping their language. A brave young girl wearing camouflaged capris and jacket, with long black braids and wisps of hair in her dark eyes, brings forth her broken English. "Church," she says as she points behind us. "Little way down. Go by two street, go … uh *come se dice destra*," and she points to the right.

"Go right?"

"*Si, destra*, right. Then go," and she points left. "You see church little way down."

"You speak English!" we burst forth at once.

"No, no," she answers humbly.

"Yes, yes, and you speak so well. *Brava.*" Her peers smile, laugh, and bow to her. The ice is broken, and we continue talking, this time in English. A few more speak the English they know, and we clap and praise them. It is very difficult being inadequate in a language and attempting to speak to natives. Jenny is much braver than I am, and so she has learned more Italian. She attempts explaining our mode of travel and our dependence on the good will of Italians. "You ask priest; his name Don Carim. He now in church. He help you," our friend encourages as she again points behind our backs.

"Okay, we go down this street two blocks, then turn right for one block?" Jenny asks. "Then turn left?"

"Go little way down and is church," our friend adds. "Ask again to someone. *Quindici minuti.*" I recognize *quindici* as a number and immediately begin counting until I get to fifteen. It's a fifteen-minute walk to the church. It's 11:00 p.m., and I imagine drunks coming out at this hour.

"*Ciao*," we chime together. "*Grazie.*"

"*Si, si, ciao, ciao,*" our young friends respond as we head in the general direction of the church. "Stand up straight, Mom, you're going to be permanently bent by the end of the summer."

"I can't stand up or I'll fall over."

"Yes you can. Your boobs counter the weight of the pack."

"My boobs don't weigh twenty-five pounds!" I protest.

"Just try it. It'll be easier on your back, too." Jenny is walking very fast, and I'm lagging behind. The streets are dark, and no one is out. "Jenny, wait for me. This is scary."

"Hurry, Mom, it's late. I hope someone is still at the church." God, I'm tired, a bit afraid, and once again, sweaty. The streets are narrow. No cars, motorcycles, or pedestrians are in sight. With each corner we round, the opposing sides of my brain engage in dialogue again.

Left: *You're going to get yourself killed.*

Right: *I wonder how old these buildings are.*

Left: *What makes you think the priest is going to help you? You're not even Catholic.*

Right: *What a beautiful Italian summer evening this is!*

"Jenny, do you know where you are going?"

"Yes, it shouldn't be too much further." Just as she says this, we see a group of old Italian men playing cards under a dim light outside the door of a bar and café. "*Dove la chiesa?*" Jenny asks. The men look at every inch of my beautiful daughter and never miss a play of cards. Italian men are egregious in their staring at the opposite sex. There is no subtleness about it. There must be no sexual harassment laws in Italy because in the U.S., a man would be hauled to jail for less. As they enjoy the sight before their eyes and remark to each other, they point in the direction of the church. They nod respectfully to me. *Dirty old men. They don't know I'm the Terminator.*

"Come on, we are nearly there," Jenny encourages. Rounding the next corner takes us from dark nothingness to the church in all its glory. The grounds are swarming with men, women, and children all talking at the same time. It is Italian chaos. There are people standing in groups, sitting on metal folding chairs in circles, and walking in or out of the church eating cake, cookies, and other goodies. The building is lit from within and forces a glow toward the night sky that blinds the stars. Jenny walks up to a group of seven men sitting in a circle laughing and talking, hands flying in all directions. The passion unique to Italians, coupled with the melodic flow of their language, explains why opera began in Italy. "*Parla inglese?*" she asks one of them.

"No, no," he says pointing to his friend.

"*Parla inglese?*" she asks again.

"A little," is the reply from a middle-aged man wearing a white shirt, black, cuffed pants that grace his ankles, no socks, worn black leather lace-up shoes, suspenders to hold the pants around his oversized belly, and a brown fedora cocked to one side. Black-rimmed Buddy Holly-type glasses frame his large, protruding eyes. "We are looking for Don Carim. Can you take us to him?" Jenny asks. Instantly all conversation stops, and fourteen eyes are on us. *Uh oh, maybe Don Carim is the Mafia boss, too.* The group is silent, and we are the center of attention. The spokesman rises and walks up to us. "What do you want of Don Carim?" he asks with a serious look on his face. I am wilting faster than a cut flower in a dry vase. I keep wiping the sweat from my face. What a sight we must be, standing before this group of Italian men who are all studying us. *Mamma* is revered by Italians young and old. Here I stand, a *mamma* from some other planet in my long black and white skirt, dirty feet in dusty blue Birkenstocks, a pack on my back, and sweat dripping off my hair. I bet I challenge their picture of a *mamma*. Next to me is Jenny, looking pretty as ever in her long, flowing turquoise skirt (recently used as a bath towel), her cascading red hair, and complete makeup displayed on her peaches and cream complexion. We are a curious couple, and I can't imagine the reception we would receive in our own country, but this is Europe where thousands of college students travel this way, right? Well, not exactly. Most stay in hostels or sleep on the ground in their sleeping bags, but doing things differently has always been Jenny, so here we stand asking for Don Carim.

Jenny introduces, "I'm Jenny, and this is my mother, Sue Ellen."

"Ah, Sue Ellen. Dallas. *Dove e J. R.?*" This reaction to my name always strikes me as hilarious, and I respond giggling, "J. R. in Texas." After the joke about *Dallas* passes, Jenny continues, "We are traveling and need a place to stay tonight, but we have no money."

"No money? *Lentamente per favore. Non capito the inglese velocemente,*" the man says. Jenny explains, more or less, that the winds are blowing us here and there around Italy, and we landed in Livorno tonight with the need for a place to stay. She attempts explaining the concept of Hospitality Club and Couch Surfing, which flies straight over his head and out of sight. The men in this circle begin commenting to one another between glances in our direction, but eventually go back to their conversations with each other. The man speaking to us motions to another man who runs into the church. The night air is thick and reminds me of the air in Houston, close to unbreathable. I hear laughter in all directions and see Italians involved in their passionate way of talking. They all seem oblivious to the hour, 11:15 p.m. Now I understand why businesses must close all afternoon. Even the Baptists don't have meetings this late! This man, whose name is Giuseppe, continues asking questions. He is interested in where we live and tells us he wants to visit New York. My quick reply is, "You must see the center of America to see America. Come to Texas," I say.

Don Carim arrives twenty-five minutes later. He is a handsome man in his forties and dressed in the typical black slacks and white shirt with the collar open showing the top of a hairy chest. His English is broken, but music to my ears as he opens with, "Hello, I can help you?" Jenny introduces us and begins telling our story to the priest. It goes something like this: "My mother and I are traveling through Italy for three months with only our backpacks. We want to stay with Italians and learn the culture and language.

We have very little money and stay with people we meet on the street. A man I met in a chat room on the computer is driving to Livorno tomorrow to pick us up, but we need a place to stay tonight. We met some kids at the train station who told us you could help." Through the entire explanation, the priest looks from Jenny to me and back to Jenny. I keep smiling. When Jenny stops talking, "the Don" does not say anything for a minute or so. He just looks at us. The chat room probably stumped him. This was before we knew most Italians do not have computers. I broke the silence with, "May we sleep on a floor in the church?" Don Carim's eyes widen, and he asks, "You want to sleep on the floor?" We both nod, and I answer, "Any place to sleep is good." He asks us to follow him into the church. The first room we see is a large banquet type room teaming with lively children and chatting adults. "Will this do?" he asks, and although I think I can sleep anywhere, my back has other things in mind when it sees the floor. My face squints from the anticipated pain when it sees the cold, hard, tile floor. Gaining control over the spasms riveting my back, I ask him if there is a pew on which to sleep. I can already feel the soft, round pillow that sits atop my pack, under my head. The priest doesn't immediately answer. He looks off into the distance as if he is thinking. He once again looks at me, then says, "Follow me." Off we go single file. Occasionally Don Carim turns around and says something to Jenny. I'm not listening. All my energies are spent staying upright and putting one somnolent foot in front of the other. The church is large, and we walk down many halls. "We are near," he says as he leads us up a flight of marble stairs lined by a black iron hand rail on the right. I lag behind, my feet feeling like cement blocks. "Come on, Mom," Jenny calls as she and the priest stand at the top of what is long enough to be the stairway to heaven. I look up, and they are standing in front of a gate. The priest unlocks the black wrought iron gate and holds it open. "My mother is very tired," Jenny assures him. *He'd have to be dense to think otherwise.* "Come on, Mom, just four more steps. You can do it." I want to tell her to shut up but think better of wasting the energy. Don Carim locks the gate behind me. Wherever we are going is behind a locked gate. *Hmmm.* We follow as he turns immediately to the right. What I see are three more milky white marble stairs. Pride is all that keeps me going. We turn left at the top of the stairs to see a large open area bare of any furniture. The priest leads us off to the right toward a dark hallway. "The bathroom is here," he says as he flips on the light switch. Suddenly the hall is lit with the power of a nightlight. A metal rolling clothes rack with five empty hangers on it greets us. Three-foot-tall windows of colored glass line both sides of the hall, and at the end is a large bathroom with a neatly tiled shower. It is clean—relatively speaking. "It is good?" he asks. Does he think we would say no? "It's wonderful, great," we answer together.

"Follow me," and he walks back out into the empty hall. Our voices echo in the hollowness.

About a block's walk from the bathroom, we follow him down a dimly lit hall with four closed doors on each side. He opens the second door on our left, and as I walk in, I know it is heaven. This priest, Don Carim, has taken us to heaven. There are a pair of twin beds, a sink with running water, one chair, a window, and a large picture of Jesus by the lime green wardrobe. My pack lands on the first bed as I round my back to stretch my shoulder blades. I will be sure he gets sainthood. St. Don, we'll call him. "I am in my office tomorrow. Come by before you leave," he instructs us. "In morning, I leave gate unlocked."

"Thank you. This is wonderful," we say. He closes the door. We wait a minute and begin chattering about heaven. "And the bathroom is just a block away," I add.

Chapter Eight

Dong Juans and Beached Whales

I open the window and lean out to see the Vespas and mufflerless cycles roaring below. Jenny props open the door with her shoe to create a little breeze. I haven't seen a screen or barricade of any kind over any window since we landed in Italy, and we must be three stories up. I wonder how people keep from falling out of windows here. How do they keep their children from climbing on them and jumping into the Grand Canal in Venice? Could it be that Italians are responsible for their actions? These same conditions anywhere in America would signal lawsuit floodgates. Jenny sits in the chair, and I sit on the bed as we relive the past hour. "I can't believe how he kept looking at me," I said of Don Carim's glances as Jenny was talking to him. "I wish I knew what he was thinking. Maybe he felt sorry for me. I do look pretty bad."

"I know, Mom, I bet he thought it would be a sin to make a mamma sleep on the floor. Italian men hold *mamma* on a pedestal you know. What is that saying? Something like Italian men respect their wives, spoil their mistresses, but the only women they ever really love are their mammas," she says with a dramatic swooping bow to me. We giggle and my body slowly relaxes from the aftereffects of the adrenaline rush at Pisa Centrale and the force I have exerted on my muscles over the past two hours just keeping me upright. Jenny pounds on my back with the karate chop edge of her hands. "Ooooo, that feels good. Will you massage my back a little?" I ask, stretching out across the bed. Jenny isn't fond of giving massages, so she digs and squeezes any loose flesh she can grab, especially around the shoulder area, until I scream for her to stop, but a rough massage is better than no massage.

"You know, we'll have to use the bedspreads for towels," I say.

"Are they clean?"

"I don't know, but they're all we have. This bedspread reminds me of a pretty, beige shirtwaist dress with a pleated skirt and rhinestone buttons my mother wore in 1959. I know it's the same fabric. I just wish I could make it through the night without having to go to the bathroom. That room has to be a block away. What do you think comes out of the walls of a Catholic church at night?" I ask, already dreading the trek through the dark halls.

"Grotesque ghouls and green goblins I'm sure. I'm glad I don't have to get up in the middle of the night to go pee. It's all in your head."

"It's all in my head all right. My bladder speaks directly to my brain, which is housed in my head. Just wait. Your day's coming. Have a few kids, and a few years later you'll be getting up in the night, too." We are interrupted by a knock at the door. Jenny answers it and is met by a humble looking man wearing Birkenstocks and corduroy pants. "Please quiet. We wake at 6:00."

"*Mi scusi,*" Jenny replies.

"Thank you," he says, and turns and walks away. Jenny peeks out the door then shuts it and cups her hands over her mouth. "I bet he is a monk," she whispers. "We are sleeping with the monks." By now we are giggly schoolgirls and have to muffle our laughs into the pillows on our beds. "We'd better get to sleep," I say as I take the bedspread off my bed, shake it, fold it, and find my shampoo and soap in my backpack. "I think I'll put my PJs on when I get back. I can just see me running into a monk in my PJs. Leave the door unlocked."

"Eeew, you're going to put your dirty clothes on your clean body?"

91

"Yeah, I don't want to scare anyone with my wet hair and PJs. I really need to wash my clothes, but I'm too tired to take them to the shower with me tonight."

I'm sure it was 1:30 a.m. before we turned the light off. Instantly Jenny's breathing became slow and steady. I lay in bed, dozing in and out of the twilight zone, only to be awakened occasionally as the cycle noise on the street intensified. My sleep deepened when the noise subsided and the gentle breezes across my wet head cooled me. My 4:00 a.m. trek to the bathroom went without episode, and if anything came out of the walls, I must have scared it.

After neatly making the beds with damp bedspreads, I write a small thank you note and leave it on my bed. As I load my pack, I pull out the yellow card and read it aloud. "Jenny, we both need to read this card every day."

"Ok, Mom," Jenny says as she puts the finishing touches on her hair with the butane curling iron. "It works great. Look how pretty these curls are." This is the first time she's used the curling iron, and I guess it's worth the three trips we made to the Venice airport to get it. "Don Carim probably won't recognize us because we look so fresh and clean this morning."

"Okay, let's go," Jenny says. I take a picture of the room, and we're off. Luckily, a cleaning lady armed with a rag mop and broom directs us to the priest's office. It is eleven o'clock. If he got up with the monks, he's already worked half a day. He greets us, "Good morning. You sleep good?"

"Oh, yes. Thank you so much. I feel like a new person."

"And you?" he asks Jenny.

"It was heavenly getting to sleep in a bed. Thank you for helping us."

"May I take a picture of you and Jenny?" I ask, holding up my camera.

"Yes, outside?" he motions toward the door. We follow him across the hall and step outside to a small, unkept courtyard. The sun casts its brilliance on the old stone cloister. Don Carim immediately begins apologizing for the poor condition of the courtyard—the fountain that didn't work, the broken-down bench, the weeds—but for me, it all looks quaint and perfect for a picture. I choose the ideal spot and the priest puts his arm over Jenny's shoulder and his body a bit close to hers. "Thank you. You both take a good picture," I assure them as I show them the picture. Whoever invented digital cameras is a genius. "I wish I had money to donate for repairing the courtyard. I am sorry," I say sincerely. "It is okay," Don Carim replies.

We both thank him profusely, and Jenny asks to use the phone to call Filippo, her Italian chat room friend. The priest escorts us into his modest office, and Jenny uses the phone, but Filippo doesn't answer. "Why don't we just ride the bus to Cecina," she says. "Where is the bus station from here?"

"Five minutes," Don Carim answers. He takes us out the door and points to our right. "Down this street five minutes." We thank him again (for some reason I keep wanting to bow to him) and walk to the bus station. For a little over a dollar each, we can ride to Cecina. We count ten stops on the schedule between Livorno and Cecina. "*Uh … Cecina … quanto minuto?*" Jenny asks the ticket clerk.

"*Quanti minuti a Cecina?*" the clerk corrects.

"*Si.*"

"*Una ora.*"

"*Grazie.*"

"We'll call Filippo again when we get there," Jenny assures me. "Maybe he was just busy the first time I called."

"Uh huh," I respond, with little expectation, but feeling rested, strong, and up to a new challenge. Thank God for last night's bed. If I had slept on the floor, Don Carim and Jenny would probably still be trying to get me up.

The bus is a modern, clean Italian version of Greyhound and takes us winding along the coast of the Ligurian Sea to visit breathtaking views of sparkling blue-green water, cloudless turquoise sky, scattered hills, sandy beaches, and sun worshipers galore. The road is bumper to bumper with cars, busses, motorcycles, bicycles, and bikini-clad pedestrians. The beach has metamorphosed into one big party. Jenny asks the lady sitting next to us, "*Che cosa?*" trying to find out what's happening. "*Festa Nationale,*" was the answer. What we understood in the sentences that followed, in rapid-fire succession, was that June 2 is a national holiday; all businesses close, and everyone goes to the beach. Later, we learn the holiday is the Anniversary of the Republic, one of the very few holidays that is not Catholic in origin. A representative form of government is relatively new for the Italians and is a stretch for the imagination. In the past sixty years, they have had no less than fifty-five different governments. At any rate, everyone is out celebrating.

"I don't see any nudes," I claim. "I thought all of Europe had nude beaches."

"I don't know. Maybe these beaches are strictly for families."

"If nude beaches are a part of the culture, I think everyone would be nude," I say, a little disappointed. The normal one-hour bus ride takes two hours today due to the congestion and intense traffic. The bus driver throws his hands up and complains, "*Mamma mia. E caseno. La programma distrutta,*" meaning the craziness has destroyed the bus schedule. I am fascinated by the liveliness of the beach goers. They look like a mass of people who have just been freed from solitary confinement. They are not lying on towels sunning themselves or reading books. The beach is splattered with brightly colored empty towels and all the participants are waving their arms as if directing a symphony, just talking. Their arms are a part of their speech mechanism. We must look paraplegic to them when we talk, as our arms are merely extensions of our bodies. Bodies are running in and out of the water, eating, walking, making out, standing arm in arm looking over the sea, changing babies' diapers, helping *nonnas* and *nonnos* (grandmothers and grandfathers) to the water, tossing balls, and generally creating a lot of commotion. What I see is a complete immersion into a one-day vacation. They will not waste a minute of this day and will enjoy every minute—another Italian talent.

After two hours of starting and stopping, we finally arrive at the bus station in Cecina. Jenny uses a pay phone to call Filippo, who answers this time telling her he'll be at the station in five minutes.

"What kind of car is he driving?" I ask.

"I don't know. He didn't tell me."

"Has he ever sent you a picture?"

"No. He'll know us. We'll just stand on the curb. Who else around here looks like an American mother and daughter?"

"True."

"He knows my hair is red and that we both have backpacks."

"Well, I'm taking mine off," I say as I drop my pack onto the dirty concrete. "I will have to take it off anyway to squeeze into his miniature car."

In exactly five minutes a suave looking Italian rounds the corner in a brand new silver BMW wagon. His Armani shades cover his face and wrap halfway around his head. As soon as he sees us, he pulls over, jumps out of the car, opens the back, and tosses our packs into the spacious trunk. Many Italians are short, but Filippo is six feet tall with dark brown hair down over his collar and scruffy growth on his face. He looks serious and offers no smile, reminiscent of businessman Marco in Venice.

"Filippo?" I ask, not sure since no introductions have been made.

"Yes, I am Filippo."

"I am Sue Ellen."

"*Sue Ellen da Dallas?*" This brings a half smile to his face.

"No, Sue Ellen of Lubbock."

"*Va bene,*" he says as he motions us to get into his car that has thirty-two miles on the odometer. Jenny climbs in the front, and I get the back seat. Filippo is smoking and turns on the air conditioner. My lungs begin looking for an escape. He looks in the rear view mirror and sees my face covered with my shirt. "The smoke you don't like? I sorry," he says as my head shakes no. Jenny proceeds to tell him about my asthma. He quickly tosses his cigarette out the window, rolls all four windows down, and turns on U2. "You like?" he asks Jenny.

"Yes, yes, of course."

"U2 is the greatest in the world," he answers as they both sing a few bars of "Vertigo." "Hello, hello, *hola!* I'm in a place called Vertigo."

"So, you are here," he says. "What you want in Cecina?"

"You said if we came to Cecina, you had a place for us to stay."

"Ah, yes," he says as he answers one of three cell phones on the console. After a minute, he hangs up and motions with his hands, "*Caseno*, always the Germans. They brings a *caseno*."

"What is a *caseno?*" Jenny asks.

"What you say in the English …uh …uh …" he is motioning with both arms, each going in opposite circles, and nothing is holding the steering wheel. "We have the word casino in English," I offer my expertise. "It means a place to gamble."

"Ah, yes, *caseno* is the disaster in English. The Germans brings the disaster." I am loving his accent and improper grammar, which encourages me to try a little harder speaking Italian. "In America you have the guns?" he asks.

"Oh, yes," we both answer.

"In Italy, if we have the guns, we shoot the Germans!" Jenny and I erupt in hysterics. "Why?" Jenny asks.

"The Germans they wants everything. They demand. They counts the spoons and plates, and two people they wants eight spoons and plates. *Mamma mia.* They counts seven spoons. They call and demands one more. *Vai a cagare,*" he sighs and gestures upward with his hand.

"The Germans they come for *vacanza* and pays apartment one week. They wants everything."

We later learned that *Vai a cagare,* used as Filippo did, is the equivalent of "screw you" in American culture. Literally, *vai a cagare* means go take a shit. Profanities in Italian are so funny when literally translated that we learn a few and throw them at each other when we need a sudden burst of energy that laughing gives. "So you don't like Germans?" Jenny asks.

"No." During this brief ride in Filippo's car, we learn Italians dislike the Germans, and everyone despises the French.

As we drive along, Filippo points out his family's hotel, called Hotel Tornese. Another couple of blocks and we stop at his office, where he takes a key from a six-foot-square board filled with keys. Filippo is all business, talking on one, sometimes two, of his cell phones at all times. He pulls up on the sidewalk in front of a two-story, 50s-looking building. "*E libero,*" he says as he motions with his head toward the apartment, "is free." Having messed up his hair with the head toss, he then runs his fingers through his thick Italian mane. We follow him through a gate and walk up the stairs lined with terra cotta pots overflowing with the dizzying aroma of rosemary, basil, mint, red geraniums, and heart-shaped vines that wander in and out of the railing. The air is thick and salty. We enter the apartment on the second floor, and sheepishly Filippo looks at us and says, "You like stay here?" Then he takes us on a tour of the rooms as he tells us towels and sheets are extra. We look at each other in disbelief. "We can't afford this," I say, looking at the two large rooms equipped with beds that sleep six and a fully furnished kitchen.

"*E libero,* is free," he answers.

"Free?" I ask.

"Only this apartment is free," he says. "I show you the safe." He opens a closet of empty shelves and behind a small door is a safe that he unlocks and says, "You put in your money and documents (passports)." I guess in their many chats, Jenny neglected to tell him our travel situation. I'm wondering if the safe is an indication of the clientele or the crime. "How long can we stay?" Jenny asks.

"Ten days only, then is reserved. He fidgets with his keys and finally says, "This I rent for 545 euros a week. I give you for ten euros (thirteen dollars) each day." I can't believe my ears, so

I repeat, "We can stay here for ten nights and pay one hundred euros? I think we can splurge."

"Yes, and beach is one hundred meters," he says as he points toward the beach. Once again, I want to grab a strange man and hug him.

"Tomorrow I call for dinner. I takes you to my brother restaurant in Bolgheri."

"We don't have a phone," Jenny says.

"I meets you in hotel 18:00.

"Thank you," we answer. As he leaves, Filippo stops at the door and says, "Is okay?"

"*Va bene,*" Jenny answers with a giggle.

"*Va bene,*" I repeat in my southern drawl.

"Yes," she says with affirmation.

"*Ci vediamo domani,*" Filippo adds.

"What?" Jenny asks.

"We see tomorrow," is his answer. The door shuts. Speechless and incredulous, we can only smile and shake our heads. "Mom, he's a Donald Trump. He owns property; his family owns a hotel; his brother owns a restaurant in Bolgheri wherever that is and no telling what else. I can't believe this," Jenny says as we walk onto the balcony that bursts with white and purple African daisies.

"When your backpack is your home and someone offers you a furnished apartment for thirteen dollars a night, I call him an angel—not Donald Trump. All this, because of a chat room on the computer?" I ask.

"Yeah, remember the trouble you gave me about that?" she looks at me with a smirk.

"Let's go see what the beach is like. I can't wait to cool off." While I wait for Jenny to change into her swimsuit, I sit at the shiny glass table and read the yellow card again. I've always considered myself a woman of great faith, but this time when I read the words, "I will not need your help," something shifted internally, like a flower bursting forth. A warmth ran through me. I felt a release where before there was tightness. Maybe I am just overly tired or feeling especially secure knowing where I'll sleep for the next ten days, but at this moment, in Cecina, Italy, I realize I haven't had great faith because I've lived under a shadow of fear. There is no faith in fear. I've been kidding myself all these years. My right brain heaves a sigh. *Finally*, it says. *Now you can enjoy life.*

We walk toward the sea on the sidewalk lined with giant pink and white oleanders, palm trees, and pine trees, past Hotel Tornese, to the beach where colorful umbrellas mark the spot. We arrive at the beach with no towels. Who needs a towel on the beach, right? The clothes we've worn all day are now cover-ups for our swimsuits. We walk bare foot on the black sand across the pebbles and into the cold tide.

"Let's go mark a spot where we can leave our clothes," Jenny suggests. We wander through the umbrellas looking for two chairs that call our names, strip to our swimsuits, and wade waist-deep into the Tyrrenhian Sea. After soaking in the cold, blue water, we return with sand-coated feet to our chairs. We sit a minute and then Jenny wants to go again. "I just want to sit here, rest, and enjoy the cool breeze."

"Come on, Mom, we're at the beach in Italy. Let's play."

"I'm tired. You go on."

I'm reclining at a forty-five-degree angle when I hear, "*Mi scusi. E libera la sedia?*"

"*Si*," I respond, having no idea why I answered since "*libera la sedia*" means nothing to me. As time passed, we learned the hard way that *libero(a)* translated by Italians means "free." *Libero* got us into trouble many times in the two months it took us to understand its Italian meaning. To Italians, free means available—not free of cost. I look over my shoulder to see a typically dressed Italian grandmother with black orthopedic shoes, knee-high hose, brown skirt that falls just below her knees, a white blouse with neat pleats on the front, and a purple paisley triangle scarf on her head. She is clutching her brown handbag. The fire dancing in her eyes defies her pale, thin body. Her daughter and granddaughter accompany her. While the daughter and granddaughter prepare for swimming, my new friend sits in the chair beside me. "*Stranieri?*" she asks. I shrug my shoulders and say, "*Parla inglese?*"

"No," was her response as she waved to her girls who were off to swim.

"*Parla italiano?*" she asks.

"*Un po.*" (Just "how little" she was about to learn.)

"*Bene,*" she responded. "*Americana?*" she questioned.

"*Si, da Texas,*" I say, knowing this reply will evoke a positive response. Everyone seems to know about Texas.

"Texas. George Bush," she says with a smile.

"*Si,* George Bush." I then attempt to change the subject so I say, "*Bella,*" as I motion out toward the sea.

"*Si, si, molto bello,*" she replies.

"*Mi chiamo Sue Ellen.*"

"*Piacere. Mi chiamo Maria.*" I think this is the first time I have introduced myself without *Dallas* and J. R. joining the conversation.

For the next hour, we two strangers attempt conversing. I fumble through my phrase book like I am groping through a dark cave. I speak one-word sentences usually ending with a question in my voice making my insecurity obvious. After a moment of thought, Maria repeats my word and comes back with a sentence using my word or idea. She speaks slowly and deliberately, using simple vocabulary with the perfect inflection on each word. I am amazed at her patience. She probably feels shredded and bloody as I rip through her language, reducing it to incredible innocence and unrecognizable utterances, but she continues encouraging me and gently helping me in spite of the fact she knows no English. By the end of the hour, my brain feels like it is trying to pull out of quicksand from attempting to recall and form words in Italian. My Spanish teacher in high school, Mrs. Skouge, would be proud that I remembered so much Spanish in my attempt to speak Italian.

Out of nowhere came Spanish words as I sought to translate into Italian what I was thinking in English.

We sit silently for a time, occasionally smiling at each other, but what fellowship is in this silence. Funny thing how silence encourages experiencing the moment, so we sit, connected in a sort of reverence, as if we share a deep secret. I want desperately to converse freely with this woman who has been so kind to me. My frustration mounts, so I jump up and pointing to the sea, say, "*Vamanos a mare.*" (Here comes my high school Spanish.) She must have understood because she rises, removes her shoes and stockings, and rigs her purse over her shoulder as she says, "*Noi andiamo.*" She leads the way, weaving in and out of the bathing beauties. When we reach the gravelly sand, she hooks her arm in mine, and we help each other balance as we yelp in shock at the cold water creeping up our legs. We stand in the no-language zone, laughing and understanding each other better than we did in all the effort we'd put forth in the past hour. Here we are, arm in arm, standing in the sea, two strangers from two continents, helping each other balance against the force of the tide and the poke of rocks against our tender feet. We stand, looking out across the vast expanse of blue water, and in the distance, I see islands. Without my asking, she begins to point as she names them, "Capraia, Elba, Corsica." Intermittent sprays of cold, salt water mist our faces, and the pleasure of this experience drugs my body—a magical drug filling me with endorphins. No matter how brief, relationships nourish our hearts. I never saw Maria again, but I think about her often and can never forget what she gave me that day.

Enough sun for one day, we head to the small grocery with ten euros. We come away with a lemon, a head of lettuce, a box of cherry tomatoes, a hunk of cheese, a large bottle of Tuscan wine, and €2.92 in change. Amazing. We decide we can eat at least two meals of the cheese, lettuce, and tomatoes. I am blessed with this break at just the perfect time, for I have a respiratory infection of sorts and cough up green crud from my lungs for five out of our ten days on the beach. I feel a bit like a queen, getting to recline on the beach, breathe the salt air, bask in the sun with the bikini-clad frauen and donne, and just rest. Europeans are definitely more comfortable in their bodies. The size of some of the women in strings on the beach resembled beached whales, while the men beyond their prime wore tight speedos with both over- and under-hang. In their attempt at being Don Juans, they were really dong Juans. I felt thin.

The next two days, Jenny went here and there with Filippo and his brother Goffredo. I begged off in favor of napping or lying in the sun. "Oh, Mom, Bolgheri is magical. Filippo took me there to meet his brother and see his restaurant. It's about fifteen minutes from here. It's exactly what you have been looking for—Italian countryside. It's a village of two hundred people nestled inside castle walls. I can't wait for you to see it, and I have a job there."

"A job! What?"

"Goffredo needs some summer help. It's just for the evenings."

"We come backpacking in Italy, and you get a job?"

"Only if it works out, something about being illegal, but you'll love Bolgheri. It's incredible."

"Well, right now I need to take a shower and get the beach off me," I say as I pull the thin bedspread off to use as my towel.

"Oh, and Filippo said we could use his office computer to e-mail if we want to."

"I still think I'm in a dream. We've been gone nine days and have had a hot shower every day. I think I'll do my laundry tonight in the shower," I said, grabbing my long skirt, capris, and two tops.

"It beats having to scrub them on the rocks at the river," Jenny laughs.

"I guess, and there's even a line on the balcony with clothespins on it."

We had cheese and tomatoes wrapped in lettuce and a glass of red wine for dinner. I never realized the value of being hungry.

Everything tastes great and satisfies. The simple life is good. "Why do you think we haven't lost any weight?" I asked.

"We probably have. It's just that we've got more muscles from walking with our packs. You've been drinking more beer, and we've both been hitting the gelato pretty hard," Jenny answers.

"Oh. I like the Italian beer, and giving up gelato is out of the question. What are we doing tomorrow?"

"I don't know, Mom. We'll decide when we wake up."

"Okay," I say as I realize how freeing her statement is as I step into the shower with my clothes to wash.

Chapter Nine

Fascism and Sea Tomatoes

"Mom, Filippo is taking us to dinner tonight at his family's pizzeria," Jenny announces as I lie across the bed thinking about my life.

"Umm, sounds good."

"Did I tell you Filippo said he wishes Mussolini were back?"

"Noooo, why?"

"He says they need one person to make all the decisions because their government is fractured, so everything is chaotic, and Filippo thinks Mussolini kept Italy better organized than they've ever been."

"Yeah, that's what dictators do."

"And get this. Italy has more than twenty political parties."

"No wonder they're fractured."

"He said he and his mother are fascists, and his father and two brothers are conservative. He told me when he was a baby, his grandmother used to sing fascist songs to him instead of lullabies."

"No way. No wonder he's serious."

"What's the percent of Italians who are fascist?" I question.

"I don't know, but we need to get to the hotel. Come on. We're supposed to meet him at 9:00 p.m., and it's 9:00 now."

"How do they eat so late and stay slim?" I ask.

"It's just their way. Come on, let's go. We get to eat out. Yipee!"

With happy Italians communing on porches, sunburned beachgoers returning home, and the clear night air all around me, I just want to mosey along enjoying my surroundings, but Jenny insists we hurry. Breathlessly, I tell her how I learned the evils of Soviet Communism, German Nazism, Italian Fascism, Marxism, Socialism, and all the other ways of living outside the United States, in elementary school in the 1950s. I remember those lessons well, particularly in my fourth grade class with Miss Elliott. Miss Elliott was an old maid, as we labeled single women in their forties back then, medium build, graying hair in a short, curly doo, and she was in love with Mozart, Beethoven, Bach, Strauss, and all the other musical geniuses. She floated, full skirt swaying, down the aisles of the classroom as if she were on the dance floor. Her arms moved in tune with her body like a ballerina's, with grace and ease as she glided between the rows of desks and up to the blackboard. She addictively watched the clock, anticipating the hour of 2:00 p.m. when we could begin music class. The onset of music class transformed Miss Elliott, and we fourth graders were mesmerized by her transformation. She escaped into her own world, complete with stars in her eyes and ethereal expressions illuminating her face, as she engaged the RCA Victor record player to play the masters' creations on old 33 1/3 LP records that she no doubt had owned for years. She guided us to listen for the stories hiding in the highs and lows of classical music. She encouraged our imaginations, and she invited us to share our imaginative stories. Our stories were accepted whether they flowed with the music or not. Reality, not imagination or art, was instilled in me at home, so I experienced immense freedom in Miss Elliott's class. The only thing that could possibly bring Miss Elliott out of music class was the electrocuting jolt of the dismissal bell. In social studies class, she made sure we understood that if we lived under a dictator such as Mussolini, we would not have the freedom to enjoy music and dancing as we do in the United States. "The dictator tells you what you can do, where you can go, the books you can read, the thoughts you can think, and even the work you must do each day," she assured us. "Just think of the poor children," she swooned. In Texas elementary schools during the 1950s, we had bomb drills and nuclear fallout drills and hid under our desks during these drills. None of this scared me. It was just an exercise we had to do, but I learned I never wanted to live under any of the bad "isms."

We talk more about fascism over dinner in the pizzeria named after Filippo's fascist grandmother, Elisa, (eh-LEEZ-ah). Filippo is convinced that freedom is okay in moderation, but Italians need a sword-wielding leader, and "Il duce" accomplished many economic successes for Italy. "I no like the competition in business," Filippo said. "Is not fair if someone open store like mine across the street and hire black man to work cheap and can charge less money than me. If man open different store than mine, is okay. With one leader, we have no competition. This is better." Those fascist lullabies must have been pretty powerful! I can't believe my ears. But, even the sword-wielding Mussolini had trouble organizing the Italian state, for after applauding Italians for years, he reduced them to stone. How can we forget that over the centuries, out of this clannish bunch came opera, the Renaissance, Christopher Columbus, Leonardo di Vinci, fashion icons Armani, Gucci, and Versace, Ferrari automobiles, the Sistine Chapel, the calendar, the piano, and much more. Filippo, who thought his hair would catch fire if he ever went inside a church, held one thing against Mussolini. He was convinced that the grand Catholic state in Italy is Mussolini's fault. "Mussolini, he give the pope land in Rome (Vatican City). The pope he live here. Italy must have religion." Filippo was reduced to tears as he told us Mussolini was shot and strung up "like a pig" at the Esso gas station in Milan. (In Italy any reference to pig is the ultimate insult.) Filippo's loyalty to fascism and Mussolini distorted his view. He thinks the way Mussolini was killed and hung is the grandest injustice of all time.

While we discuss politics and religion, the personable pizza maker meets each patron walking through the door with a robust smile and greeting. Andrea, the Napolitani (from Naples) manned the pizza oven with a watchful eye, and his pizzas were cooked to perfection. "In Napoli water is the finest for pizza." According to him, the water mixed into the dough is what makes the dough good or bad. Evidently, there is something special in the water in Naples, so Naples has the finest pizza in the world. I ordered the white pizza with mozzarella and covered with arugula and fresh basil leaves. Jenny ate the margherita pizza covered with cheese, fresh tomatoes instead of tomato sauce, and topped with arugula, and we had the house wine, which comes from Bolgheri. Filippo told us these were personal pizzas, but each one could easily feed three people, and there were no Styrofoam boxes for the leftovers, so we ate the whole thing.

"We go to Bolgheri in two days," Filippo says, "you stay in apartment there."

"Mom, you'll love it. It is beautiful," Jenny assures me.

"Goffredo needs help in restaurant. You must not say this. You have no documents. My father go to jail if control know this information."

"You mean, if I work for Goffredo, they will put your father in jail?"

"My father is the first of the family," he says, with a sudden sadness. "My father must not go to jail."

"What is the control?"

"*Polizia.*"

"Jenny, you'd better be careful what you say about the illegals back home because you're going to be one," I say. "Oh boy, this could be a real adventure," I think, envisioning an Italian jail.

"Bolgheri is just what you came to Italy to see, Mom."

"Bolgheri very beautiful. You like it," Filippo agrees.

It's almost midnight and we are still eating and drinking. Filippo orders *grappa,* which he says Italians drink after dinner. "Is for digest," he says. *Grappa* is made from the grape skins. This clear drink arrives in beautiful, tiny, fluted stemware and looks quite harmless. Filippo raises his glass to toast and says, "Salute" (health to you). Jenny and I oblige the toast and both take a dainty sip. Flames erupt in my esophagus and shoot straight out my ears. I can feel the *grappa's* muscle wrap around the contents of my stomach. "Whoa," I screech, sucking in air and grabbing the napkin to wipe the tears pouring from my eyes. "What is that?" I demand, placing my glass a distance from me. "You like? Yes, is *grappa*. Is good for digest," Filippo again assures me. *Yeah, if you're a fire-breathing dragon.* Jenny manages to get hers down while trying to keep a straight face. (I'm glad I'm not twenty-one anymore and have to be cool.) Filippo motions the waitress who is instantly by his side. "What do you like?" he asks us.

"You mean we're going to eat again?" (I'm incredulous.)

"What you want."

"Water, please, water," I say.

"Water is good to rust the gut," he replies.

"I'd like to put the fire out in my gut."

"And you?" he looks at Jenny.

"I'd like a cappuccino," she replies. The waitress stands frozen. Filippo sneaks a look over his shoulder hoping no one heard Jenny's request. The pizzeria is quiet, and all eyes are on Jenny. Filippo says, "No, no, no cappuccino. You wish wine, beer, a drink?"

"All I want is a cappuccino," Jenny repeats. Filippo looks at the waitress, takes a deep breath, and nods his head for the waitress to go.

"What's the deal?" Jenny asks, as she looks around at the people staring at her as if she had an arm coming out her head. He leans in and whispers, "You must not take the cappuccino after tomatoes. Is bad for you. Cappuccino is for the breakfast." Must be one of those holdovers from Mussolini's day I think. There are many rules concerning food. It is a religion here. Wine is not considered alcohol but part of the meal; drink wine not water; no cappuccino after tomatoes; a digestive is required. Sounds governed, doesn't it?

Dining here is opposite dining in America. Here water is brought in four-ounce glasses, and there is no constant refilling. In fact, there is no customer service in Italy. No one is in a hurry, the waiter takes care of ten tables by himself, and tipping is evidently an American custom. A cover charge of one or two euro is assessed each table. This charge entitles you to a basket of Tuscan bread and use of the silverware. What if you don't want a basket of bread or silverware? You have no choice in this matter. You will have a basket of bread and silverware, damn it. Oh, and the receipt you receive has nothing on it but the total, usually handwritten. No itemizing here. Heck, this is Italy. Next time there may be two receipts. So what if we're late? Next time we might be early. I've been here for two weeks and still haven't seen a clock or a calendar except those for sale with pretty pictures of Tuscany for tourists to take home. I love it. Their attitudes toward life are stress free.

We spend our last day in Cecina at the beach. The sea air is heavy with mist that grays the turquoise sky holding the famous Tuscan sun. After sunning a few hours and splashing in the salty water, Jenny decides we should walk down the beach looking for a locals' hangout, so we walk the entire length of the beach and into the piney woods, but find no locals' bar. "I guess we need to go the other way," Jenny says, so we walk, dodging the Juans and whales, wading in the cold water past our sunbathing spot and on to the other end of the beach to find an outdoor bar built up and out over the rocks. The tide splashes over the rocks every few seconds, barely missing the bar patrons sitting with their feet propped on the wood surrounding the deck. This bar seats no more than six on the deck and maybe ten more around small, umbrella-covered plastic tables with folding chairs, and the bartender stands at an open-air counter. We walk to the counter and order two beers, introducing ourselves to the bartender. Behind us we hear, "*Bella, bella, oh, bellissima,*" and turn to see a tall, brown-eyed Italian coming our way with wallet in hand wanting to pay for our bottles of beer. "*Americani?*" he asks.

"*Si,*" Jenny replies. "*Parla inglese?*"

"Yes, please sit with me, and my friends. My name is Davide," (DAV-ee-da) he says, with all his attention focused on Jenny. Davide is six feet tall, built like a football player, and looks a bit like comedian Will Farrell. His dark curly hair barely touches his shoulders. He is wearing khaki pants, black rubber flip-flops, and his peach-colored shirt is unbuttoned, framing his broad chest. We introduce ourselves and follow him to the white plastic table shoved up against the building for shade. Davide's two friends, both in shorts and t-shirts, rise to meet us. They are Marco and Danny. Marco is mid-forties, and Danny looks seventyish although we later learn he is eighty-two. Davide is theatrical in his body language and script. He wastes no time in beginning his pursuit of Jenny. After a brief flirty exchange with Davide, Jenny turns her attention to Marco and Danny asking them if they are locals. The three speak varying degrees of English, and once I know they all speak my language, I am much more comfortable. The men snicker and comment to each other in Italian as they watch a man in the distance walking our way. "What's funny?" Jenny asks.

"This man he is Tarzan in his mind," Davide answers. We turn to see a stunningly bronze man with thick white hair walking barefoot toward us. He is most likely the dong Juans' idol, since he has kept in touch with his abs. He is wearing a neon-pink, extremely tight Speedo covered in flowers in shades of orange and pink. I am struck by his glistening tan. He stops shy of the bar and sits on a rock at the water's edge. Davide and Marco are shaking their heads and rolling their eyes in disbelief, but Danny is just smiling. He is probably in the same age category as this man and wishes he had the guts to wear a neon-pink Speedo.

We talk the afternoon away exchanging information on subjects ranging from gardening to the Italian birth rate and everything in between while we all improve our Italian and English vocabularies. Their talk of WWII as if it were yesterday reminds me of the one year I lived in Alabama where they are still fighting the American Civil War, and it comes up in conversation at least once a day. Davide's knowledge of English is the greatest of the three, although he uses the least number of words since most of what he says is woven between phrases of desire directed toward Jenny as he pets her hand and showers compliments over her beauty. Marco, tall, nice looking with salt-and-pepper hair, serious and philosophical, is distraught because he wants nothing more than to marry and have a family, and he can't find an Italian woman who is willing to cooperate. "Italy is first country in world where woman don't want have baby. I can have German woman, but I not want German woman. I want Italian woman, but Italian woman not want baby. I want many baby, *tanti bambini*." He has pursued his dream of the perfect Italian family for years and is so heartbroken by his predicament that we have to change the subject, asking him to explain Italian income taxes. "*Porca miseria*," (misery of the pig) he begins. "The government they take all, 65 percent," he announces, as we stare at him in disbelief. "65 percent?" we ask. He continues, explaining how the government gets most of the remaining 35 percent, also by hook or crook—mostly crook in his opinion.

Danny's eyes are bluer than the sky against his thinning, blondish hair, and his smooth skin defies his eighty-two years. His tanned face gives him a ruggedness that melts with his soft-spoken manner. Retired and widowed, he spends most of his time traveling around the world visiting relatives. He was born in Croatia, and his parents moved to Italy seeking a better life, so he was raised in Italy. He has a son in Los Angeles, a daughter in New York, two daughters in Cecina, and brothers and cousins scattered in Croatia and Italy. "All invite me visit to them," he says, motioning with his arms. "I go. I go in Italy, in Los Angeles, in Croatia. All the time I go." Listening to him apply the melody of Italian to English is delightful. He has returned from two months in Croatia to care for his grandchildren whose parents are visiting in the states. He seemed proud of the fact his grandchildren are staying with him. "I go to my grandchildren and look see they are good," he says as he jumps on his bicycle. "I return." Thinking the grandchildren are young, possibly great-grandchildren, I ask their ages. "Thirty and thirty-one," he replies. "They are good boys. I go make little dinner for them," he says, as he pedals away.

"Did he say his grandsons are thirty and thirty-one?" I ask.

"That's what he said," Jenny laughs, shaking her head. We look questioningly at Marco and Davide in search of some other information, like Danny's thirty and thirty-one-year-old grandsons need him to make them dinner because they were missing arms, legs, or possibly brains, but Marco and Davide seemed to think an eighty-two-year-old *nonno* watching over his adult grandchildren is perfectly normal. Of course, Davide, thirty-six, still lives with his parents.

"You are easy," Marco says, smiling at us.

"What?" Jenny asks, indignantly.

"You are easy," he repeats, this time opening his arms in an outward motion.

"What do you mean, easy? In America when someone says a girl is easy, it's not good."

"This is so fun," I add, laughing as I lean back in my chair and enjoy the breakdown in the languages. "You make easy in your conversation. Italian women no make easy." Davide intervenes and explains to us that we are easy to talk to. We are open in expressing ourselves, and we are friendly. According to Davide and Marco, Italian women have none of these qualities. Danny, just returned from his grandparent obligations, sits listening and nods in agreement with the other two, but doesn't comment. "Not all American women are open and friendly," I suggest, which leads to a brief explanation of the different parts of the United States and how Southerners are more open and outgoing than in other parts of the country. Once again, our Americanism is an asset to us. These men are captivated with us because we answer their questions about life in the good ole USA—at least from our perspective and experience. Our three-hour conversation turns to four, and we are having such fun that Davide suggests we go with him to Castiglioncello to his special place where we can watch the sun set. "Is so beautiful. You must see."

"Yes, yes," Danny and Marco agree. "Is beautiful." Danny wants to go home and clean up after sitting at the beach all day, so he once again jumps on his bicycle and pedals away. Jenny, Marco, and I attempt climbing into the back seat of Davide's eight-hundred-year-old, green Fiat Panda. We do so by dodging the torn and falling ceiling fabric, a four-foot-long spear gun, black wet suit, swimming flippers, goggles, gloves, orange construction-worker vest, various size thirteen shoes, and one empty pizza box. We three resemble six circus elephants trying to climb into a cardboard box since none of us wants to sit on the exposed and rusty springs standing tall from the foam padding that is bursting through the three-foot-wide back seat. Davide is behind the wheel with his seat belt on, waiting for us to settle so we can pick Danny up and head off to watch the sun. "*Dai andiamo,*" (come on let's go), Davide calls. "We lose the sun. *Dai andiamo.*"

Somehow, we manage to seat ourselves. I am in the middle and have the choice of facing Marco or Jenny because in order to miss the protruding springs, I have to sit sideways facing someone. I choose Jenny. Davide and Marco begin a conversation in rapid Italian, arms waving, while Davide maneuvers the street to Danny's house. One honk sends Danny running from his front door in clean clothes and freshly combed hair. He jumps into the front seat, locks the seatbelt, and we are off speeding down the streets, swerving in and out of cars, ignoring stop signs, roadblocks, and pedestrians to get onto the highway for the eight mile trip to Castiglioncello, when Davide abruptly says, "We are five. The insurance say for four. *Porca miseria.*" The three men begin discussing this problem, and Davide insists that one of us ducks down so any passing polizia will see only four people. "Mommy," Davide calls to me, "You put your head down, please?"

"You're joking, right?" I reply. There is a two-inch clearance between the side of my head and the front seats, I'm not sure where one of my legs is, our three bodies are touching, and he wants me to duck down. "Sure, okay," Jenny and I continue laughing, while the three men persist discussing and gesticulating about the fine for carrying five people instead of four when suddenly the little green Panda whips off the road and stops in front of a small white building standing alone in the middle of nowhere. "What pizza you want?" quizzes Davide.

"Anything is fine. We like it all," Jenny answers. Davide looks at me with his forehead raised. "Anything," I respond, amid my laughter. All three men unload and go inside the pizzeria continuing their concern over the fine for going against the insurance. Everything is drama in Italy. Talking and gesticulating incessantly. Everyday life is their exercise. This must be their secret to staying slim and trim. "I thought Italy didn't have fast food," I say.

"Looks like a joint to me," Jenny adds.

"I'm not sure how much longer I can sit like this," I say as I attempt reclaiming my lost leg. Almost as soon as they enter the building, they return to the car carrying five white boxes of piping, piquant pizza that Danny holds on his lap. Davide peels out and bounces the little Fiat back onto the road, where he announces we will arrive before the sun sets. Then Marco and Davide begin to argue. *Oh, no,* I think. "What's the problem?" I whisper to Jenny.

"It sounds like Davide owes Marco money," she says. "And I guess Marco paid Davide's part of the pizza. That's the best I can understand." Marco, already serious, was not happy when he realized Davide had gotten to him again. Marco would have it no other way but that we go immediately to an ATM, so Davide could pay him back now. The brief stop at the ATM was all Marco needed to make him happy again.

Miraculously, I unfolded my body and exited the Panda when we arrived at Davide's "special" place. "My parents rent this apartment, but I can use when is not rented," he says with a wink at Jenny. He grabs all five pizza boxes, and we follow him down an old, four-foot-wide stone stairway with a black wrought iron rail on our left. The building guides us on the right. At the bottom of the stairs, we turn right and descend another twenty steps, spiraling to sea level. We look and see the sun hanging sleepily over the horizon. "Wow," Jenny and I breathe. "Gorgeous." Davide unlocks the door, and we enter a small apartment with a glass wall facing the sea. No matter which window I look out, I see a spectacular picture. "We eat later. We go see the sunset," Davide instructs as he places the pizza boxes on a table. We walk down two small ramps to the sea. I am speechless, and my eyes tear at the sight before me. I've never seen anything so magnificent in my life. We are in a private cove with no voices but ours. The landscape around the cove is a high wall of ancient earth sprinkled with stone houses, and perched atop a ridge in the distance is a peach-colored castle. Before us is the sea, lit by the slowly descending sun casting its flames into the sky. The scene is wild and simplistic at once. The majesty of nature is so awesome and in its presence I feel small yet grand. I stand still as my surroundings imbue me. Even though the guys live on the beach, they, too, stand quietly soaking in the sight. I try to speak, but once again only three-letter words are available. "God," is all I can say.

Boulders, arranged perfectly as stepping-stones, lead out to a small concrete platform built just above the water. Davide has jumped the rocks and is inviting Jenny to come onto the platform with him. She lifts her long, turquoise skirt and tries balancing on a boulder. "I can't. I need help," she cries. The very words every knight wants to hear—a damsel in distress—and Davide has played the role many times. "Hark, I cometh," he calls, and after falling into the water twice, he arrives to give Jenny balance. We are all laughing as Davide clowns some more and kneels as if in proposal. He then carefully helps her to the platform and leaves her there. He skips back across the rocks to the walk where Danny, Marco, and I are standing. Davide sheds his shirt and pants and is now in his underwear. I look twice to see it is not a swimsuit but black briefs. He jumps into the water that is mid-calf deep and motions to Jenny. "Come and play," he implores. "Leave your dress and come in." He's probably hoping she is in her underwear, too, and is not the least bit concerned that her mother is watching. Jenny can't respond because she is doubled up in fits of hysterical laughter. Both Danny and Marco look at each other and do the lower eyelid pull, an Italian gesture meaning be alert, this guy is clever, although they don't seem the least bit surprised that Davide's behavior is out of the ordinary. Jenny and I are squealing amid our laughter, as if this is the first time we've seen a male in his underwear. Under normal circumstances, back home, I'd be embarrassed, but tonight I laugh until my sides hurt.

As the sun drops behind the horizon, Jenny and Davide come back on shore. Jenny rings the excess water from the bottom of her full skirt, and Davide climbs back into his clothes. We lean against the stone wall behind us and watch the stars pop. A seat for two has been hollowed out of the wall and Danny and I sit in it. "Come, we eat," Davide instructs. *This really is a love nest,* I think, as we go inside to our pizzas. We sit around an old, wooden table with rickety, wooden chairs. The pizzas, *frutti di mare* covered with shrimp, oysters, clams, and prawns (this was a unique experience); *quattro stagioni* (four sections) with a section each of artichoke, mushrooms, sliced sausage, and peppers; *quattro formaggi* (four cheeses); and Italy's most popular *margherita,* lay open our gastronomy. Davide serves us local red wine. Once again, it is after 10 p.m., and we are eating and drinking. Davide's wine is mmmmm good—bold and penetrating. Sipping my wine and putting the conversation in the background, I imagine being immersed in peaceful prettiness every day. The wine permeates deep, full, and warm, like being seduced for the first time.

Davide jumps up and still chewing says, "Come, I show you the octopus."

"Octopus?" Jenny asks.

"Yes, my little octopi."

"What?" I ask, still in my dreamy state.

"Come. I show you," he says as he flips a switch and outdoor lights shine across the rocks and boulders. We all follow, but only Davide and Jenny wade into the water. "There. They go around the rocks. See."

"That's a baby octopus?" Jenny asks.

"Yes, yes. They hide here," Davide assures as he disturbs the rocks.

"They'll get me," Jenny squeals, as she rushes back to the safety of land.

"Jenny, Jenny, I protect you," he promises, smiling like the Cheshire cat.

"No," she rejects. Danny and I are once again sitting in the wall as Marco leans against it. "Are you teasing us?" I shout to Davide.

"Teasing?"

"Yeah, you know, joking?"

"No is not joke. Come see," he says as I step on the first boulder.

"Where?" I ask, not trusting him.

"I get one for you," he says as he digs his hand under a rock and comes up with something red.

"Look, is a sea tomato," he says, showing us a round, red creature. He holds it carefully as we lean in for a look. It's a beautiful red anemone that is closed. "My uncle he hunt these for aquariums," Davide says.

I begin humming "Volare," the Italian song sung by so many American entertainers. Maybe these three Italians can teach me the rest of the chorus. "Do you know the song 'Volare'?" I ask Danny and Marco. They both respond with a blank look. "You know, *volare, oh, oh, cantare, oh, oh, oh, oh,*" I sing.

"*Volare, oh, oh,*" they sing together.

"*E cantare, oh, oh, oh, oh,*" echoes from the edge of the water as Davide lifts Jenny off the last boulder and onto the walk.

"*Nel blu dipinto di blu, felice di stare lassu,*" Danny sings, swaying in time with the melody, and then Marco and Davide join him for the next verse. Jenny and I sing the chorus, learning the words we didn't know after the "*oh, oh, oh, oh*" part.

How we enjoy each other's company under the stars in this secret cove. We adjourn to the kitchen where Danny, Marco, and I wash, dry, and put away the plates, forks, knives, and wine glasses. Davide brings out the *grappa*, and the three men drink their quota, but thank God, they accept our refusals. Italian men must endure this horrid drink to put hair on their chests. "We go to Ice Palace get gelati," Danny suggests. "Is from me," he says, offering to pay as we head up the forty stairs still singing the chorus of 'Volare'. This time Danny rides in the backseat with Jenny and me. If bicycling keeps the body agile at eighty-two, I think I'll become a devotee.

The Ice Palace is teeming with late night gelato addicts. It's nearly midnight, and we feast our eyes on a kaleidoscope of thirty-five flavors. Jenny chooses dark chocolate with tiny specks of cayenne pepper and gets a second dip of ricotta with fig. I choose mandarin and mango, then Danny encourages me to get a third dip. I choose peach. We find an empty table and chairs on the patio. The moist night air wraps itself around me, and I want to melt into the night. It's been two weeks since we left Texas, and I've fallen deliriously in love with Tuscany.

Chapter Ten

Buff Grandmas

Since I have no idea what my next sleeping arrangement will be, I plan to sleep late on our last morning in Cecina, but I am promptly awakened at 7:00 a.m. by noisy chattering accompanied by clanging and hammering sounds on the street below. It's Sunday, and instead of getting ready for Mass, these Italians are setting up their money-changing tables. Canopies line both sides of the street, and all traffic is detoured for a few hours. The shopping begins early and ends at noon. Items for purchase cover the gamut, with something for everyone no matter their age, size, nationality, or need. Men and women, boys and girls, young and old, engaging in commerce—Italian style. Chaffering, haggling, dickering, all in melodic Italian. "Jenny, get up. It's a party on the street," I shout from the balcony. "Come on, let's go."

"No," she moans, covering her head with the pillow.

"Come on. We might not get to go to one of these again," I urge.

"I'm sleeping."

"Come on, get up."

"You go, then come back and tell me about it."

"Party pooper." I quickly dress and spend the next two hours on the street perusing tables of aprons, lace, women's and men's fashion, shoes, cheap jewelry, kitchen collectibles from the 1980s,

119

lush and juicy clementines, pears, apples, bridal fabrics by the meter, and espresso makers of all sizes. I watch the women swarm the produce tables, discussing each pear, apple, and tomato they touch. Each piece is compared to another, sniffed, caressed, denied, or embraced. This communion is a female dominated event although the oldest of the male gender are also represented at the fresh fruit and veggie tables. I watch three women at one table interrupted by a man (holding an eggplant) shopping at the next table. He steps closer to the women, and taking a pear from one of the women, turns it over and over, putting in his two cents and prompting a heated discussion about the fruit. The vendors from both tables join in the debate. I am blown away by the passion I see in this discussion. It's about pears, for God's sake. Food is not taken lightly in Italy and is a personal philosophy with its discussion becoming an emotional event. I know I'd be a better person if I had understood what they said. It was most likely equivalent to a semester of nutrition and dietetics study at any university. Back home I race through the grocery barely giving the fruit any attention, just dropping them into a bag. What am I missing? If I spent as much time with a pear as these Italians did, I don't think I could eat it. I'd have a relationship with it—and how do you eat something you have a relationship with?

Nothing is rushed in Italy, and for accomplishment-oriented Americans, every day is a lesson in patience. Seeing, smelling, tasting, and touching are what matter most. One particular vendor attracts my attention as I listen to his jovial verbiage and watch his extreme animation. I stroll to his table and nonchalantly, yet gingerly, lift a clementine from the mountainous pile of eye-pleasing, orange fruit, each with the stem and a leaf or two intact. Taking my clues from the pros, I caress it, smell it, and hold it lovingly. I move to the pears and spend the next ten minutes choosing three. My mangled attempts to speak well of these beauties, bring a smile to his face and a brief lesson in Italian. The vendor attempts to help me deliver a complete sentence since my communication has thus far been one-word sentences. I choose three pears, four clementines, and two tomatoes. Finally, after much encouragement and repetition, I say, "*Vor..rei ... tre ... pere, ... quat..tro..clem..en.. ti..ni,..e due pom..o..do..ri.*"

"*Brava, bravissima,*" he praises, to my embarrassment as all around respond to his outburst. He puts the fruit in a plastic sack and makes sure I see him put in two extra clementines. "*Per la senora Americana,*" he says. "*Grazie, grazie,*" I answer, trying to clip the end of the words to cut off my southern drawl. "*Grazie a lei,*" he responds with a broad smile as he hands me my fruity fortune.

While I'm learning how to shop for fruit, Filippo stops by and wants to move us to Bolgheri. "My mom is at the street fair," Jenny tells him.

"Is good. We go at 1:00 p.m. I come here *a l'una,*" he tells her. When I return, Jenny informs me we need to pack and be ready at 1:00 p.m., so we pack our lives back into our packs, retrieve our documents from the safe, and stand waiting for Filippo at 1:00 p.m. No Filippo at 1:30 or 2:00. "You stay here. I'll walk to the hotel and see if they know where he is. Maybe I can call him from their phone."

"Okay," I agree and sit down on the steps to get high on the narcotizing aroma of the herbs lining them. My nostrils flare to absorb the maximum advantage of this live herbal essence.

No hint of the street fair remains, not even a flyaway sack. I gently brush my hand across the needles of the rosemary bush. It's 2:30 and no Jenny or Filippo. Finally at 3:00 p.m., Filippo's car speeds to a halt right in front of me. "Come on, Mom," Jenny calls. "Are you taking a nap?"

"No, I'm high on rosemary," I say, grabbing my pack and reluctantly climbing into the backseat where the residual odor of cigarettes snatches the remnants of heavenly aromas from my nasal passages, and I'm wishing I'd stuck two pieces of rosemary up my nose. Evidently, the Germans' demands had tied him up for two hours. He seems not the least bit sorry that we had been waiting so long. Waiting is just part of life in Italy. The music of U2 is once again filling the car as Filippo tells us he has tickets to see the band in Germany in September on his birthday. This will be his third U2 concert. Talking about U2 is the only time I have seen Filippo excited.

From Cecina Mare, we drive east two and a half miles to the main town of Cecina, then into the countryside past acres of tomatoes, where four people holding paper bags, sneak a few of these ruby jewels and quickly race back to their cars. "I take you in country near Bolgheri. Is very pretty," Filippo says as he looks back at me. "Great," I respond, wondering how anything could be more beautiful than the green I am seeing now. The intense green that fills our eyes daily will surely change their color by summer's end. We round a corner to see an expanse of Tuscany's gold mines arranged in perfectly straight rows, grapes on one side and olive groves on the other. We gaze across fields of vineyards on rolling ground with a sprinkling of tan or salmon-colored stucco buildings. My favorite thing about buildings here is that none are exactly alike (no tract housing), and businesses and residences coexist. "My parents marries here," Filippo says, pointing to a small stucco building with a cross on top.

I stare out the window, practically salivating. "I told you you'd love it, Mom." Filippo makes a sharp left turn and stops. Before us is a narrow two-lane road, lined on both sides with double rows of cypress trees growing very close together and all stretching skyward as if they were reaching for freedom. "Is very famous this road and once have two thousand four hundred cypress tree," Filippo says, slowly emphasizing the two thousand, four hundred. I am staring in disbelief. "Why is it famous?"

"Very famous poet, Carducci, write about this. He live here when a child. All school children come here to see cypress tree and read his poem." These skyward growing evergreens are so thick and tall that we can see nothing but the road-lined trees for two and a half miles. Filippo peels out and speeds down the road, cypresses whizzing by. "Please slow down. I want to enjoy this famous street," I say.

"Is here every day," he responds, lifting his heavy foot.

"Tell us more," I beg.

"Trees, they very old," he adds. We laugh, which brings a smile to his face. "We are easily entertained," Jenny tells him. At the end of this famous corridor, we unexpectedly meet a castle right in front of us, complete with Roman walls protecting the town. Filippo slowly drives through the arched entrance, introducing us to Bolgheri. "This is entrance and exit," he informs us. "Is one way to arrive and leave. Maybe we see Count of Bolgheri. He is little, fat man." The road narrows to one lane as we drive past the original church built in A.D.1000. Next, on our right, is an *enoteca* (eatery that also sells wines, cheeses, and other food and gifts) with outdoor tables and chairs occupied by those waiting for what I would come to know as the best bruschetta in all of Italy, lovingly prepared by the owner. My mouth waters, just thinking about it. The Tabacchi shop is next on our right, and on our left is Bolgheri's tiny park. Five wooden benches are scattered around the area and are filled with men enjoying local talk. "Where are the women?" I ask. Filippo answers, "The women they work." The little park is shaded by large trees, with what appear to be emeralds growing under them. "Who is that?" I ask, pointing to a bronze statue of a woman sitting on a bench. "Nonna Lucia," Filippo says. "Very special woman for Bolgheri."

"What'd she do?" Jenny asks.

"She is mother of poet Carducci." We continue, creeping our way up the slightly inclined, narrow road. The ancient buildings house Bolgheri's two hundred residents. A footpath leads between two rows of buildings. Engraved in the stone of the building is the name of this narrow path, Strada Giulia. Filippo stops outside Goffredo's restaurant. As Filippo goes looking for his brother, we sit in the car gazing out the window at the countryside easily recognizable as Tuscany with cypress trees sprinkled here and there. "Jenny, this street makes a U. It's one block up and one block down the other side. Bolgheri is tiny."

"Can you believe we're going to live in a town that's protected by a wall?" she marvels.

Filippo returns and says Goffredo hasn't arrived yet. "We goes to flat now," he says as he pulls the car over and parks. We walk around the building to the large wooden front door with the number eighteen in stone next to it. Our new address is via Lauretta Eighteen. Filippo reaches his fingers into a shallow stone vase attached to the wall and retrieves the key. "We keep key here," he says, "then who use apartment can go in."

"Should we leave the key outside, too?" I ask, wondering if everyone in town knows where the key is kept.

"*Si, va bene,*" he says as he opens the door. "*Madonna!* (spoken when one is incredulous). Tomorrow I have clean for you. Lady come from hotel and clean."

"Don't worry about it. We can clean it," Jenny offers.

"No, no, lady come. *Porca miseria.*"

"How old is this building?" I ask.

"Mmm, many century," he answers. "You must remember, you not speak to anyone your work with Goffredo," he reminds Jenny. I'm wondering how this community of two hundred people who live literally on top of each other won't notice Jenny working for Goffredo, but Filippo's problem was with outsiders knowing this, since one of them could be an undercover agent. If Jenny is waiting tables and the undercover agent is dining here, he will see she is working. No one has to say anything. I guess they know what they're doing. Oh well, I'm going with the flow. Whatever happens, happens.

Filippo begins our tour with the one-room living/dining/kitchen combination in typical Tuscan décor with bricks on one wall, plaster on the other, and wide beams on the ceiling. A brick fireplace is at the bottom of the stairs. A small TV sits on a chair by the fireplace. We walk up the brick stairs that sink in the middle from hundreds of years of use. At the top of the stairs on our right is a hallway with two bedrooms and two twin beds in each. Old mirrored wood dressers and large mahogany chiffarobes wait to be of use.

Both bedrooms have windows whose green wooden shutters open into the room and another pair of shutters opens out to the air and the street below. The building directly across the street shows some modernizing, with metal pipe running vertically in three different places hiding electric wires. A clothesline mounted on a pulley system stretches the length of four windows on the outside of the building. "Mom, this can be your bedroom since it's closest to the bathroom. I'll take the other one."

"No," I protest. "It'll be more fun to be in the same room." Over one bed is a picture of Jesus with some children, and over the second bed is a picture of the Madonna and child. "I get this bed," I call.

"I know. It's closest to the door," she answers.

"Is okay?" Filippo asks. We look at each other smiling, once again in disbelief.

"Here is bathroom." We follow Filippo into a huge room broken into three sections. The floor of the entire room is tiled in white six-inch tiles. The walls are white. The entry is complete with hooks on the wall and a fake spider plant on a white plant stand. One step up, takes us into the bidet, toilet, sink, and mirror section complete with a small window next to the toilet that opens out to view the neighbor's balcony. (I later learn this the hard way.) To our right is the shower domain easily six-by-seven-feet and tiled in green. The wall opposite the showerhead has a built-in recessed area that is large enough to sit in. We both gawk over the shower. Actually our eyes pop out since until now we've showered in stalls barely large enough to turn around in and impossible to bend over in to shave our legs. This shower's size reminds me of the public school showers in which we were forced to lose our modesty after each junior high physical education class. It could easily accommodate six at once. We exit the bathroom, and Filippo shows us the wooden stairway that leads up to the attic room, which houses a drying rack for clothes and a couple of folding chairs. From the looks of the floor, I knew we shared this place with some members of the rodent family.

125

Filippo turns to us and says, "Flat is okay? You like? I call for cleaning tomorrow."

He wants to know if this is okay. This apartment is at least twice the size of the generous rental in Cecina.

"How much will Goffredo charge us?" I ask, wondering if this will be work in trade for a place to stay and concerned about the price if not.

"You speak with Goffredo. Is good for you here. You like?"

"It's great," Jenny answers.

"Thank you, Filippo," I add, not believing our good fortune and resisting my desire to once again grab him in a bear hug.

"I go now. Tomorrow cleaning lady come."

"Can she bring us some towels?" Jenny boldly asks.

"*Si, si*, I send towels in restaurant laundry. *Ciao, ciao.*" Filippo shuts the door and once again, I find myself in familiar territory—incredulity. "Why is he doing this?" I ask.

"Doing what?"

"Helping us so much. Everyone we come in contact with is making our lives simple. It's hard to comprehend." We later learn there are no rooms to rent in Bolgheri. Diners come for an evening of Bolgheri's magic and world famous wines, then return home when the businesses close. The D'Andrea family holds this apartment just in case they need it for anything. "Do you think you'll get paid for work or will this be your pay?" I ask, looking at the china cabinet housing plain white china and sterling silver. "Well, I guess we'll find out soon. Let's go see the rest of Bolgheri."

"What do you mean? We've seen it all."

"No, I mean go into the shops and meet people," Jenny says as the social butterfly in her emerges. We drop the key in the stone vase and we're off to the store next door. Over the door is a sign that reads "Artigianale." Inside is a tiny room full of jewelry made of rocks and stones from Argentina. Artigianale means made in house by a craftsman. A petite, blond woman greets us with, "*Buona sera*." We both answer with our rendition of the same and she instantly responds with, "Americans?"

"Yes, *parla inglese?*" I ask.

"Oh, yes," she answers, "I worked in New York for two years."

"Good, maybe you can help my mother learn Italian while I'm working. She needs a lot of help," Jenny smirks, lifting a beautiful necklace from a display. "Ooh, what stone is this?" she asks.

"Is tourmaline and peridot." We chat with Nicole who was born and raised in France, came to Italy for vacation when she was twenty, fell in love with an irresistible Italian, and has lived in Italy her adult life. She and her husband retired from jobs in Milan and moved to Tuscany. She drives the fifteen miles from Donoratico daily to work in this one-clerk store in Bolgheri. "My husband and me, we buy land in Tuscany to build a house and retire. We give government plans, and we wait seven years, and still we have no permit to build our house."

"The government has to okay your blueprints, and you've waited seven years?"

"Yes, Tuscany is very special to government. If you want put window in house, you must propose to government. If you want take window out of house, you must propose to government. The government is not in hurry to help you. My husband say, we wait no more. We sell land and live in house we now live in." Jenny and I look at each other thinking we must have misunderstood something, and I am remembering the summer we had to replace the gas line from our house to the meter in the alley, which then had to be inspected before the gas could be turned back on. We were impatient with the twenty-four hours we had to wait for the city's inspector.

Nicole stands in the doorway pointing to the right and tells us we must walk up into the hills and see where the Duke and Duchess of Bolgheri are buried. "Go straight in the trees." At this moment, a trim lady standing as straight as an arrow with dyed purple/gray hair combed perfectly in an old lady doo comes running across the street, waving her arms as her white skirt flows and her high heels click. Her face is as bright as new glass, and her arms are sculpted like a body builder's. "*Andata a ballare,*" she announces. (I've been dancing.)

"*Com' e?*" How was it, Nicole asks.

"*Bene, sempre bene,*" was the reply accompanied by a smile. Nicole introduces us to Giustina (joos TEE na) and tells us she goes dancing three times a week.

"*Piacere,*" we both say. (pleased to meet you)

"*Americane?*" Nicole tells her we are staying in Bolgheri a while.

"*Per che?*" Giustina asks. Nicole says Jenny will be working for Goffredo.

"*Ah, bene,*" she responds. "*Ci vediamo (see you later),*" Giustina calls as she waves and goes back across the street to her apartment.

"Giustina is eighty-four years old," Nicole says.

"No way. You're kidding," I respond.

"She could carry both our packs," Jenny adds.

"Every day she fill two bucket with water at community, oh what is word in English … (she is twirling her fingers around in a circular motion). You turn and water come," she adds.

"Faucet?"

"Yes, she carry water from community faucet every day. Why, no one know. She have water in apartment, but she carry water for her plants."

"Wow. No wonder she's buff. She carries a bucket of water in each hand up this incline?"

"Yes," Nicole nods, "and up the stairs to her apartment," she says pointing to the top floor of the three-story building across the street. The three of us smile and shake our heads in disbelief.

"*Ciao, Nicole. Ci vediamo,*" I say as we leave. I love the sound of these two words, *chee-vay-dee-AH-mo,* we'll see each other again.

We walk up into the spectacular countryside, past an old cemetery that is surrounded by a stone fence. A lock hangs from the black iron gate. We peer in to see twenty-nine crosses of weathered wood or rusty iron in various sizes standing over graves and some leaning to one side or the other. We continue walking, taking the incline slower as it gets steeper. "Whew," I spout as I stop for a rest. "This whole place is uphill. The street in Bolgheri is uphill, the countryside is uphill, wow."

"We'll get some leg muscles," Jenny says. "Wouldn't it be great if we went home slender and muscled up from walking through Italy?" she dreams.

"Yeah, no eighty-four year old I know looks or moves like Giustina. I don't think she knows she's eighty-four. Can you believe her?"

"Yeah," I puff. "She puts me to shame." The quiet chatter of birds accompanies us as we continue our search for the famous graves. "Look, there's something. Maybe that's it," Jenny says as she picks up the pace.

"I hope so," I tag along breathlessly. The hills are sprinkled with Judas, poplar, olive, and pine trees. A gazebo-shaped, stone and granite structure stands before us. Twelve pillars support this memorial to Bolgheri's famous family, the Gherardescas. We climb the three shallow steps to the center where a granite table holds a book of stone engraved in Italian. We are unable to read but no doubt a tribute to Duke Della Gherardesca and his family. We walk around this open structure to see a cement bench where a gray-haired, slightly built woman sits. Beside her on the bench is a piece of newspaper covered with pine nuts. She holds a rock in her hand. She looks up at us with a smile exposing her only three teeth. Her blue eyes scintillate in the lone ray of sun streaking through the towering trees. Her muscular body defies her eighty-seven years. Her face, drawn with wrinkles, is as beautiful and natural as this Tuscan setting. Looking at her gives me a feeling of belonging to all of history, as our surroundings testify to the accumulation of thousands and thousands of years. It's deep, yet heartening, reassuring, and safe. I look at her and know all of Italy. All boundaries of language, culture, age, and distance disappear. She's wearing a tan, sleeveless cotton dress, thin from age, with an olive green print on it. A pale green, stained, and frayed apron is tied around her small waist. She continues cracking open the sections of pinecones with her rock and harvesting the nuts as she talks to us. Jenny sits beside her and introduces us. *"Mia mamma, Sue Ellen, e mi chiamo Jenny."* Elena says something neither of us understands. *"Lentemente, per favore,"* Jenny begs her to speak slowly, to which Elena responds in even more rapid Italian. We both listen carefully as she nods her head as if she thinks we understand every word. She looks at my blank face that clearly reveals my level of understanding and then turns to Jenny. *"Capito?"* she asks. (Understand?)

"Si, capito," Jenny answers.

"What'd she say?" I ask.

"I think she comes here every day to gather pine nuts to put in her pesto."

"Wow, you're getting good."

"Quanti ani habita?" Jenny asks her how long she has lived in Bolgheri.

"Sono qui quando in la pancia della mia mamma," she responds, pointing to her abdomen and telling us she has been here since she was in her mother's womb. Looking at Elena in this setting, I realize how much we miss in life. Beauty is everywhere, but we are too busy to see it. We get bogged down in life's details to the point we forget we're living it. Knowing Elena climbs these steep hills daily to crack pinecones with a rock speaks to me. I know that living here is truly an experience. Since time isn't important to them, Italians can be present for every moment. I am beginning to think about and see life differently. I'm becoming more open to strangers and differences, and I can look at the sky, the grass, the history all around me through different eyes. This gives me a strength I've never had before. Back home, when I'm living the rat race, it's hard to see other possibilities. I think of how many days in my life I am so spent there is nothing left for me to recognize as me.

Italy is thousands of years older than America, yet less spoiled, and she's showing me another way. It's amazing how much time

Italians spend with their friends and neighbors daily. They are rich in a way that we are poor. We live sterile lives, ceaselessly racing ahead of ourselves toward progress and achieving bigger and better goals. Consequently, America is wealthy, creating opportunities for all, and we cast those opportunities out to all who will take the bait and join life in the greatest country on earth. We are the most generous people in the world when it comes to money. Americans gave over $300 billion to charities in 2006. Our compassion comes through our pockets. We as individuals are happy to share our money, but we don't share ourselves, like I see Italians doing. I'm not talking about volunteer work, but a day-to-day sharing from the heart, because you're in touch with your heart. Life is very different here. The average Italian couldn't have as much money as the average American. Surely if they did, they wouldn't live on top of each other—or maybe this is what America will look like in a few thousand years. So many people that we have no choice but to live piled on top of each other.

Many Americans live in someone else's reality through TV shows, never realizing what's happening in their own lives. How many people recorded the OJ Simpson trial and watched it every night even though they did not know anyone connected with it? They gave up weeks of their lives, addicted to someone else's drama. Do we ever stand back and question ourselves? Is this all there is to life? We're irresistibly addicted to the rapturous discovery that defines technology's progress. We stay connected via Google, MySpace, YouTube, Facebook, instant messages, cell phones, text messages, e-mail, occasionally a phone call, and even less often a personal visit. We can avoid talking to the clerk at just about any store by going through the self-checkout lane. Having lived in a time without PCs, I realize how technology has stolen our opportunities to socialize. I remember studying China with my young children. We were in the library looking for books that would help us, and Jenny runs up to me motioning for me to follow her. "Mom, I saw a Chinese lady reading a newspaper in the children's area. Maybe she can help us," she whispers, pulling me in that direction.

"How do you know she's Chinese?"

"She's reading a paper with Chinese words on it, and she reads from right to left. I watched her. Come on."

"You go talk to her and ask her if she can help us, then come tell me what she says." Jenny, age six, struck a conversation with this woman, and before we left the library, our new friend had offered to come to our house with all sorts of hands-on learning tools from her native land. Today a study of China would take us straight to the computer for our research. We'd enjoy pictures and videos of China and never leave the house, exercise our imaginations, or communicate with a real live person. More often than not, I resist new thoughts and feelings of a different way. I'm clutching to my old ideas while feeling the excitement of the far side of me changing.

Here in Elena's forested getaway, I'm reminded of my childhood when my grandmother took me with her for a few days every summer to the mountains of southwestern Arkansas to visit her cousin in Caddo Gap. Grandmother's cousin, Cousin Ola, offered us a feather bed to sleep in that was on her screened-in porch where we could watch the fireflies light the black night as we drifted off to sleep. Every night, Grandmother and I would roll into the middle of the bed making it difficult to crawl out in the morning. Cousin Ola cooked on a wood-burning stove, commanding that cooking machine like George Patton and his army. Turnip greens were my least favorite food, but they melted in my mouth at Cousin Ola's. Cousin Ola had no indoor plumbing, and one dark night when the crescent moon offered little light, Grandmother took me up the hill to the outhouse. The trees rustled just as we got there, scaring me so that I peed my pants. Out the back door was an old, concrete well with a rope threaded through a pulley system and tied to a metal bucket. It was magic when we lowered the bucket out of sight and pulled it back up full of clear, cold water. Each time, Cousin Ola warned me not to lean too close lest I fall in. She would look very sad as she told me of my fate if I fell into the dark, cold water. Never daring to ask, I'd peer into the well wondering how many boys and girls were at the bottom. Like Bolgheri, Caddo Gap had one road, a dirt road that curved slightly through town and ended at the mercantile. One entered the store by stepping up on a wooden porch and opening the screen door. This rectangular building held any child's delight. A walk down the center of this room was a walk down memory lane even in the 1950s. Both sides were lined with bins holding everything from penny candy to socks, nuts and bolts to fishing lures. I spent hours touching everything and listening to the adults talk about the weather and whether or not the fish in the Caddo River were biting. Finally, I would buy a stick of cinnamon candy for a penny before skipping back up the dirt road to the house.

At home, we went swimming in a concrete public pool whose water was chlorinated and made my eyes burn, but at Cousin Ola's, we walked across the two-lane highway to swim in the Caddo River where the water was clear and cold and had a gravelly bottom. Once, something swam through my legs. I jumped and screamed, but Grandmother and Cousin Ola just stood in the waist-deep water talking. I loved how they were absorbed in each other, enjoying their infrequent visits. They always knew where I was and never prevented me from exploring and taking a few risks. "Grandmother, something went through my legs," I screamed.

"Probably a snake," Cousin Ola answered, without turning her head. I got out of the river as fast as I could and carefully walked barefoot to the swinging bridge whose sides were made of rope with wooden slats to walk on even though some of them were missing. As a child, the bridge's height was scary for me, but the thrill and challenge the swinging bridge offered were more than I could resist and certainly safer than swimming with snakes! The bridge swayed with each step, and I didn't dare look down at the moving water, get dizzy, and lose my balance. I gripped the rope in the same way I grip the armrests of the dentist's chair (a white-knuckled death grip), and with each step I'd look into the woods of scrubby oaks, cedars, and ethereal white dogwoods all around me. Each time I stood on the bridge, I wondered if I'd make it across or if I'd fall into the river, and sometimes I just went halfway, stood there swinging, then ran back and climbed down. Caddo Gap was my secret place. Grandmother was my favorite person and her being a part of my secret place endeared her to me even more.

We had discovered Elena's secret place. She knew we had come to see the famous graves, so she pointed to them and said, "*Di la* (over there)." We walk away from her, looking for the graves. The graves are flush with the ground and barely recognizable are the names of the Duke and Duchess Gherardesca. A serenity and magic permeate the air, and in spite of the stillness and calm, I can feel the land's energy. Jenny is right. I love Bolgheri.

"*Ci vediamo*," we both say, waving to Elena as we leave to walk back down to town.

"*Ci vediamo*," she replies. Vineyards and olive groves come into view all around us as we walk back to Bolgheri. "Well, tomorrow's going to be a disappointment," I say.

"Why?" Jenny asks.

"What could tomorrow possibly bring that could equal today?"

"Oh, Mom, you're such a hippie. I can't wait to see the shops."

"What shops? I saw mostly eating-places. Did you really understand what Elena said, or were you just guessing by her hand gestures?"

"Maybe a little of both."

"Great. I wonder what she really said."

"I think I'm understanding more and more Italian," Jenny brags.

"Good. So as long as we're together, I'll be able to communicate."

"No, don't depend on me. You need to learn Italian, too."

"I know. I want to. I'd love to be able to communicate with these wonderful people, but I don't know if I can."

"Just forget about conjugating verbs, and you'll be okay."

"Would you stop that? I get it okay."

"We'll see who gets hung up on Italian verbs. Let's go have a glass of wine and some bruschetta."

Chapter Eleven
Lunar Landing Module

As we stroll the promenade, hundreds of swallows dip and sway in the fiery sky, shooting upward then suddenly, as if they hit a dead end, turn diving earthward in a majestic swoop, drawing loops in the sky. They entertain us in a glorious display of graceful dance before settling into their mud homes for the night. We stand looking at something too beautiful to be real. The atmosphere, the sky, the pixilating air, the vines and purple plumbago creeping along the old stone railing, together with our feathered friends imbue our surroundings with magic. Words, powerful as they are, cannot do justice to nature's seduction. Bolgheri must be experienced. Since our Texas departure, on May 25, everything on this trip has been fresh and dramatic. I thought at some point the drama and wonder would either end or at least settle down. I was wrong. "Goffredo is right," I whisper to myself.

"Right about what?" Jenny asks.

"There *is* magic in the air."

"I knew you'd love it here, Mom."

The next week, Jenny goes to work daily at 5:00 p.m., working in Goffredo's restaurant, La Taverna del Pittore, until the magic hour of 11:00 p.m., when the patrons, saturated with wine and satisfied gastronomies, dreamily wander to their cars. I help take the outside tables down and carry the candles and flowers inside. Each night, at the midnight hour, Goffredo insists we have leftovers from the kitchen and a glass or two of wine. I sit outside La Taverna's front door at a table for four next to the stone wall, where a fuschia bougainvillea climbs to the roof, inflaming the wall with royal color. On the other side of the entrance to La Taverna are three tables under the canopy of an orange tree covered in tiny, green fruit. The wafting aromas of roast pork, basil, and garlic seize me, all forcing my tongue into dialogue with my stomach. These aromas can change your life.

Having worked in restaurants back home, Jenny was entertained by the slack "health standards" she observed in Italy.

"Mom, get this. The cooks' cigarettes dangle from their mouths as they work."

"Well, I guess a little ash never hurt anyone," I answer.

"They pour what's left from the wine bottles on the tables into one bottle and use it to cook with the next day."

"I wouldn't waste any of that wine either. It's red gold."

"They drink wine while they are working, and they let me wear flip-flops! The eggs, milk, cheese, and even meat sit on the shelves for two or three days without refrigeration. The only thing they refrigerate is bottled water."

"Ooo, meat and milk sitting out? Hmm, I don't know about that one," I say.

Every day we attempt communication with the local shop owners and walk into the countryside to feast our eyes on vineyards and olive groves. Each night, when we are supposed to be sleeping, we hear the scamper of little clawed feet and hope those claws don't join us in our beds that sink in the middle making it difficult to get up quickly. Before I climb out of bed to go to the bathroom, I survey the path with my key chain light. Then one night, while Jenny is working and I am at home watching Italian TV (to immerse me in the language), a rat (not a mouse) runs out from under the china cabinet. This guy was definitely displaced. He belonged across the ocean in the New York City subway system. I ran out the front door and around the corner to tell Jenny. "Could you ask Goffredo for some rat poison?"

"We're too busy now. When you come to help us later, you can ask him," she says, so I walk to Nicole's shop and ask her to write, "there's a huge rat in our flat" in Italian so I'll be prepared. "Oh, no," Nicole exclaims. "You cannot live with the *topo*! Goffredo will kill the *topo*." Everything is so dramatic, exciting, and passionate to the Italians. I love it. She takes a cash register receipt and writes, *"speriamo di non vedere il topo sta sera in casa,"* (We hope we don't see the rat in the house tonight) and hands the note to me with the promise that she knows Goffredo will take care of the problem.

When I go to help take down the outdoor tables and chairs, Goffredo asks me to sit with him and enjoy a glass of wine. His eyes reach into your soul, simultaneously revealing his. One look from him melts my heart with kindness, love, and gentleness all rolled into one fantastic gift. I'm not sure how Italian women resist this soul-snatching, but I feel like a schoolgirl. The invitation to sip wine with him distracts me from my mission—rat poison. "Come on, Mom, help me."

"No, Jenny, *la mamma* make wine not work," is Goffredo's reply, and with a smile he adds, "I make the English."

"Yes, and it is good," I tell him.

"No, no good. I make practice for you," he says. Ah, practice, the word that wins every teacher's heart. "Goffredo, we have a rat in our flat," I blurt as my fingers walk across the table.

"Che?" (What?) I take the slip of paper from my pocket and read, *"speriamo di non vedere il topo sta sera in casa."*

"Che?" He again asks, taking the paper from my hand and reading it. *"Un topo in casa?"* He asks, with a look that fuses shock with horror.

"Si, il grande," I assure him. A huge grin that could melt an iceberg spreads across his face as he says, *"Buona, parla italiano per mi? Buonissima."* (Good, you speak Italian for me?) He rattles off several Italian sentences that broke the sound barrier, and all desire

I had to speak Italian limped off to hide in the shadows. "Jenny, can you help me?" I shout.

"What, Mom?"

"The rat I saw in the apartment could gnaw my leg off," I say. "How do we ask for rat poison? We need poison."

"I'll go ask Oliver," and she skips off to the restaurant next door and asks a waiter whose English is quite good. One wouldn't think that exterminating a rodent could be so involved, but in Italy everything is involved. Italy is invigorating and exhausting at the same time. "*Veleno per topo,*" she returns and tells Goffredo. His eyes widen, he sets his glass down and says, "We go." Goffredo rises and we three march to the apartment, single file. He looks under the china cabinet and all around the living area for signs. "*Domani,*" (tomorrow) he says.

"*E grande,*" I emphasize with outstretched hands indicating the *topo's* size. "Jenny, its tail was a foot long. I saw it."

"Don't exaggerate, Mom."

"Well, that's the pot calling the kettle black. You're the queen of exaggeration."

"Eeez beeg?" Goffredo responds. "*Domani, le da veleno,*" indicating he would bring the poison tomorrow.

"*Si,*" I say, once again holding my index fingers about twelve inches apart. "*Il topo e grande.*"

Goffredo leaves with a distressed look. "Oh, no, I hope we didn't make him feel bad," I say.

"I don't think he feels bad. Italians just want everyone to be happy, and they'll do just about anything to make and keep you happy."

Word spreads quickly in a village, and the next morning, Bolgheri's matriarch, Lina Serini, comes knocking on the green shutters of our side window that stands open. Lina's another one who doesn't know she's in her eighties. I guess when you look in the mirror and see sixty, you don't know you're eighty-three. Must be the olive oil. Standing next to Lina's four-foot-eleven-inch frame is a tall Italian grandmother, Francesca. Both are dressed in sturdy shoes, knee-high hose, and crisp shirtwaist dresses. Leaning into the open window, they both speak at once in Italian as Francesca hands me a small box. I see by the picture on the box that it contains the sticky pads to trap mice. If one can be inhumane to mice, sticky pads provide the way. I went to visit Jenny when she lived in New York City, and the apartment building's exterminator had littered her apartment with these pads. In spite of the party the mice held for our entertainment in the center of the living room each night, only one of them ended up on the sticky pad. One night as I wrestled the royal-blue couch whose springs bit into my back, I was disturbed by a heart-wrenching screech. I didn't dare get up for fear I'd step on a rodent, so I lay still listening to the intermittent, faint yell for help. The next morning we found a mouse glued to the pad desperately pulling his legs and emitting a sound that must scramble transmissions to the human brain, for I felt sorry for this warm-blooded varmint. Neither Jenny nor I were willing to touch it, so we called on the services of a friend who came to our rescue and carried the mouse-clad pad out to a bag of trash on Manhattan's West 44th Street sidewalk.

Yesterday, a large tomato rested on the windowsill, but today Lina, Francesca, and I stare at the puny remains. "*Mangia, il topo mangia,*" I say, pointing to the remains of the red, juicy fruit. "*Si, e grande,*" Lina says, looking at Francesca who nods in agreement. The two Italian *nonnas*, whom I had just met, have come to my rescue. "*Grazie mille,*" I say, with a smile and a nod as the two women proceed to show me with hand gestures how to use the sticky pads. I quickly peel off the covering of one pad and put it under the china cabinet where I had seen the four-legged monster. Lina and Francesca continue peering into the open window, and not knowing what else to do, I invite them in, motioning to them as I open the front door. They gratefully decline and back away waving and chattering. I put another sticky pad upstairs in our bedroom between the dresser and the wardrobe and another in the attic.

Each night at dark, geckos surround the lights both inside and outside Nicole's shop. "They eat mosquitoes," Nicole says, when I point to three crawling across her wall. She assures me they will only help us, so we remain calm the first night we see one climbing the brick stairs to join us in the bedroom. We watch to make sure we don't step on him and thank him when he hangs out on the wall near the open bedroom window, knowing he'll grab the mosquitoes that fly in. We name him Gecky and call him our pet. I get up the next morning and check to see if maybe we've caught two rats instead of one, but no such luck. There is Gecky, stuck with no chance of escape. He lifts his neck and looks at me wide-eyed, anticipating. "Oh no, I'm sorry, Gecky," I say, holding him at eye level. "Jenny, we caught Gecky."

"Way to go, Mom." Not knowing what else to do, I walk downstairs and out across the street to put him in the two-gallon trash bucket attached to a pole outside Giustina's apartment. As soon as he feels the outside air, Gecky raises his little head and cranes his neck around tasting freedom. "I'm sorry, Gecky," I say as I drop him into the can. I grieve that little guy for days and throw away the remaining sticky pads. Two days later, Goffredo brings us little square pouches of poison that something in our apartment devours nightly. The victims evidently crawl off to die somewhere else, since we never see any signs. We are assured that no matter the intruder's size, it will die after eating the poison packets, but without evidence of death, I am not trusting, and my eyes scan the floor most of the time.

We make a trip into Cecina to apply for Jenny's work permit. I can't wait to get to a computer to check my e-mail and see if Jake has written. We wait two hours. I didn't know two hours could feel like weeks until I sat in a room the size of a sardine can, sweating with nine visa-seeking Romanians. Jenny doesn't sweat. This is a skill she learned during her beauty pageant days. She sits calmly and dryly with her knitting needles and yarn while I walk into the sour-smelling hall for a breath of fresh air. Italians aren't concerned with whose turn it is, or if they wait forever for whatever it is they are waiting for. Time just means conversation and another glass of wine. So, when the door under Room Nine opens, we sardines swim toward it hoping we get caught, which we finally did and cooperated all we could in the question and answer process with a language barrier the size of Mount Everest. The process is reminiscent of my experience in the early '80s, waiting outside Montgomery Ward in a pack of crazed females who trample the manager when he unlocks the door at 7:00 a.m. so the first fifty of us can race to the prize. I remember being in the midst of this gang, realizing my life was more important than a Cabbage Patch doll. We paid one hundred euros for what we understood would be health insurance. We are told Jenny must prove she has twenty-five hundred euros in a bank account in her name. There is no chance of getting her work permit without this proof. Somehow, this lets the Italian government know she has enough money to stay past her three months' travel passport. I wonder over how many glasses of wine that regulation was cerebrated?

We headed to an Internet café, where five computers crammed into a tiny basement assure the owners no one will use a computer longer than ten or fifteen minutes lest he die of heat stroke or lack of air. I took a deep breath and walked down the flight of stairs into the hot basement. "Jake's in Torino and leaves today to hitchhike to Nice, France. He says he's stayed with Couch Surfers in Milan and Torino. Thank God, he's safe."

"He'll be okay, Mom."

"Easy for you to say. You've never been a mother."

"Come on, let's go get gelato before we meet Goffredo."

"I think I'll try fig and ricotta, or maybe chocolate and chilies. I'm feeling 'outside the box.'" My salivary glands stand up anticipating gelato flavored with figs and ricotta cheese. The barista scoops me a generous serving. "Mmm, try this," I say, shoving my cone to Jenny's lips.

"Outside the box? Maybe. Try mine." The sting of red chiles against chocolate wrinkles my nose.

We hop the bus to avoid the two-and-a-half-mile walk to Hotel

Tornese so we can hitch a ride back to Bolgheri with Goffredo. Nightly, Goffredo picks up the fresh laundry for his restaurant. We sit waiting outside the hotel, watching the tourists walking to and from the beach, when Goffredo pulls up in his mother's Toyota Land Rover. I sit in the back seat between the boxes of freshly folded towels, napkins, and tablecloths, enjoying conversation half in English and half in Italian, as Jenny and Goffredo bounce their second languages off each other.

Each evening, Lina Serini and three other *nonnas* converge at the top of the road next to La Taverna to watch the nightly restaurant activities begin. The workers set up their outdoor tables and dress them with colorful tablecloths, napkins, crystal, candles, and flowers, and I'm sure things wouldn't have gone as smoothly without the *nonnas*, even though they never move off their benches. They sit and watch the set-up, visit with each other, and leave after the restaurants' businesses are in full swing. Lina and Elena are present each evening, and as I pass them at 5:00 p.m. on my way to help Jenny set up tables, I try speaking to them in Italian. It had to be the highlight of their day, for they all try to help me pronounce words as they correct each other and me. When they finally realize what a slow learner I am, they one-word banter with me until my tongue twists into a pretzel, then I'd throw up my hands and claim I have to go to work. "*Lavoro*," I say to escape, and I'd leave them giggling, talking, and gesticulating.

Daily, I walk the dirt roads up into the hills where nature engorges my senses with her arousing aromas, tempting textures, cascading colors, and symphonic silence. I sit on the gnarled, holey, unearthed trunk of my favorite olive tree, listening as each enchantingly distorted trunk jumps at me with its own history. These fantasies fuel my desires for a new and different life, and the art in each trunk fascinates me. The young olive trees have normal tree trunks, but the old trees' trunks split several directions, like they've been struck by lightning multiple times. They have both large and small holes bored into them by critters and are twisted into shapes that create spectacular nooks and recesses. On my left is a large olive grove, where I see the Tuscan breeze barely lift and stir the slender gray-green leaves. How glorious it is! The young leaves glisten in the sun, while the newly birthed fruit, confident of this year's harvest, hides behind the remaining dried blossoms. On my right, stretches a world famous Ornelliaia vineyard, whose arrow-straight rows carry my vision on and on to the Tyrrheanian Sea. In front of me in the distance are cypress trees standing guard on ridges and a castle whose walls guard Bolgheri's magic. I picture the Romans stealing these mighty cypresses for their houses or sea-faring galleys. Filippo said Bolgheri is the only Tuscan town that has resisted the grip of commercialism. Bolgheri invites you to dine and experience the magic, but then you must leave, for there are no rooms to rent here. Behind me, roll the hills of Tuscany, wildly acquainting me with the color green, which until now I've never fully savored. Nicole told me the smell of olive oil permeates the air the entire month of November when each family brings their harvest to be pressed and bottled. "We have seven trees that give us oil for the year," she said. Between the olive grove and the vineyards stands a mighty fig, whose enormous leaves shade its tender, naive fruit. I've never seen a massive fruit tree. It must be thirty feet tall and thirty feet wide, and I hope I'm here when the figs ripen.

I reflect on the acts of kindness that serendipitously come our way. At our every turn, goodness has greeted us. Each person who housed us during these past two weeks and the D'Andrea brothers who offered a job and a place to stay, are all from different walks of life with one thing in common—kindness—a kindness that is not premeditated, offered with no expectation, and given to strangers. It's a generosity that comes from an everyday compassion for humanity. How do I pass it on? I think I could house and feed couch-surfing strangers for the rest of my life and never repay what's been given me in so short a time. I've been remodeled on the inside. Maybe it's not about housing and feeding, but listening, hearing, and being unconditionally friendly and open. The Italians haven't labeled us, and they are open to a relationship with each day's reality, even if it includes two nutty Americans. I pray I'm a blessing to all I meet and can adopt this open-hearted kindness.

"Mom, you up here?" Jenny calls breathlessly, as she climbs the hill to my favorite spot. "Goffredo says we have to go back to the police station tomorrow. Evidently Filippo's policeman friend said he has to go with me this time."

"Good, while you do that, I'll get my hair cut and colored at that little salon by the hotel."

"Can you help me talk to the salon ladies and tell them what colors to use?"

"I'll be at the police station with Filippo. Just take the colors Tim wrote for you. They're made by an Italian company, right?"

"Yeah."

"Then they'll be familiar with them at the salon. You'll be fine. When you talk, just don't worry about verb conjugations."

"Oh, shut up. Hey, how are we going to see Italy if you have to work? Is this the end of our vacation? There's two and a half months left," I ask.

"I don't know. I'd like to stay a year and learn all I can. This job will let me stay."

"Goffredo won't need you after the summer season will he?"

"Maybe not, but I bet I can get another job. I *really* want to live in Italy."

"I wish I were brave enough to go it alone, but it wouldn't be fun without you. Are you sure you want to do this?" I say.

"I'll ask Goffredo if I can go for a week or two."

"Well, that's better than nothing. I guess if we have to stay in Bolgheri for the summer, I'll become a poet. I'll just sit here and write all day. No, I can't do that. Maybe I could garden for someone."

We rose at 8:00 a.m. the next day, dressed, and walked to the arch by the castle to hitch a ride into town. Jenny stands firmly planted with arms held straight out in front of her, hoping to stop the car.

"Jenny, please don't get hit."

"They'll stop."

The two-door Fiat slows to a stop and the driver rolls down his window.

"Cecina?" Jenny asks.

"No, Bibbona," is the response. Jenny steps aside as the little box on wheels shoots through the arch. Three cars go past before we get a ride. Today our savior is a happy man in his '50s, balding, who introduces himself as Oscar. We climb into his roomy VW Jetta and off we go. Jenny asks him what kind of work he does. "*Che lavorare?*" she asks, and he spends the entire twenty-minute ride telling us, in Italian, with an English word here and there, about his thirty-five interesting years as a horseracing jockey. All I understand is that he didn't get to eat much while he was jockeying, but by the scant distance between his belly and the steering wheel, he has definitely compensated for those lean years. He drops us in Cecina, where Jenny heads toward the police station to meet Filippo, and I board the bus for the ride to Cecina Mare. "Good luck in the sardine can," I say.

"I bet Filippo will take me directly to the person in charge. That's why he's meeting me."

"Just come to the salon when you're finished," I call.

"Okay."

Armed with the note card containing the Italian hair color numbers that Tim puts on my hair, I enter a salon that blasts me into the past. The green, linoleum-topped counters and retro pictures of '50s, '60s, and '70s hair models hang on the cream-colored walls and are perfect accents to the outdated dryers, washbasins, and heat lamp resembling a lunar module with four metal arms jutting in different directions. The room smells of cheap rose perfume. There are three beauticians and one client, an older woman, getting her hair styled. "*Buon giorno, senora,*" says the stylist as she leaves her client and walks toward me.

"*Buon giorno,*" I reply, to which she adds, "*Americana?*"

"*Si da Texas.*"

"*Va bene.*" (It's good.) Showing her the card and giving it the old college try, I attempt to tell her what I want as she gestures like she's trying to pull something out of my gut. She finally grabs the card, studies it, and calls the other two beauticians for a consultation. She shakes her head, no, as she begins stroking my hair. I'm standing, head bent forward with six hands in my hair as they jabber and pull my hair this way and that. I can't understand a thing they say, and as soon as the verdict is in, I am informed in broken English, "No," she says pointing to one of the numbers on the card. "Theez eez no gooood. Theez *e scuro* (dark)." They all stand back and nod their heads in agreement. One of them says, "You have the light skin and blue eyes. Dark color is no good for you."

"But he uses all these colors," I protest as they continue shaking their heads, no. A tiny voice from a remote place within me says, "They are passionate about hair. Sit back and enjoy this. They're going to do what they want anyway."

The process went as they planned, and they all had their hands in it. One applied the color, one shampooed and rinsed, and one cut and styled. I spent twenty minutes under the lunar heat lamp. Three hours later, I emerged much blonder than I entered, and they all nodded in agreement, pleased with their work. A trip to the salon is always an exhilarating experience. I go once every other month. Each time I leave, I feel like a new person. The feeling is what I imagine I would experience if I'd lost ten pounds, found a cure for cancer, and raised my children to be happy adults all in two hours. I'm on top of the world, and I feel beautiful, strong, and powerful. Today is no different. I love my blonder, shorter style, and I thank them as they wave goodbye.

The English-speaking beautician, who washed my hair, told me she and her husband lived in Detroit for twenty years, and they loved America. "The United States, oh, she is wonderful. We love her," she claims.

"Why did you move back to Italy?" I ask.

"Oh well, you see, oh well, it is in America when you are old you go to "nursery," she says, with a long face and a drop in her voice. "But America I love her, *capito* (understand)?" she says in an apologetic tone. She and her husband decided they would move back to Italy before their children took this American mindset concerning their old parents and nurseries. She continued, "In Italy if you are old, your family care for you. If you have no family, your neighbor care for you. This is the way in Italy. All help when you are old. I don't want go to nursery, *capito?*" she says, with a pleading look on her face. The ground quaked, my heart twitched, and something gnawed at my gut. I live in a part of the world that values the young, and I am fast becoming old in that young society. It's terrifying how the value of our elderly is discounted when their working life is over, or they seem no longer useful. Many are put into homes where they die lonely and abandoned by those they loved most. "I am sorry," I say, looking at her, and the gnawing in my gut continues.

Jenny asked Goffredo about time-off for backpacking, and he told her if she wanted to work for him, she would have to be back July 15 for the "crazy" busy time. "What planet are we on? You're kidding right?" I ask.

"Can you imagine what a boss back home would say if you worked a week then asked off to go traveling?" she says.

"No, I can't. You tell me."

"What the—? Get out of here!"

"They'd put us in the nut house, and are you ready for this?"

"Yeah, what?"

"Goffredo paid me for this week's work."

"Uh, uh. No way. Your work wasn't in trade for the apartment?"

"He's too good to be true." We continued our outrageous thoughts as we repacked our packs. "Where should we go first?" I ask.

"Siena, I guess. There's a Hospitality Club member there, and he e-mailed me his number. I'll call him when we get to the train station tomorrow." I fall asleep, reading Rick Steves' section on Siena.

Chapter Twelve

American Women Escape Italian Asylum

"Let's see, today is June 19th, so that gives us twenty-five days to see how many adventures we can have. I still can't believe he gave you time off with pay!" I say.

"Yeah, how cool is that? I hope we meet some really nice Hospitality Club and Couch Surfing members."

"I want to go to Gimmelwald. It's my favorite place in the whole world," I add.

"Mom, I don't want to go to Switzerland. We came to travel in Italy."

"I know, but we're so close. Jenny, I have to go back to Gimmelwald."

"I'm not spending my money on an expensive train ticket to Switzerland when I don't even want to go. Why don't you go up there by yourself, after I come back to work?"

"Come on, Jenny, it's more fun with you. I'm not ready to travel alone. Okay, I'll pay for your ticket. I'll pay for the hostel, too, if that's what it takes to get to the Alps again. If I run out of money, we can always come back here. After visiting Florence and Rome, you'll probably need the peace and quiet of Gimmelwald."

"You and your peace and quiet. You know I love crowds."

"Okay, let's say goodbye to everyone and get to Cecina."

"Maybe we can do some real hitchhiking. You know, like from town to town. That's what everyone does when they go backpacking," Jenny suggests.

"Didn't Goffredo say it's illegal to hitchhike on the highways? Besides, we've been hitching from Bolgheri to Cecina. Doesn't that count?" I say, to rolling eyes and a shaking head.

"He was talking about the expressways not the back roads," she says.

Oh, God, please spare me.

Before boarding the train in Cecina, Jenny uses the payphone to call her Siena contact who says he'll pick us up at the train station at our arrival time, 5:24 p.m. We board, and as soon as the train begins its monotonous sway, Jenny promptly falls asleep. For two hours the train snakes in and out of hills in the Tuscan countryside, unveiling what until now I had only seen in obese coffee-table books of Italy. As Jenny snores, we pass miles and miles of fields painted thick with rich, yellow-gold sunflowers. Emerald green vineyards creep gently over hillsides, and silver-leafed olive orchards perch obliquely along sunny slopes. Scattered here and there are patches of golden wheat that look as if they've been added for contrast. Phenomenal. When I can't stand it any longer, I wake Jenny, begging her to share this experience. She mumbles, "I'll see it later."

"You may never come this way again," I advise.

"Uh huh," is her only response. Oh, to be twenty-one again. The train stops and the de-boarding activity begins. "We here already?" Jenny says, stretching and bouncing to her feet.

"You missed two hours of awe. I don't want it to end. I want to stay right here and see what comes next."

"What you'll see if you sit here is the ticket man's boot kicking you off for having no ticket. Ours is good to Siena. We're here, so let's go. I have to find a payphone to call this guy again," she says, watching me swing my pack over my shoulder. "Look at you putting your pack on by yourself. Good job, Mom. You're getting strong." Suddenly I feel like a child and fall in line behind my mamma.

"Don't patronize me," I whisper in her ear as we stand in line to get off. "I thought he was going to pick us up at 5:24 p.m. Isn't that why you called him from Cecina?"

"I guess he knows not to trust TrenItalia's schedules. Remember they don't tell time over here," Jenny says as she spots her target, drops her pack at my feet, and walks toward the red phone box attached to the wall. A minute later she returns and says, "Well, he's on his way, and he speaks English, but he says he can't keep us both. Don't worry. We're not splitting up."

"Didn't he know we are two?"

"Yeah, I told him, but I figured we wouldn't take up any more space than one cause you can sleep on the couch, and I'll sleep on the floor beside you. Maybe he'll change his mind," she says, with a confident air.

We move outside the station to a line of cars loading and unloading people and baggage. "What car are we looking for?" I ask.

"A black Fiat, but he's looking for my red hair, so he'll probably spot us first."

"A black Fiat. Of course, what else would it be?" I laugh.

"I think he's your age, so look for an old man," she smirks. "This is him, I bet."

"This is he," I correct. A balding man about my height gets out of a black Fiat wearing wrap sunglasses, jeans, brown leather loafers, and a white t-shirt with Mickey Mouse center front. "Jeeen-ee," he calls in our direction as he opens the back of the car. A sunscreen of Donald Duck on a sky-blue background decorates the back window. I approach the open space by backing up to it and letting my pack slide off my back. "This is my mother, Sue Ellen." Jenny introduces. "Hello, thanks for picking us up. I'm so glad you speak English."

"Mom, I'll get in back. You can sit up front." As soon as he opens his mouth to introduce himself, a feeling washes over me. Something I cannot identify immediately, just an odd feeling.

"We go to McDonald's for ice cream," he announces. McDonald's? Hmm, Disney characters, McDonalds, American icons. Maybe he thinks we'll feel comfortable at McDonald's since we're Americans. Almost immediately, when we get in the car he begins chastising Jenny. "My Hospitality Club profile says one person."

"But we won't take any more space than one. Mom can sleep on the couch, and I'll sleep beside her on the floor."

"No, not possible. You stay," he says, and then pointing to me, "She cannot." (So much for age before beauty.) You must respect HC profile." He continues his barrage of verbal bludgeoning explaining why only one can stay, none of which made any sense to me, but he made clear he keeps one at a time, preferably female. I get it. He's out to change the world one female at a time.

"We can't split up," Jenny replies. "If Mom can't stay with you, neither can I." The more he talked, the more resistance I felt toward him. He was a negative person, but what I felt was much more than negativity. He told us what a horrible city Siena was, that he had grown up here, and it had never been good to him. "Is horrible city," he emphasizes with his Italian accent. "I don't know why you want be in Siena," he adds as we pull into McDonald's. He opens the back and tells us to take out our packs. "Can't we just leave them?" Jenny asks.

"No," is the punctuated reply. Inside McDonald's, he tells us to sit down while he orders. "What are we going to do?" I whisper.

"Don't get excited. We'll figure it out." He gives us each a cone but has nothing for himself. "You're not having—?" He cuts short her question with a magnanimous wave of his hand and sits across the table from us. He leaves his sunglasses on and seems discomposed that there are two of us. He asks about our Hospitality Club and Couch Surfing experiences. "They've been great, and we've even gone home with a guy we met on the beach," Jenny says. "People here are so nice."

"You cannot do that," he says. "Is not good. Why you travel like this?" My friends back home would agree. The longer we are with him, the more uncomfortable I feel. It's not what he says, so much as how he says it. His shoulders are bunched, and he carries anger in his body. His body is aggressive in a degrading way. He can dislike Siena if he chooses. Yes, he is a negative person. He hasn't revealed his eyes to us. Yes, he's annoyed and annoying, but it's deeper than any of this. It's not an intuition, but it's coursing through me. I can't identify it. I haven't experienced this feeling before.

"Can you take us to a computer?" I ask. "It's getting late."

"Yeah, maybe there is another HC member we can stay with," Jenny says. "Do you know another HC member in Siena?"

"No," came the unequivocal response.

"Do you have a computer we can use?" Jenny asks.

"I cannot take you to my flat," he says.

"Is there an Internet café or hostel near?" I ask.

"Yes, we go to hostel," he says as he practically runs ahead of us to the door, which he opens and lets close in our faces. Grabbing Jenny's arm I whisper, "Something's wrong," and she nods in agreement. "I'm not sitting up front with him anymore. He gives me the creeps," I say.

"Okay," she answers as she opens the door for me. The ride from McDonald's to the hostel is a short one, and he begins attacking Siena, George Bush, and our mode of travel. "I am born in Siena. Is bad place to live. Siena is no good for me." The more he spoke, the more agitation rose in his voice. "George Bush is mad man. He is bad man."

"No, he's not," I counter, defending my President.

"Mom," Jenny warns, with a tone of voice I remember using to quiet my children. Trying to change the subject, she asks his line of work.

"I know the stars," he answers. "I help people."

"You're a fortune teller," Jenny guesses.

"No, I do not tell the fortune. I know things." He seemed to enjoy the guessing game, so he continues. "People come to me for know more."

"You're not a fortune teller, so you must be an astronomer," Jenny guesses. I'm in the back seat not believing what I'm hearing.

"Astronomer?" he questions. "What is astronomer as you say?"

"It's astrologer," I mumble from the back.

"You are an astrologer," is Jenny's last guess.

He blurts with the urgency of projectile vomiting, "I am psychic," then pointing to me he says, "She is devil." If there had been any way, I would have bailed out of the back seat leaving Jenny to fend for herself. I sink into my seat and encourage my shoulders to consume my head. This man just called me the devil. My heart flip-flops inside my breast, then something pricks it, and I feel a stinging heat tear through my chest cavity. Oh my god, is all I can think looking at my front to see if I am bleeding. Now I understand. Our spirits clash, and he must feel the tension if I do.

"My mother's not the devil!" Jenny objects. "How can you call my mother the devil?" My lungs cave. The air has just been sucked out of me. "The devil," I gasp. At once, I feel totally weak, wounded—and horn-mad. I have no idea what a psychic could do to the devil, but I'm in the cross hairs. I look in the rearview mirror to see if I've grown horns, my eyes are red, or I'm on fire. We pull up in front of the youth hostel, get out, and grab our packs all while this man keeps his eye on me. The hostel with its large, clean, common room inspires a prayer. "Please, God, let them have an empty bed." The clerk is already shaking his head, no, as we approach the desk. We ignore his indication and ask for any available bed. "*Un letto, per favore?*"

"*No. No letto sta sera,*" he replies. I point to the couch and say, "Ask him if we can sleep on the couch." Jenny points to the couch with raised eyebrows and says, "There? *La?*"

"No," comes the answer.

Jenny turns and asks the self-proclaimed psychic, "Will you take us to the Internet café?"

"Yes, is near," he answers. We thank the hostel clerk and turn to leave. At this moment I feel like I've left my body. Where am I? Have you ever suffered a moment of what could be called "temporary insanity"? It takes you somewhere else. Here, outside the hostel in Siena, I have such a moment. I get back into the car with the man who has just called me the devil. Temporary insanity. I've heard you get it from your children. Maybe it's true. Tension oozes from our three bodies and bounces off the walls of this claustrophobic, black rectangle as it rolls down the street. *Have you lost your mind?* something inside me asks.

Yes, I calmly answer.

Have you lost all reason and sense of self preservation? was the next question.

Evidently.

What are you doing in this car?

I don't know.

The George Bush tirade continues as the psychic equates us with our President. "You are the same as George Bush," he says, turning up the volume on his voice box.

"What do you mean?" Jenny asks.

"He is independent, and you are bold and think you do anything you want." After being called the devil, I didn't consider this an insult. "Please take us to a Catholic church. Maybe the priest will let us stay," I say. He slams on the brakes stopping dead center in the street, looks at me from behind his sunglasses and announces, "I cannot take you to church. Is not possible."

"Why not? We slept in one in Livorno," I say.

"You are devil. I cannot take devil to church. You must understand this." I don't know why, but I wasn't afraid. I just had an overwhelming desire to deck him. In my fifty-six years, I have never wanted to hit anyone until now—well maybe my children once or twice. My warring spirit has pulled out the stops and is recruiting my whole body to move to action. How can this be? Yesterday I sat in the countryside wrapped in thoughts of peace, understanding, compassion, kindness, and love of all mankind, and now I want to punch this guy's lights out! The energy coursing through me at this moment, if harnessed, could light the globe for decades. "Maybe the priest could exorcise me," I suggest, between clenched teeth. "Please just take us to a church."

"No, no," he booms.

We are still sitting in the middle of the street, cars honking and pulling around us, hand gestures flying, and people leaning out their windows in our direction, shouting obscenities as they careen down the street. We would learn, as the summer progresses, that this driving behavior is the Italian norm. More than once, we were passengers in a car flying down the freeway when it suddenly stopped and backed up at fifty miles per hour because the driver had missed the exit. This is a thrill beyond words, and more than once, my life flashed before my eyes as we sped in reverse into oncoming traffic. Returning a few hand gestures of his own, our driver jumps back into traffic. We arrive at the Internet café, and Jenny logs onto both the Hospitality Club and Couchsurfing sites. It is possible to find an empty bed in a few minutes online, but it wasn't happening tonight. No one in Siena was logged on at this particular time. "Now what?"

"Can you take us to a convent or monastery?" Jenny asks. He thinks a moment and says, "Yes, I take you there." The sun is behind one of the mountains, and he removes his sunglasses for the first time. His eyes are dark, but not brown. They are dark blue and anxious like they could burst at any moment. *If he thinks I'm the devil, why does he want me in his car? I don't understand. How is a monastery or convent different from a church?* I had developed a trust for the Italian people and culture, and so I continued getting into this man's car. This time the Fiat drove straight out of Siena and up into the beautiful surrounding hills. Tree-lined, serpentine roads took us up and up through a forest to the top of a mountain. The little Fiat grew claws that clung to the pavement despite the speed we were traveling. We stopped when the road ended. It was in a tranquil wood where only the songs of birds pierced the silence. This man, who thinks I'm the devil, has brought me to heaven.

Our surroundings create a natural desire to be quiet and listen. We take our packs and hurry ahead of him to the door. I ring the bell, and a second later, we hear the latch release, and we push the massive wooden door open to reveal an inviting courtyard. We quietly walk around this garden paradise where stone benches beckon the weary to sit under the protection of bird of paradise trees, Gothic planters of geraniums, and ivies climbing a stone wall in the direction of the next door. Jenny pushes a small button near the second door, and a smiling nun in full-length, black and white habit greets us. *"Buona sera,"* her sweet voice welcomes as she opens the door and motions us into a receiving room.

"Buona sera," we each respond with a nod and a smile. Jenny begins her attempt at telling our story. A blank stare is a telling picture and this nun has one. A tiny frown between her eyebrows appears. "Try again," I encourage Jenny. The nun bows her head and asks us to excuse her. *"Scusi per favore,"* she says as she leaves. Jenny and I bounce our ideas off each other about the best way to explain our dilemma in Italian. The psychic has seated himself on a bench behind us and is listening. The nun returns five minutes later with two additional nuns in tow. Jenny begins her request, but the psychic steps forward with his story. The tone of his voice is not pleasant although he is respectful of the sisters. I assume he omitted the devil part since the nuns didn't run screaming for cover. Once again, they excuse themselves, this time returning with a piece of paper containing three telephone numbers, looks of apology, and well wishes. What we understood was there is no room in this inn, but if we call one of the numbers, maybe there would be help. Had they felt his vibes? If they did, do they fear for us?

The three of us leave this sanctuary as quietly as we had entered. The serene environment has calmed my "devilish" nerves and given me hope, until I look at our chauffeur who has taken the piece of paper from Jenny and, after giving it a brief glance, wads it up and shoves it into his pocket. He slowly backs the car away from the premises, then returns to his reckless speed, taking us back down the hill, the little car hugging each corner on two wheels. He excitedly says, "I know the place, yes, they take you. They must take you. Yes, I know," he says, with an intoxication in his voice.

"Where?" Jenny asks.

"A place I know. They will take you. Yes, they will." The more he says, the more excited he gets, and the faster he drives.

"Okay," Jenny says.

Once down the hill, he drives through town and starts up into hills on the opposite side of Siena. Five hours we have been with this nut, and he gets more volcanic with each passing minute. We twist our way to the top of another remote hill. Darkness surrounds us, and unpleasant ideas skip through my head. Could this be our end in the dark, wooded stratosphere surrounding Siena? The car stops in a graveled lot, and a stark, three-story, modern building rises before us. There are no cars, no people, no signs of life. "I leave you. I cannot help you. You must do this alone," he says. *Freedom at last*, I think as I start to follow Jenny out of the car.

"I'll go in and see if we can stay," Jenny says. "You stay here, Mom."

"No," I protest as Jenny shoves her seat back into place, smashing the backpack that is on my lap into my chest. "You stay here. I'll go in," she says, gritting her teeth. There are times in a mother's life when her children make it clear they don't want her anymore. I never thought my time would be in the dark of night at the top of a remote mountain, in the hot plastic backseat of a two-door Fiat with a man who thinks I'm the devil.

Jenny disappears into the building. Nerves tingling, I sit clutching my backpack. The silence is deafening as the 'devil' and 'psychic' sit together. Numbers of apparitions, abstractions, and apprehensions race through my head. I imagine ghosts converging on the car, coming for me. I see him turning around and smiling with fanged teeth, laughing hysterically as he ties me to a tree, while fire shoots from his eyes lighting my feet ablaze. I see him driving off, leaving Jenny and taking me to hell with him. Then, "I will not need your help" booms inside my head. The yellow card, yes, I read it this morning. The visions leave me as I sit hugging my pack and repeating the words, "I will not need your help."

In what seems an eternity, Jenny returns, gets into the car, clicks her seatbelt, and says, "It's the nut house. You tried to leave us at the nut house."

"They will keep you, no?" he asks.

"What?" I ask.

"Yeah, it's some kind of asylum. There were doors on either side of the hall, and they were all locked. I had to go to the top floor before I found anyone to ask and they were the cleaning crew. They told me it was some kind of institution for the insane."

"You mean the cleaning crew speaks English?" I ask.

"The crazy sign is universal, Mom," she says as she draws small circles in the air near the right side of her head. "They did this and then pointed to the closed doors."

"They let you stay," he says, emphatically.

"No they won't," she snaps as he peels out and the black box bounces off the gravel onto the paved road.

"You are relative of Condoleeza Rice," he shouts. I have no idea where he was going with this, but Jenny cuts him off as she points to her arm, "We're not related. Wrong color."

In a sarcastic tone, he says, "Now you pray to your star for place to stay."

"What are you talking about? What star?" Jenny asks.

"George Bush is your star. Pray to him to see if he give you place to stay." This was getting too weird for words.

"Please take us to the main plaza," I plead. I am desperate. This guy is a raving lunatic. If we get out of this one, we'll chalk it up to experience, insanity, or whatever column on our list needs something added to it. "You want Piazza del Campo?" he asks.

"Please," I say.

"Yes," Jenny adds. "Well, we knew we'd have to sleep outside sometime, didn't we?"

"I feel not good I cannot help you," he says.

159

"He feels bad since the nut house wouldn't take us," I mumble.

"It's a good thing, too. Now do you know why I wanted you to stay in the car? How would we have gotten down off that mountain? It's got to be ten miles out of town," Jenny exclaims, starting to giggle. "Can't you just see the headlines? American Women Escape Italian Asylum. Or maybe it would read, Two Nuts In Italy Found In Straight Jackets."

It is 10:00 p.m., and we escape the darkness of secluded hills to the well-lit central plaza of Siena. Piazza del Campo hops with college students from around the world. The feeling of barbed wire coursing through my veins for five hours vanishes, and I look forward to sleeping on the thousand-year-old bricks that extend from the center of this plaza in a slight incline to meet the buildings that surround it. Soon we hear American spoken. We stop to visit with a party of six college students from Delaware hanging out and enjoying themselves. They are attending the summer session at the local university, and as we talk, we share our experiences with them. "Wow. What a cool mom. My mom wouldn't go backpacking with me," one of the girls says.

"Mom *is* cool," Jenny praises. "Wait till we tell you what happened here in Siena," she begins and recounts our experience with the psychic. I'm not sure these American students believed her since they kept saying things like, "Uh, uh. For real?" and "No way."

"My mom would take the next plane home," adds a boy.

"Mine would have screamed the whole time," another says.

"So now we're looking for a place to stay," Jenny says.

"You could sleep on our floor, but it's full already," a cute, freckle-faced girl offers.

"I'm happy to sleep out here. I'm just glad to be away from that psycho," I say. "It's beautiful out here. There's a breeze, and I can lean on my backpack and sleep staring up at the star-filled sky." The truth is, I can't believe I'm saying this.

"Yeah, sometimes we sit out here talking all night and then watch the sun rise. All you need is a bottle of wine," a boy says.

"Sounds good to me."

"Can we spare five euros?" Jenny asks.

"Why not. This is a special occasion. We survived."

"Well, if it's a special occasion, you need something besides wine. Here wine is just food. I don't think Italians could eat without it," adds the freckle-faced girl.

"What do you think, Mom?"

"We're in Italy. The more Italian wines I taste, the better."

"Okay," Jenny says, and heads toward a bottle-lined window on the opposite side of the plaza.

"It's not too bad out here," says one of the boys. "I've spent more than one night here."

"Well, anything beats the nut house," I say.

"No joke," they all laugh.

It's been years since I voluntarily stayed up all night, but having my ego pumped up by college students and feeling the intense energy my body released when we left the psychic, I thought I could stay up one night if I had to.

"Wait till I tell my mom I met someone her age who slept out in the plaza on a backpack," another girl says. "I didn't know moms could be cool," she adds. I don't remember a time in my life when anyone called me cool. I love it.

"We've gotta go. Good luck to you."

"You, too," I answer, leaning against my pack. The kids move on, and I sit on the warm bricks, waiting for Jenny. Fifteen minutes pass and no Jenny. "You can do this," I say aloud.

"Sure you can," accompanied by howls of laughter, bursts forth from within me.

You lost this one, I respond mentally, *I'm doing this cause I'm cool.*

I hear the familiar, "Mom," in the distance. "Mom, Mom," Jenny shouts as she runs toward me, a bottle of wine in each hand. "We have a place to stay tonight!" she says breathlessly.

161

"You're kidding."

"No, there's a nice California couple over there. They're visiting their daughter who is my age, and they said we can sleep on their couch."

"You asked them?" I was incredulous.

"No, they offered when I told them how cool you are. Come on and meet them. They're your age."

"Oh my god. I hope they don't change their minds when they see me."

"You're ok, Mom, you're just sweaty, but what else is new?" Suddenly I was uncomfortable. Why? I was about to meet my fellow countrymen, peers, but they were probably dressed nicely and clean and looked real, not cool. I wiped the dripping sweat from my face, around my hairline, and off my neck with my soured, wet rag that was my constant companion. "I need to rinse this out soon. Help me up," I say as I reach a hand upward toward a smiling Jenny.

"Come on before they leave," she says, pulling me to my feet.

"We're staying with Americans in Siena?" I laugh.

"Well, maybe not if you don't hurry. They're over by the wine store."

Sweat continues dripping from my hair. I must have a slow leak on top of my head. I look frazzled. I am filthy. I remind myself of Fagin, the hapless outcast, in *Oliver Twist*, with one difference. I'm enjoying this lifestyle—until now. I'd forgotten how peer pressure feels. I try to poof my hair, but it's stuck to my head like flies to honey. The disbelieving comments of my friends back home sound in my head:

"That kind of travel is for college kids."

"You would sleep in a stranger's house?"

"You're going to do what?"

"Have you lost your mind?"

"You're nuts!"

I swallow my pride and nearly choke on it. I've spent the past three weeks with Italians and never felt this way. Now, facing an

American couple, who is offering help, makes me uncomfortable. Every part of me is having fits of self-consciousness. "Should I wear my pack or carry it?"

"Whatever's easiest," Jenny says as she hoists her pack over her shoulder. "Come on." I decide to carry it with one hand. I follow Jenny across the plaza as I look down at my dirty feet.

"There they are. Hi, this is my mother, Sue Ellen," Jenny proudly announces, as she gives me a little hug for support.

"John Ward," the man says, extending his hand. "My wife Evelyn, and our daughter, Jessica."

"Jessica has spent this semester going to school here, and they've come for a visit," Jenny explains. The Wards manage pleasant looks on their faces, but I'd love to know what they are really thinking. Probably, oh my god, what have we gotten ourselves into? This woman's a street freak or something dangerous. They were clean, affluently dressed, and if they had negative thoughts, they feigned both body language and facial expressions. John and Evelyn looked at me as if I were neat, clean, hair and makeup in place, and they smiled making me feel comfortable. This was an unexpected emotional moment. I stood reveling in their warmth washing over me.

"When Jenny told us you were willing to sleep out here on the street, I imagined myself doing the same," a wide-eyed Evelyn says. With a half-laugh I say, "I hope she didn't ask if we could stay with you."

"Oh no," John steps into the conversation. "No, I knew if she was Jessica's age that you were probably our age, and I wouldn't want to sleep out here."

"She told us some of your adventures, and I want to hear more," Evelyn says.

"We have two available couches and you are welcome," John offers.

"Thank you. You are so kind, and I really appreciate this," I humbly respond. They are so kind; in fact, they don't mention their available shower.

"Come on, girls. Let's stop and get some pizzas on the way home," John says, interrupting Jessica and Jenny's conversation.

"We've got the wine," Jenny says, holding up her two bottles.

"Great. Let's go." The walk to their apartment, with a stop for pizzas, gives us time to learn the Wards love living in northern California and working together in a home-based business, but they are most happy their only child has completed her study abroad and is coming home.

We enter the centuries-old stone building and walk upstairs to the Wards' spacious two-story rental, which is like nothing we have seen thus far in Italy. The rooms are huge with magnificent, wooden, floor-to-ceiling bookcases shined to a high gloss to match the floors. Trendy furniture compliments the opulent burgundy, velvet drapes hanging from the twenty-foot ceiling and flowing in the breeze that sweeps through the large, screenless windows. The fully equipped kitchen flashes new appliances and sparkling white counters. It feels more like Times Square than old Italy. Evelyn gives us thirsty terrycloth towels and washcloths. I begin to feel like a queen as I shower in the clean, spacious bathroom. We eat pizza and drink both bottles of wine as we sit around the table, conversing like long lost friends and learning how Jessica's backpack and all its contents were stolen out from under her feet as she slept on a bench at the Bosano train station. Finally, at 1:00 a.m., John retires. We girls continue until the late hour holds us in its tiring grip. "Do you girls eat breakfast?" Evelyn asks.

"I'm not much on brioche and coffee," I say. "That seems to be what Italians eat for breakfast."

"John has to have his breakfast, and you are welcome to join us. Are bacon and eggs okay?"

"Wow, bacon and eggs, a real American breakfast. I'd love it," I answer.

"Okay, don't worry about getting up early. We'll just have a leisurely breakfast. We're going to Florence tomorrow to the embassy to replace Jessica's lost passport, but as long as we get off by early afternoon, we're okay. Good night. I hope you sleep well."

"We will thanks to you. Good night."

We stretch out our clean but weary bodies on two separate couches that are four feet wide and eight feet long with big, fluffy pillows to cradle our heads. The cool evening breezes lull me, and I begin drifting off, thinking about the good in people.

"Those kids thought I was cool. I'm cool, and I could have died today. I wonder how differently this day would have gone if we'd just stayed at McDonalds. We knew he was weird," I say.

"Doesn't it make you feel powerful?" Jenny responds.

"Huh? You mean that I didn't die?"

"Yeah?"

"No, it scares the shit out of me."

"Well, you can get right over that. We've got a month to go, and if this is any indication of the adventures, it's going to be fun. You weren't ever really afraid of him, were you?" she asks.

"No."

"Then what's the big deal?"

"You're right," I say. "But I do think his Hospitality Club profile should include that he's a psychic and a nut case. Don't you?"

"Mom, you're funny. Good night."

"How do you sleep with the constant noise of high-pitched scooters zooming around?"

"They're monotonous music. I don't even hear them. Shhhh, tomorrow's Florence, mmmz-z-z-zzzzzzzzz."

Chapter Thirteen
The Answer Is No

Lying on the supple couch while morning breezes grace my head, I dream I'm singing on the stage of the Metropolitan Opera where I stand in a sea of bluebonnets. Wow, what dreams accompany satisfying sleep! My opposite is Donald Trump singing as Siegfried, and I am Brunnehilde. We roar our love for one another in Richard Wagner's "Die Walkure." Our voices and movements, so tied to our passion, envelope our spellbound audience and lure them into the roles. In their seats, each is Siegfried or Brunnehilde. My glorious moment of Viking maidenhood is invaded by the ear piercing screams of cycles on the street below giving birth to another day in Italy. Not wanting to leave the spotlight, I struggle to hold my dream, a delicious impossibility. I lose to the day's realities bearing down on me. I'm conscious. The dreams I can remember occur between 6:00 and 7:00 a.m., that hour just before dawn when some mystical spirit tranquilizes everything, and I drift suspended between the bona fide and the unknown. "Donald Trump?" Laughing aloud, I ask myself, "Where did he come from?" Realizing no one else has stirred, I am first in the bathroom. The bright, cleanliness awakens me, and the soap's citrus fragrance renews my senses. I'm ready for the day.

Returning, I shake Jenny's shoulder, "Get up, Jenny, let's get out of the bathroom before anyone else gets up."

166

"Huh?"

"Come on. Wake up," I say, continuing to shake her right shoulder.

"You go," comes the mumbled reply.

"I have. I'm ready. Get up. It's your turn in the bathroom. Come on. It's so clean and smells like oranges."

"What's the rush? Is anyone else up?" she asks.

"Not yet. That's why I want us to get out of the bathroom before they get up."

"Gimme a few more minutes to make up for those I missed listening to you snore. Did the books jump off the shelves last night? You were sawing 'em," she says, turning over to bury her face in the oversized pillow.

"I was singing Wagner with Donald Trump at the Met," I tell her.

"What?"

"Yeah, I dreamed I was Brunnehilde."

"What a wake-up call. Mom singing with Donald Trump," she laughs.

"Come on. Evelyn will probably be down here soon to start breakfast."

"What time is it?"

"Seven."

"Seven! I can't get up at seven. Go back to the Met."

"Wish I could."

"You girls are up early," Evelyn says as she descends the stairs with a white terrycloth robe tied around her tiny waist. I wonder what it would feel like to wear a bulky robe and still have a tiny waist.

"Well, one of us is up," I answer, stuffing my PJs back into my pack.

"Sleep well?" she asks.

"Yes, thanks to you."

"Good," she says, entering the bathroom.

"Is Jessica hard to get up in the morning?" I ask.

"Oh, yeah," came the answer from behind the bathroom door.

"Jenny, get up," I say, digging in her pack for the Rick Steves' book.

"What do we need to see in Siena? How far is it to Florence? Do you have a contact in Florence? Get your lazy butt up!"

"Would you chill? Yes, I know someone to stay with," she says, dragging herself to a half sitting position on the couch.

"Good God, we're in Italy. How do you sleep when there's so much to see?" I ask.

"I'm here to learn the culture more than to see things," she responds. "Anyway we don't have to see it all."

"We probably won't see it all, but it's fun trying. How is it I have so much more energy than you? I'm thirty-five years older!"

"It has to do with death," she answers, nonchalantly.

"How does death give you energy?" I ask, confused.

"I don't know. I've just noticed," she says.

"Oh, you mean the older you are and the closer you get to death, the more you appreciate each hour?"

"Something like that," she says.

"It's called wisdom," I say.

"Yes, teacher."

"Good morning, ladies," John hails, from the top of the stairs.

"Daddy, please, it's too early," Jessica answers from the loft. John dances down the stairs in his red and tan golf shirt tucked neatly in his khaki walking shorts. "Excuse my father. He jumps out of bed every morning with enough energy to run a freakin' race," Jessica informs us as she slinks after him in her lime green pajama bottoms, tank top with bright, pink polka dots, and her disheveled blond hair not knowing which way to turn. "Mom and I get tired watching him."

"I love it," Evelyn says as she emerges in her long, khaki pants and white shirt. "If it weren't for John, Jessica and I'd have trouble getting up," she adds as she joins John in the kitchen.

"Can I help?" I offer.

"We've got it covered don't we, honey?" she says, shooting John a smile.

"You bet," John smiles back as he hands Evelyn a carton of eggs from the fridge and puts four pieces of bread in the toaster. "So what sights are you ladies visiting today?" he asks as he sets the table.

"I'm not sure. What do you suggest?"

"What do you think, Jess?" John asks Jessica.

"I guess the cathedral & il Campo are musts," she says as she goes back upstairs.

"Where are you staying tonight?" John asks.

"Who knows," I say. "Could be another exciting one. Jenny says she has a Hospitality Club contact in Florence." Jenny, wrapped in a blanket, sits up, stretches, and answers, "Yeah, he has unlimited space so he says. He's the number one HC host there."

"Hey, look, she's up," I say as Jenny gathers her necessities to take to the bathroom. I quickly fold the sheets and put the decorative pillows back on the couches.

The apartment fills with the heavenly aromas of bacon, eggs, toast, and black coffee. "Everyone want coffee?" John asks as he holds the coffee pot in the air.

"No thanks, I'll have water," I say as everyone else shouts, "Yes!"

"How about some orange juice?" Evelyn offers.

"Mmm, I'd love some." John places a juice glass by my plate. The scrambled eggs and toast make their way to the table and are placed in front of me as I sit down. Jessica plops her pajama-clad body in the chair beside her father. "I haven't seen bacon and eggs or toast since I've been in Italy. What a treat!" I say. Halfway through breakfast, Jenny emerges from the bathroom with hair and makeup ready to meet royalty. She fumbles through the mess she's made on the floor beside her couch. "I'm about to eat your eggs," I say. "Better hurry."

"No you won't," comes the fiery reply.

"Boy, it's amazing what makeup can do for a girl. A few minutes ago she was comatose, and now she's ready to fight," John grins.

"You know," I say as I compare what I'm wearing to the freshly pressed cottons on the Wards. "I purposely brought cheap, knit clothes thinking I'd be sleeping on benches and brick roads and have no access to ironing. These are just a month old, but my scrubbing them in bathroom sinks has peeled them to slick and shiny. Even when I'm clean, I look homeless."

"You are homeless," Jenny says.

"I'm amazed at what you two are doing," says Evelyn. "I could never do without the comforts and securities I'm used to."

"Ask me at the end of the summer. I may say the same," I laugh.

"If you last till the end of summer, you'll be ready to do anything," John adds.

"Mom, ready to do anything? I hope so."

I sit enjoying the warm breakfast inside me and observing my hosts interacting as a family. John's enthusiasm has rubbed off on Jessica who teases him. "Siena's own golf pro right here," she says. "Did you bring anything but golf shirts?"

"Nope," came the reply as he holds her down until she cries "uncle."

"When do we need to leave?" I ask.

"No hurry. We can all leave together," John says.

"I want a picture of you two before you get away," Evelyn adds.

"We can take pictures when we're all outside in the Tuscan sun," John suggests.

"Ok." I rise and begin clearing the table. "Thank you so much. That was delicious. I'll think about this breakfast all summer when I'm facing sweet rolls and cookies."

"Yes, thank you," Jenny adds. Evelyn and I team to clean the kitchen. I rinse and she loads the dishwasher.

Jenny repacks as I look around and under the couches for anything that might have strayed like a "thong," earring, or lip liner—Jenny's necessities of life. "Are we ready?" John asks. "We are." For a moment, I forget I'm here to immerse myself in Italy. A fleeting wish to go with the Wards comforts me with thoughts of money, my own language, security of having a man around, and an organized day. It's easy to forget we're supposed to be travelers lost in the wide-open spaces of feminism.

With John holding the door, the five of us head down the long flight of stairs. We arrange ourselves in front of the door on the street for several pictures. "Will you promise to come to Lubbock?" I ask. "How can we ever repay you? You may have saved a life, mine!"

"I can't promise we'll get to Lubbock, but you are welcome anytime in northern California," Evelyn counters. "It's beautiful where we live."

"You girls have fun today, and take care of yourselves. Keep in touch," John says.

"Keep in touch? How? I have no e-mail, phone number … nothing." We all dig around for paper and pencil and exchange contact information. Hugs and waves good-bye send us in different directions. "Good luck at the consulate's office," I shout back up the street.

"Thanks. You girls have fun." These abrupt acquaintances are hard on the psyche. I learn just enough about someone to want more time with them and then we're off to meet another stranger. I'm bummed out, wondering if I'll ever see any of my new friends.

Jenny and I walk around il Campo once again, take a few pictures, then head to the dark-green and white striped cathedral, which hasn't opened yet but where a short line of anticipants stand waiting. We take our places at the end of the line behind a family of four. Mom and Dad are dressed as typical American tourists, shorts and t-shirts tucked in with brown belts. Two young girls sit at their feet drawing on sketchpads. The girls have on jeans and t-shirts from Sea World and Six Flags. A pink backpack rests at one girl's feet and a lavender pack is on the other girl's back. "Hello," I say.

"Hi," Jenny adds.

"Americans?"

"Yeah, I guess it's pretty obvious," the dad admits.

"Italians say they can see us coming a mile away. Do you think we all look alike? Is it our dress or our hair? I always thought Americans were a melting pot of looks," I say.

"Maybe, but after being here a week, I think I could pick out an Italian in any group," he adds.

"My name is Sue Ellen, and this is my daughter, Jenny."

"Brad and Helen from Portland," he introduces, then pointing to the girls, "Jaclene and Sarah. We all nod and exchange nice-to-meet-yous. "Sounds like you're from Texas," Brad says.

I laugh. "How'd you guess?"

"I grew up in Dallas. I'd know that accent any day."

"Looks like you have two artists," I say, looking at an involved drawing of Jaclene's. "How old are you, Jaclene?"

"Nine," she answers. Her drawing is a detailed picture of a cobbled street in typical Italian style with various buildings around and a fountain of lions in the center.

"Look at this, Jenny, can you believe it? She's nine. Wow, are your sketches for sale? I would love to buy one."

"Can you teach me to draw a stick figure?" Jenny asks.

"A stick figure?" questions Jaclene, wrinkling her nose.

"Is your drawing of something in Siena?" I ask.

"It's Assisi," Jaclene answers as she adds more details to the monk's robe.

"We were there yesterday," her mother says. I stand amazed at what I'm seeing on her sketchpad. "Assisi. Isn't that the home of St. Francis? I read he's the original hippie. You'd probably love it there. Mom's a hippie at heart," Jenny says.

"I'd love to buy your picture. Could I?" I ask Jaclene.

"It's for Grandma," she answers. "I'm sending it to her so she can see Assisi. It's so beautiful there." I glance at both her parents who are casually observing their daughter's artwork.

"You can buy mine," Sarah exclaims showing me her picture

of a dog sniffing three daisies while the smiling sun looks on. Her drawing is fresh and alive.

Oh, Sarah, it's very nice," I say, trying not to show any comparison to Jaclene's.

"How old are you?"

"I'm seven," she proudly announces.

"And how much for your picture?" Sarah looks to her mother for help, but gets only a smile.

"Mmm, can you buy it for one dollar?" she asks.

"Would one euro do? I don't have any dollars, but you can spend a euro here in Italy."

"Okay," she says, carefully tearing the drawing from her sketchpad. I set my pack down on the step and begin looking through my money pouch.

"Here you go," I say, handing her the gold colored euro coin.

"That's not a dollar," she objects. "It's cents."

"No, honey, it's one euro," her father points to the "1" on the coin. A bit disappointed that it was not a bill, Sarah takes the coin and shoves it in her pocket.

"Thank you," she says.

"No, *thank you*," I emphasize. I'll put this on my bedroom wall and remember the two young American artists I met in Siena.

"Put your things away, girls," Helen says. "The line's moving." Both girls hurry to pack away their pads and pencils. "Well, it's only 10:20 a.m.," Helen brags. "Not bad for a 10:00 a.m. opening."

"It was nice visiting with you," Brad says.

"Thank you, nice to meet you. I hope you enjoy your stay. How much longer will you be here?" I ask as we walk slowly toward the door.

"Two more weeks, but we hope to go to Bavaria, also," he answers. "And you?"

"Until the end of August," I say.

"I'm hoping to stay for a year," Jenny adds.

"They're serious travelers," Helen says.

"No, just beggared backpackers," I answer.

173

We all enter, and the two girls stay close to their parents, listening to what their dad reads from a guidebook about the art and the structure they are seeing.

"Those are unusual girls," I whisper.

"Yeah, they're not making noise and running away from their parents," Jenny observes.

"They're probably scared to death," I say, pointing upward. Jenny's eyes widen as she stares into the faces of one hundred seventy-two heads of past popes glaring down on us.

"I hope they don't think those are the real heads," Jenny laughs. As I look down the line of heads, each one looks more dictatorially forbidding than the one before.

They are scary," I say, darting my eyes to meet the floor. "Look," I breathe, pointing to the beautifully inlaid marble under my feet.

"I'm digging these columns," Jenny points to the timberland of columns populating the room.

We continue strolling through this thirteen century edifice packed with Renaissance art. I'm thinking about Jaclene's drawing. Her shading, proportions, detail are years beyond her gentle age. She's just passing time and having fun with her pencils and sketch pads--so young and uninhibited. "I wonder when Jaclene is your age, what she'll be doing with her talent."

"Does it matter?" Jenny asks, pointedly.

"Well, yes. She has a gift. It would be terrible to waste it."

"Teacher mode," Jenny sings. "I know you can't help it, Mom." Her comment resounds the words of an accountant friend, who told me years ago, "Teachers can't resist any teaching opportunity. Those of us who aren't your students feel talked down to. I was married to a teacher for twenty-three years; I was in a fourteen-year relationship with a teacher; several of my friends are teachers. You're all the same. It's an occupational hazard. There's always something I need to learn, and you're gonna teach it to me. You all think you're experts. You don't get it. Not every situation needs to be a "teaching moment." Just talking about it gets me riled," she said, frustrated. I never told her my thoughts on the obsessive compulsive often boring nature of accountants. That's one teaching opportunity I passed up. Nor could I tell her about the year I opened an online trading account for each of my adult children for Christmas. I was tired of buying them toys, clothes, watches, CDs, electronic gadgets. I'd spent years and thousands of dollars on such presents, so one year I set up a Scottrade account in each of their names and deposited one thousand dollars in each account. Their ages were eighteen, twenty-one, and twenty-eight at the time. All lived in different states, and all were single. What a great way to help them learn about investing and trading. Right? *This is a hands-on gift they can play with for a year*, I thought. They will have to do the digging and researching—and learning. I patted myself on the back. It was a brilliant idea. The goal was to return the next Christmas with their statements in hand to make a comparison. The person who had earned the most would win a monetary prize. The prize amount would be secret until next Christmas morning, but I assured them it would be well worth it. They could not withdraw any of the account money until the following Christmas, and they couldn't deposit any of their own money, just what accumulated from their investments. There is not a competitive bone in any of their bodies, so I thought a little sibling rivalry would spark their interests. There were no other gifts that Christmas. How could there be? The day they left to go back to their adult worlds, they departed like puppies with their tails between their legs. My enthusiasm for this project didn't rub off on them, but I was convinced they'd all enjoy it once they began trading.

Months passed and no one mentioned that they were doing anything with their accounts. I assumed they were all keeping their activity secret, since it was a contest. In June, I sent an e-mail to them inquiring. To my dismay, not one had bought or sold a thing, so I gave a little nudge, "Come on guys. Just get started. It'll be fun once you get into it." The oldest reluctantly began investigating into stocks and trade activity and talked to some of his experienced friends. Jake, the twenty-one-year old, who has a degree in finance and had spent a semester investing university monies in an invitation-only class, clung to his one thousand dollars. He didn't want to lose any of it and figured he'd be that much richer come next Christmas if he didn't take any chances. Jenny, the eighteen-year-old, long ago labeled math as hostile, and even though there was a dollar sign involved, she wasn't interested. One year later, they all arrived home with their monthly statements in hand. Jarrod, the oldest, was the only one who had attempted any trading. He had turned his thousand dollars into fifteen hundred dollars and won the prize. Jake and Jenny were incredulous that he hadn't shared the hot stock with them, and they had the nerve to look disheartened. We went back to clothes and CDs after that Christmas.

"Earth to Mom, what're you thinking about?"

"That Christmas I gave you guys Scottrade accounts."

"Oh, yeah, the teaching present."

"It could have been so great," I say, looking at my watch. Jenny, it's 2:00 p.m. We need to head to Florence," I say, taking the last bite of my facaccia and tomatoes. "Can you call ahead to your contact?"

"I don't have his number. I'll have to go online again."

"Why is it always a 'he'? Do females keep travelers?" I ask.

"Sure, but none have responded to my requests so far. Let's see. From this map, looks like it's only a mile or so to the train station," she says.

"Let's take a taxi," I suggest.

"For a mile?"

"For a block," I answer, pointing.

"How'd you know the station was there?"

"I opened my eyes."

"Good one, Mom. One up for Mom," she announces with a devilish grin.

Vineyards, orchards, and sunflowers, greet us along the way. I've read so much about the magic of the Tuscan sun, and it's true.

It casts a golden softness that infects everything it touches giving eminence to each leaf, twig, and petal. I soak in nature's symphony like a kid with her nose smashed against the candy store window, drooling, but the show ends too quickly as the train slows to a creep and arrives at Santa Maria Novella terminal, a huge, inviting depot. We step off the train to kiosks of souvenirs and newsstands. We stroll through the building taking it all in. A door opens in front of us to Florence, and the big city slaps us in the face. It's noisy, hot, and swarming with Americans. "Let's go back," I say as we walk across the traffic circle, narrowly missing contact with several speeding Vespas, busses, and racing Fiats. "Venice filled my need for city. Let's go somewhere small."

"Mom, we have to see the David again, and remember how we had to hurry through the Uffizi last time? It's Florence! The spirits of Michelangelo, di Vinci, Raphael, and all the other geniuses are here. Who knows, maybe we'll go home artists. Look, there's the dome," she says pointing to the brick-red top of the Duomo."

"Don't walk so fast. It's too hot. My liver's roasting," I huff.

"What a drama queen you are!"

"Drama queen whose organs are cooking."

I trudge along behind her feeling sick to my stomach. "We have to sit down for a while. I need some ice."

"Come on, the buildings are air conditioned," she says.

"Let's go straight to the Hospitality Club guy's house and sight see tomorrow," I suggest. "I really don't feel good." Dragging myself around the next corner, I am met by the white, pink, and green marble work of art—the Duomo. As did Jenny, I stopped in my tracks, my eyes climbing the building. Goose bumps cover my sweaty body. A fluid joy overtakes my ill feeling and washes through me. The last time I saw this Duomo was in 1998. I'd forgotten the 'heavy' that comes on you when you see this enormous work of art. No matter how hard you try, you cannot ignore the emotion that takes you when you round the corner and Florence's Duomo stops you dead in your tracks. We stood staring at it. For a moment, the swarms of people and noise are insignificant. "I forgot how cool it is," Jenny says, and childlike, I add, "Those tiny pieces of pink and green marble make me happy."

"Seeing this is worth a trip to Florence. Now aren't you glad we're here?" she asks.

Florence has many Americanized businesses where clerks speak at least some English, and signs with ads like "We have ice" tempt any American. I don't remember so many Americans in Venice, but then when we were in Venice, I was trying to adjust to the foreignness. "Florence must be the landing place for American tour groups," I say.

We stand for a moment watching masses of Americans shoving their way, by mere size of their clans, through crowds, shouting at one another, seeming oblivious to the fact they are standing in the middle of ancient history.

"How do they not notice what's around them?" Jenny asks.

"They are too busy being quintessential travelers."

"Let's go inside and cool off," I say. We walk into the stone coolness of the Duomo, and as soon as I find a seat, Jenny drops her pack at my feet. "I'll go call Marco. I saw an Internet café across the street. Stay right here so I can find you."

"Don't worry. I'm not moving," I say, leaning my head against the wall behind me. The relief from the heat and the cool darkness are all I need to revive me. "The outside of this building is definitely its calling card," the woman sitting next to me comments, "not much in here."

"Yeah, but it feels great," I reply.

Jenny returns twenty minutes later with the news, "He didn't answer his phone. Don't worry. We'll call again later."

"Great," I answer, sarcastically.

"Every time we've needed a place, we've found one. Well, haven't we?" she asks.

"I guess so. It's just daunting. Here it is early evening and we are wandering the cobbled streets of another strange place," then lightening, I add, "I admit when you escape with your life time after time, it becomes fun—in a demented way."

"That's the spirit," Jenny says, smiling and locking her arm in mine. "Come on, let's go find a cold one and some tomatoes."

I stop at a showcase of what seems to be a thousand different pizzas. We enter, and I choose a piece of white pizza (no marinara sauce) covered with arugula, fresh tomatoes, and basil, and a cold Peroni. Jenny gets a piece of the Italian favorite, margharita. In 1998 when we were here, beer wasn't cold, there was no ice, and soft drinks were room temperature. Those American tastes of iced drinks are now in Florence. "Mmm, so good," I say, with a mouthful. Jenny pulls the yellow card from her pack and says, "Read this."

"I'm eating. Read it to me," I mumble.

We walk on and on through hot, humid, venerable Florence, stopping to peer into windows at designer shoes. "Jenny, we have to get serious about a place to stay."

"Don't worry. It'll happen," she assures.

"Yeah, I can't wait. Let's call that guy again."

"Where's your adventure?"

"I lose it every time I get tired and it's late. Just a weakness of mine."

"A little faith here, okay?"

"Okay. But you seem oblivious to the fact that there could possibly be danger and/or consequence to being female in the twenty-first century." We round another corner to be greeted by the huge Piazza della Signoria. A band is playing and spectators have gathered, some swaying to the beat, some dancing. I spot a stone bench up twenty or so steps in the wall of an ancient courtyard. I motion to Jenny that that's where I'm going. Steps conquered, I drop my pack, sit down on a stone bench, and lean against the adjacent wall. My skin absorbs the coolness of the stone. A stone that's thousands of years dirty and billions of people dirty. I don't care. I stare straight ahead and listen to the music coming from the plaza. I can feel the world in my feet. I glance toward the crowd to make sure Jenny is there. That mother thing is constant. I can see her in a sea of people as if she were the only one. Her copper hair glistens in the moonlight brushing her neck and flowing over her backpack. She sways to the funky, folk music, cheers, and claps as the song ends.

I'm as relaxed as one can be on stone, and close my eyes recalling the scene from my dream earlier this morning. Vikings, bluebonnets, and Donald Trump with his lips pooched out. What an ominous thought. The familiar, "Mom," interrupts my reminiscing. "Mom." I open my eyes to see Jenny in her long turquoise skirt and white shirt, eyes sparkling. Beside her stands a young man who is flashing me an excessively winning smile, complete with two rows of over-sized, luxuriantly white teeth framed by a pair of plump, velvety lips. His eyes are black as coal. He is dressed in a pressed blue shirt and clean beige linen pants. His black hair parted on the left and combed to perfection sits on his collar. "This is Vicky," Jenny shouts over the music. "Vicky?" I question. It's hard to hear a girl's name while staring at a boy's face. "Yes, Veekee," the young man says. "Vicky, this is my mother, Sue Ellen."

"Soo Al-len," he carefully repeats, nodding and extending his hand. I push myself up to a sitting position, reluctantly meet his hand, and smile. "Nice to meet you," I say, while shooting a questioning glance at Jenny. *God, please don't ask me to do this.* "Vicky said we can stay with him tonight."

"No," I say, shaking my head.

"Come on, Mom, it'll be okay," she light-heartedly assures. Vicky begins declaring that I can trust him. I cannot understand much of what he says even though it's in English. I shoot Jenny a definitive *no* with my piercing, blue eyes. "Vicky, I need to talk to my mom," she says as she nods toward the plaza. Vicky looks at me and says very slowly and deliberately, "Me, safe." Then he walks off toward the music. "Jenny, I'm exhausted. The answer is no. It's okay to go home with some Americans my age."

"That's not what we came here to do. What's wrong with you? Carlos wasn't your age or American, and we went home with him. Look, Vicky's a nice guy."

"That's what everyone said about Jeffrey Dahmer," I respond, feeling weak.

"Look how clean he is."

"No," I say, battling to keep my defenses up."

"He said he houses people all the time. He walked up to me and said he knew I needed a place to stay since it was 11:00 p.m., and I had a backpack on."

"And we're supposed to trust him because he's observant? No. I don't feel safe with him."

"You don't even know him."

"Neither do you," I counter.

"You're prejudice because he's Middle Eastern," she accuses.

"No, I'm not. I don't know why I don't trust the situation, but I don't."

"You're just tired, and it clouds things," she insists. Vicky wanders back, and I stand up and say, "Thank you for you offer, Vicky, but we can't stay with you." Jenny crosses her arms over her front and shifts her weight to one foot. "And where will we stay?"

"I safe," Vicky says, trying a different pronoun. The concert in the plaza is over, and the crowd is dispersing. I can hear and follow his words easier. "You my mother. She my sister," he says, pointing to Jenny. "In Nepal, I keep good mother and sister," he says, flashing his pearly whites. I study his mouth as he continues his convincing monologue on what excellent care he takes of his mother and sister and how many travelers he houses. I swear his smile is painted on. "How old are you?" I ask.

"Me?" He thinks a minute and says, "Nineteen."

"Come on, Mom," Jenny says, taking my hand as Vicky jumps to get my pack. "I take?" he asks.

"We are getting a room tonight," I say. emphatically.

"Remember how great last night turned out? We have no idea. It could be better tonight," Jenny says. "If we got a room every time you wanted, we'd be back home by now. Come on. It'll be okay."

"Yes," Vicky begins again with his scintillated assurances.

"Why are you here and not taking care of your mother? Where is your mother?" I quiz.

"Nepal," he says, and what follows was not an answer to my

question. He didn't say he is going to school, working, vacationing, or anything that would have satisfied my question of why he's here, but my defenses are at an all time low, and I succumb when Jenny says, "We'll ride the bus, so you won't have to walk." Without saying a word, I allow myself to be dragged by the hand and led to God knows what while my instincts continue shouting, *no*.

Vicky's effusiveness gets on my nerves. His talking is almost a nervous talking. Fortunately the bus stop was only four blocks away. Arriving, I lean against the bus stop pole and ask, "Do you live alone?"

"My brother and two," he says, holding up three fingers.

"Three roommates? No. That's it. We're not going any further," I say, looking at Jenny with my wisest, most matronly expression weakened by the oblivion in my eyes. "He has roommates that he hasn't consulted. Do you get the picture?"

Vicky interrupts, "No, no, is okay. They go. Is good."

"Jenny," I say, incredulously as I whisper in her face, "Think about the possibilities. Four Indian men. Two of us. The answer is no." I turn to Vicky and say, "You are a very nice man trying to help us, but we cannot stay with you. Thank you." I pick up my pack and begin to walk off. Just then, the bus roars around the corner and stops next to me. The doors open. No one de-busses. "Come on, Mom," Jenny says, taking a step up to the bus.

"But we have no ticket," I protest.

"Is good," comes Vicky's response, as he grabs my pack and gently leads me toward the door.

"This is it, Mom, come on." The bus is packed. Standing room only. The windows are down. It's nearing midnight, and the smells emanating produce a soured-sewer odor—an olfactory hallucination. It's not possible to breathe through the body odor. I hide my nose inside my sweaty shirt. Jenny and Vicky continue conversing as the roar of the bus and the exhaust fumes waft through the windows adding to the stench. I look at Jenny, who is enjoying every minute of this situation. She is intoxicated by the experience with the Wards and its outcome. Her youth knows no bounds, and she is ready for anything. I fear our adventures will have to 'one-up' the Siena experience to keep her adrenaline flowing. I imagine that by the end of the summer, our travel adventures will have taken on extreme sports status.

"See, Michelangelo here," Vicky says as he points to something I can't see in the darkness. "Look, Mom, it's Michelangelo's house." (We later learn the property belonged to the great artist, but the house was not his.)

"Can we get off?" I ask.

"No," he answers. He says the same thing at each stop. I look at my watch, 12:30 a.m. "Jenny, I think we're going in circles."

"Vicky, lives here. He knows where we are," was the answer, but each time I looked at Vicky, he was staring out the windows in all directions and carefully watching the street signs as they passed. A look of concern covers his face and he speaks to some guys in Italian. A passionate discussion of bus stops ensues, and picking up a familiar word here and there, I understand we're on the wrong bus. Great.

We de-bus at the next stop and join the group of young people waiting for the next bus. Three girls in summer dresses and high heels chatter over one of their new purchases. A guy dressed in freshly pressed white slacks and pale blue shirt unbuttoned to expose his hairy chest and gold chain leans against the building smoking a cigarette and enjoying their conversation. I'm trying to keep it together. My feet are numb, and my thoughts are disjointed. I'm not sure I could give my name right now, but it's too late, too hot, and too unbelievable to give up. "Little more," Vicky says, holding his thumb and forefinger an inch apart. My pack hangs helplessly slung over his right shoulder. "We go," he says as the bus squeaks to a halt. I spot a seat and throw myself into it.

A brief ride and we arrive in Vicky's neighborhood. The houses are piled high on each other, and beat-up, run-down cars line the streets. The street's smells come at us brazen and bloodthirsty.

"Here," Vicky says, pointing upward. "I ask to them." He leaves my pack with me and disappears into a building across the street. I can't believe I'm doing this. Tears fill my eyes. "I can't do this. Look at these houses, Jenny. Open your eyes. Breathe this air."

"Whoa. Calm down," Jenny says, as we hear men's voices cursing through an open window, one of them Vicky's. "*Cafone.*"

"*Vaffanculo.*"

"*Dai, figlio di mignotta.*" At this moment, I could crawl into a trashcan and hide. Vicky returns with a bloody lip. His smile is gone, and he is not standing so tall. He continues touching his busted lip with the back of his left hand. "I'm sorry," I say. "Please take us to a hostel."

"Who hit you?" Jenny asks.

A shake of his head is Vicky's reply. The three of us walk quietly for what seems like days at this delicate hour of 2:00 a.m. Vicky opens the door of a hostel and says, "I help you. I know someone. Is little more," he says, pointing down the street.

"No, Vicky." He speaks to the clerk who shakes his head, no. "No bed," Vicky says, again attempting to get us to follow him. "Is little more." I wipe the tears streaming down my face and muster all the composure available to me as I walk to the desk. The Italian words flow from my mouth surprising all of us. "*Posso prendere il taxi?*" At this moment, I see stars swirling around the room. "I'm going to faint," I say.

"Mom, sit here," Jenny says, pulling me to a bench. She holds a bottle of water to my mouth and I drink. "Mom, please don't faint."

"Is taxi," Vicky shouts urgently and runs out and greets the driver.

"Can you make it?" Jenny asks.

"I will," I say, taking a deep breath.

The female taxi driver is standing at the rear of the car with her left arm on the trunk lid and a cigarette dangling from her mouth. I'm jerked to my senses when I see her five-inch-long, black underarm hair flapping in the breeze. Vicky tosses my pack into the trunk and Jenny adds hers. The lid slams, and we wave to a dejected-looking Vicky. "Thank you," Jenny shouts to him as she slides into the backseat. "Hotel," I say.

"Are you okay, Mom?"

"I'm numb and dumb," I answer. The taxi driver continues waving her odorous armpits as she talks. I follow her arms with my eyes. Each word slurs into the next. The taxi abruptly stops, and the driver points to the train station on our left and several hotels on our right. She jumps out and opens the trunk, waiting for us to retrieve our packs then announces, "*quindici (15) euro.*"

Jenny, in disbelief, questions, "For four blocks? *No, quindici!*" The driver flips her head, waves her right arm in the air in a circular motion, and responds in a biting tone, "*Americane.*" She then puts both hands on her hips, stands tall, and emphatically says, "*quindici.*" I hand Jenny the money pouch. She pays the fifteen euros. "Jenny, I can't walk around looking for a room."

"Okay. Can you lean on the side of the building? I'll go in." I spent the next few minutes consciously breathing.

The first hotel is three hundred euros. The second hotel is one hundred fifty euros, but the clerk is willing to call his friend around the corner and ask if he has a room for less. We walk around the corner to a pension and for sixty euros have clean sheets and towels and a shared bathroom four doors down the hall. I stand under the shower for ten minutes renewing myself. It is 3:00 a.m. when I lay my head on the pillow. *If* I make it home alive, I'm going straight to the nut house where I belong.

Chapter Fourteen
Thieves

The hives of scooters that usually buzz me into consciousness lull me this morning. Six hours of prone position and solid sleep gave the inner me an opportunity to distill the varied ingredients of the Vicky debacle and emerge renewed and eager to meet a new day. Florence is beautiful to me once we begin pounding the pavement in the brilliant Tuscan sun. I have my rose-tinted glasses on today, and my senses are keen. My eyes are alive, seeing shimmering radiance in everything. Florence's centuries-old art resonates romance. Love appears ubiquitously—in the air, between the lips of the two lovers leaning against a massive column, amid the clasped hands of an elderly couple shuffling along carrying their daily produce, and nestled in the downy feathers of turtle doves. Italians are poetry in motion. I see females at the height of feminine elegance, live fashion ads sitting atop motor scooters as they ride to work. Art oozes out every nook and cranny of old structures. It is easy to see how food, fashion, and flings meld into Florentine art.

"You're springy this morning. Do you feel better?" Jenny asks.

"I do. I'm primed. Should we make reservations at the Accademia or the Uffizi?"

"We don't need a reservation. We'll just take our chances. There are only two of us. It'd be different if we were a group," Jenny says as she lifts the pay phone receiver and dials her Hospitality

Club contact. I walk to the next shop and look at the window's faded display of drugstore offerings. The guidebooks say we need a reservation. I stroll back toward Jenny to hear, "Okay, the Duomo steps at 2:00 p.m.? *Ciao, grazie.*" She turns and handing me the phone number says, "Would you please put this in the small zippered pocket and get the book? Guess what? This guy's name is Marco, too. That's the third Marco we've met. He can't be here until two o'clock, and he's on a cycle, but he says he'll help us get on the right bus. So we have four hours to see the Uffizi or the David or whatever you want," she says, opening Rick Steves' book to the Florence map.

"Four hours, hmm. The Uffizi it is," I say. "Let's go."

We head south, making our way through the narrow streets lined with cars and cycles. "What are you laughing at?" Jenny asks.

"Look at the numbers over these doors," I say, stopping and pointing. "201 is between 35 and 6A. How'd they do that?"

"It's Italy. It's creative chaos. I'm sure it makes perfect sense to them."

"Whatever," I answer. "Well, I guess considering how many civilizations this land has been through, it's a wonder there is any organization. Goethe said you have to visit Sicily to understand Italy. Guess we'll have to go to Sicily."

"Sicily is a long way from here, but I'm game. You want to go there from here?" Jenny asks.

"Why not?"

Old stone, graffiti, even political signs reach out to me. Everything is art. "It should ... be ... here ... right around this corner ... yessss," Jenny says as we turn the corner where the great courtyard of the Uffizi gallery presents itself.

"Looks like we should have phoned in a reservation," I say, raising both eyebrows with an 'I told you so' smirk. "Look. The line stretches out of sight and is at least five deep."

"I'm not standing in that line. We'll never get in. Come on, we'll just cut close to the front," Jenny says, with the confidence of a serial burglar.

"You mean cut in line?"

"Yes, I mean cut in line. Come on."

"Jenny, I can't cut in line. It's wrong."

"Mom, we're not robbing a bank. No one'll care," she says, heading straight for the front of the line pulling me along. "If they do, we'll just find a different place to cut in. No biggie." I stop, breaking loose her grip. "I can't do that. I've spent my life teaching kids not to steal, you included."

"Mom, people do it all the time."

"Really? Think about what you're saying."

"Grand, I know what's next, 'Would you jump off a bridge—?' No, Mom, I wouldn't jump off a bridge just because everyone else was doing it, but I don't put cutting in line *once* in the same category as jumping off a bridge. Gaah, come on."

"My adult child wants to cut in line. Where was I when you began losing your grip on right and wrong?" I ask, but what I'm thinking is, *I'm a failure.* Jenny stops, turns to face me, and with the heaviness of a gangster who is giving you one more opportunity to comply with his wishes, she says, "Look. I don't do this every day, but this is different. There are just two of us. We have less than four hours. Do you want to see the Uffizi or not?"

"Not if I have to cut in line."

"Come on. It'll be our adventure for the day," she says, in her cheery tone.

"Maybe people expect this of college kids, but I'd melt right into the sidewalk if someone called me on it. Besides, old people don't cut in line."

"How is it you've lived so long and are so naïve? We'll find some friendly Americans, then it won't feel like cutting."

"I can't do it."

"Okay, but I'm going through the Uffizi," she says, with a toss of her head as she points her body toward the front of the line. I stand watching my daughter cross the plaza and dance over the retaining rope nudging her way forward. I think about all the conversations I've had with children about the evils of stealing. I'm fifty-six years old, and I've never given cutting in line a thought, ever.

This reminds me of when I was sixteen, and two of my friends asked me to cut afternoon classes to go riding around in one of the girl's new cars. At first, I was horrified. My rich classmate's father owned some nightclubs in town; I had been to their house (castle) once, and my friend's bedroom suite was as big as the two-bedroom house I lived in. Her private bathroom was larger than my mother's kitchen/dining room combination. She was asking me to drive around in her brand new 1966 Mustang fastback (four on the floor), shiny black with red interior, that her Daddy had given her a week ago for her birthday. I drove a 1956 red and white Ford (three on the column) that was as long as a city block. I felt sick at my stomach just thinking what my Daddy would say if he ever found out. I loved him so, and he would be very disappointed in me. Besides I was a good student and enjoyed school. Why would I want to jeopardize my grades? That thought fueled my answer, "No, I can't."

"Come on. I'll let you drive," she said. That afternoon was the greatest. We three laughed and sang at the top of our lungs until we were all hoarse. I got to drive a new Mustang, and winding out those first two gears was a thrill.

Wondering what I'll do for the next four hours, I turn away knowing I can't join Jenny. I browse through the plaza reading the inscriptions under the statues on both sides of this wide courtyard. Life-size statues of Leonardo, Machiavelli, Galileo, Michelangelo, and other fathers of Florence stand on pedestals looking down at me. Jenny smiles and motions discretely when she sees me looking her way. I look back down the line, which stretches the length of the building, turns the corner, and strings along the bank of the Arno River. I amble along this line looking at the scores of people Jenny has cut off. I stop and think how long it will be before they all get in the door—maybe not today. If the gallery only allows six hundred in at once, and those six hundred can stay as long as they want, and there are forty-five rooms, and a bazillion pieces of art, and the line hasn't moved yet, and if I went to the end of the line, maybe I would get in by this time next week. An old thought moseys in and settles itself among the prospects of cutting in line. It grabs my attention flashing across my internal screen like an annoying computer pop-up. *Remember how you've always said it would be fun to go to another country and be someone you're not?* My still, small voice moves into alarm action and its siren screams, *No, you'll be sorry. Don't do it.* I look toward Jenny, then down the line, and … I undergo an attitude adjustment. I watch my fear slink off through the statues and hide behind Leonardo da Vinci. With fear gone, I begin plotting my crime. I'll nonchalantly stroll around like I'm looking for Jenny, who has been saving me a place in line. I'll act surprised when I find her and quietly slip in beside her. *You'll be sorry. Next, you'll be stealing something. You know how you hate it when someone cuts in front of you. You have labels for them—low life, scum bag, #%*+*, and *#%**. Those people probably got here while you were still sleeping. They have been standing in line for hours, but go ahead. Once you're comfortable with crime, there's no end. Who knows where this one act will lead you? Next, you'll be going nude to the beach.* That thought actually appeals to me. Nudes are the real deal, completely without pretense, but right now, I have to pretend … *if* … I'm going to do this. My sense of right and wrong, what I'd learned and live, what I taught my children, went somewhere. Ignoring the small voice within, I continue my fantasy while browsing the statues and vendors around me. Intermittent glances toward Jenny reveal a perfectly comfortable redhead visiting with the people she has cut off. *Should I? I'm such a puritan. I need to do something off-color to relieve the monotony don't you think? Well, that's justification if I ever heard it.* "Just do it," I whisper to myself as I walk toward the crowd. I begin at the end of the line and squeeze through the hordes lining the stone wall of the great Uffizi. As I near Jenny, my heart races in preparation for flight in case the mob gives me the boot. Jenny smiles as I snuggle in beside her. "Thanks for saving me a place," I say, not daring eye contact with anyone.

"Mom, you're too much." I lean nearer and whisper, "Are they friendly to cutters?"

"We're still here," she whispers back.

"Did you ask them if you could cut?" She laughs aloud, then whispers, "You don't ask." I sheepishly look at our victims. They are engaged with one another, too busy to glance our way. It worked—this time.

Another ten minutes and we are herded in the door where we purchase our tickets and go through security. "Come on. I'll race you to the top," Jenny challenges, looking up the wide flight of stairs we must conquer before we can feast our eyes on the treasures awaiting us.

"I've already cut in line and now you want me to race up the stairs. Not today. I'll get there when I get there," I say, watching her take the steps two at a time. Halfway up, she turns, and waving her arms in the air, sings in an upbeat tempo, "We're breaking the law, breaking the law, breaking the law." This is an old joke that spontaneously burst forth one day, years ago when I accidentally turned the wrong way on a one-way street. After realizing my mistake, I announced that I was breaking the law, to which this little catchy tune was born. "We're breaking the law, breaking the law, breaking the law." By cutting in line, I've joined the ugly American category. The very people I disdain. I hang my head and trudge up the stairs.

Once on the gallery floor, great windows line the corridors exposing a breathtaking view of Florence. Each window frames a perfect picture of multi-colored domiciles nestled in the hillside keeping watch over the puke green of the Arno River. Busts of Roman greats mark the path into the gallery rooms. We wander in and out of rooms for hours, stopping to enjoy what, until now, we've only seen in books. Hushed voices lend a reverence to these rooms. Then we enter the vastness of Botticelli's room. Immediately on our left, in six-by-nine-foot glory, is Botticelli's 'Birth of Venus.' I peer into the eyes of Venus, whose innocent beauty moves me. Jenny steps closer to a tour group and listens to the narrative on this painting. I don't want a narrative. I don't want words. I want to experience it. Surveying the room, my eyes meet Botticelli's equally magnificent 'La Primavera' on an adjacent wall. The longer I gaze, the more Botticelli's work stirs me. I have a sudden desire to hug everyone in the room. A barely controllable urge to shout, "It's huggy-wuggy," overtakes me. "Huggy wuggy" was one of Jake's favorite childhood sayings. He used it often to express exhilaration, bliss, thrill, and any other exaggerated sense he was having at the moment. I am having 'a moment.' A 'moment' happened to me once before when I visited New York's Metropolitan Museum of Art where I stood gazing at Monet's bridge. I remember feeling as if I could cry if I let myself. This surprised me, and later I told a friend who said, "You were touched by art. That's its power."

The people in front of me float through the moistness in my vision as I unconsciously fold my arms around myself. The magnitude of this art excites and calms me. It gives me goose bumps, then warms me. I stand absorbed in the genius and energy of Sandro Botticelli. I think I understand the bumper sticker, "Art Saves Lives." I get it after all these years of wondering what it means. Artists know who they are. They are willing to meet their minds every day. They are comfortable in the depths of their souls. Their work is intimate, yet artists are not afraid to paint, write, and create what is at their core, no matter how everyone else might receive it. Art has a spiritual strength and connection. Yes, art saves lives.

"Mom, it's 1:45 p.m. We have to get to the Duomo to meet Marco."

"Okay," I sigh, not wanting to break the spell. She tugs my arm, and I dumbly follow her out of the building. On the street, the heat and humidity breathe down my neck and slap me out of the art stupor. "I could have spent all day in Botticelli's room."

"I know, Mom. We'll go back sometime, and you can sit there all day, but now let's top off great art with gelato," Jenny says as she darts into a corner shop. "Maybe they have something weird like broccoli and jalapeno." The variety is overwhelming, so I choose the colors that draw me to them. Today they are peach and pear, the cool colors.

Smelling the hot dampness of my body, I sit on the Duomo steps, crunching my cone. Jenny drops her pack at my feet and says, "Don't run off now. I'm going to look for someone I don't know." I sit soaking in the surroundings, listening to people admiring the pink, green, and white Duomo exterior and watching a girl holding a sign over another girl who is asleep on the marble step. The sign says, "I'm not dead, Mom, just sleeping." Some people are taking pictures of her. Jenny is at the far end of the steps talking to a man dressed in long black pants, a black turtleneck, and a black poofy vest. I must be hallucinating. I am drowning in my own sweat, and this guy is wearing a turtleneck and what looks like a down vest. This is the guy we're staying with tonight? Jenny points in my direction, and they slowly make their way toward me. "Mom, this is Marco, and guess what? He lives in the country."

"Hello, Marco," I say, extending my hand to touch his gloved one. "Thank you for keeping us."

"Is pleasure," he says, with a nod. "You ride bus. I ride motorbike. To bus now?" he says, pointing in the direction of the bus stop. Not only does he have on a turtleneck, it is a thick, sweater turtleneck. I feel weak just thinking about what that must feel like. He is completely covered except for his face, and he is wearing black leather gloves, a black, knit ski hat, and carries a helmet.

The bus arrives just as we do, and Marco steps up to the driver speaking in Italian.

"We don't have tickets," I say to Marco, who waves us down the aisle of the bus.

"Where do we get off?" Jenny asks.

"He take you," Marco answers, pointing to the driver. The two men have a shoulder-slapping, hand-shaking exchange, and Marco waves to us as he leaves the bus. Glad to be sitting for a while, I wonder if the bus's atmosphere would be any different if a Botticelli painting were hanging for all to see. Does the setting of marble floors, reverent voices, open spaces, and beamed ceilings have an effect on paintings? I decide, no. Genius is genius no matter the setting.

"I hope he didn't forget us."

"I'll go ask him," Jenny says. She returns holding up two fingers. "We get off after two more stops, or maybe he meant we get off at the second stop. I don't know. Hopefully he'll tell us." At the third stop, the driver motions to us as he looks in his rearview mirror. We grab our packs and hurry. "*Grazie, grazie*," we say as we jump to the ground. The bus speeds away, leaving us looking for Marco. Instead of Marco, we see all of Florence sprawling below. "Wow, look at that view. We are in the country."

"Here, here," Marco calls from across the highway, turtleneck, down vest, knit hat, and all. We cross the highway and listen to his directions for our walk to his house. "We down and down and then my house." He rides his scooter down a steep hill as we descend two levels of cement steps that lead from the highway to a graveled path below. Marco dismounts and from here walks beside his scooter. A rock house sits before us. We continue around the house and down another terraced slope to a narrow, Tuscan-style, suburban street. Single-car garages connected in a row complete one side of the street. Garages are something we've not seen in Italy. We stop at the end so Marco can open the black, iron gate. Small, shiny beads decorate his face. He's glistening as they say in the pageant world since beauty queens don't sweat. My back itches, and looking at his clothed body sends claustrophobic creatures crawling up my neck. We continue our descent. A dozen pregnant peach trees greet us as we walk the path through them. On the far side of this grove, an open meadow of tall grasses teased by a random, invading weed carries our vision to a wooden shed leaning insecurely to the left. We follow Marco into this slouching barn through its generous opening where he parks his scooter. Old, rusty sickles, hoes, and hand tools untouched by at least two generations hang on the wall to our right. Dangling from the rafters are several old tires and inner tubes keeping company with some oxidized chains. On the left, six dilapidated bicycles lean feebly against the wall, wrapped securely in dust, some with and some without tires and seats. Two retired motor scooters, both with flat tires, persist in standing upright in the center of the dirt floor. We walk out the distant opening of the shed where Marco points to a small house covered in vines and announces that his mother and sister live there. Huge orange trumpets welcome us as we walk under a pergola of trumpet vines. We emerge from the trumpet canopy to a thicket of hazelnut trees and thirty-one junk cars from the 50s and 60s scattered, all blooming where they were planted. Three white tents are set up in the distant end of this acre. "My brother was used car salesman," Marco says as if littering one's land with dead cars was expected from any used car salesman. Volkswagen bugs, Fiats, Saabs, a couple Studebakers, and some European specimens I didn't recognize have found their final resting places. Some are windowless, others topless, tireless, or headlight-less. Variegated ivies curl in and out, up and over, tickling red geraniums and blue morning glories that trail out windows or sprout from missing headlights. A bird of paradise tree grows from within the shell of an unrecognizable vehicle. Faded black, white, green, and orange paint murmurs through the rust reminding us of what once was. Every crack, broken window, and missing door burgeon vegetation. I stop to enjoy this landscape, imagining shoppers browsing through these cars when they were all mechanically sound and ready to drive off the lot. Only in Italy can one find a used car lot that has evolved into living art—a tin lizzie gallery.

Behind all this is Marco's house. We enter a small kitchen and a now sweating Marco immediately seats us at the table. "Please, please, you must rest," he says, removing his gloves. He gives us both small glasses of water with one ice cube each that he retrieves from his dingy white 1960s, five-foot-tall refrigerator. He sets a tall glass pitcher of water in the middle of this round, black Formica dinette set. He leaves us with our water and returns momentarily with two talkative girls whom he introduces as Lila and Rosa from Brazil. Lila and Rosa give an obligatory hello and return to their previous activity on the computer in the next room. "They stay three months," Marco says.

"You mean you are willing to keep people for three months?"

"Yes, is good travelers learn Italian. Come in here, your bed." He opens a door, immediately off the kitchen, to expose a room barely large enough to hold a set of bunk beds and still allow the door to close. A miniscule fan sits on the windowsill. You sleep here. Girls sleep in tent."

"This is where Lila and Rosa sleep?" I ask. "No, we can't take their beds."

"Yes, you mamma. You have bed. Is good."

"Lila and Rosa won't agree," Jenny says. "Mom can sleep on a couch, and I can sleep on the floor."

"No, mamma have bed. Mamma tired." *He is one observant guy.* Could it be the steady stream of saline solution oozing from my pores, or my reluctance to get up from the table to take the home tour?

"Girls sleep in tent. *Si,* is good."

"This won't have a positive effect on international relations," Jenny says. "Brazillian Duo Forced to Sacrifice Bed for Americans."

We continue our tour as we pass the computer that two chatting girls hover over. Marco tells them in Italian that Jenny and I will have their room and they will be temporarily sleeping outside. The chatting ceases and they both look at us blankly, but Marco quickly says in an affirmative tone, "*Is mamma.*" They accept their fate and return to their e-mails. Tucked behind the computer area is a small bathroom with only a toilet and sink. "Shower is up," Marco says, pointing upstairs. We climb the stairs to a landing where two, disheveled bedrolls are in the way. "Two boys of Lithuania and Nepal," Marco says, kicking one of the bags out of the way.

"You have other guests?" I ask.

"*Si, si,* is good. I am Hospitality Club leader," he proudly announces. Two large, freestanding bookshelves back up to the wall on our right. Their burden is such that each shelf sags in the middle. I survey the books, open a couple, and notice they are on health. "I love books," I say.

"You read in Italian?" he asks.

"I wish. Maybe someday." Next are his bedroom and an adequate bathroom where we may take a shower if we want. He even offers us towels.

We return to the kitchen where Marco opens a drawer and taking a key says, "The rules: all cook for himself and clean for himself. Now I give you key. The gate you buzz," he says pointing in the direction of the outside gate. "Someone come and open for you. Now you must rest and eat." Marco still in full Arctic dress, returns to the fridge and proceeds to prepare a plate of watermelon and cantaloupe wedges circled with fresh pineapple rings. "You eat now. I go for travelers."

"*Grazie,*" we both say weakly, suddenly realizing our exhaustion.

"There are already six here, plus him, and he's going to meet more? Wow, what fun. It's going to be a party," Jenny says. "So far there are two Americans, two Brazilians, one Lithuanian, and one Nepalese. Did I say that right? Is it Nepalese?" My lips are wrapped around a watermelon slice extracting the cool juice.

You do not realize how exhausted you are until you sit a while. I want to stroll through the sprouting car lot just out the back door, but my brain doesn't communicate this to my legs, so I sit. "What will we eat tonight? We didn't bring food," Jenny says.

"I'll get by with this," I say, looking at the empty plate. "I'm so tired I don't think I could eat anything else."

"What's the deal with all his clothes?" Jenny asks.

"Maybe he's going on a sweat diet or something."

"He seems a bit reserved, but I think he's super intelligent. He's just on another level, kinda like Jake."

"I question the intelligence of anyone who wears a ski hat, turtle neck sweater, down vest, and gloves in the middle of summer," I say. "Speaking of Jake, I hope he's okay."

"Well, if Lila and Rosa ever get off the computer, we'll check e-mail. Maybe Jake's written, but I'm not about to ask them to use the computer. They've already been forced out of their beds for us," Jenny adds. We sit and stare at each other until two guys come in and introduce themselves as Tom from Lithuania and Hari from Nepal. Tom is eighteen and Hari is twenty-five, and they met here at Marco's house yesterday. Tom opens a can of soup and dumps it into a pan to heat. Hari boils water for rice. They both lean against the counter facing us and ask about our country. "Is beauty, America, yes?" asks Tom. "My dream New York City," he says with a smile.

"No, not New York. Come to Texas," Jenny says, with her broad Texas smile.

"Texas? You Texas? Yes, I go Texas." We laugh and attempt sharing where we have traveled. Their English is sketchy, but not as sketchy as our attempts at Italian. It doesn't matter though since all attempts and goofs become food for laughter. The most fun for me is when I say something and the person to whom I'm speaking stares at me as if he were attempting to look inside my brain to understand what I said.

Soon another couple arrives, a beautiful young girl from Mexico named Ana, and Fons, a boy from Germany. They have been traveling together since Ana attended language school in Germany last month. Ana is twenty-one and fluent in French, Spanish, German, and English. She's so fluent in English that she has no accent even though she says she grew up in Mexico. We learn that her reason for coming to Florence is for language school. For a month, she will spend seven hours each day in Italian classes. Don't I feel stupid with my one language! Marco never returns. None of us has any idea where he is, and while we are all disappointed that we don't get to visit with our host, we have a great time together. At 9:00 p.m., in come Crystal and Kenneth, two college students from Singapore who were both traveling alone until they met on the train to Florence two days ago. Small world. From 9:00 p.m. until midnight, we ten tell about ourselves as best we can, have fun with our languages and attempts in Italian, and laugh, and laugh, and laugh. Ana, a unique girl of twenty-one, a linguistic genius, and well-spoken, and pretty, says language is not what she wants to make her life's work. She wants to be a nurse. Fons is a massage therapist in Germany and wants to study herbal healing. Crystal and Kenneth are both business majors. Lila and Rosa aren't ready to commit to one occupation. Hari, who has walked across India and Pakistan for peace, currently sells cell phones, but his heart is in the spiritual realm. He wants to write books on and promote camps for teaching children meditation and yoga. Tom is just glad to be old enough to travel and see the world outside Lithuania. How do ten people, representing four continents and five different languages communicate so much in a few short hours? The answer is what makes traveling in this crazy fashion gratifying, engaging, entertaining, and educational. Who would give up this experience for a clean bed at the Marriott? Ana and Fons share their cheeses and tough bread with us. Crystal and Kenneth brought a bottle of wine that we all taste. Lila and Rosa drag their bedrolls out to a tent while I profusely thank them. I don't think I'm their favorite person. We're all ready for bed and still no Marco. We joke about staying in Marco's free hostel. After a fun evening, we all say our good-byes and exchange contact information since Kenneth and Crystal are moving on to Rome tomorrow, and Tom and Hari are headed to Milan. I wish them safety and sanity in their travels, and Tom asks, "What san ee tee?"

"It's travel a different way," says Kenneth.

"It's not sleeping in a park," adds Crystal.

"It's not sleeping in strange places," says Ana.

"It's boring," Jenny says.

"Sanity is good mind," adds Fons.

"San ee tee, no fun, yes?" says Tom, to which we all laugh and nod in agreement although I question my corroboration on this one. Once again I find myself in the company of intelligent, fun-loving youth from around the world. Our conversations and camaraderie warm my heart and make me wish we could all go live in an Indian ashram.

Chapter Fifteen

A Scare

My body aches for the cool mountain air of 10,000 feet, a taste of crisp spring water, or a big fan blowing in my face, but all I have to offer it is an untiring faucet, so I keep drinking. "It's not possible I haven't lost any weight," I say to Jenny as I get into my pajamas. "Every day I walk, sweat, eat tomatoes and bread, walk and sweat some more, eat gelato, then walk and sweat some more. We've been doing this for three weeks now, and my clothes still fit."

"I haven't lost any either. We're building muscle from walking and climbing. We're strong."

"Whatever."

"Well, we are," she says, digging in her pack for a brush. "Tom and Hari want to go into town and see what's going on. I'm going with them," she says, pulling the brush through her tangled ponytail.

"Jenny, it's nearly midnight. Please don't go. You don't even know those guys."

"What do you mean? We spent the past five hours talking to them. I'll be okay, Mom, just go to sleep."

"You know I can't sleep knowing you could be in danger, and I'll wake up when you come in, and then I can't go back to sleep for the rest of the night. Besides you promised not to leave me alone."

"You're not alone. There's a houseful of people here, and they all love you. You can go with us if you want to."

"Please don't start this late night stuff. You said this wasn't what we were coming here to do. You said you wanted to spend time in the country writing and painting and doing totally different stuff from what we do at home, and we're in the country now. That's what appealed to me about this trip."

"Yeah, but I've never been out at night in Florence, Italy. Mom, it's okay. I'll be back in a while. Go to sleep, or get your clothes on and come with us," she says as she's out the door.

One thing my mother forget to tell me is that sweet little children grow fangs and claws when they grow up. I trusted Jenny to do what she said. That is why I'm disappointed. I did not see this coming, and I don't want to spend the summer alone every night in a strange bed. I had visions of being creative together and doing things we don't have time to do at home like painting, writing, learning Italian, getting friendly with the locals, and learning how to make pasta the Italian way. *Don't let this ruin your summer,* a voice within calls. I stand looking at the sinkhole in the bottom bunk. The sheet on the bed is thin from use. I wonder when it last saw soap and water. Staring at the sagging mattress, I spend a few seconds talking myself into putting my body on the grimy sheet. What other choice do you have? Once in, the mattress holds me in its crater, not allowing movement all night.

Jenny comes home sometime after 2:00 a.m. "Everything was closed," she whispers. "That's why we are home early."

"Early? What dictionary do you use?" I spend the remainder of the night trying to doze off again. At home when I cannot sleep, I get up and do something. Here I lie in this bed that envelops me, smell the humid night, plan how I'm going to get out of bed, and listen as the birds begin the day. Marco is not around when I wrestle out of bed at 8:00 a.m. I'm not sure that in my absence I could leave ten strangers in my house for any length of time. Is that an American mindset? Maybe my trust in mankind needs an overhaul. Knowing how long it will take me to get Jenny up, I begin nagging her. "Get up. Let's go." I would prefer beginning the task of finding a bed for the night early in the day, but she thinks that's planning ahead too much. Every fifteen minutes I jiggle her leg, arm, and back and say, "Get up. Let's go." Finally, at 9:00 a.m. she gets up. "Would you hurry? I'm so hungry I could eat a whole pizza. I took a spit bath in the downstairs bathroom because the shower was occupied every time I checked," I say.

"Okay, a spit bath it is."

"Since Marco gave us each a hand towel, we have the luxury of using one end as a washcloth and the other end as a towel. I remember once I forgot my toothbrush, and Grandmother had me brush my teeth with a washrag as she called it. It was fun with the terrycloth tickling my gums. I'm sorry you never got to meet Grandmother. We are staying one more night aren't we?" I ask

"If you want to. Doesn't matter to me."

"Let's. I love knowing I have a bed to lay my weariness in."

"Mom, you're so dramatic."

"Think our packs will be safe here?"

"What's in them that anyone would want?"

"Good point."

At 10:00 a.m., we are off through the car gallery, around the shed, in the peach trees, across the open field, beyond the iron gate, and up to the bus stop. "I wonder who will open the gate when we buzz tonight," I say.

"Why do you worry about everything?"

"I'm not worrying. Just thinking ahead. Speaking of thinking ahead, when we get to town, we're going straight to the Accademia to make reservations for this afternoon. I'm not cutting in line. I'll probably think about that every day for the rest of my life."

"I thought it was kinda fun. Think you'll go to hell?"

"Maybe."

We find the Accademia that houses Michelangelo's David and make a reservation for 2:30 this afternoon. "Let's visit a few free museums and then go shopping," I say.

"Can we go shopping and then visit the museums?" Jenny asks. "Although, shopping is no fun when you can't buy anything."

"True, but we're shopping in Italy! That's prize enough!" I reply.

I have shopped in New York, Dallas, and Los Angeles to name a few and never feasted my eyes on the fine fashion I saw in Florence. After fondling fine leather shoes, we decide the Italians keep the best for themselves. "It's like potatoes," Jenny says. "All the restaurants get the Grade A potatoes, and the grocery stores sell us Grade B or less. Italy keeps the finest shoes. Do you blame them? They're so gorgeous." I can feel their smooth suppleness through the glass. As we browse the street markets, I want to stroke and smell the leather items. We listen to Americans trying their haggling skills and wish we had room to take home a scarf.

Talking with a local man over our lunch of an oversized piece of pizza and a cold Peroni, we learn some Italian trivia. In Italy, prisoners receive daily pay and three consecutive days off from time to time. Unfortunately, recently a prisoner on his three-day leave shot and killed a carabinieri (policeman). All diamonds sold in Italy are G grade diamonds or better and by law must be accompanied by a certificate. Dogs are allowed in groceries and restaurants. Unless you have a journalism degree, you cannot receive credit for your writing. You can write an article, but a degreed journalism major's name is given credit. We sit for nearly two hours visiting with an Italian man who takes the opportunity to brush up on his English. With Jenny around, there's never a want for anyone to talk to. She takes every opportunity to practice Italian, and she attracts Italian men like flies to a picnic. They are interested in this lively redhead, even with her mamma sitting beside her. Italian men are shameless in their attention to females. I love it.

We arrive at the Accademia where a long line stretches down the sidewalk, but we have reservations this time. Rick Steves says of those without reservations, "Walk briskly past the 200-yard-long line, pondering the collective IQ of this gang, to the reservations-only ticket office," which we do and are ushered in. Standing on a six-foot-tall pedestal before us in creamy white marble is Michelangelo's five-hundred-year-old statue of David, the young shepherd boy who slew Goliath. One's initial response, especially if one is a post-menopausal female, is: if only all vigorously healthy young men would wear simply a sling draped over their left shoulder, how thrilling life would be. David's thick, loosely curled hair tickles the nape of his broad neck. His focused expression is tense with anticipation and concentration on his goal. His furrowed brow, wide eyes, and flared nostrils expose the power that surely surged through his every cell the moment before he killed the giant. Scanning David's perfect body, I see every muscle taut with determination, expectation, and aplomb. David is anatomically divine. A twenty-six-year-old Michelangelo chiseled veins so true you can see them pulsing. The skin on David's toes has the weathered finish of a sandal-clad outdoor worker. The details in every square inch of this fifteen-foot statue dumbfound me, and I stand gazing in awe. I have one question that I pose to Jenny.

"David is a Jew. Why is he uncircumcised?"

"Oh, I didn't notice," she says. Silent, we stroll through the remainder of the museum searching for anything that might match the David. We are disappointed and take one last step around the powerful piece of marble before walking out the door. We spend the remainder of the afternoon sitting in Piazza della Republica, enjoying listening to and watching people as our minds assimilate what we saw in Michelangelo's David. On our way to the bus, we pick up some cheese, bread, tomatoes, and clementines to take for dinner.

Marco is home when we get there and opens the gate for us. "We missed you last night," Jenny says.

"*Mi mamma* need me," he answers.

"Is she all right?"

"*Si, si,* in times she need me."

"Are there any new travelers tonight?"

"No. They come. They go. You here tonight?"

205

"Is it okay?"

"*Si, si, va bene.*"

"Tomorrow we are going to ... where are we going, Mom? Sicily?"

"I want to go some place small. Gimmewald, Switzerland."

"How about Cinque Terre? Remember that one night we stayed in Vernazza, when we came in 1998? I think there's a Couch Surfer guy there. I'll check when the computer is available."

"Lila. Rosa. You give computer," Marco says. He turns to us and shrugs his shoulders, "They are in computer all day." Once again, Marco asks Lila and Rosa to yield to us. They are resistant at first, involved in instant messaging, but they stop and return to the computer as soon as we have checked our e-mail.

"I do want to go back to Cinque Terre. I remember its quaintness," I say, leaning over Jenny's shoulder.

"Boy, that's luck. Look. Piero is logged onto Couch Surfing. I'll ask him if we can stay tomorrow night," she says, typing madly, then pausing for a reply. "Yea, he says we can stay with him one night."

"Yessss, I have a bed for tomorrow night. Oh, that feels good. Let me check my e-mail to see if Jake wrote."

"Ok, but let me check all my accounts first." Between My Space, Couch Surfing, Hospitality Club, and three different e-mail accounts, it could be a while. I pass the time sitting at the kitchen table writing in my journal. My weak attempts at describing what I saw today make me wonder why I even try. "Jenny, it's my turn. I want to see if Jake wrote."

"He did. He's in—"

"Don't tell me," I interrupt. "I want to read it myself." I breathe a prayer for Jake's safety as I read. "He's in southern France and had a good hitchhiking experience. He said he got picked up by two old, rich women in a Mercedes convertible who let him ride with them for an hour. Now he's working on an organic farm, in trade for room and board. He hasn't found any dancing yet. The dancer is picking lettuce and raspberries eight hours a day. Bet he's beat every night, no pun intended."

We eat our *pecorino* (sheep's milk cheese), bread, and tomatoes. I browse through Marco's books finding some on alternative health, which I've seen back home. We retire earlier tonight (11 p.m.) with no new people to greet and Marco coming and going. He seems quite content to open his home to all who need whether he gets to know them or not. "When can we spring for a real meal?" I say, putting my feet on Jenny's bunk. "At some point our bodies will turn on us and we'll get sick. We aren't eating balanced meals."

"What's unbalanced about tomatoes, bread, cheese, fruit, and gelato?"

"Protein."

"It's in the cheese. Fat's in the cheese. Dairy's in the cheese. Carbs are in the bread, and there's lots of fiber in the raw fruit. Oh, and sugar in the gelato. Besides, neither of us looks like we're suffering."

"Okay, so we're eating fat, protein, carbs, and fiber—and gelato, my fave."

"Uh, huh."

"Mmmm, I can't wait to get to Cinque Terre," I say, remembering what I can about our one night visit in 1998. "Let's stay in small places from now on."

"Uh, huh."

"Can we get up and leave early?"

"Uh, huh."

"Pay attention to me. What are you doing?"

"Writing in my journal. Okay, you can turn out the light."

Once again, we leave the house at 10:00 a.m. and make our way to the train station. Looking at the schedule, we see we've timed this just right. The train leaves at 12:27 p.m., arrives in Monterosso at 2:54 p.m., costs about fifteen euros each, and gives us two and a half hours to sit back, relax, and watch the Italian Riviera come into view. "We change trains in Pisa. This time please stay on the train," I say as we board. An hour into the ride, I smell something burning and look around to see other people's noses wiggling. The train slowly screeches to a stop. A thin cloud of smoke floats down the side of the cars. All remain seated, continuing their conversations as the smoke thickens. My sensitive lungs tighten in the suffocating smoke, and I cover my nose and mouth with the neck of my shirt. Several people begin closing the windows. Jenny strikes a conversation, asking what she can in Italian, with the family of four seated across the aisle from us. Evidently delays are par for TrenItalia, and no one is worried.

"*Americane?*" asks the father.

"*Si, da Texas.*"

"*Bella la Texas?*"

"*Si, molto bella,*" Jenny says. She continues, telling about our travels.

"Jenny, something's on fire. It has to be with all this smoke," I say. A tall woman in four-inch heels and dark suit gets up and walks to the next car. She returns in three minutes telling us the difficulty is *meccanico*. Papers and books begin moving as people fan themselves to circulate the thick air. A man tries the door, but it is locked. He looks up at the emergency handle but doesn't pull it. Conversations continue, now laced with agitation and movement back and forth across the aisle. After ten minutes, a man runs through our car waving his arms and shouting, "*fuoco, fuoco.*" This middle-aged Italian continues into the next car yelling "*fuoco, fuoco.*" We all stand and begin moving about in the car from window to window trying to see through the smoke outside. "What's wrong?" I ask.

"I don't know, but that man was shouting, 'fire fire,'" Jenny says.

"Great." Another ten minutes and a man in a green, official TrenItalia suit escorts us off the train. Jenny understands the man to say the brakes are on fire. The entire train evacuates, and hundreds of us pace up and down the side of the train like expectant fathers in a hospital waiting room. Forty minutes later, we are herded back onto the same train. The train lurches forward, and we creep into the Pisa station at a snail's pace because we have no brakes to stop us.

We change trains and continue our trip. The scenery gradually changes from the buildings of Pisa to blue water. The sun rains sparkling diamonds that dance on the water's surface as the tracks run parallel to the Ligurian Sea introducing us to the Italian Riviera. We snake in and out of mountain tunnels, and once in the Cinque Terre, at each stop the train empties and fills with swimsuit-clad beach hoppers. The Cinque Terre are five quaint, thousand-year-old villages whose colorful houses cling to cliffs that overlook the sea. From a distance, the houses look like Legos snuggled in the hills. A mile separates each village, and they all have their odd fascination to newcomers. The muddy odor of dampness, seaweed, raw fish, and salt infuse the air, and a relaxed atmosphere replaces the hustle of Florence and the frenzy of the smoking brakes.

Once in Monterosso, we detrain and enter the bar twenty feet from the tracks, where Jenny asks the bartender if he knows Piero. "*Si, si,*" he says with a musical emphasis on the two words. Obviously taken by this feisty redhead attempting to speak his language, he says, "*Ah bella, bella, mi amico, Piero, per fortuna sta sera,*" he says, winking at Jenny. I understand him to say his friend has fortune tonight. *Yesss*, I understand what he said.

"*Grazie,*" Jenny says, pointing in the direction she understands we are to go.

"*Si, si,*" he points.

"He's cute," Jenny says as we walk down the stairs to beach level.

"Cute? He's a hunk," I answer.

"Whoa, now," she teases. "He said Piero lives at the end of this street in that direction, so let's go." It is hard to watch where I'm going with nature all around. Piero is not home, so we acquaint ourselves with Monterosso, have a gelato, stand gazing at deep purple bougainvillea tumbling down the front of a white stone building from three stories up, and sit looking out over the white beach and the endless scintillating sea.

An hour passes and we again walk to Piero's. This time a balding, mid-thirties, blue-eyed Piero greets us. After the initial greetings in Italian and English, we take the tour of his tiny, one-bedroom flat. He has no kitchen, and the couch (our bed) in the living room folds out barely missing the thirteen-inch television with a rabbit ear antenna on top. He informs us that we can stay only tonight since he has other couch surfers arriving tomorrow. "And the day after?" Jenny asks.

"My brother come for two days." I'm standing nearby, smiling ever so gratefully that I have a bed. "Are there other HC or Couch Surfers in Monterosso?" I ask, thinking ahead.

"No. Only me," he smiles proudly.

"Mom's obsessed with where she's going to sleep," Jenny says. Piero gives a blank look, and Jenny makes one more attempt at explaining my obsession.

"What ob-shss-shon?"

"Something you constantly think about. Mom constantly thinks about where she will sleep." Piero accepts his incomprehension, and we move on. Today is June 24, and he tells us that tonight in old town will be a huge celebration of St. John the Baptist. "Will be many people," he says, encouraging us to go early to find a place to sit. "Is big party with ... how to say ... ," his hands form a bursting circle as he looks for the right word. His gesturing sends waves of air brushing my cheek. "In English is—" a frustrated Piero continues searching for the right word. He gets a cigarette lighter and pretends to light something, throws it into the air, and makes an explosion sound only guys can make. "Fireworks?" Jenny asks.

"*Si, si,* fireworks. In Italiano, *fuochi.*"

Absent of cars and motor scooters, Monterosso's narrow street lazies along the beach leading us to the old, original town of Monterosso. The air is tight with excitement as young and old anticipate tonight's celebration. Once in old town, we follow Piero, who looks for just the perfect spectator spot. "Jenny, hold my hand.

I need help. I don't trust my balance," I say as I precariously climb over boulders and squeeze through people. Piero finds us just the right spot to sit on a huge boulder, and at 10:00 p.m. the volunteers begin lighting luminarias and setting them on the water. At 10:45 p.m., hundreds of pink, yellow, green, and white luminarias are released in the cove so the gentle tide can slowly carry them out to sea. There are no loudspeakers or master of ceremonies to announce what's happening; no band to entertain; just a group of volunteers and a mass of onlookers crowding the street and covering the rocks lining the bay. What unfolds in the next twenty minutes is, bar none, the most beautiful fireworks display I have ever seen. Once the luminarias drift out to sea, fireworks erupt from the water and shower over us. One after another colorful shooting stars fire in rapid succession to thrill the crowd. Cheers, oohs and aahs, and applause explode with each. The display and the crowd's appreciation of it bring tears to Jenny's and my eyes. Jenny's favorite holiday is July 4, and my tears come from the memories of fun and family togetherness that Fourth of July outings have always brought. After the last firework blasts into the night sky, we sit watching the luminarias drifting farther apart and deeper into the watery abyss. We make our way off the rocks and head straight for the gelato store with hordes of others thinking about the frozen delight. Until you've experienced a display case heaping with creative combinations of flavors, you cannot imagine the ability it has to bring elation to both young and old. We three stand, gelato in hand, watching until the luminarias are out of sight.

We walk back through the tunnel and into new town. Jenny asks Piero about local night life, to which he answers with a flirty grin, "I take you."

"Can I go?" I ask, looking at Piero whose expression turns to a question.

"Sure you can," Jenny responds.

"I wish we could just go home and go to bed."

"You can," she says.

"Yeah, I know."

Intermittent light breezes challenge the thick night air and chase the sweat from my brow. The rhythmic sounds of the tide draw me aside to listen. Nature has such power. I stand for a moment lapping up the moonlight like a cat at a bowl of cream. This is one of those moments when a writer can carefully arrange word upon word on an organized heap in an effort to describe something that words can never adequately express. "I buy *birre* for you," Piero says pointing to a seaside bar. Over cold, Italian beer, we visit learning more about our host and sharing the wonders of Texas with him. We learn that Piero travels in the Rome area two weeks out of each month as a computer parts salesman. He didn't tell us about the remaining two weeks. Maybe he has some secret life for those two weeks each month. Once again, I go to bed at 2:30 a.m. in a strange place, while Jenny and Piero stay out. Fueled by tiredness, my disappointment broadens.

Jenny and Piero come in at 5:00 a.m. "How was it?" I groggily whisper.

"Fun. You really should come with me some time. People drinking don't care how bad your Italian grammar is, and you get lots of practice."

"Your desire to learn Italian is greater than mine. I wish I could stay up, but I can't."

"Didn't you love the fireworks display? How cool was it coming straight out of the sea!" Jenny exclaims.

"I admit it beats anything I've seen back home, including that July 4 we were in NYC." Jenny was asleep before she had completely stretched out. I did go back to sleep but woke with daylight.

Backpacks on, we say goodbye to Piero and hop the train for the mile ride down the tracks to Vernazza in hopes we can find the old man and woman we stayed one night with in 1998. Vineyards spring from the steep hills, and I can't imagine how a farmer tends the vines, let alone harvests them. The colorful apartments with equally colorful laundry tell of another time, another way, another world.

"What did they do to the beach?" I ask, knowing something's different.

"Looks like they hauled in some black sand and widened it."

"The sand is gray. I don't like it."

"Look, that wasn't here last time," Jenny says, pointing to a small platform jutting out to the sea and holding a dozen small tables protected from the sun by an overhanging canvas. Vernazza has several open-air restaurants, and at night more pop up as the little plaza fills with white clothed tables covered with umbrellas. "I wish we knew that man and woman's name. It'd be too cool if they are still alive and we could stay with them again. They were the cutest." We have no luck tracking them, so we decide to enjoy ourselves sunning, splashing, visiting with all who wish, and finding no bed for the night. Late afternoon, we hop on the train to visit Corniglia, the only village away from the water. After hearing of the four hundred steps leading up to Corniglia, I opt for the shuttle bus ride that takes us to this delightful town sitting high on the hill. The spectacular views would have been worth the four hundred steps—well maybe. We sit in the tiny square, cooling off near a fountain. "So where are we going to sleep?"

"We can always take an overnight train up to Switzerland," Jenny says.

"I'd still like to stay here in Cinque Terre until we see everything."

"I can't believe you said that. I thought you wanted to get to Switzerland."

"I do, but we're here, so let's check it all out."

"Let's try Vernazza one more time." We shuttle back to the train and head to Vernazza where we mosey in and out of places and ask about the little old man and woman whose names we don't know. The cool sea breezes wisp through the hair of those sitting in the plaza. There's a friendliness and relaxation in the air that is very inviting. It is much smaller and quieter than Monterosso, probably because my crowd, the older crowd, is here.

Having no luck finding a bed in Vernazza, Jenny hitches us a ride in a small fishing boat from Vernazza over to Monterosso. At midnight, the vast expanse of sea is black, as soon as we lose the lights of Vernazza. For a few minutes, I can't see anything, and it reminds me of the summer when I was six and Daddy took us to Carlsbad Caverns. Once our tour group reached the big room deep in the cave, the lights were turned off, and we were asked to stand and listen to the cave's sounds. I heard drips of water, and bats flew about. Spasms of terror shot through my body, and I clung to Mother's hand. I learned what it would be like to be with no light—cold and scary—but now I look up and the stars spill into my vision, then we round the cliff jutting into the sea, and the lights of Monterosso brighten the way. I make an effort to say a few Italian words to this nice man who has given us a ride, and I listen to his and Jenny's conversation. With a grin as big as the sky, this man compliments our efforts to speak his language, we thank him for the ride, and we hope we have shown him a little bit of friendly Texas.

Back in Monterosso, we walk along the beach and head for the pubs. I admit it is fun when I am the center of attention among twenty-year-olds. They have no idea how their attention blesses me, entertains me, and gives me hope. I order a salad and two pieces of facaccia to go with my ale. I'm eating after midnight, but a full stomach puts a different outlook on the upcoming possibly bedless night, at least for a while. "Mom, are you already tired?" Jenny asks, noticing my face leaning into my left hand.

"It's after 1:00 a.m.; I'm going to find a bench. This will be the night to sleep on a bench." Jenny follows me out of the bar and says, "Why don't we sleep on the beach?"

"Don't ask stupid questions."

"Why is it stupid? I bet kids sleep there every night."

"Kids being the key word," I say, turning away. "Kids with bedrolls or sleeping bags."

"Mah-ahm." (Only kids can make mom a two-syllable word.)

"We'd freeze on that damp sand if the mosquitoes didn't carry us off first."

"If it's cold enough to freeze, there won't be any mosquitoes," she answers.

"As hot as it is during the day, I bet it gets really cold next to that water at night." Some boys from Iowa University whom we had met earlier see us and one interrupts, "Hey, what are you Texas gals doing?"

"Deciding if we would rather sleep on the beach or an iron bench," I answer, with a bit of sarcasm in my voice. "Which would you choose?"

"You don't have a room?"

"It's not part of our plan," I say, glancing at Jenny who is smiling at my boldness.

"Why didn't you say so. Hell, we've got an empty bed. You're welcome to it." Limp with relief, I ask this three-sheets-to-the-wind Iowa boy, "Can we go there now?"

"Sure." His two buddies nod in agreement. The real trick will be in the morning when they wake and see us there. Will they remember this moment?

"Here," he says, lifting my pack and offering me his left arm. "I'll take you." He is tipsy, and I am drunk tired, so we should have a good walk. Looking at Jenny, I say, "There are still gentlemen in the world." My escort stands taller. "Does your mother know what a wonderful son she has?" He broadens his shoulders, standing even taller, and says, "I don't know."

"I'll call her and tell her." He looks at me, smiles, and says, "She'd be asleep now. She goes to bed at 10:00 p.m."

"Lucky duck."

Thankful for a strong arm to pull me up the constant incline, I hold on tightly for the two-block walk. "Here we are," he says, opening the door to a modern building. "It's upstairs." I let go of his arm and grab the rail, following him to the top of the stairs where he opens a door to a generous room with a king-size bed, a full bed, and a set of bunk beds. "No one sleeps here," he says, pointing to the king size bed. My eyes widen.

"Joe and I sleep on the bunks, and Tommy sleeps in that bed. Oh, yeah," he continues, crossing the room and sliding open a door. "There's this deck if you want to use it, and the bathroom's over here." A step up and we are met by a modernly furnished bathroom.

"You okay now, Mom?"

"Yes. Thank you so much. You're my hero," I say, smiling at this six-foot tall boy fresh off the farm in Iowa.

"Well, I guess we'll go back and finish up the evening," he says.

"See you later," Jenny says as she drops her pack and heads out the door. This time, I'm neither surprised nor disappointed with the news. I hit the shower where the day's sweat and grime slide down the drain as I wash out my underwear and t-shirt. I slip into my pajamas, hang my washed items on the deck fence to dry, peel back the bedspread, feast my eyes on clean sheets, climb in, and fall into a deep sleep. At 3:00 a.m., the three guys stumble in and fall immediately into their beds without a word. Within five seconds, they are all snoring like freight trains. I lie awake wondering where Jenny is and she walks in an hour later.

The following is an excerpt (written by Jenny) from an e-mail we sent to friends following this incident.

This is what really happened. After another great night in Italy, I walk to our bed for the night in the room of three Iowa boys. I am enjoying the pure peace of Italy at 4:00 a.m., breathing fresh air, remembering the friends we have made and adventures we've had, and just all around loving life, when I hear a horrible sound. Tensing my muscles, I know I don't have the strength to run anywhere, and I don't know what could make such a horrible sound, then I realize that the open window I am walking past is evidently where the earthquake is coming from. As I walk up the stairs, this monstrous noise becomes louder. I arrive at the door of our room, and I really start to get scared. I slowly open the door and think that there has to be a bear, a mountain lion, and a screeching peacock in my room! Oh my god! What am I supposed to do? I don't even know where the light is, so how can I see these animals before they tear me to shreds? After trying to adjust to the terror, I slowly open the door to see that this sound of death is coming from no animal, but from my sweet mother! What has possessed her, and how do I find an exorcist at this hour? Even after I realize I am not going to die a slow, painful death, I am still afraid. When I strain my ears, I hear one of the boys snoring softly, and I know first thing in the morning, mom will tell me all about how she couldn't sleep because those boys were snoring. Ha! Finally, I whisper in Mom's ear, "Roll over. You're snoring." Sure enough, the first thing she says is, "Those boys have been snoring all night."

Chapter Sixteen
Sleeping With An Italian

It is hard for me to stay in bed after 9:00 a.m., no matter how little sleep I have the night before, but this morning the wide, clean bed beckons me, and I stay a few minutes longer. Jenny drags herself up at 11:00 a.m. and showers. While she is showering, I sit on the deck to enjoy the morning air. Good thing, too. I would have forgotten my shirt and undies I rinsed last night. "Let's go," Jenny whispers, over my shoulder.

"This shirt didn't get dry, so I think I'll put it on. It'll keep me cool for a while." I carry both to the bathroom with me, roll up my clean underwear and lay them on the sink while I change my shirt. Jenny opens the door and whispers, "Are we going to leave them a thank-you note?"

"Yeah, can you write it? My note pad's in the outside pouch," I say.

"Okay." We leave a thank-you note for each person who has extended kindness. It seems so little for what has been given to us. Fortunately, those who give to ad-libbing travelers, give from a place in their hearts that does not keep score. No ledger is kept. You scratch my back and I'll scratch yours, or if you share your bread with me, then I must give you something of equal value— this seems to be an American fairness doctrine. It's easy to help strangers when they have experienced tragedy, but the help that has

218

been given us comes from those who know we only live once, and if we are to do anything good for our fellow man, we need to do it when the opportunity arises. My eyes have certainly been opened to the good in people. Our travel experiences have unlocked a place in me that only faith in the goodness of strangers can open. I have no doubt that each act of kindness that has come our way has done so through the blossom that opened in that person because of a seed planted by another act of kindness. We will offer our help and give of ourselves wherever we can.

The boys never stir when we close the door behind us at 12:00 noon. Out on the street, I pick up the pace, feeling the warmth of my own blood driving my muscles. Jenny tells me about her night and the compliments she received on her good Italian, then she says, "I can't believe those boys could sleep through the noises you were making. Mom, it was scary."

"They weren't sleeping. They were comatose; there is a difference. Speaking of sleeping, I can't do this another night," I say.

"Do what?"

"Wonder where I'll be sleeping at 1:00 a.m., finally go to sleep somewhere, and then get woken up whenever you decide to come in. I just can't do it anymore. An hour or two of sleep doesn't cut it for me. You kids can squeeze the benefit of six hours out of two. I did it when I was your age, but I can't anymore. I'm going to Riomaggiore and rent a room. I've never been there, so I'll kill two birds with one stone—see Riomaggiore and sleep," I say, picking up the pace.

"Don't worry, Mom, we'll get a place to stay earlier in the day."

"Yeah, well, I've heard that before and it hasn't worked."

"I haven't let us down yet," she says in a pleading tone.

"You have a short memory," I say, and hurrying on, "I have to sleep from time to time, and I trusted what you said about staying in small places and doing things differently—*and* never leaving me. My heart pounds and my blood rushes as I realize how tired I am just thinking about repeating this pattern night after night. "You're letting me down. I mean—" my words skid to a stop as I walk faster and faster. "I'm just tired. I want you to have fun, too, it's just that I hoped … I put stock in what you told me, and I believed you when you said you wanted to paint and write and do different stuff. Looking for a place to sleep after 1:00 a.m. is definitely different, but it's not the different I thought you meant. I know you're a social butterfly. I just thought you'd be more considerate. I'd hoped—" I speed up as my voice cracks, tears fill my eyes, and my words lose their shape. "I need quiet and good sleep, and if I'm paying for a room, I'm not opening the door for anyone after 10:00 p.m. If you don't want to stay with me, it's okay. In fact, I'd rather you didn't, then I don't have to worry about whether or not you'll interrupt my sleep. What difference does it make if we run out of money, if I'm sick or dead? I'm going to Riomaggiore," I say, walking straight for the tunnel into the new part of Monterosso to catch the train, not once giving a thought to the consequences of getting separated.

Walking faster and faster, I think to myself. I know she loves crowds, cities, and late nights. Why did I come with her knowing this? Jenny is who she is. Why did I think she would be different in Italy? Maybe I read into what she said. Maybe all those together things in the quiet of Italian villages were no more than a thought to her. It's what she said she wanted to do, but now that she's decided to stay for a year, she's thinking differently about this trip. She wants to create opportunities for herself by meeting as many people as she can. Wait, she already has a job. In three weeks, she'll be back in Bolgheri working for Goffredo. I'm just tired. I'll feel better tomorrow. No, it's more than sleep. I came with expectations for these three months. I made it clear to Jenny that I did not want to be alone in a foreign country, but that was something she didn't comprehend. Jenny would have made the trip alone. She made the rules and told me those rules when she asked me to come with her. Her rules: no money, no itinerary, no security. Did I not hear the 'no security' part? I heard it, but I didn't comprehend. I'll be more independent. If I need sleep, I'll rent a room. If my money runs out, I'll go home. It's simple. But I don't like being alone. The longer I think, the madder I get at myself, and the faster I walk.

"Mom, wait," Jenny's voice echoes in the tunnel. Not realizing the space between us, I turn around, and in a second I see her as the child, adolescent, and adult I have known and the stranger she could one day become. The Jenny I see, stands in a long, flowing dress with flowers that look like my May garden springing up from the hem to meet the bodice. The dress is covered by a layer of off-white voile. The waist is marked by a two-inch wide, rose-colored, velvet ribbon. She wears an Easter basket on her head. I have to smile, remembering that Easter she was sixteen. Not concerned about what her peers might say, she made her own Easter bonnet by attaching a bed of green Easter grass on top of a piece of pink felt then gluing fuzzy yellow baby chicks around the grass. She put a small straw basket filled with tiny eggs and flowers in the center of it all. Do you know any sixteen-year-olds who would be caught dead in a long dress with an Easter basket on their head? Jenny is the only one I know, and her uniqueness is one of her endearing qualities. But, this is Jenny, and she is an adult now. I need to see her as an adult. At that moment near the end of the tunnel in Monterosso, Italy, an emptiness bores through me as I let go. Jenny is my youngest and my only daughter, and she is an adult. A dread grips me as the fear of the loss of a connection I have enjoyed becomes real. If the relationship changes, is it lost? Yes, the original is lost, but I know our relationship has to change to remain healthy. We are two adults. She will not be living at home any longer, she will be living in Italy. What better time than now to begin making emotional adjustments? What better place than alone in Italy where children never completely leave home? What better scene than Italy where the strongest emphasis is placed on family togetherness and loyalty at all cost? A bit of illogicality seizes me. I feel an uneasiness about her independence, and mine. As a breathless Jenny nears, I verbalize a favorite Bill Cosby routine in an attempt to lighten my thoughts. "I brought you into this world, and I'll take you out ... make another one look just like you ... don't matter to me."

"I know, Mom," she answers, smiling.

"And don't you forget it," I add. I guess our trip could have ended here, but we walk silently toward the train station. Children are the greatest teachers. They can bring indescribable joy and unutterable suffering, while cracking you open and exposing your secrets without even trying. Having adult children, I have learned that parenting gets harder once the relationship changes. They need you, but they don't. They want you, but they don't, and in their effort to grow up and be independent, each step is precarious and often dangerous, and you can just watch and pray they don't do something to ruin their lives. Those beings grew inside me. Without me, they would not have survived. Then came all the years of care and worry and sacrifice and protection and guidance and support and love that a mother (whose depth of feelings for her children are measureless) pours into each child. Then suddenly they are adults, and their wanting and needing are now on their terms. I want them to be happy and independent, but at the same time, the loss throbs like a boil that cannot be relieved. It is the loss of a relationship that nourished and fulfilled, and the loss is permanent. My chest is leaden. The same heaviness I remember feeling at seven years old when a strange man closed the lid on the casket where my Aunt Lois lay. No one had explained death to me. In my childhood world, the concept of death was as foreign as that of child abuse. I knew nothing of the two. Aunt Lois was sick, but I got sick every year with tonsillitis and no one put me in a box. Mother, Daddy, and I had visited her in her home a few days ago. She sat on the couch in her white robe with pink roses on it and looked weak and pale. Now we stand in a dimly lit room at a box where Aunt Lois is sleeping. I think she feels better. She looks so pretty. She lies so still, and my desire to see her get up from the box creates an illusion. I think I can see her chest rise slightly with her breath. A man in a black suit and stone face closes the lid on the box as Daddy takes my hand and we walk away. Every muscle in my little body trembles. Clinging to Daddy's hand, I turn to see if Aunt Lois got out of the box or maybe the man opened the lid, but no she didn't … and no he didn't. Being too afraid to ask questions at this moment, I carried fear of being alone, fear of the dark, and feelings of claustrophobia with me for forty more years.

"So what are you going to do?" I ask.

"If you're getting a room, I'm going to see where it is."

"I'm serious about the locked door after 10:00 p.m. tonight."

"I know, Mom." We take the four-mile train ride to Riomaggiore, and once off the train, we stand gazing at a bright, colorful mural bigger than life depicting the men and their amazing work building the Cinque Terre. I had not realized the extent to their work until I walked through the pedestrian tunnel and came to the main street. The street is at least a sixty-degree angle! How many men and animals must have dropped by the wayside dragging rocks up, up, and up to put this place together? Immediately on our right is a window with pictures of real estate, so I bounce in and ask about renting a room. "Mom, can we just walk to the hostel and see if they have a bed first?"

"No," I growl, showing my teeth. Then I add, "You can stay in the hostel if you want." Twenty minutes later, we are making our way through paths between buildings, up flights of stairs, and into a room with two beds and a bathroom that was obviously an afterthought. The sink juts out in front of the toilet like a night watchman. A tiny shower hides behind the open door. I shut the door to see a two-foot-square stall that had been enthroned a foot off the floor. As if that weren't challenge enough, the shower door opened inward, so to get into the shower, you had to simultaneously leap up and squeeze into the miniscule opening. I placed my hands on my hips measuring the width of my body against the shower then say, "Okay, *si, per una noche?*"

"*Si, si, una noche.*"

"*Grazie,*" I reply. We leave our packs on the beds, walk back to the office where I pay sixty euros (ninety dollars) and get the key. "The leg muscles Riomaggiorian's must have!" My quivering thighs look to my calves for help. Fire shoots through my calves like jumping razors. *All this just to acquaint ourselves with this little town.* "If I can walk up those stairs again, I'm going to get my swimsuit on and spend the afternoon in the water. Dehydration and extreme exercise in the heat are self-torture. Whew," I puff. "I'm glad I don't live here."

"You'd have legs like Laura Lane if you made these climbs every day."

"When you put it that way, it might be worth it," I admit. Rummaging through my pack for my swimsuit is the first time I realize I left my freshly washed undies in the Iowa boys' room last night. Blood rushes to my face, and I smile. *What a way to start their day! They were so drunk last night, they'll spend hours trying to figure where those granny panties came from.*

Riomaggiore's beach is rocky and sandless. I sit, allowing the salt water to splash over my legs, cooling my sweaty body. Jenny joins the sun worshipers. My mind wanders in the quiet between us. Can I welcome what will be to come? Can I instigate it? I've seen women my age traveling alone. Just take a step outside your comfort zone. It is the only way to meet an uncomfortable challenge, and you know it. *Outside the zone ... outside the zone ... mamma is gettin' outside the zone. That'll be my chant.*

"I've got to have something to eat," I say.

"I saw some cherries that looked really good."

"Let's get some on the way home," I say, glad I have my fanny pack with me. The aroma of ripe fruit wets my mouth. "Mmm, it's hard to decide. I want one of each."

"Mom, let's go in and get some cheese."

"Go ahead and choose." The shopkeeper interrupts my olfactory and tactile affair. Not happy that I was fondling the fruit he asks with a slight frown that warped his broad face, "*Aiuto?*" (May I help?)

"*Si*," I answer. He takes a small brown bag and lifts a handful of cherries. With a question mark on his face, he holds the bag and the cherries slightly elevated. "*Si, si*," I answer. I guess we will pantomime. Carefully I point to the clementines and show two fingers. He takes another sack and puts two clementines in it. I point to the peaches, and he again obliges. *"Punto,"* I say, which really means 'dot,' but I have heard Italians use it to mean the end or period—end of thought. We enter the store by stepping down two stone steps. The eight-by-ten-foot room has a refrigerated meat and cheese case and a butcher with two cutting machines. In front of the case on opposing walls are wines, bottled and canned goods, and paper goods. Six customers attempt shopping elbow to elbow.

We sit on the square, slurping our juicy fruits and savoring cheeses aged to perfection. "I can't wait to sleep tonight. I can already feel it. Don't even think about coming in after 10:00 p.m."

"How many times are you going to say that?"

"As many as I want. You kids are the ones who taught me about deafness."

"A bit testy are we?"

"Let's go, I'll feel better after a shower," I say, trudging toward the rental. The shower is a giant worth conquering. I carefully choose what I will take in the shower with me due to the space limitation. No washing clothes tonight. Once in the tiny cubicle, I push my face into the side of the opposing wall and 'suck it in' so to speak so the door will close. The space is so tight that I cannot bend over to shave my legs. Washing my body is more of a thought than a reality since my elbows kept hitting the shower walls, so I stand, enjoying the comfort of warm water spilling over my tired body. I emerge feeling slick and clean and ready for sleep. The close proximity of the buildings prevents any breeze from entering the open window in this part of Italy that has not discovered ceiling fans. Heated conversation between two lovers on the street below hangs on the window in the still night air. I fling myself into the twin bed with the wrinkled brown bedspread at 8:00 p.m. Jenny leaves looking for nightlife in Riomaggiore. In the two hours I am alone, the only thoughts drifting through my head are of green meadows, wildflowers, cowbells, and the heavenly Swiss alpine air.

Renewed by rest and sleep, we both are back to our fun, and we spend one more day in the Cinque Terre to visit Manorola, which reveals itself to be the quietest and most beautiful of the five, in my opinion. The main drag dead-ends into deep water, where huge boulders become diving platforms for swimmers. At one end of the diving area, standing erect, is a beam piercing the sky. There is no launching dock for small boats, so the I-shaped beam retrieves boats from the sidewalk, lifts them over the water, and sets them afloat. Space is at a premium here and the number of small boats parked can be counted by a three year old. A long stretch of walk, wrapping around a cliff and meandering along the sea, creates the *via dell'amore*, lover's lane. Benches and rock ledges positioned against the cliff invite those strolling to sit staring into the mirage, pose for the perfect pictures, and draw in the therapeutic sea air. The day passes slowly and pleasantly, and I soak in Manorola's peaceful beauty, wrapped in the warm feeling of the friendliness of nature. "Mom, let's go back to Monterosso and just see what happens."

"Okay. We're leaving tomorrow anyway." When I'm rested, I admit I enjoy this loose travel agenda of 'stay if we want, go when we want, and drift with the wind.' Our journey is birthed as we go along. Lackadaisically, we lounge on Monterosso's white beach until the moon beams soften the water. The sea is ominous and foreboding at dusk, but I think I could stay right here and be lulled to sleep by the foamy tide. Jenny is off socializing and soon brings a new friend to meet me. "Simone, this is my mom." I look to see her standing next to a tan, glistening, young man. "Simone is a lifeguard."

"Hello, Simone." Simone smiles affectionately. His gentle brown eyes are inviting.

"Hal-lo," he nods.

"Simone says we can stay at his house tonight since his roommate is out of town."

"Really? Are you sure?" I say to an oblivious Simone.

"He's just learning English," Jenny says, then turns to Simone, and they exchange a few phrases in Italian. "Simone has to work a little longer until everything is locked up, then he can take us to his house if you want. "Great," I say, with anticipation in my voice. "Thank you, Simone."

"Wahl-coam," he says, slowly and a bit insecurely. (I know exactly how he feels.)

At 11:45 p.m., we are walking to Simone's house. We walk past Piero's, turn a corner, and continue a block or so up a hill to a wooded area. "My legs have turned to spaghetti," I say, stopping and leaning against a tree. "I have to rest. This incline is too much." Jenny translates for Simone who turns and relieves me of my pack. He leads the way into the woods. It is very dark, even with the flashlight he carries. I am putting one foot in front of the other looking at the ground when we begin climbing rugged, concrete steps built into the dirt and so steep I have to grunt to get up them. "These steps are a foot tall! Where are we going? This must be the stairway to heaven." I huff.

"Good one, Mom, you can make it," Jenny says, breaking from her conversation with Simone. A small pipe rail suddenly appears on my left, and I grab it encouraging my upper body to help by pulling me along. "Geez, I thought I had walked and climbed enough to be stronger than this," I say, stopping again.

"These stairs are pretty steep, but you can make it, Mom." The stairs continue stacking themselves on top of each other. "Wait a minute," I say, thinking of an excuse to stop and rest. "Will you ask Simone if I can use his flashlight?"

"What for?" Jenny asks.

"I just want to see something." Jenny descends a few steps and hands me the flashlight that I point illuminating where we've been. I count the steps, and we have just climbed ten of them.

"Come on, Mom."

"I'm going to count and see how many steps it takes to get to the sky. Eleven, twelve, thirteen, fourteen ... huff. ... twenty ... puff ...

twenty-nine … grunt. … forty-four … gasp. … sixty-one … I'm feeling light-headed. My God, are we there?" Simone is chuckling at my exaggerated moans.

"*Mi mamma stanca*," Jenny tells Simone that I am tired. She might need to learn the word for dead, soon. The total of seventy steps takes us to Simone's house that is a two-room apartment. We enter the kitchen/living room that has a hide-a-bed couch. A dark, wooden, rectangular coffee table with a stack of books for one leg, stands in front of the tan and very stained couch. The table holds a dirty pair of socks, a black boom box with a broken handle, and a scratched-up frying pan with a nut, bolt, and two AA batteries in it. Simone shows us a bathroom with shower, tub, and white tile walls where several tiles are missing pieces as if they have been hit with a hammer. The floor is tiny black and white hexagonal tiles that make my vision swim. An oval mirror the size of my face hangs over the freestanding sink. A pile of towels and clothes rest helplessly under the sink. A roomy bedroom with a dresser and full bed is where Simone takes us. The dirty beige walls, peeling and spotted, look like a skin disease. This is his roommate's bed. *Hmm, Simone sleeps on the couch and the roommate gets the bed, so this must be the roommate's flat.* Jenny understands Simone to say that Giuseppe is gone for three days to visit his girl friend in Milan. Trying to be brave, I send Jenny out without a struggle. At 12:50 a.m. I am alone in a strange bed, and the youngsters have gone back to town. At first, a few spooky thoughts jump through my head, but I remind myself of my independence and that high-walled comfort zone that I'm climbing out of. After ten minutes of yoga nidra, I float away to dreamland in the quiet of this elevated atmosphere.

A few hours later, when I'm in the death grip of deep sleep, the glaring overhead light reaches down pulling my eyes open. Groggily, I blink as incomprehensible words bring life to my ears. My eyes pop open, and I see (as best I can without my glasses) the form of a man leaning on an obliging wall pointing to me and saying whatever Italians say in such situations. My heart drops into my gut, splat. I shriek, grab the sheet, and pull it to my quivering chin. Terror grips, my mind convulses, and I belch all twenty-five Italian words I know peppered with Simone's name five or six times and laced with a few special English words. Adrenaline pumping, thoughts rip through my mind: *I need a plan. My life could be at stake here. I'm going to kill Jenny when/if I see her again.* Then I focus briefly and say with the rapid fire of an automatic weapon, "I am Simone's friend ... Please don't hurt me ... *Mi amico Simone ... Simone mi amico, per favore, mi amico Simone, per favore—*" He continues drooling drunken Italian words that drip from his mouth like black-strap molasses. I want to scream or fly out the window, but I don't. To interrupt my hysteria, he says with a downward motion of his arm, "*Allora, va bene,*" and stumbles into the kitchen, flips on the boom box, turns the volume to max, and hits the repeat button. For the next hour, I hear him banging pots and pans and singing at the top of his lungs the song that Eminem sings about killing Kim and stuffing her in the trunk of his car. The same song, over and over for an hour, is now tattooed on my mind, and I pray he doesn't understand the words in English. This must be Giussepe, home from a visit gone sour with his girlfriend, and he finds me in his bed. The ceiling light is on, but I'm not moving, so I remain in the bed with the sheet over my head, my fingers in my ears, praying that he will put the pots and pans on the stove instead of against my head. *Wait until I get my hands on you, Jenny!*

Jenny and Simone return an hour later. Simone flips off the boom box, and he and Giuseppe begin arguing rather loudly. Jenny walks in the bedroom and shuts the door. "I'm going to kill you," I calmly announce.

"Is that the roommate?" Jenny asks, ignoring my statement.

"How could I know?"

"Didn't you talk to him?"

"Didn't I talk to him? What do you mean, 'didn't I talk to him?' His rendezvous evidently turned upside down, he returns home, getting drunk on the way, and finds a strange woman the age of his mother sleeping in his bed! She is not only old and strange, but she speaks a foreign language, and you want to know, 'didn't I talk to him?' Yes, I talked to him! He woke me from a dead sleep, and I pled for my life in English while he drooled Italian down his front."

"You don't have to get excited about it," she says.

"What? Don't get excited." Thankfully, Simone interrupts us when he comes into the room, looks at me quaking under the sheet, and tells Jenny we all *tutti* will sleep in the bed together. Jenny looks at me and bursts out laughing. "Okay," she says. "We're sleeping with an Italian man tonight, Mom." What's left of the night ends in this double bed with Simone on the left, Jenny in the middle, and me clinging to the right side of the bed while Giuseppe sleeps on the couch.

Chapter Seventeen

Has Anyone Seen George Clooney?

"It seems dumb to spend money going someplace I don't want to go. Why don't you go? You'll be okay," Jenny says.

"But I don't want to go alone," I say, looking at her with a tinge of loneliness, feeling her slip away.

"Mom, you're the most careful person I know. You could go it alone if you wanted to."

"Going it alone wasn't part of the deal remember? I don't think you realize just how much I have depended on you this trip. Besides, I get twice the fun out of something when you share it with me. Good grief, it's Switzerland, Jenny! Those of you who are brave just don't understand those of us who aren't. How 'bout we can stop in Lake Como. It's in Italy, and who knows, maybe we'll see George Clooney. Isn't that where he lives?" I add cheerfully.

"And what are the chances we'd see George Clooney?"

"Well, there's a chance, right?"

"Do you want to go to Lake Como?" Jenny asks.

"I'd love to see Lake Como. I want to see everything I can," I nod, smiling.

"It's all so expensive," she sighs, dragging herself to the ticket window. She informs the clerk we want to go to Lake Como. "*Ah, il lago bellissimo,*" he assures. They have a brief exchange, and then Jenny turns and asks, "Which station for arrival?"

"There's more than one? I don't know." She shrugs her shoulders and leaves the decision to him. Taking the tickets, she politely thanks him, turns to me, and says, "I hope you're not going in hopes of seeing George Clooney. He won't be there."

"How do you know?" I ask.

"He's filming now."

"Oh, it pays to read the Enquirer, huh?"

"I didn't read it in the Enquirer. I think I read it in People magazine." Screeching metal is our clue and we rush to the ramp.

Jenny sleeps the three hours to Milan where on arrival we race to change trains. Once aboard, we scan the seats for two together. The train is arranged in groupings of four seats, with two seats facing forward and two facing backward. I prefer to sit facing forward, and today we are in luck. We find a cluster where both forward facing seats are empty. "*Buon giorno,*" I say to the girl sitting in the seat facing me as Jenny tosses our packs into the overhead rack. The girl briefly glances my way with a hint of a smile but no word, then darts her eyes downward. Usually I'm met with a big smile when an Italian hears my Texas drawl, a drawl that somehow is exaggerated when I attempt Italian.

Another hour to Lake Como and again Jenny sleeps. I split my attention between the changing scenery and the girl sitting across from me who looks to be in her late twenties. She is dressed in a short gray skirt. Her powder-white, bare legs end in gold leather sandals with yellow rhinestones across the instep. Tucked into the gray waistband is a simple, sleeveless, white blouse that buttons up the front. She neglected the top three buttons exposing the roundness of her breasts. A psychedelic-colored scarf of geometric design is tied tightly around her slender neck with one of the tails tickling her cleavage. Her dyed red-brown-blond hair hangs over her left eye, curves at the corner of her mouth, and ends beneath her chin. The right side is cut short, exposing her silver and gold hooped and dangled ear. She is oblivious to her surroundings as she strokes, sniffs, and sucks on what appears to have been a small piece of cloth but is now about six strings, five inches long. She fumbles through her immense gold bag in answer to the annoying ring of her cell phone. She talks for two minutes then promptly returns to the strings pulling them repeatedly through her lips from left to right. She opens a paperback novel titled *L'Animale Morente* and begins to read taking the strings with her into her story. She reads for ten minutes, closes the book, and sits twiddling the strings between the fingers of her right hand as she stares out the window. A stray thought enters, and she transfers the strings to her left hand while her right hand searches the depths of her handbag. She retrieves a bottle of brilliant orange fingernail polish. The same color of a double knit pantsuit my mother made me in 1969, the year we college girls began wearing pants to class. She deposits the strings on the front of her blouse near the collar so she can open the polish. She meticulously paints the left thumb and forefinger, replaces the cap, and sets the bottle on the window ledge. Taking the strings to her nose, she sniffs them, and then pulls them across her nostrils with the elegance of a ballerina extending her arm to a prince. She holds her pets between her lips and strokes them with her freshly painted fingers. The strings remain between her lips as she paints the remaining nails on her left hand. She recaps the polish and returns it to her purse. I am fascinated thinking the strings must be soaked in something that is calming and pleasing to her. I stretch my olfactory nerves, flaring my nostrils and breathing in slowly and deeply. I smell nothing but stuffy air. She begins chewing the strings until they disappear behind her pale lips. She tenderly removes the strings from her mouth, lays them across her lap, and strokes them with the lacquer-less fingers of her right hand as if she were apologizing for the moist darkness of her mouth. She lifts the strings, tickles both cheeks with them, and returns them to her lips briefly. I knew I should have been a psychology major. I would love to study this one. In fact, on my first day as a freshman at Oklahoma State University, I told my advisor, "I want to be a child psychologist." Peering over her reading glasses, my advisor pulls my test scores from a folder and says, "Are you sure? To do anything in psychology, you'll have to go to school for at least eight years." This was my first day, and the four years ahead of me seemed an eternity. My advisor burst my bubble. Her tone and stiff look assured me I did not want to attend school for the next eight years, so I did it my way and became a teacher and mother—real life psychologists. The girl's phone rings again. She answers and gives two replies and returns the phone, accompanied by the strings, to her purse, which she zips shut.

Jenny is still sleeping as the train pulls into Como. The girl stands and retrieves a duffle bag from overhead, which she quickly throws into her seat and frantically unzips the purse pulling the strings from it and quickly caressing her left cheek with them. She walks down the aisle, purse in right hand, duffle bag slung over left shoulder, and strings hanging from the left corner of her mouth. I want to follow and learn more about this interesting person, but I turn to Jenny and say, "We're here. Wake up."

"Huh?"

"Here, wipe the drools off your face," I say, handing her a napkin. "You missed the most interesting person."

"What do you mean?"

"Never mind. You wouldn't believe me." I will forever wish I had made an attempt at conversing with the girl.

Just outside the station is the bus stop. A crowd of people stands waiting. The schedule indicates three busses. La Vespa, the hostel where we plan to stay, is not listed as a stop. When the door opens on the first bus, I ask the driver, "*La Vespa?*" He smiles and says, "*Ah La Vespa, si, in prossimo autobus*," and points behind him. "That was easy," I say proud of myself for gaining this bit of information. "He said we need to be on that bus."

The streets are narrow, not allowing busses and delivery trucks to share the space, and the bus always yields to the trucks, so we sit idling. It's amazing, a trip around Lake Como takes two and a half hours and not because of distance! "I can't believe this," Jenny says, tensely.

"Yeah, you'd think they would widen something. Look at this. Did you know Lake Como is a melted glacier? If this is what happens when glaciers melt, we should be encouraging it. It's a fairy land," I say, wishing I could turn my head three hundred and sixty degrees to take it all in at once.

"Yeah."

"What's wrong? Do you feel sick? PMS?"

"No."

"Spoiled maybe?" I ask, raising my eyebrows to no response. Maybe she's tired and doesn't know it. She has never behaved this way on any of our travels together. She rolls with the punches and change doesn't bother her. The fear that someday I might lose her dizzies me.

The bus pulls up to the front door of La Vespa. We thank the driver and hop off. "Well, we're here. Let's see what hostel life is about," I say. We enter an unkept building with the simplicity of 60s art on the walls. A painting of a yellow hand shaking a white hand is over the front door. A sea with an orange and white sailboat bearing the number five on its white sail glides through the blue waves painted on the wall to our right. "Has a bohemian feel," Jenny comments.

"Yeah, it's 60s hippie." The common room is equipped with foosball tables, couches, a bar, three tables and chairs, and it opens to the beach. The building is next to a campground with tents and fifth wheels parked in a fenced area. We walk outside to see two long picnic tables sitting in the sun. No one is in the water. I can't say I blame them. The beach is more dirt than sand, with pieces of broken shells scattered—not too inviting. Two young boys in their swim trunks kick a ball up and down the beach competing with fancy moves, both attempting to outdo each other. We walk back inside looking for someone to help us check in. I can't believe I never thought about calling ahead for a reservation. Hmm, randomness is becoming comfortable. I walk to the bar where a man stands with a distant look in his eyes. "*Il letto per sta sera?*" I bravely ask. Without a word, he grabs a key from a pegboard behind the bar and heads directly to a room by the front door. Two twin beds with red iron headboards butt up against the wall in front of us. A bold, yellow sun resembling a new-age tattoo on steroids has been painted on that wall. This sun is reminiscent of a wannabe artist who strives to be metaphysically correct and who has some knowledge of the Dali Lama and Santa Fean culture. The clerk questions us, and I question him, "*Il bano?*" He motions, and we all ascend the stairs outside the bedroom door to the second floor where we find a community bath similar to the old college dormitory baths. "Okay, Mom?"

"Yes, for one night," I say. Jenny tells him we'll stay one night. I obediently follow him to the cash drawer to pay and get the key.

The people and the building bring back memories of the 60s, but the music is, well, disturbing. We have to yell to be heard over it. "What kind of music is this?" I yell.

"Techno/trance," Jenny yells back.

"It's kinda creepy. I wonder if they ever turn it off."

"Bet you could get any drug you wanted around here," she says.

"If they play this music all night, I'll need some drugs. Oh well, we won't be here for long. It's already 4:30 p.m. We'll leave in the morning and find a different place to stay."

"Mah-ahm. Let's go on to Gimmelwald."

"We came to see Lake Como. I love the hazy feel in the air. It's so different from anywhere we've been. We're going to the other side of the lake tomorrow, so we'll try the hostel over there for a night."

We hang out at the hostel all evening watching mostly guys play foosball and toss Frisbees. Two Asian girls survey the common area, look at each other, and retreat to their room. We sit eating a slice of pizza and drinking a cold beer in the cooler night air when a German man, with a somewhat elastic age, asks if he can sit at our table. "Sure," Jenny says, as I hide my stuffed mouth. "Hello, I'm Jenny, and this is my mother, Sue Ellen."

"Pleased," he replies with a nod. "I am Birn." His thick, blond hair is of a man in his thirties, but his face and body are a sagging sixty. He is recently divorced and wandering around Italy trying to reinvent himself. The poor guy just kept buying beer as long as we kept listening. I retire at midnight. Jenny comes to bed at 1:00 a.m., falls instantly to sleep, and I lie awake until someone cuts the blaring music at 2:00 a.m. My old bladder drags me up the stairs at 5:00 a.m., after which time I lie in bed hoping to fall asleep again, until an electric charge shoots through my body when the music blares at 9:00 a.m. Jenny never hears it.

We ride the ferry to Bellagio and walk the shops that, from the window dressings and prices, cater to George Clooney's crowd. "Oh, this place is beautiful! Clean, old, green, and quiet," I say. We drop into a small café with yellow walls and foot-square black and white tiles arranged in a checkerboard on the floor. We order the cheapest sandwich, an open-face toasted grilled cheese with a pineapple ring on top. A heavenly sprig of basil garnishes the pineapple. I would have topped the pineapple with a sprig of mint, but the fruit and cheese spring to life in collaboration with the basil. The store offers six flavors of their own gelato, obviously celebrated, given the length of the line that stretches out the door.

Relaxed and happy tourists fuel the ferry ride around Lake Como. "George Clooney house? Yes?" A Japanese lady jumps up and down with her finger on her camera's button. "George Clooney?" she asks. Someone else overhears and passes the news along, and soon the ferry buzzes in different languages that we are in sight of George Clooney's house. A symphony of cameras releasing shutters in harmony point in the direction of what we all hope is the celebrity's home since we'll take a picture back to our friends.

The next stop on the lake is Menaggio, where we find another hostel. La Primula Hostel sits on a hill and overlooks the tarnished pewter lake outlined by surrounding green hills. What a picture! I'm ready to give my back a break and rid myself of my burden, so we climb the hill in hopes La Primula will have a vacancy. A covered balcony alive with scarlet geraniums stretching their long necks toward the sun greets us. The balcony buzzes with people playing cards, exchanging stories, writing in journals, and setting tables for dinner. This hostel is family-oriented with several couples and their children here. We arrive just as a downpour begins. My mother used to say the devil is beating his wife when it rains while the sun is shining. Today Mrs. Devil gets a good beating for forty-five minutes. We sit idly on the balcony watching the steam rise from the pavement below. Friendliness is on the menu here, and we find ourselves in a game of Scattergories with two women from California and two college girls from Scotland and one from Croatia while the rain pounds itself out beyond the balcony rail. We are to share a room with two girls from England, whom we never get to know since we are in bed before they come in, and they leave before dawn. In the remainder of daylight, between rain showers, we walk the streets enjoying fantastic views at every turn.

La Primula charged us nine euros each ($12) to sleep and eat. What a deal! Tonight's dinner is four-cheese pizza, and breakfast will be bread, jam, and coffee or tea. Jenny's conversation is limited though friendly, but her light is off, her radiance gone. When I'm around a low energy person, I feel like I'm trying to climb Mt. Everest, and no matter how much effort I put forth, I make no progress. The hostellers around dinner are mature, refined, somewhat reserved, relaxed, and happy. Most retire around 10 p.m., but Jenny and I remain on the balcony enjoying the sights and sounds of the water as lights on boats and ferries illuminate their way. "Tomorrow is Switzerland," I say, imagining the alpine air all the way to my bones. "Gimmelwald, I can't wait." I ask Valentina, the tall woman manning the office, if she knows where to find the number for the hostel in Gimmelwald. "*Si, si,*" she says pulling a book from a drawer. She finds the number and writes it down on a piece of paper. "Have change?" she asks, and before I can answer, she motions me to sit at her desk. "Come," she says. I sit and look at the number. "Do I dial 011 or 001 first? I can never remember. Is this the country code?" I say confused.

"I call," she says, taking the phone and dialing the number for me then handing me the receiver.

"Thank you."

"You welcome." I go to bed knowing that Gimmelwald's Mountain Hostel is booked, but we will have our own little apartment a few yards away from the hostel for three nights.

Jenny gets up easily with a deadline. Our train leaves at 9:40 a.m. and, if the force is with us, will arrive in Interlaken, Switzerland, somewhere around five hours later. Valentina assures us the bus ride to the station in Varenna will take no more than fifteen minutes, so we enjoy our bread and jam at 8:30 a.m. We say our good-byes and walk to the bus stop. The stop is across the narrow street from a parking lot that edges the lake. We watch as a teenage girl helps an elderly woman across the street. The girl opens the car door for her elder, bends to kiss the old woman's forehead, waves good-bye, and walks back across the street entering the building she left. The aged woman is in an ancient blue Saab. Taking orders from the white-haired dame, the blue vehicle lurches forward as the woman looks only to her right before making a left-hand turn. Pulling out, grandma sideswipes the white Volvo on her left that is minding its own business in a designated parking place. "Uh-oh," I say. "Should we go help?" The woman glares at the Volvo with a look of contempt and continues her left turn taking out the Volvo's headlight as she jerks around the car and up the street. We stand bamboozled, speechless, mouths hanging as if unhinged, both pointing to the white Volvo with its new, blue, three-foot-long crease, ending at a dangling headlight. "Oh my gosh," Jenny howls. "I can't believe it. She never got out of the car to see the damage."

"She couldn't get out."

"Mom, she just dented that car and didn't leave a note or anything."

"Maybe they don't have car insurance here."

"Or hit-and-run laws."

"Did you see the look on her face when she realized she had hit it?"

"Yeah, it was like, 'get the hell out of my way.' Then she just pulls on out." We stand laughing in disbelief at what we have just witnessed as the bus door opens.

No one is manning the ticket counter in the one-room Varenna station. Another ticket seeker says we can buy on the train. According to the schedule, the next train arrives in fifteen minutes. "Have you seen the bathroom?" I ask.

"It's over there," Jenny points outside to a building with black silhouettes of a woman on one door and a man on another. I drop my pack at her feet, walk down the sidewalk, and enter the ladies' room. I open the stall door to see salmon-colored tiles on the wall and a brick floor. Perfectly centered in the bricks is a white, porcelain square, maybe two feet by three feet, with two raised places (shaped like feet) complete with ridges for traction. A three-inch-diameter hole sits a little back of center on this thing. I giggle thinking about what's going to happen. In Texas we would call this 'squat and aim.' There are no rails on the walls to hang onto. In fact, you couldn't reach the wall. You are on your own and desperately out of luck if you have weak knees, legs, back, or poor balance. I'm laughing so hard that I almost can't complete the task. Luckily no one else is around—I hope. The flushing mechanism is not apparent to me, so I begin looking for something to pull or push. On the wall near the floor is a black rubber circle. I push the circle with my shoe, and water rushes over the porcelain. The whole thing is disgusting. If the City/County Health Department, or the Centers for Disease Control, not to mention personnel representing the American Disabilities Act saw this, they would riot in the streets.

The wheels clack along the tracks as the romance of Italy, where you can literally smell the sun, joins hands with the austere Swiss/German scene. The homes morph into dark rugged wood with window boxes gleefully spilling color. Every home is set perfectly on a green pallet amid dancing flowers. Each country has a charisma that is all its own, a part of its history and character, and Switzerland's is not on the same page as Italy's. The air hangs like a sentimental shroud over the foothills, veiling all. I don't trust my words, so I yield to what novelist Henry James said, "One can't describe the beauty of the Italian lakes, nor would one if one could."

At the Italy/Switzerland border, a newer, more powerful Swiss engine capable of making the demanding climb into the Alps, hooks up to help us complete the journey. Vicissitudes in elevation slow the train to a creep as it struggles up the mountains. In a little over five hours, we arrive at Interlaken West station, buy a bus/gondola combo ticket, and board the bus that takes us on a thirty-minute ride through the countryside to the gondola. The closer I get, the more antsy I am. I wonder if Gimmelwald will still look as it did in 1998 when we visited, or have the developers stolen it? I remember no motorized vehicles and an atmosphere from another time. Men stood on the sides of steep hills cutting hay with scythes then stuffing it into burlap sacks or tying it to their backs and hauling it up the elevation to old barns. *Oh, please let it be the same, with the same hundred souls living here.* I have experienced the heartbreak of what we call progress. I spent the summers of 1968,1969, and 1970 working in a candle store in Central City, Colorado, an old mining town that had maintained its 1859 charm and was a delight to all who visited. I returned to Central City in 2001 to see a ghost town with every building empty and boarded and the air dead. The heart and soul of a mountain town ripped away. At one end of town stood man's god, money, in the form of a flashy gambling casino. It was pitiful, and I wish I had never gone back.

"It's getting cold, Mom," Jenny shivers.

"I know. Isn't it heavenly? Maybe I can toss my sweat rag. You brought a sleeve."

"Yeah, but I need a coat."

"Here, I'll share my body heat," I say, putting my arms around her as we walk to the gondola. Twenty-two of us board the gondola, a glassed-in box that hangs from a cable. Butterflies take flight in my stomach when my eyes tell my feet they have left the ground. Up we go with a clear three-hundred-and-sixty-degree view of paradise. The wonders of nature snatch my breath. I find myself gasping when each waterfall, wildflower, verdant meadow, cowbell, or majestic peak comes into view. "We're in the Al-lps," I sing.

"My mom loves this place," Jenny attempts explaining my behavior to those around, but no explanation is needed. Anyone who loves peace and nature in the exceptional realm, experiences Gimmelwald's addiction sooner or later. "Oh … I hope it hasn't changed," I say as we step off the gondola in Gimmelwald.

"Well, here's the cheese hut just like it was last time," Jenny points as we round the corner and pass the dark wood hut reeking of aged cheese. Wildflowers tickle the wood, and tall grasses, green as the Emerald City, make a soft bed for two young hikers resting in the shade. We continue our climb and see the one-room schoolhouse. "It's the same … yesss," I say, twirling around, my arms extended out to the side like Maria von Trapp leading her crew over the Austrian border. "I just might hug a tree." Just as it was seven years ago, on our left is a fence covered in blooms white as snow. "After we check in, let's go to the barn," I say. The barn is the winter home of Gimmelwald's cows but in summer is cleaned out and fresh straw spread on the floor. The cows, donned with different size bells, are sent to graze on hillsides posing for pictures while hikers rent space in the barn to lay their weary bodies.

The hostel walls hold all of Gimmelwald's noise. It brims with happy travelers who, once in Gimmelwald, experience heaven and want to stay longer, many tossing their itineraries to bask in divine essence. The view from the front porch of the hostel is humbling, a look at God's face. Through the air's misty veil, I see the rugged beauty of the Alps that look near enough to touch. As if an artist's brush painted white lines down the mountains, narrow waterfalls plunge from top to bottom. Snow caps the highest peaks. This is the backdrop for alpine meadows collecting flowers and warm chalets dribbling down hills. One could never know the severity of winter seeing Gimmelwald in July—except to notice the pipe that is anchored on each roof holding that roof intact against wintry winds. I could sit here for the rest of my life, but I go back in, pay for the apartment, get the key, and take directions.

Fifty yards up the road, we enter a typical Swiss house at ground level. Five wooden pegs holding scarves and jackets greet us. A pair of bulky hiking boots rests on the floor below them. To the right of this wall, a narrow stairway shoots up revealing nothing about what or who is upstairs. We walk down the hallway on our left toward the back of the house. I open the door to a spic and span modern kitchen with a wooden table and two chairs surrounded by wood cabinets and tiled countertops. Pale blue linoleum carries us from the kitchen into the laundry/bathroom with both washer and dryer and a bathtub deep enough to swim in. A small living room, adjacent to the kitchen and carpeted in worn, tan indoor/outdoor, holds a nondescript beige couch. On the opposing wall stands a built-in bookcase and desk. A thirteen-inch non-functioning television sits on the desk. At the end of the couch, sunlight filters through lace. I pull aside the lace to see the Alps in all their glory. On the other side of the bedroom door stands a plain wooden wardrobe. The bedroom is small with a dresser and twin beds on opposite walls. The beds are covered with white down comforters. It's July 1, and we need down comforters to sleep comfortably. "Ahhh, I love it."

"This is cozy," Jenny says.

"I think I could live here forever. I wonder if I'd ever tire of this."

"You could stay here, Mom, and write. I'm sure you could find something to do. Why don't you ask?" *She doesn't miss an opportunity*, I think to myself.

We spend the next three evenings playing games with the happy hostellers and listening to accordion players. The hostel's staff offers a delightful menu. We splurge and have Swiss fondue. One night we have cheese fondue and one night chocolate fondue with a plateful of juicy strawberries, apples, pineapple chunks, and bananas for dipping. The third night we have mouth-watering pizza and what I've come to realize is my favorite beer, Feldschlosschen. It is like old-home-week with mostly Americans staying here. Our first night, we play chess and checkers with five Mormon boys from Utah who later ask if they can use our washer and dryer. I feel like a fraternity house mom with guys coming and going in the apartment. The second night, we loan our couch out to a boy named Andrew from Chicago, who has arrived late with no place to sleep, not knowing how popular Gimmelwald's hostel and cow barn are. While it felt abnormal, it gave me a chance to return the goodness that others have extended us.

The cow barn has been remodeled since we were here in '98. It now has a shower and a new bathroom. I remember it being a barn with one large floor area. Now short temporary partitions provide a stall effect and some hint of privacy for those on the straw. Before the remodel, a space rented for two francs. Now the price is twenty-four francs. Don't you love the entrepreneurial spirit? Jenny stays at the hostel until the wee hours of each morning, so my days are spent hiking and exploring alone—definitely outside my comfort zone—while she sleeps. I sit leaning against a pine tree staring at the sky's rapidly moving clouds and listening to the Alps. Maybe I'll see a cow in the sky again. During our visit in '98, we witnessed a cow being transported via helicopter. The cow was secure in a harness dangling from a rope under the helicopter. The pilot flew low enough we could hear the moos for help from the bovine victim. When I asked, I was informed by a local with an "Isn't this how everyone moves livestock?" tone in his voice, that things are transferred from one mountain to another by helicopter. My musings continue to be interrupted by a sign I saw on the wall in the hostel. The sign says, "Nanny wanted for one-and-a-half year old. Begin work in December in Murren. Contact Francine at 035-879-7700." *I think I'll apply for that nanny job.*

Chapter Eighteen
On My Own

Today is July 4th, and we have spent three nights in Gimmelwald. Jenny is counting the minutes until she can get back to Italy, and I am hanging on to the Alps, knowing that my willingness to take action is all that will keep me here. For the first time this summer, we are wearing our $1.99 paper-thin rain ponchos to protect us from a misty mountain mush. "It's so cold," Jenny says, shivering in the dampness. "It'll warm when the sun breaks through," I promise.

"Are you going to ask for a job? If not, we need to head south," she says as we stroll toward the gondola station.

"You never know till you ask," I say, feeling confident no job is available. "That's what my mother used to tell me."

"Yeah, my mom told me the same thing," she says with an endearing glance.

"As much as I love new places, new things, starting new endeavors, it's kinda scary since this is a foreign country, and I'm the foreigner."

"You should stay if you want. Nothing's going to happen, and what are the odds that you would ever have an opportunity like this again?"

"True. But then you're by yourself in Italy," I say, my thoughts clinging to her. I would go insane if something happened to her in

Italy, and I wasn't there. Sometimes I think I could die, I love her so. *Let go. Just let go,* comes an echo from within me.

"Remember, I was coming by myself in the first place," she says.

"I know. It's just uncomfortable for me to be serious about this." *You need to put on your big girl panties and stay. You know you want to.* "Will you go with me to Murren to check it out?" I ask.

"Are you going to ask about the nanny job?"

"Yes."

"Let's go," she says, her arm in mine leading me to the ticket window. Jenny insists on walking arm in arm when we're together. I love it.

Petie, with the purple and orange punk rock hair, is the German who keeps everything and everyone organized and happy at Mountain Hostel. She told me the lady who put up the nanny ad is at Hotel Alpenruh in Murren. "Go to Murren and meet Francine. Hotel is near station," she had said. So we go, and with each rise up the gondola cable, my energy, anticipation, dread, and desire escalate. I begin chatting nervously, my bustling words falling over each other like dominoes in a pile. I feel an urgency to say everything I can right now. I may never see Jenny again. Five minutes later, we arrive in Murren, and as soon as we leave the station, we look toward town up the main walkway. The entire town tumbles down a mountain, and in that tumbling, an eruption of Switzerland invades our senses as colors and scents, intensified by the misty air, rush to welcome us from all directions. We see rugged Swiss structures clinging to sloped earth. Pots of edelweiss decorate perfectly groomed steps and porches; pregnant flower gardens judiciously occupy every square inch of land; hanging baskets cascade from eaves, each one more manicured and colorful than the one before and all set against the backdrop of the Alps. Again, Jenny loops her arm in mine. We stand staring—our silence spontaneous, neither wanting to spoil the awe-inspiring moment. Together we look and listen, and I know this moment is immortal because I have shared it with someone I love, someone close to my soul, Jenny.

"Yep. Looks like heaven to me," she says, breaking the trance. "Well, are you going to stay? Are you going to be a nanny in Switzerland?" Reluctantly, I pull myself back to reality.

"Yes."

"Okay. I'll sit here and wait," she says, pointing to a bench. "Let's not complicate things by having to explain that I'm going back to Italy and all that." I hesitate, collecting my thoughts. I am about to ask a stranger, in a country where I am foreign, to give me a job. I don't know what the big deal is, but I feel the same nausea, shortness of breath, and weakness I remember feeling at age six when my mother drove me to the convenience store two blocks from our house so I could return a baby bottle I had stolen. Mother parked the car right at the front door, in clear view of the counter. She said, "I'll wait here. You go tell the man what you did, say you are sorry, and return it." At that moment, I had wanted to throw up and my knees began to shake. "I can't breathe," I pleaded.

"Go on. You have to do this," Mother said. Meekly I walked into the store and up to the counter. The man greeted me with a smile and a "Can I help you?" His congenial nature returned strength to my legs as I set the bottle on the counter, bowed my head, and said, "I'm sorry I took this. My mother said I had to bring it back." Not knowing what to expect, I kept my head bowed and darted my eyes upward toward him. I was relieved that Mother did not hear what he said to me. "Thank you, sweetheart. It's okay. Now run along." I'm not sure what I expected, but it was not for him to say, "It's okay." This was the first time I experienced my mother being disappointed in me. It wasn't what she said, but the message in her body language. I could feel her disappointment, and I was grateful that Mother kept this to herself, for my father was the love of my life, and I couldn't bear the thought of causing him sadness. From that moment, I knew my actions could hurt others, and this understanding played a big part in my ability to say no to temptations I faced through those growing years.

I walk into the hotel. The lobby is inviting with soft chairs and a couch near the multi-paned window that looks out over a terraced rock garden full of colorful columbines, sweet alyssum tumbling over rocks, petunias, and pansies. Magazines are spread neatly in a fan shape on the coffee table. I walk straight to the desks that are closed off from the seating area by a three-foot-tall wooden partition with a swinging gate. "May I speak to Francine?" An attractive, slender woman in a gray-green suit rises from her desk, walks out of the area, and says in a gentle voice with German overtones, "I am Francine. Can I help you?"

"My name is Sue Ellen, and I saw your ad for a nanny in the hostel in Gimmelwald. I would like to apply," I say with surprising ease.

"The position is filled," she says. A rush of relief consumes me, but instead of thanking her and leaving, what I say next comes from a place within me that until now, I did not know existed. "I love your town. This is the most beautiful place I've ever seen. I have to stay here, but I have no money for a room. I am willing to do any type of work in trade for a bed. I will cook, clean, pull the weeds from the gardens. I'll do whatever you want. Can you help me?" Without a moment's hesitation, as if she had expected me, she says, "Yes, my husband need help in restaurant on mountain. I call him now. You go there." Her petite body returns to her desk as adrenaline, nerves, vigor, and verve all engulf me. I didn't move a muscle. I couldn't.

Francine speaks to her husband in German. The guttural sounds of this abrupt language change her look from soft to hard. She hangs up the phone and takes a card from her desk. "I show you room now." I follow her down two flights of creaky stairs wearing worn carpet. Once in the basement, she points immediately on our right to a bathroom complete with toilet and a built-in sink with white-tiled vanity where a green pot of artificial ivy sits. The room glistens and has an antiseptic smell.

The next door in the hallway is marked with a sign that says SPA-hotel clients only, to which Francine emphasizes the information on the sign by saying I'm not considered a client. "I understand," I say, nodding. We continue down the carpeted hall to the end. She opens the door before us to reveal a white tiled room just large enough to accommodate a glassed-in shower and one white plastic chair. There are two other doors at the end of the hall, and the room closest to the shower remains closed. The next room is for me. She opens my door and a ten-by-ten-foot room dressed in hospital white except for gray carpet and drapes greets me. On my right is a plain wood wardrobe just like the one in our apartment in Gimmelwald. On my left is a sink with a three-inch wide glass shelf above it. Over the shelf is a two-by-two-foot mirror. Francine flips a switch and a light brightly illuminates the area. Before me is a king size bed with huge down pillows and comforters covered in pressed, white cotton. Wooden nightstands guard either side of the bed, and matching foot-tall lamps with plain white shades sit centered on the tables. A television hangs in the corner near the ceiling by the window that Francine opens to invite in the alpine air. "Is good for you?" she asks humbly. What I want to do is jump in the middle of the down pillows and roll in the down comforter; but I exert all my energy to keep myself collected. If she only knew that not once this summer have I slept in anything clean much less pressed. I swallow my collection and say with a giggle, "Quite nicely, thank you."

"Good," she answers, walking to the door. She hands me the key, and I follow her with the eager anticipation of a child being led into a toy store. At the top of the stairs, she points to a pegboard and says, "Please put key here each day when you go." Then she walks to the window, turns her body in the direction I am to go, and says, "Walk to water trough then go left to station. You speak to Jon. He can talk about work. Here is pass for train."

Pulling myself back from my ephemeral moment and trying to keep my feet still, I say with way too much energy, "Thank you, thank you, thank you." I practically run out the door to find Jenny sitting where I left her. "I'm going to be working in trade for a room, and I couldn't be any more excited if I owned the hotel. I can't believe it. I think I just got a job. I am staying in Switzerland! The nanny job is filled or at least that's what she said, so I asked for any type of work, and you should see the room I'm going to be in, it's white with down pillows and comforter, it has a TV, I never dreamed … I've never worked in a restaurant before, I can't even make coffee, I might get to work on the mountain—. Come on, it's this way."

"Way to go, Mom. You never know till you ask," Jenny says, hooking her arm in mine as we begin walking.

"Well, it's not for sure. It was too easy. I just asked her and she said yes. Now I have to meet her husband's approval. He's the one that needs help. I can't believe I'm going to stay here alone. Oh no, can I do this? I don't know if I can. It won't be any fun without you," I say, stopping for a breath.

"You'll be too busy to miss me. Just wait and see. I mean look at all this peace and quiet and nature."

"I've never had fun alone. I've always had someone to share the fun with. I don't know if I can have fun alone." My words continue stumbling over themselves as we walk up the street in the direction Francine had pointed. The street is a paved way wide enough for one car, and thank God there are no cars in Murren. We pass the grocery, bank, a tourist shop, and a yarn store. "Let's go in, Mom. It's a yarn shop." We enter a tiny room overcome by musty odors. Before us is one display case with three pair of handknit socks, all knit in horizontal stripes, and four solid color ski hats. On the wall to our left hangs a simple shelving unit stuffed with muted color yarns. A basket sits on the floor with several more balls of yarn. A stern woman with salt-and-pepper hair pinned in a bun at the nape of her neck, walks through a curtain hanging over the door behind the case. She stands looking, with no smile to greet us. I suddenly feel unwelcome. We both smile and say hello. Her response is akin to a grunt. "Are you open?" I ask, not sure whether to make a run for it or continue my attempts at communicating.

She answers my question with a vinegary look. "O-p-e-n?" I try more slowly this time maintaining my smile.

"Yes," she flatly replies. We quietly linger looking another sixty seconds and then Jenny says as she opens the door for me, "Thank you."

Once outside Jenny grabs my arm dragging me up the street and says, "Well, she's fun. Maybe you can be her new best friend. She needs some sunshine."

"I don't know if I'm that bold. What might she and I have in common?"

"Well, you both knit."

"True. I bet she can spew some twenty-four letter German words. She frighteningly reminds me of my ninth grade algebra teacher, who made sure I forever hated math."

"The Swiss aren't as friendly as the Italians. I want to go back to Italy," Jenny says.

The sun has cleared the mist, and we can see in the distance. I stop to admire blue thistles, four feet tall, leaning happily against a white picket fence. "Jenny, I've never done anything alone. Even that first summer I went to Colorado when I was in college, I went with a friend. What if I have an asthma attack or my heart gives out when I'm hiking? There's no hospital here. As much as I want to do this, I'm not sure I can," I say, nervous energy fueling my tongue. "There's the water trough, so we turn left here." We stop and fill our water bottles from the waterspout continuously pouring cold mountain water. "Mmm, taste this. I'd love to take this home," I say.

"Wonder how many deer have peed in this water," Jenny says, reminding us of a Saturday Night Live segment. We continue to our left, walking up a steep hill to the funicular station. "Look. This just keeps going up," I say, looking up the mountain where the train will take us, then turning around looking from where we've come. "Good grief, this place is built on a cliff! Look, it drops off and there's another village down in the valley," I say, leaning into the incline trying to keep my balance. A friendly blond, blue-eyed lady is manning the station. I show my pass and buy Jenny a ticket. We walk through a turnstile and up three steps to the first car. These cars are glassed-in and slant into the mountain. They sit on tracks and are pulled up the mountain's face via a cable that runs between the tracks. The climb is nine hundred and twelve feet in three minutes.

The car's other occupants are two couples (my age) dressed in walking shorts, windbreakers, and stout hiking boots. They are from England and not voluntarily friendly. The women have walking sticks and the men carry small packs on their backs and cameras over their shoulders. We strike as much conversation as we can with unwilling subjects. Our conversation is interrupted by a loud beep and a red light flashing by the door, followed by the door closing. A smooth jerk and we are off. Jenny and I stand holding the rail by the door, faces pressed to the glass, enjoying every breathtaking view of our three-minute ride that's practically straight up. Grazing near the tracks are five black and white very contented cows whose bells tinkle when they raise their heads to look at us. "I could never eat beef again if I looked into those soft eyes every day," I say.

"Mmm, I could eat a juicy rib eye right now," Jenny muses.

The train stops, and the doors open to two choices. Go left up the stairs and into the restaurant, or go straight and enter the great outdoors. Jenny goes straight, "I'll just be sitting out here, good luck." Once inside the restaurant, every direction I look is a different view of the Alps. The restaurant has two indoor dining areas and an open-air deck where twenty-five tables with either two or four chairs sit. The deck is at the base of a gigantic ski hill that in summer is covered in velvety green. Footpaths for happy hikers leave the deck in all directions. I stand for a moment letting my eyes brand this sight on my memory. In the distance, a gondola rises. I have the urge to run up the hill singing "The hills are alive with the sound of music," and then I remember why I'm here. I walk back inside to the cafeteria-style counter and ask a girl if I can see Jon. She smiles without a word, leaves, and returns with a man with light brown hair and blue, blue eyes. "Hello, I'm Sue Ellen. Francine sent me."

"So you vant to verk," he says, crossing his arms over a middle-aged tummy.

"Yes. I love Murren and this countryside. I've never seen anything so beautiful, and I want to stay as long as I can."

"You vash dishes?" he asks, motioning me to follow him. "Yes, I wash dishes." He takes me on a grand tour of a spotlessly clean, well-equipped kitchen that gleams from top to bottom in stainless steel counters and cook tops with wheels of cheese here and there. "You verk four hours each day? Is okay?" he asks.

"Yes, of course," I grin.

"Every day?"

"Yes. I wash dishes for four hours every day and can stay in the hotel?" I ask, making sure I understand the trade.

"Francine take you to room? Is good?"

"Yes, yes," I say, shaking my head affirmatively.

"Ok," he says. "You verk each day. You eat each day."

"Eat?"

"Yes, Chef Thomas is good cook. He prepare food and vee eat together." I can only smile. I'm going to get a meal everyday plus a bed in trade for my washing dishes four hours a day!

"Tomorrow you verk at 10:00 a.m.," he says as we walk to the counter to meet Lenka and a smiling Chef Thomas who is six foot four inches if he's a foot tall.

"Jon, I don't speak German," I say, once again humbled that they all can speak my language to some degree.

"Is okay. Thomas, Heidi, and Lenka speak little English, and if you need, you ask me."

"How long can I stay?"

"One veek or two," he answers.

"Thank you, Jon. I will see you at 10:00 a.m. tomorrow."

I run out to Jenny, who is sitting on a bench with her head back basking in the sun. "Jenny, I'm going to wash dishes. I might get to stay two weeks!"

"Really? Great, Mom," she says, jumping from her seat and matching my excitement.

"Yes, I'm staying," I say, turning around with my arms outstretched. "I get to look at this every day. Jon says I can work four hours a day and will get one meal here. I don't know whether to laugh or cry. I can't believe it."

"Mom, I'm so happy for you. This is your bliss. I can just see you doing yoga with the wildflowers."

"Look. What's that?" I say, pointing up a hill.

"Looks like one of those long horns like in the Ricola commercial. Let's go," Jenny says, once again hooking her arm in mine and walking toward the activity around the horn. A man dressed in traditional folk clothes with a black felt hat, suspenders with edelweiss embroidered on them, a white blousy type shirt, and black pants holds the horn. We join eight others who are asking questions. This horn is eleven feet long and curves to a bell shape at the end, which rests on the ground. It has no finger holes, keys, or valves, yet the mellow, reverberant sound made by this talented player will calm any nerve. As in the long-running Ricola cough drop commercial, communities used the alpenhorn to communicate with each other. Walter plays a short tune then offers to let anyone who wishes blow into the horn. A couple of college kids who obviously play horn in their schools' bands have no trouble sounding the horn. Jenny and I step up and try our lips. First try, Jenny blasts out a fine G. My first attempt fails, but with a little encouragement, I am able to succeed although my face turns bright red, and my cheeks puff like someone has blown bubbles into them. "Veensday eve at 7:30 in sports complex is Folklore. You come. I play. Is nice evening," he says.

"How many people live in Murren?" I ask.

"Is possible two hundred," he answers. "And many rooms for skiers." Later, Jon tells me there are fifteen hundred rooms for rent in Murren.

"Well, I guess I better head down the mountain," Jenny says as we part company with the alpenhorn player. A hollowness grips my gut. My palms get clammy. The dreaded moment arrives. I must say good-bye to Jenny. Separation anxiety sets in. I only remember one of my children experiencing this as a toddler and it wasn't Jenny. "Yeah, I guess," I say. *Send her off with a smile.*

"Can we just sit on that bench for a while enjoying the scenery together?" I ask, attempting to keep her near. "I need a picture of us together in the Alps." She follows me to the bench where I sit with my arm around her. "How would you describe this view?"

"Dramatic in an elegant way," she answers.

"It defies my description. How can I e-mail this back home?" I say, looking over miles of orchestrated mountain meadows in a chorus of wildflowers, half a dozen rustic chalet-type farmhouses sprinkled here and there, distant waterfalls, and snowcaps against blue sky all in perfect harmony. "Thank you for sharing this with me," I say. The land has a reverence I cannot ignore, and the experience becomes holy sharing it with someone I love. "It's interesting the feel that places give," Jenny begins. "In Italy everything is carefree, inviting. I don't feel that here."

"Yeah, in Italy things just are. It's loose, relaxed. This looks manicured, pristine."

"Mom, I need to get going. It'll take me eight hours to get to Cinque Terre."

"Okay. Let me take my pics before you run off."

As we walk toward the funicular station to go back down the hill, my mind moves into self-preservation mode. My thoughts move away from what's about to happen, to the light-hearted. *She's certainly not feeding your illusions of traveling the world together in harmony and conviviality is she? In spite of the fact that you've spent the past twenty-one years teaching her about life, you're the one who's learning now.* I snicker at the truisms running through my head.

"What's so funny?"

"Nothing."

"What are you laughing at, Mom?"

"Myself."

"Mah-ahm, tell me."

"Nothing, Jenny, it's just me. Come on. Let's get you down the mountain." There's silence between us, walking arm in arm through tiny Murren toward the cable car station. Jenny has been quiet, listening to me jabber, and hanging close keeping her arm in mine. I ride the gondola back to Gimmelwald with her. It is sprinkling again and a man takes our picture in our matching purple rain ponchos. "What if I need to talk to you?" I ask, realizing the depth of the separation about to take place since neither of us has a cell phone.

"I don't know yet. We'll communicate with e-mail until we can figure it out. I can go to Hotel Tornese, and you can call me there. We'll figure it out, or since I have a job, maybe I'll buy a cell phone."

"I have to hear your voice, Jenny, and know you're okay."

"I know, Mom, we'll talk." The car operator steps into the cable car. We hug, and her warmth fills me. *It's okay not to get frantic. Just allow this experience to be what it will be.* I step back, smile with a quivering chin, and let her go. She walks through the turnstile and boards. The door closes, and a teary-eyed Jenny waves as the gondola drops out of sight. With a heavy sigh and realizing our relationship, as I've always known it, is over, I walk to the ticket office to buy a ticket for the ride back up to Murren. "One way?" the clerk asks.

I hesitate, then say, "No, I think I'll hike." Ready to make a stronger connection with this land, I begin the fifty-minute uphill walk. I take my time, sit on every available bench, take pictures of flowers, think, cry, and an hour and a half later, the ground levels off in Murren, my new home. I'm in Switzerland, Jake's in France, and tonight Jenny will be back in Italy. I smile just thinking, *If my friends could see me now.* I have to find a computer and write home. No one will believe it when I tell them we are in three different countries.

Chapter Nineteen
Died and Gone to Heaven

Chocolate. I need chocolate. The cold dampness of the day and my sudden loneliness necessitate a cup of hot chocolate, so I stroll, looking for the perfect chocolate spot—past the volunteer fire department, grocery, bank, and water trough, to a tiny cafe called Staegerstuebli. As soon as I open the door, I'm juxtaposed to a café in Luckenbach, Happy, or Turkey, Texas, where light streams through all windows shouting, "welcome." The tables are covered with either blue or red vinyl checked cloths. Their chairs are a comfortable mix of wood and plastic. The three blue checked tables are occupied, and all occupants are involved in a spirited conversation in German. They all acknowledge me with a glance, and I return a smile. I sit at a table for four nearest the door and pick up the paper menu that luckily has a few English words on it. I do not see hot chocolate on the menu, so I ask the waiter/cashier/cook/bartender who is standing behind the bar looking my way, "Hot chocolate? Hot cocoa?" The sound of my voice interrupts the conversation. All participants momentarily look at me like my blouse has disappeared, then quickly return to their table talk.

"One?" he asks.

"Yes," I nod, relaxing to my language. Movies and opera have been my only contact with the German language, and during the five minutes I wait for my cup of comfort, visions of WWII movies come to me as I listen to the German discourse. Two burly men dressed in coveralls and heavy boots sit at one table. Another man, also dressed in work clothes, sits at an adjacent table. Seated at the picnic table is a family of four with dark-haired mother, blond father, and two tow-headed preschoolers. All four are dressed for hiking, complete with matching hiking boots, and the younger boy sports a green Peter Pan hat. The holder for the salt, pepper, and sugar has been moved to the adjacent table. I am entertained by the amount of food spread across the boys' faces, dribbling down their fronts. They carry on a private conversation rocking back and forth, giggling, playing with food, standing on the benches, beating on their chests, and swallowing their tongues in bold attempts at conquering German. Even though I do not understand a word the five adults are saying, their tonal inflections and facial expressions assure me the news never changes. The same day-to-day challenges confront people no matter their geography, and German words certainly make life's challenges sound severe.

My eyes catch 'a hearty soup' following a listing in German on the menu. When my hot chocolate is delivered, I point to the menu and ask for a bowl of the hearty soup. "One?" the waiter/cashier/cook/bartender asks.

"Yes, please." Realizing the locals are keeping a nonchalant eye on me, I give my best friendly face. The face that says, "I was your favorite teacher, remember?" or "I look like your long lost cousin, don't I?" I'm indefinably strange to them, and they glimpse at me with odd curiosity. My blond hair and blue eyes fit in, but my facial features and clothing do not. In spite of my efforts to look neutral in the way I've dressed, I am a fashion *faux pas* and it is hard for people not to look. *I wonder if I'll make any friends here. Forget it. You're here for a short time. Just eat your soup, go home, and make friends with those heavenly down pillows and comforter.* This is exactly what I do, and I am lulled to sleep by the pitter-patter of an evening shower falling outside my open window.

My first morning on the job, Jon, the manager, does not arrive until after 11:00 a.m., so Chef Thomas keeps me busy. He is six feet four inches tall and nearing three hundred pounds. He is built like a lumberjack, with a baby face and hands the size of lunch plates. He could throw a telephone pole into the next county all the while smiling, which comes easy to him. "What can I do?" I ask him. He motions me to follow as he fills a bucket with hot, soapy water, drops in a rag, throws a towel over his shoulder, and grabs a squeegee at the door. I follow him outside to the deck where he sets the bucket on the first table and says, "This," as he carefully scrapes last night's rainwater off the table with the squeegee. "Yes?" he asks.

"Yes," I smile, and then he says, "This," as he shows me how to wash the table with the rag and soapy water. Steam rises from the table in the cool morning air until Chef Thomas wipes the table dry. "Yes?" he asks. I nod affirmatively amused that this Paul Bunyan with the white apron is showing me how to wash a table. This is definitely not Italy. Same scenario in Italy would find us looking at the tables, retreating back inside, and sitting down with a glass of wine to discuss the project, but this is Switzerland, and work is important. With a swoop of his arm, he indicates I am to carry out this maneuver on all thirty-one white, plastic tables and their accompanying chairs. I begin my task, which is frequently interrupted by my standing as a statue, staring in the face of nature's magnificence. Thirty minutes later, my job complete, I go to him and ask, "What next?" He gently puts his hand on my back and directs me to a stainless steel counter with a large wooden cutting board. A cardboard box with forty or so fat, white onions sits next to the cutting board. Without a word but sure of his connection with me through eye contact, he selects one onion and shows me how to peel it with a small knife carefully taking the two outer layers off and cutting the ends from it. *I can do this,* I think. I've peeled onions before. Chef Thomas's precise handling of the knife and onion, and his delicate peeling from the onion only what is necessary, puts him in the realm with those who chop vegetables as a spiritual practice. Cooking and cleaning have been necessary evils for me all these years of housekeeping and raising kids. What's the use spending hours preparing something lavishly beautiful and romantically gourmet when the kids scarf it down in seconds and prefer peanut butter and jelly anyway? I have friends who get high reading cookbooks. I never understand them. I would rather be pulling weeds in the garden, but the kids would never eat the weeds no matter how I offered to prepare them. Chef Thomas puts the small knife down and picks up the largest butcher knife in existence. He checks in with me via eye contact and a smile, and then I must have blinked, missing his 'faster than the speed of light' demonstration. Before me are two mounds of onions, one diced and one sliced. *How did he do that?* He points to the diced pile and says, "ten," and to the sliced pile and says, "twenty." He hands me the knife that looks three feet long and says, "Okay?"

"Okay," I answer, staring respectfully at the gleaming blade. He then sets two plastic containers behind the two piles of onions and returns to his duties at the stove. I am so preoccupied with the size of this knife that I have to measure it against my arm. I place the blade's tip at my wrist, and the end of the handle meets my shoulder. I am a foot shorter than Chef Thomas, and I'm standing at a counter trying to cut thirty onions into precise sections with a knife the length of my arm! I fumble with the tool whose weight alone is daunting, and my focus is on preserving my ten fingers. My slicing is uneven and slow. Three onions into the thirty Chef Thomas sees I'm having problems, comes back, and gives me another exhibition of his slicing prowess. This time I don't blink and actually see the split second demo yielding all slices uniform in size—amazing. No words are exchanged, just smiles, as he lays the behemoth beside the cutting board. Since Chef Thomas has twice shown me how to slice an onion, I figure any attempt at doing it with precision will be appreciated.

I had damaged thirty onions when he calls across the kitchen, "Sue Ellen need eat." Hey, I like this guy. He has two plates piled to overflowing in his hands and motions me with his head to follow him. The waitress, Lenka, has arrived and together we are served. "*Danka*, thank you," Lenka and I agree. On the plate before me is a hunk of meat. I don't mean a slice or even a piece but a hunk of meat with a fried egg on top. Covering the remainder of this large dinner-sized plate are potatoes (German style), mixed with cauliflower and blanketed with a warm, creamy, cheese sauce. The meat looks like Spam but certainly doesn't taste like it, and Lenka tells me it is called meat cheese. It's great. While I eat, Chef Thomas surveys my work. The expression on his face, when he looks at the damage I inflicted on his precious onions, is reminiscent of the same look my mother had when she realized she had failed to improve my posture after making me walk around the house during my junior high years with a book balanced on my head—mild disappointment. The chef doesn't ask me to slice onions again. Without a word between us, except for an occasional mmm and lip smacking from me, Lenka and I eat everything on our plates. It is 11:30 a.m. and the first thirsty and hungry hikers of the day are beginning to line up at the counter placing their orders with Lenka.

Jon enters, has a friendly back slapping exchange with Chef Thomas, and asks me if the food is good. "Mmm, delicious," I say, patting my full tummy.

"Vee eat before vee verk," he says.

"Great." If I eat this hearty every day, hike, and lift racks of dishes, my shape will have to change. After my lunch, Chef Thomas puts me to work cutting carrots with his favorite 'sumo' knife after giving me a one-carrot demonstration. I am better with the carrots but only because I secretly abandon his knife in favor of one that is half the length of my arm.

As soon as dirty dishes are brought to the sink, I begin scraping food from them into a trash bucket. I set the dishwasher racks over the sink so I can load them and spray them with the overhead sprayer hose then put them in the dishwashers below. A steady stream of dirty pots and pans comes to me while the dishwashers are busy. These commercial pots are so huge I can get lost inside one. Jon sees me washing them by hand and he instructs me to put them in the dishwashers. "They're full," I say, pointing to the working machines.

"Vait till empty then use." I'm thinking to myself that the chef may need one of these pots before I'm able to let the dishwashers complete the task, and I have to keep him happy; he's feeding me every day. The washing cycle is thirteen minutes from the moment I push the 'on' button until the light goes off. I open the doors to rushing hot steam, grab the racks, and heave them up onto the counter, letting the dishes air dry and cool a moment so I can return them to their proper places. I follow this regimen without ceasing until 2:00 p.m. when Lenka comes to me and says, "Jon say you need make finish."

"Okay, thank you." I understand this to mean I'm finished for today, so I quickly wipe the counter, and remove my apron and put it and the towels in the plastic laundry receptacle. I can hardly move. My upper body and back are tired. My trapezius muscles are screaming at my deltoids, or visa versa. *Tomorrow lift with your legs, you nut.* I go to Jon to say good-bye, and he says, "You vant eat? drink?"

"A cold beer," I answer, half joking.

"Is all?" he asks with surprise in his voice.

"You mean I can have one?"

"You sit," he says, motioning me to the nearest table and chair with one hand as the other pours me a glass of the ice-cold golden brew. Alois, his four-month-old long-haired dachshund, looks at me from his bed next to the wood-burning stove.

"Thank you," I say as he sets the glass before me. I sit by the window looking across the deck into the vastness of this beauty and think about the five of us working here. Chef Thomas is native Swiss. Jon is from the Bavaria region in Germany. Lenka is from the Czech Republic, and Eva, who came in an hour ago to help cook, speaks German as well as Portuguese and Spanish and is from Portugal. When I leave, the sun is shining, the sky is blue, and in spite of my tiredness, I need to walk around in this gift of nature I've been given. Staying near the restaurant, I investigate the wildflowers on one of the footpaths and sit on the ground, leaning against a log to bask in pure essence. Two hours later, I drag myself to the funicular for the ride down the mountain, stop at the grocery for a couple bananas, take a hot shower, and go to bed at 7:00 p.m.

On my second day of work, Jon and Francine leave for vacation to take their eighteen-month-old, Hans, to see his grandparents in Germany. Chef Thomas is now in charge, and he keeps me busy until 4:00 p.m. most days, or until I go to him in a state of total exhaustion, at which time he says, "Sue Ellen need eat," and he offers me a dessert. Today he presents me with a five-inch-square piece of the most delicious apple pie in the world. Eva made it.

"Yummy, thank you," I say, my eyes rolling toward the back of their sockets in ecstasy. This delicacy has a hard crust spread with an apricot glaze, a layer of egg custard, a layer of sliced apples, and is topped with a lattice crust and more apricot glaze. Eva speaks no English, but I know she understands my animated compliments. She is a very interesting twenty-one-year old. She's average build with long black hair that she keeps in a ponytail at the nape of her neck. She makes little eye contact with her black eyes, and she works like a team of draft horses. I am sure she could command any army, and she can almost keep up with Chef Thomas in the slicing department. Eva never slacks and goes from one self-engineered task to the next as if each day she were trying to out-task the day before. Italy would benefit from Eva's organizational skills and work ethic. Well, maybe not. Then it wouldn't be Italy.

After work each afternoon, if it is raining, I sit in the modest hotel lobby reading anything I can find in English. Today I sit reading amid three different conversations simultaneously sounding—one in German, one in Japanese, and one in broken English. All three groups are within arm's length of each other. I don't know why I find this fascinating, but I do. I have learned many interesting facts about Switzerland whose authentic name is Confederato Helvetica. We Americans refer to their money as Swiss francs, but the Swiss call it CHF (Confederato Helvetica Francs).

Switzerland boasts the greatest number of European millionaires, and they have more banks than dentists in this country the size of Vermont and New Hampshire combined. According to what I've read, the Swiss invented vitamin pills, DDT, plastic wrap, and the modern formula for life insurance, and of course, their famous watch guts. On the days when rain is intermittent, I investigate the shops and check my e-mail at a hotel called the Guesthouse that is at the other end of Murren. The shopkeepers make little to no attempt at conversation acting indifferently to customers. I am quickly realizing how much I need human interaction. The constant stimulation of social settings tires me, but at the same time, I want to talk about what I'm doing with someone, so the experience is deepened and complete. The lady who operates the funicular is always smiling, friendly, and appears to enjoy chatting when I come and go to work, but she has not invited me to join her at any other time. I have to remember that it is my desire to make friends around the world. The people of Murren may not feel the same way. Maybe I scare them. Maybe I'm too friendly, too urgent, too needy.

I've become intimately acquainted with the small grocery store where I buy bananas, apples, Nutella, and several Lindt yogurt/apricot chocolate bars to enjoy in the evenings. Today I visit Murren's tiny bank to get some francs. A German-speaking couple are there visiting with the teller. I am not acknowledged as I walk in, so I stand waiting until the teller finishes her conversation with them. I am ignored for some time. Realizing their conversation is strictly social, I interrupt, "Excuse me." All six eyes turn to me with condescending looks. I wait while they stare at me as if my presence has contaminated the room. They continue looking at me and making comments to each other. I begin to feel very uncomfortable. The teller has not invited me to the window. What was probably fifteen seconds seemed like an hour, so I invite myself to the window, rather sheepishly, like I am doing something wrong. I give the teller my debit card and say, "Fifty francs please," to which the couple snickers and the teller smirks a grin like teenagers do, making you want to slap them. "ATM out," she says pointing.

"Oh, thank you," I say as she returns the card. "Where can I get a map of the surrounding area, you know, one with items of interest?" This is more than any of them can handle, and their snickering turns to disbelief. They look at each other and then at me like I have my head on backward or something. Suddenly I don't like it here. Feeling insulted, I back out of the bank and out of their sight, make sure my clothes are still on my body, and never visit the bank again.

On Wednesday, I attend the Folklore evening in the sports complex. It is great fun, with a tourist-friendly slide presentation of the area accompanied by the music of a local brass band, a men's chorus, and two alpenhorn players. Everyone is warm and friendly, and I meet an American couple from Chicago who are almost as fascinated by the Alps as I. At the end of the presentation, the alpenhorn players ask for three volunteers to come to the stage to play the alpenhorn. *What the heck. Go for it.* A twelve-year-old boy from Canada goes forward, a teenage boy from Germany follows him, and I am the third. We all introduce ourselves and tell where we live then take turns blowing into the horn. We are given a genuine certificate signed by Walter saying we are alpenhorn players. I walk home guided by the moon and feeling the security of mountains wrap around me, but an inner loneliness clings to me, not having someone to share it all with. There are no police in Murren; people from around the world are here; and I've never felt safer. Travel teaches us things we don't know about ourselves. I need people, or maybe I just need someone to talk it all over with.

Every day a new group of Japanese tourists keeps us frantically busy from 11:30 to 1:30. These groups range in size from twenty to thirty. Lunch at Allmendhubel is part of their package deal along with a room at Alpenruh and one dinner there. For one day and one night, they come to see the scenery, take their pictures, taste Swiss food, and then leave. The other customers who come through are hikers, trickling in four or five at a time all day long. Many of them are from England. The Swiss are crazy about the Brits and welcome them with open arms. The British are given credit for conquering these Alps. They were the first mountain climbers here and founded the ski industry. A statue of an Englishman, Sir Arnold Lunn, stands proudly in a small park by the train station, which is at the opposite end of town from the cable car. This man organized the first slalom and world championship downhill races right here in Murren. The majority of hikers are German, Swiss, and British, and the most interesting thing to me is how many of them travel three and four generations together—Grandma, Grandpa (sometimes the greats), Mom, Dad, and the kids all hiking through the Alps. The number of seventy and eighty year old hikers who hike these mountain trails with relative ease is impressive. I wouldn't doubt if some of them are nearing ninety.

The afternoons that are too rainy or I am too tired, I retire early, put on my yoga CD (a real trick, since all I have is a personal CD player) for an hour of stretches followed by a shower and TV. Mostly I watch *Mr. Ed the Talking Horse* in Italian or the *BBC* in English depending on my mood. The other options are German cartoons, German *CNN*, or American movies in German. Since even a talking horse makes Italian sound beautiful, *Mr. Ed* is usually my choice. Every night I sleep to the rhythm and sweet smell of rain, which together make the most effective sleeping pill. Rain comes rarely in west Texas, and these rainy nights affect me like drugs do an addict. As the week progresses and I lift more and more loaded dish racks, muscles are awakened in my back, legs, and arms that I didn't know existed, and after five days, I can now get out of bed without screaming.

Today while walking to the other end of town to use the computer at the Guesthouse, I stop to look out over a sloping meadow where two young chamois are grazing. I turn to leave, and behind me is a cute, petite, blond, hair cut in a short, spicy, summer style that makes her turquoise eyes twinkle. She is fresh as rain and is pushing a stroller with two darlings in it. "What cute girls," I

266

comment on her blond children, one as round as a butterball, and the other with eyes and a smile that has already stolen my heart.

"Thank you. This is Lily and Claire," she says strapping round Claire in. "Are you going to use computer? I see you there."

"Yes," I answer. "That's where I'm going."

"I am Elise," she says, pushing the stroller up the hill with ease.

"I am Sue Ellen," I say, huffing and puffing.

"I see you in hotel," she says, "but you have no room there." I have not seen her before, but she has seen me, *hmmm*.

"I'm at Hotel Alpenruh. Do you live here?"

"Yes, my husband, we have hotel."

"Great," I say happy to meet a friendly local. "Your English is quite good."

"No, no, I am French," she says, "but my husband he is from Scotland. He speak good English."

"And the girls, what language do they speak?" I say, watching Claire straining against the seat belt.

Laughing she says, "Claire is not talking. She is one-and-one-half, and Lily is just beginning to speak. She is vague," she says of three-and-one-half-year-old Lily.

"Vague?" I question.

"I speak French to them. Bran speak English to them, and their nanny speak German to them."

"Ah," I answer looking at Lily knowing she'll be tri-lingual once she gets it all sorted out. "Wow," I add, "that's a lot for a little girl."

"We have good hamburgers here," she says as we enter the hotel, "come to eat one sometime."

"Okay, I will. Thank you," I say, waving good-bye to them as I enter the computer/game room. When I check e-mail, my only connection with my world, I think back to the planning stages of this trip. I would not have come if anyone had said I would be alone in Switzerland, yet here I am, and it was my idea. Jake writes, "I have ten more days here, and then I'm coming back to Italy. I'm out of money. What are you doing?" Jenny has sent me her cell phone number with a *call anytime* at the end of her message. She writes what fun she is having working with Goffredo in Bolgheri. It feels good to hear from two of my children.

Chef Thomas continues to feed us hearty Swiss meals daily. These meals have been: pork with fried potatoes smothered in gravy accompanied by a green salad with cucumbers, red, green, yellow peppers, corn, kidney beans, and tomatoes; beef steak, baked potato with creamy sauce made of sour cream and herbs; pork sausage, gravy, and French fries; lentil soup with potatoes, carrots, and hunks of beef and sausage; a whole chicken each with rice and vegetables; and my favorite, kaseschnitte mit ei, which is a piece of whole wheat bread soaked in red wine then covered with ham, tomatoes, onions and two fried eggs on top, all floating in white cheese. The day we are each served an entire chicken (not a Cornish hen but a whole chicken), my eyes pop a ways out of their sockets, to which Chef Thomas asks with trepidation, "No?"

"Yes," I laugh in answer. "It's so big." Neither Eva nor Lenka bat an eye at the size of their chickens. They just dive in and enjoy.

My first week is up the day Jon and Francine return from vacation, and I beg, "Please, can I stay longer?" Jon smiles, opens his cell phone, and calls his wife. "Yes, you stay again one veek. Francine say she need room next Thursday."

"Yes," I say, clapping my hands. "*Sweet, another week in Switzerland.*" The restaurant runs much more smoothly when the manager is here. We all sigh and are grateful our leader has returned after a five-day absence. Jon, who is five foot ten and fortyish, reminds me of a young buck. He's German, feisty, quick, and way ahead of everyone else's game. He is one sharp guy, and each day when I arrive for work, I find him standing on the deck peering through binoculars. He hunts these mountains, and each time he sees wildlife, he gets a thrill. "Look, look," he says, pointing and handing me the binoculars. "Chamois." Another day he spots a herd of mountain goats. Chef Thomas shares in the thrill of seeing this fall's prey and the two retire to the kitchen where Jon arranges for them both two tiny mounds (nostril size) of a greenish powder and places them in the recessed area between the thumb and first finger. Together they count to three then snort this stuff while keeping their eyes locked on each other. They chase the snort by chugging a glass of tea and locking hands in a brotherhood handshake. They offer me a snort of their powder one day when they see me watching them, but I never get my nerve up to try it. Jon promises me it is nothing more than a menthol-type product that clears the sinuses, but by their looks the first second after the snort, it does everything but take the tops off their heads. I think the man with the least expression after the snort wins. Chef Thomas's eyes water and he blinks the tears away, but Jon never flinches.

One sunny afternoon, Jon asks if after work I'd like to walk home, and he would take me on a wildflower tour. Every Thursday morning at 6:30 a.m., he takes a group of tourists from the hotel on a flora and fauna hike. He has asked me to go, but I cannot get out from under the comforters that early. Two in the afternoon seems a more friendly time to enjoy nature. "I'd love to go," I answer, feeling honored that he would take his time to do this. Jon and Alois, who has to jump through the grasses on his three-inch tall legs, lead the way. I have seen edelweiss growing in pots, so I ask him if he can take me to see this national flower growing in the wild. He stops and points across to the distant mountain and pulls out his map. On the map, he shows me exactly where he has seen wild edelweiss. The terrain he's pointing to is not for the faint of heart. "You vant go?"

"Mmm, not today. I'll be happy seeing it in pots." He stops and un-pots a young edelweiss from the restaurant's deck, carefully wrapping the roots and dirt in plastic. "I veel plant, so all can see in vild." Not far from the restaurant, Jon finds the perfect spot, protected by trees and behind a fence, so the cows can't get to it. I climb the fence after him and watch him plant the young edelweiss. "Now I show edelweiss to tourists." Jon walks thoughtfully through the meadows, stopping to name every species of flower. The vast number of different flowers is nothing short of astonishing. Every meadow we come to is more spectacular than the one before. Some meadows are a single glorious color and some are multicolored. There are fields of blueberries, hazelnuts, wild roses, and unusual flowers. He points to alpine orchids, which have typically orchid-type leaves, but flowers are very different from tropical orchids. "I can't believe there are orchids in the Alps," I say.

"In two veek cows come here. They eat all herbs and flowers."

"Oh, too bad," I lament, grateful I get to experience this color before the cows devour it.

"They must eat flowers. Flowers make good cheese, so vee see flowers now, then cows eat." My thrill increases with each new field of flowers. "I find for you Man's Dream. It smell of vanilla," he says, walking bent at the waist surveying the ground before us. "I see it last veek in this area. Yes, is here. No human has eat it," he says, laughing robustly, then pointing to the ground, "Go, you must smell." I look down to see one flower with a three-inch stem.

"Can I pick it?"

"No, is just one. Is for cows to eat."

"I know," I say, "it makes good cheese."

"Yes," he answers. I lie down on the ground before the deep magenta flower and sniff. Indeed it smells like a bottle of vanilla has just been opened under my nose. "Mmm, beautiful." Here I am lying flat on the ground with my nose in the flower, and now I have to get up. I try desperately not to move like a hundred-year-old (even though that's how I feel) as my tender muscles scream at me. I awkwardly regain my upright posture, and just as I stand up I see a short distance before us, four chamois playing in and out of the trees and over a hill. These animals have an antelope-type head and antlers that point back. Their bodies are more like a mule deer's body. We stand for minutes watching them romping, then they spring out of sight. "Chamois are the most shy and human cannot get close for picture," Jon says.

We continue across a marshy area where the field is covered with white flowers that look like old, white-haired men. Jon points out what he calls *wascholder*—an evergreen bush whose berries, in fall, are blue. He says they pick the berries and cook them with the wild meat. We start up a hill and right in front of us less than twenty-five feet away stands a young chamois buck. Jon freezes in his tracks, not believing his eyes. The three of us stand like statues. Jon quietly, with no motion, takes his cell phone from his pocket. I push the 'on' button on my camera, which makes a sound, but the chamois doesn't move. He stands looking at us. He changes positions as we snap picture after picture. If I didn't know better, I'd say he was deliberately posing for us. We took three different poses of him, and then before he bounced off, he gave us a side shot. Jon looked at me and said, "You can't book that." The shyest of animals had allowed three predators close enough for pictures.

Sunny afternoons I spend sitting among the wildflowers, on the top of a green hill, at a waterfall, near a farmhouse, or gazing at the Alps while musings from the left and right sides of my brain mingle as if it were natural. I've died and gone to heaven, I just know it. How can anyone be normal and see this spectacle day after day? I take a supply of Kleenex to wipe the drool from my face since my mouth is permanently gaping in awe. In the distance, I hear the symphony that Swiss cows, sheep, and goats make. Cows wear the largest bells, sheep the medium bells, and goats the smallest bells. This is the Alps' version of the Mozart effect, and it heightens my appetite for the sounds, colors, and smells that permeate everything. Every scent that makes my spirits soar comes to me in this air—peppermint, chocolate, ripe peaches, fresh baked bread, rosemary, lavender, and rain. There is nothing more thrilling than leisurely basking in the presence of greatness. I stare at the Eiger, Monch, and Jungfrau, the three brutish, dominating snow-capped peaks before me. Nothing is as thrilling, except possibly receiving an unexpected, six-digit check in the mail from a distant relative you didn't know you had.

Chapter Twenty
Two More Weeks

"You 'vant see Schilthorn?" Jon asks as I'm cleaning the deck tables.

"I would love to see Schilthorn, but it's often in a cloud. Besides, I hear the tickets are expensive."

"I geev you tee-ket," he offers. "Someone geev it me. You vant?"

"Yes, I'd love to go."

"The view ... fantasteek," he emphasizes, taking the ticket from his shirt pocket.

"Thank you, Jon," I say, slipping the ticket into my pocket. "How generous of you." I continue my cleaning and begin thinking about the James Bond movie 'On Her Majesty's Secret Service,' where in one scene, the Schilthorn blows up and everyone skis down this very mountain. I'd love to see this as a winter wonderland. Chef Thomas calling, "Sue Ellen need eat," interrupts my thoughts, and just as we all sit down to my favorite dish, a group of fifteen middle-aged Americans converges on us. For me it was a pleasant surprise, but no one else was happy with a group this size not making a reservation and the kitchen was a little slow in meeting the demand, much to the Americans' dislike. Earlier, Jon had come to me and said, "I need you help make a terrace."

"Sure, when?"

"I veel call you." About an hour later, he came again and said, "We need make terrace."

"Okay," I say, stopping my work to follow him, but we didn't make it outside because someone engaged him in conversation, and Eva grabbed me to help an English-speaking customer with the German menu, which I can't read, so I always point to *kasechnitte mit ei*, which I can describe because it's my favorite and say, "It's the best." Thirty minutes later, I hear clapping thunder and pouring rain and see Jon scurrying on the deck trying to bring things inside. I run to help and once the shower subsides, I look at a drenched Jon who says, "Ve did not make terrace. Ve make mess." After some discussion on the terrace subject, I understand that he wanted me to help him take the condiments and trays off the tables and bring them in. He knew a shower was coming, but my understanding of the word 'make' means to create something. He said, "make a terrace," which I thought meant to set it up or add something special to what was already there. He meant we needed to put it back into a deck.

Somehow, I ended up staying until four o'clock, and by the time I reached the street, the shower had turned to mist, a heavenly mist that I loved walking in. After an hour of yoga and a shower, I decide I can't face fruit, crackers, and Nutella for dinner again, so I treat myself to a meal in Alpenruh's restaurant. A bowl of minestrone soup and a hard roll are my choices. Soup is cheap comfort food. The restaurant is busy and a table for eight is occupied with Lenka's family who have come from the Czech Republic to see Lenka, her husband, and their beautiful one-year-old, Ana. The table next to me has two young men, probably in their early twenties, a man I guess to be their grandfather, and his wife who looks twenty years his junior. They are obviously Americans and it feels like old home week listening to English without British or German accents. Most Europeans who know English have British teachers. I think I'll go home and gather a load of Texans to teach English here with a Texas drawl. I hear the grandfather telling WWII tales, not shying from the vibrant details. The boys listen raptly, and the way they look at him reminds me of my two sons as young boys sitting around the kitchen table with their grandpa listening to his WWII experiences. I eavesdrop intently, imagining my father and father-in-law sitting in camaraderie with this man, all three warriors recalling individual encounters. The gratitude I feel when I think of all those willing to serve sweeps through me, and I want to stand and sing the national anthem, but I control myself thinking there might be a better place and time.

While the waiter serves their table multiple courses and bottles of wine, I sip my soup wanting to listen as long as I can. Each spoonful of warm soup fills me with satisfaction—laced with emptiness. When I think it is probably apparent to him that I am indeed eavesdropping, I rise to leave, and on my way out, I stop at his table. The first words out of my mouth are not hello, not an introduction, but "Thank you for serving my country." Startled, he leans back in his chair joining the six other eyes at the table that are now on me. "I couldn't help hearing that you're a WWII veteran. My father served in the Navy, and my father-in-law flew a B-17."

"It was my pleasure to serve," he says, adding, "It's my country, too."

"Where do you live?" his wife interrupts.

"Texas," I answer. The conversation explodes as they tell me they are from Paris, Texas, just about ninety miles from where I was born and raised. They own a house in Murren, and for the past twenty-five years have been spending every summer here. "It's our launching pad for exploring Europe and Asia," she says. "We leave for Poland tomorrow." We continue talking like friendly Texans, but never introduce ourselves. I thank him again and turn to leave, noticing a Japanese couple at the next table.

It never dawns on me that there might be something to do in Murren at night. Really, what can two hundred residents and as many tourists do every night? Surely everyone is as tired as I am. A few evenings I take my notebook and pen and sit outside on a bench making every effort to be creative. If I can't get inspired to write in this setting, there wouldn't be any place to be inspired. It seems that every time I sit to write, the cool night air hypnotizes me, and I stare, searching the sky. No smell of summer here, no sultriness or biting insects, just the perfect writing atmosphere. I sit savoring my surroundings and cease to exist, becoming a part of my environment, yielding to a place deep within me that would love to disappear in Murren. First, my mind takes flight as I fantasize about conquering the jagged rocks piercing the sky, or what it must be like to grow up in the middle of God's palette. During these evenings devoted to meditative thought, I emerge powerful, realizing I'm doing something I've never dreamed of— living by myself in a foreign country. Then my mind goes blissfully blank, and none of my thoughts ever reach the page.

For two weeks, I've resisted buying a cowbell, but today I decide I can't live without one for my garden to remind me of this heavenly air when it's 110 degrees in the shade in west Texas, so I buy the medium-sized bell with a leather collar and Murren printed on it.

On my way to the post office to ask about shipping rates so I can mail this bell home, I jump into the phone booth just outside the post office door. This has become one of my favorite places. In the privacy of this booth, I call Jenny and spend twenty minutes at a time chattering. My words chase each other like horses on a track in an attempt to bring her into my experiences. She says nothing. I talk the entire time, reveling in the fact that my listener understands every word, cliché, idiom, personal inflection, and alliteration pouring from me at top speed. "You really miss me, huh, Mom?" Jenny says, at the end of twenty minutes when I stop to take a breath. "Wow."

"You know I miss you. I didn't think I could ever travel alone. Sharing with someone is important to me. Oh, how I wish you were here. Hey, look a tiny truck. It's the first vehicle I've seen here. It looks like a Tonka truck, and it's carrying trash bags. How cute."

"Mom, guess what?" Jenny interrupts. "Something really cool happened to me last night. Three guys were at the restaurant and when they found out I was American, they asked me to sing our national anthem. They said they love the sound of this song."

"Did you?"

"Yes, and they loved it. I think they were from Italy, England, and Scotland."

"Ohhh ... I wish I had been there. I love to hear you sing."

"I get to sing Happy Birthday from time to time, too. How much longer are you staying in Switzerland?"

"As long as they will let me. I'm not sure this makes sense, but I feel young even though my muscles ache every night. I think breathing this air day after day and being in spectacular nature, has given me back some of those years I lost when you kids took my breath away with your antics, like the time you swallowed a hearing aid battery, and I just knew it would explode in your stomach; or when Jake sucked a blow dart down his throat; or when Jarrod nearly cut his finger off the first time he used his pocket knife; or when he and I were bicycle riding, and he breezed past the stop sign ignoring my shouts for him to stop, and all I heard was screeching brakes as a truck skidded to a stop; or when you fell off the skateboard and were knocked out as a knot the size of a goose egg grew on your forehead; or when Jake ran his car up a telephone pole when he was seventeen—you know, kid stuff that makes a mother old."

"Oh, Mom."

"Don't 'oh, mom' me. Your day's coming."

"Ok, Mom. What's Jake doing?"

"Well, he's out of money. How long did he think six hundred dollars would last? He's still in France working on the organic farm and coming here soon, then I guess we'll come back to Bolgheri. That's all I know."

"Okay, Mom, well, gotta go get ready for work. I love you."

"Love you too, Jenny." Each time I talk to her, I'm as snug as a bug in a rug. I step out of the phone booth, take a deep breath of gratitude, and stand looking at the picture perfect garden across the street. It has to be hard trying to pull weeds or even harvest onions while standing on such a slope. How opposite these Swiss gardens are from a cottage garden! English cottage gardens are a bit wild in comparison to these. In an English garden, anything of delight grows together obscuring the ground giving the garden a crowded look. Swiss gardens are organized in rows, manicured, pristine, even scrubbed, cleaned, repaired, and freshly painted just like everything else here. Nothing squeaks or creaks including the post office door that is now *locked.* "Damn."

I stop to check my e-mail and send a few. Jake is on his way to Murren. "Perfect timing," I whisper to myself. Saturday is my last night here. *Sure hope he makes it by then.* He's hitchhiking. God keep him safe. I close out my computer and go to the bar to pay. Elise is working today. "Hi, Elise."

"You have been here long time," she answers. "How long are you staying?"

"Saturday is my last day," I say, handing her my money. "I'd give anything to get to come work here in winter."

"You would? We need a nanny for our girls in ski season. You would like this?"

"Are you kidding? I could spend the winter here and take care of your girls? I'd love it."

"Possibly. I will speak with Bran. You can come here tomorrow at five when he will be here?"

"I'll be here," I say as I float out the door making plans. I go straight to the phone and call Jenny to tell her, but she doesn't answer. I think I might burst with this news, so I decide to spring for a call to a friend back home until I realize it's 1:00 a.m. in Texas. The possibilities of such an opportunity swarm my head all night, and I wake tired.

Standing at my stainless steel sink with my head in a huge pot, I hear Jon calling my name. "Sue Ellen, come to meet Shannon." I follow him into the dining room to meet a pretty young girl

277

from California who has been Hans's nanny since November. We exchange introductions. "Sue Ellen veel go away Sunday, so Saturday night I make fondue for you," he says proudly.

"Real Swiss fondue," I say, licking my lips.

"Yes, and Jon's fondue is the best," Shannon assures me.

"Shannon like the hiking. She know all the paths."

"Tomorrow is my day off. We can go hiking after you finish work if you'd like," Shannon says.

"I'd love it. I get off at 2:00," I say.

"Oh, I need tell you. Tomorrow Francine say you verk her garden. No need verk here tomorrow. Is okay?"

"You mean I can weed her garden?" I say, bursting with energy.

"Yes, yes, you say you like the garden. When you complete, then you go hike. In morning, see Francine. She geev you tools. Put all veeds in corner by rhubarb plant. You cut some rhubarb and bring to me, okay? I make rhubarb pie and cake."

"Oh, I can't wait," I say, rubbing the palms of my hands together like I've found a prize.

"Have you been to Schilthorn?" Shannon asks.

"No, every afternoon when I get off, it's cloudy."

"Not today," she says, pointing outside.

"If it holds, I'll go today."

"Let's meet by the cable car at noon tomorrow. Will that give you enough time to weed?" she says.

"I don't know. I haven't seen the garden."

"It's not very big."

"Okay, I'll start early. It's so nice to meet you. I better get back to my dishes. See you tomorrow."

Realizing it is Thursday and Saturday is my last night here, I begin the dread of leaving. I've learned so much about myself and know I can function outside my comfort zone, and even though I haven't made any friends, I love the quiet uniqueness of Murren. "Jon, thank you for letting me stay so long. Can I come and work another time?"

"Uhmm, no," he says, raising his eyebrows. "You are American. My government have contract with other countries, but the USA, Canada, New Zealand, Australia, and some Eastern European countries not verk here."

"Even if no money changes hands?"

"Yes. Is not ... in the law."

"You mean what I've been doing here is illegal?"

"Uhmm, yes. People in these countries can come for university study or get nanny pass. Is all, no other verk."

"Wow, I've got to talk to the labor department when I get home. The United States needs a contract with the Swiss government. I can't believe it. Anyone can work in America. Gee, I'm an illegal alien. Thank you for being illegal with me, I guess," I say, with a puzzled smile.

"Yes, I am sorry for this. One time ve have boy from university in Australia come for three months to practice his degree in hotel and restaurant. Ve love this boy. He is best at his verk, so ve correspond to government, and ve call government and ask for him stay. Ve tell them he is best, and ve need him, but government say, no, he come on university pass, his time expire, he must return to Australia."

"Really?"

"Yes, so you see?"

"Yeah, I see, but I could be a nanny?"

"Yes, you get nanny pass. Now you go to Schilthorn," he says, looking at his watch. "Tomorrow Francine's garden."

"Who will wash dishes?"

"Me," he says, with a grin. I leave wondering why Jon and Francine let me stay and have this experience ... wow.

At half past two o'clock, I take the cable car out of Murren for the twenty-minute ride to the famous Schilthorn. For someone who is altitude challenged, hanging in a glassed-in box in mid-air does to my stomach what I imagine it would feel like if a butterfly farm sprouted inside me. This glass box creeps along and from time to time stops, causing a bouncing up and down that makes my stomach flip-flop and lodges my heart in my throat. The 360-degree view of sparkling green meadows and rolling hills outlined with Alps and iced with clear, blue sky keeps my attention, and just as I forget and look down, a lady clinging to a pole squeals releasing her own feelings of anxiety. Two college boys standing beside her grab her arms and help her sit down on the bench that is attached to the cable car's wall. "Are you ok?" One boy asks kneeling beside her.

"Maybe you should put your head down for a minute," the other says. She looks at them with stars in her eyes.

"Whew," is all she can say. The boys keep watch over her. "It's a crazy feeling when you're moving and your feet aren't on the ground. Made me dizzy," she says.

"Look up, not down," the boys suggest. She stands again and grabs the pole. "I think I'm okay. Thank you."

"Maybe you should stay seated," one boy says.

"I would miss the view," she laughs.

I could have easily frozen and stopped breathing if I had let myself. I avoid elevators and when they are glassed-in, it really makes me uncomfortable. Confined spaces make me nervous, and hanging in mid-air like this brings out my acrophobia tendencies. I heave a sigh as we arrive at Schilthorn to see Piz Gloria Restaurant looking like a flying saucer perched on top of a rock. First, I check out the gift shop where *James Bond, 007* and skiing souvenirs crowd the walls and cases, then I wander through the hallway down to the basement and watch a clip of the movie. Next, to the deck, where the thin air and mysterious sensations of being at 9,744 feet create a sort of dreamy, light-headed feeling as if I'm about to float away. I grab the rail as the wispy air, filled with a misty dreaminess and the feel of actually being above many of the peaks, overwhelms me. Enough of the out-of-body feeling, and I'm back to my comfort zone, a restaurant, Piz Gloria. I find a table next to the window. This circular restaurant makes one revolution per hour, and in the course of that hour, over two hundred mountain peaks as well as sights as far away as the Black Forest in Germany come into immediate view when their names appear on brass plates at the base of the window.

A waiter, standing tall and dressed in crisp white shirt and black slacks, approaches my table with a menu in his hand. I greet him and tell him it might take me a while, as I want to see every peak. "You remain as you veesh," he says in staccato German.

"Thank you." I graze the menu and decide that no one can ruin ice cream, so I order the "007," a fifteen-dollar creation with five flavors of ice cream topped with different fruits. Why not? *God, I wish someone were here to share with.* I begin mentally running through a list of friends I think might enjoy this with me, but none are here. I look at the tables around me to see if there might be any lonely prospects. In front of me are two empty tables and beyond them sits a woman in a suit, alone. A family with grandma, mom, dad, and three children all under ten, sit at the table in front of the lady. *In two months' time, you have talked to a lot of strangers. You wouldn't be sitting here had you not been willing to walk up to a total stranger and ask for a job. Go on. All she can say is no.* I leave my seat and walk toward the woman not believing I'm actually doing this. I would never do this back home. From the back, I can only see straight black hair to her neck, narrow shoulders draped by a celery-colored jacket, and a head bowed over the menu. *What if she's a he or a cyclops? I'll ask anyway.* "Hello," I say, smiling as I stand slightly in front and to her left. The oriental face lifts to look at me. Orientals are great with English. "Would you like to sit with me?" I ask, pointing to my table.

She answers by widening her eyes.

"I see you are alone. I'm alone, too. Would you like to sit with me?" Not sure how to read the look on her face, I then begin a form of charades. I point repeatedly from her to me and then to my table and say, "With me?" She is now intrigued and begins to smile. Either that or she's about to scream. I now get my body involved and begin to move in the direction of my table as I reach my arm toward her motioning for her to follow. It was similar to the feeling I had the first time I tried to get my horse to walk with me instead of following me. *Let's go*, is the thought. She looks at my table, and says, "Ohhh," then rises and takes her menu and purse and follows me to my table where my Texas size sundae sits.

"Beek," she says, which I interpret as 'big.'

"You speak English," I say, smiling.

"Leet-lee," she says, holding her thumb and forefinger an inch apart.

"Where do you live?" I ask, eager to get to know her.

"Yes?" She asks, with a question mark running the center of her face. I repeat the question to be met by the same expression.

"I live in Texas, USA," I proudly say.

"Ohhh," she says slowly.

"I Korea." The waiter interrupts us and asks for her order. She points to a menu entry as I take a picture of my divine ice cream topped with pineapple, mangoes, strawberries, apple slices, banana slices, and two figs. "You vant lasagna?" the waiter asks.

"Yes?" she answers. The waiter attempts, in his heavy German accent, to describe the lasagna. "Ohh, yes," she answers.

We try many times to communicate using very different English. I try extremely hard not to speak louder, only slower, but it doesn't always work. She throws out one word at a time, seemingly as bait. I feel like a dog jumping for each word, chewing it, attempting to make it into a thought. At first, she looks hopeful, but later, hopeless. I think she wonders what she's gotten herself into. We give it our best, I have to say, and I fill in the blanks understanding her to say she has business in Interlaken and wants to visit Schilthorn. After this, silence reigns between us as she picks at her lasagna. I offer her some of my ice cream, and she takes one spoonful of vanilla. I find myself fidgeting with the paper napkin, shredding it. How is it I can ask a total stranger to sit with me and then I fumble the communication? Where is Jenny when I need her? She loves language barriers. My companion and I never exchange names. Maybe that is our problem. We are two women at Piz Gloria. We both know ten English words: yes, no, go, big, move, work, boo-tee-ful, good, English, and you. That seems to be the extent of commonality. Maybe I should try to arrange the words in short sentences for her like 'You beautiful' or 'You move' or 'You work good' or 'You go big.' Who knows what she might make of that. She isn't as interested in the scenery as I, and she leaves just before one revolution of Piz Gloria is complete. "Chow, chow, you, move," she says as she leaves, with more enthusiasm than I had seen from her.

"Okay, you, too," I say, waving goodbye. What could 'you move' mean? Maybe she thinks I'm moving here or I should move here or maybe she thinks I made a good move in asking her to sit with me. Who knows? I must say I almost love my time at Schilthorn, and with this experience, I am less fearful of the language barrier.

I stop by Francine's desk at 8:00 a.m. the next morning. She asks me to sit a minute while she talks to the kitchen staff. When she returns, she leads the way up the hill to their condo-type house. She opens the laundry room door, a room separate from their house, where inside are a white washer, a beige dryer, and the biggest, red, hot-water heater in the world. No rakes, no hoes, and the only shovel I see is a snow shovel. On the floor next to the dryer are three plants and a hand trowel. New garden gloves rest on the washer. She hands me the gloves and trowel then picks up the rose bush and walks outside. I grab the potted sunflower and edelweiss. She places the flowers where she wants me to plant them. She chooses a shady spot for the sunflower. She goes back into the laundry room and returns with a little green watering can with a spout. "If you need water, go inside to kitchen," she says, handing the can to me.

"There is no faucet out here?"

"No," she says, acting a bit surprised that I think there should be. I have to speak up for the sunflower, so I suggest we find a sunny place for it.

"I want Hans to see from window," she says, pointing to the living room window.

"Oh, okay." Inspecting the yard, I find the garden runs

down two sides of the house and boasts a variety of weeds. Like everything else here, the yard has a steep slope that ends at the corner in Jon's rhubarb patch and is still ten feet above the street below. "May I have a bag? Jon asked me to cut rhubarb and take it to the restaurant." She goes into the house and returns with a paper bag with handles. "Here. Is okay?"

"Perfect, thank you."

"I must go now," she says.

"Francine, thank you for letting me do this. I love working around flowers and digging in the dirt." She wrinkles her nose and says, "Good."

I look at my tools then I go searching for an outside faucet. Maybe she just doesn't know they have one. No faucet. It is heaven. There's so much moisture that they don't have to water anything. With a hand trowel, I'm going to dig a hole deep enough to plant a rose bush and water the hole with a cute, spouted watering can. This is going to be fun! I apologize to the sunflower as I set it into the ground in the shady spot, then move to the edelweiss. To be so celebrated in alpine lore and song, it is not a pretty flower. It's a small, puffy, velvety, grayish-white spidery-looking thing with a seedy center. Digging in, I feel the earth glove my hands. This is rich, Swiss soil—moist, dark, and loose. I feel my gardening expand as I touch edelweiss and blue thistle. I'm an international gardener now! The weeds quietly yield to my touch. Several times during my two-hour weeding and planting on a forty-five degree slope, I have to grab the tall blue thistle lining the house to keep from tumbling down the hill and landing in the rhubarb patch. I make half a dozen trips into the kitchen to fill the watering can just for the rosebush. I cut the rhubarb, sack it, and stand back to admire my work. Not a weed in sight, beautiful. I return the tools to the laundry room and head to the train with rhubarb in tow. It is 10:55 a.m.

"Jon, here's the rhubarb. Did I cut enough?"

"Oh, is good."

"The garden looks great," I brag. "No more weeds."

"Francine veel be happy. She do not like her hands dirty," he says, with the same wrinkly nose as she. Now I make rhubarb cake."

"Sounds great."

"You go hiking?"

"Yes," I say, starting to leave. "Oh yeah, and I forgot to tell you I saw Schilthorn yesterday. Thank you for the ticket. I have never seen anything like that view."

"I'm glad you like it."

"Well, see you later," I say, waving.

Shannon and I walk past the schoolhouse at the end of the main street and up a path into the countryside.

"What a cute schoolhouse," I say.

"Yeah, I think it's cool how the communities share the children's education."

"How's that?"

"The kids from Murren, Gimmelwald, Stechelberg, and Lauterbrunnen all come here for their first four years of school. Then in fifth and sixth they all go down to Stechelberg. Seventh through ninth grades are in Gimmelwald, and high schoolers go to Lauterbrunnen."

"How would you like to ride a cable car to school?"

"Well, if that's the only way ..."

"In 1998, my daughter and I were in Gimmelwald, and we knocked on the school door. I'd have given anything to get to teach there. It was a one-room schoolhouse then. The teacher let us peek into his classroom. I think he had seventeen students in grades one through twelve. It was great seeing all ages together. So have you enjoyed being a nanny?"

"Love it. Jon and Francine are the greatest, and Hans is so cute."

"So how'd you get the job?"

"I was at the hostel and saw an ad, came here to Murren, and they hired me. I'll be ready to go back home by December even though I'll miss them and especially little Hans."

"Oh, my gosh," I say, stopping to stare at the intimidating view before me. "You have to forgive me. I'm probably older than your mother and I need to stop every now and then, plus I get terribly distracted by this scenery."

"No problem," twenty-four-year-old Shannon says. "You haven't seen the best yet. That's where we're going."

"I appreciate you letting me go hiking with you. I haven't walked deep into trees or too far away from voices by myself. I'm afraid of getting lost."

"This is what I usually do on my days off. Who wouldn't?"

"Really." We walk through wooded areas and wildflower-strewn meadows for a good forty-five minutes. "I applied to be the next nanny when I saw Francine's ad in the hostel, but she said they had already hired someone."

"Yeah, they hired a guy for next year. Hans will love that. He's all boy."

"Do you know Elise?"

"Yeah, and Bran?" she asks.

"Well, I'm going to talk to them this evening about the possibility of coming back for ski season to be their nanny."

"Cool. You'll love it."

"I don't know if I could actually stay here a whole year. I mean I take care of my eighty-eight-year-old mother who has dementia. I know I'd love it here and all, but I've never done anything quite so drastic, but we'll see. It sounds like great fun. Have you been to Italy?" I ask changing the subject.

"No, I haven't been to Italy, but I've been to Denmark, Germany, and Switzerland."

"As a group, they aren't as open and welcoming as the Italians," I say, expecting her to disagree. "I've been lonely here. They're painfully reserved."

"Yeah, you have to work at it. It's too bad we didn't meet

sooner. You could have gone with me to Guesthouse. That's where everyone meets in the evenings."

"I wish I had, too, but I've been so tired at night," I say, having to turn up the volume on my voice with the sound of water getting closer. "This is Murrenbach," she says, as we cross a bridge and continue into the woods where I have to grab trees to help me up the incline.

"How do you know where you're going?" I ask, seeing nothing but trees.

"I've been here many times," she says.

"Tell me about you back home."

"I live in California. I have one brother who travels a lot and has stayed in Denmark this past year. He found a girl he couldn't leave. My parents are the greatest. I finished school a couple years ago, and I've been traveling some, too, and then fell into this job for a year. Just over this hill, and we'll be there. And you?" Between huffs and puffs trying to keep up with this youngster, I spit out an extremely abbreviated version of my life as an adult. "Do this as long as you can. Once you settle into real life, there's no escaping," I advise.

"So I've heard." Shannon, who has been leading me, steps to the side, and with a smile on her face and a wave of her arm, she says, "You first." I step past her then pass through a thick foliage overhang feeling the deafening roar of water. I look back, and she's standing watching me. She waves me forward, and I continue. A mist kisses me, and my next step takes me into an enchanted fairyland. To my right is a curtain of falling water. An old path goes under the falls and around the pool. The sun's rays filter through a tangle of vines across the mist, hanging little rainbows and lighting the wildflowers that dance on the earthen wall. Tears well in my eyes, my heart lightens, and I feel something open inside me. A few minutes later, Shannon joins me. Words are not audible, so we stand—she smiling, I awestruck.

Pulling myself together after this experience is difficult. I feel like I have escaped from somewhere or something. "We'll take a different route back," she says. Not knowing what to say, I resort to the familiar. "Is tonight fondue night?" I ask, "I'm hungry."

"No, I think Jon said Saturday. Have you ever been to the restaurant inside the station?"

"No. I've eaten fruit, nuts, crackers, and Nutella in my room most nights. Can you go to Guesthouse for a burger tonight?" I ask, hoping for the company.

"Sure."

"I'm supposed to meet with Bran and Elise at five. It shouldn't take long. 6:00?"

"Yeah." Waterfalls, cows with tinkling bells, a secluded house, fragrant meadows, wildlife, and a summer shower all accompany us back into Murren.

My senses overloaded, I retreat to my room to think and take a shower, and then at five I meet Elise. "Where's Bran?" I ask.

"He is at home with girls. We go now," she says, walking out the door, up the hill, and around a corner to their condo with a sunny living/kitchen area downstairs and two bedrooms up a very narrow stairway. "Bran," Elise calls up the stairs. "Sue Ellen is here." A tall, handsome Bran speeds down the stairs and greets us, smiling. "Come in and sit here," he says, directing me to a rocking chair in the sunny room as Lily comes to me like she's always known me. The younger, Claire, with fat red cheeks chooses to hang back with her pile of toys and watch. The next thirty minutes is a two-way interview. I have a million questions for them about the nanny job, and they want to know as much about me as possible. "You are the perfect nanny. An English teacher for my girls," Bran says, almost as excited as I am about the prospects. "I will begin the work for your documents right away."

"I'm probably leaving Sunday or maybe Monday, but I can always call you."

"Good. Come by before you leave." By now both girls are in my lap. Lily is trying to explain a drawing of hers. "She is learning three languages," Bran says. "She is confused."

"That's okay. She'll figure it all out and be tri-lingual," I say as Claire rolls onto the floor.

"Elise will take you to see where you can live," he says, snatching Lily from my lap and tossing her in the air. I say good-bye to the girls and follow Elise back to the hotel chattering about how exciting this is. Four winter months in Murren! We walk through the kitchen and laundry rooms, through a swinging door, and up two short stairways to a hall full of rooms that remind me of a hospital ward in a 1940s war movie ... old tile floor, white walls, and rooms close together. "This one is empty," she says, unlocking a door. When she opens the door, the bottom falls out of my dream. In this white room is an army cot covered with a white comforter, a white, metal, free-standing cabinet that is two feet wide, a white, wooden, straight-backed chair, and a small oval mirror over the chair, all in a six-by-seven-foot room. "Ohhh," my voice slides downward. Looking surprised at my reaction, she says, "This is where all the help stays. It is three hundred francs a month."

"*Three hundred francs?*" I gasp.

"You can stay another place, but is difficult to find an empty room in winter season and very expensive."

"Oh," I say, taking in a breath. "I just wasn't expecting something so small. Uh ... and the bathroom?"

"Down the hall," she says, leading me to a room that we had to step down into. *Keep your mouth shut. Maybe you can find something different.* In this afterthought of a room is a metal shower stall, toilet, and sink (all white), a gray, concrete floor with a drain in the center, and no mirror. How badly do I want this experience? "How many people share the bathroom?" I ask.

"Oh, six or eight."

"Boys and girls?"

"Ye-e-s-s," she says slowly with a puzzled look on her face, like I'm speaking a foreign language and she has to think about it.

I'm too old for this.

Chapter Twenty-one

A New Travel Partner

Our conversation over burgers is mostly subdued with outbursts of excited anticipation. I'm still wrapped in the soft feeling that came over me as I stood at the waterfall in the enchanted forest while simultaneously rhapsodizing the possibility that I might be a nanny for four months this winter caring for two Swiss angels. Ultimately, my fiery excitement over the nanny job wins out. "Would you like to see where I live?" Shannon asks. "It's down the mountain."

"Sure. I've never been down Murren's mountain, only up."

"Well, let's go," she says, jumping up.

Shannon lived down, down, and down through part of the residential section.

"Where are we going, Stechlberg?"

"No, not that far. Here we are." Shannon's house rests on a small plateau. "Six people live downstairs, and I live up," she says pointing to the ceiling, "and this is the common kitchen."

"Nice." We climb the narrow stairs to a short hallway with a bathroom on one side and a huge bedroom on the other. Wooden pegs covered with Shannon's scarves, jackets, ski hats, and coats hang on the bare wood wall at the end of the hall. "Wow, this room is huge," I say looking into the bedroom.

"Come on in. Yeah, I'm really lucky. It's big enough to have visitors. My parents have been here, my brother came one time, and my parents are coming back in two weeks."

"Have you ever housed backpackers?" I ask.

"No, but I could." I survey this huge room with plenty of empty floor space even though a king size bed sits against one wall and an inflatable mattress the size of a full bed is on the opposite wall. Multi-paned wood windows look out over the mountain's steep slope. The windowsill is covered with various vines and candles. "This is nice, Shannon. Elise showed me where I would stay if I come back this winter, and ... it's scary it's so small."

"You mean one of those rooms upstairs in the Guesthouse?"

"Yeah."

"Yeah, I've seen those."

"So how'd you get to stay here?"

"Jon just told me I was living here."

"He's great isn't he? Lots of fun," I say. *What if Jake doesn't get here this weekend? Do I dare ask her?*

"They really are nice people."

"Uh, Shannon," I pause, "my son is coming sometime this weekend, but I don't know when, and tomorrow night is my last night at the hotel. If he doesn't get here until Sunday, could we spend one night with you before we head back to Italy?"

"Sure. You and I can share the bed, and he can have the mattress."

"I checked with the hostel, and they are booked solid all weekend," I add.

"Oh, yeah, they're always booked. No problem. You can stay here for a night or two."

"Thanks. That's a relief." I smile as I think about the yellow card that's propped up on the ledge over the sink in my room.

My last day at work, Jon prepared an American type brunch complete with bacon, eggs, orange juice, and German-style hash browns. It was a beautiful Saturday, and a festive air permeated the restaurant. A folk band was to play on the deck for three hours. This was a monthly Saturday event, and visitors flocked to take part in the Swiss musical brunch. The extra business kept me in the kitchen, too far away to hear the music. *I wonder if Francine was pleased with my weeding. Maybe I can weed around the hotel, too.* This energized thought created such a diversion that I hardly knew when I was heaving dish racks in and out of the dishwasher. There was never a break in the flow of dishes coming to me, so I missed the party on the deck, and the musicians were long gone when I left at four.

Only Jon and Chef Thomas remained and were engaged in their daily ritual of snorting 'menthol' and chugging tea. "You vant?" Jon asks, tempting me with the green powdery snuff.

"No thank you." I look up at Chef Thomas and thank him lavishly for the mouth-watering, hearty sustenance he has prepared these past three weeks. "Ah, Sue Ellen need eat," he says, with a grin spread across his baby face.

"Come to Texas sometime, and we'll ride horses."

"You have horse?" he asks, with a surprise on his face that makes him look like a ten-year-old boy.

"Well, I know some people that do."

"Yes, I like," he says, pretending he is galloping on a horse, to which Jon spits a sentence in German, and they both laugh. "You come to Texas anytime, okay?" Turning to Jon, I say, "Thank you again, Jon. I have enjoyed being here. You and Francine gave me something I've only dreamed about. Please bring Francine and Hans to Texas."

"Oh, Texas, yes, yes, someday ve come to Texas," he says, not at all convincingly.

"I would love to show you where I live. It is very different from Murren. Just don't come in summer. It's too hot." He extends his hand to shake mine and says, "You are velcome."

"Hope you guys are here the next time I come to Murren."

"We veel, we veel be here. Tonight the fondue," Jon reminds me.

"I'll be there." I leave, not believing this three-week experience.

Why would they do this for me? Have they ever before let a wanderer barter for a room? I leave trying to calculate the odds.

During the three-minute ride down the funicular, life in Murren occupies my mind. Murren's children have an extreme vulnerability about them, even the teenagers. How could they not, living day to day in poetry? This is not the real world. Have they ever breathed big city's air or endured its noise or smelled the stench of vomit and urine in the French Quarter while on family vacation in New Orleans? Where do they go on vacation? To the mountains? They are all Heidis!

When I get back to the hotel, Francine is at her desk. "Francine, did you like the garden after I weeded? Is there anything else I can do?"

"Yes," she says. "It is fantastic."

"Oh, good. I've noticed a few weeds outside here. Would you like me to pull them? I have a few hours before Shannon and I meet Jon for fondue." Her eyes sparkle as she steps from behind her desk. "You want pull more weeds?"

"I'd love to."

"The gardener is away to vacation. Come, we find gloves." I follow her just outside to a tiny metal shed filled with 'things,' and among the things are a pair of gloves, a watering can, and a hand trowel. She digs a little further and says, "And here is sack for weeds. When you complete, put sack here."

"Okay, thank you." I begin work in the small, terraced rock garden at Alpenruh. A foggy mist has settled over Murren, and I think about my good friend, Rachel, back home in the blazing sun, weeding my huge garden for me, wishing she were here to enjoy the cool.

Jon makes the fondue but is too busy to join us, so Shannon, Hans, and I sit down to his special recipe. The warm, soft bread torn into bite-size chunks absorbs the fondue like a sponge. At the risk of sounding like a food slut, my first taste is nothing short of orgasmic. I didn't know cheese could taste or feel like this. "Mmm, how many different cheeses are in here?" I ask licking the creamy drip off my finger.

"I'm not sure, and he won't give me his secret. Do you taste wine?"

"I don't know. It's so ... mmm ... divine. We Americans just think we know what Swiss cheese is," I say savoring the next bite. "Yum, my idea of comfort food is changing." We sit dipping, relaxing, enjoying, and talking until thirteen-month-old Hans can't take it anymore. "Maybe Francine is home now," Shannon says. "This little guy needs to go to bed, huh, Hans." Hans rubs cheese over his right eye and through his golden hair. "Yeah, we need to go. If you need to stay at my place tomorrow night, just come to Jon and Francine's house. I'll be there till nine."

"Thanks, Shannon. I'm getting a little anxious about Jake getting here."

"Don't worry. He'll make it," she says as she walks off pushing Hans in the stroller. 'Don't worry' rolls out of young people like gumballs from a machine.

Sunday morning I stuff into my pack what I haven't shipped home with the cowbell and leave my room, permanently. I'm once again a roaming backpacker. With no electronic connection to Jake, all I can do is wait. I go see if Elise and Bran are working, but they aren't, so I visit a couple of hotels, asking locals about the availability and cost of a room a little larger than the institutionalized corridor Elise offered. I am told during high season there are more workers than rooms. I am convinced that if I found something larger for the same price or if I find anything at all, it wouldn't be in Murren.

"Hi," I say, to the funicular operator. "I have to say good-bye. It's been nice meeting you."

"You leave?"

"Yes, but I might get to come back in winter."

"Yes?"

"Yes. Do you know Bran and Elise?"

"Oh, yes, and girls."

"I might get to be their nanny this winter. I'm really excited. Do you work in the station all year?"

"For the season, I teach to ski."

"Wow, you do? What fun. I always wanted to be a ski instructor."

"For fourteen years I do this," she says.

"Well, maybe we can ski together if I come back."

"Ok," she says as we wave good-bye. I knew I should have been a ski bum in Colorado when I had the chance. Then on my days off from nannyland, I could teach skiing. I'm going to be a nanny. Everyone thought I was nuts to come backpacking at my age; what will they think now? Which children's books should I pack to read to the girls? I'll pack Jarrod's favorite, Richard Scarry's *Big Book of Words*; Jake's favorite, *The Hungry Caterpillar*; and Jenny's most-loved *The Cat In The Hat*; and then my favorites, Tomie de Paola's *The Art Lesson*, and The Berenstein Bears books.

For the remainder of the day and into the night, I sit near the cable car station waiting for Jake. Before 9:00 p.m., I go to Francine's to tell Shannon that we do indeed need to stay with her for tonight—at least one of us. "Come to Guesthouse. I'll probably be there," she says. "Tell you what, just take my key. If I'm not there, go on up to my room. I'll get someone else to let me in if the door is locked."

"Are you sure?" I say, taking the key. "Thanks."

"See you later," she says.

I sit outside the cable car station watching the sunset. The stars come out then quickly disappear into light rain, the kind that smells sooo good. I go inside and plant myself in a recycled gondola car that is now an Internet point. Fifteen minutes costs the equivalent of six dollars. I step in and sit for a minute. *You better not. You've already paid twenty dollars for computer use today. You know Jake's out of money. It's July 22. You have another six weeks, and you know you'll have to help him or he'll just go into credit card debt. Better he than me. He's twenty-four, I'm fifty-six. He has longer to pay the debt. I'm not using my card. This trip is not about having fun in the conventional way. It's about everything else. Gee, I hope he's not on the last gondola of the day.* I sit watching six people walk through the station, then I wander around looking at pictures of Murren's history encased in a glass display on the wall. On another wall hang the first skis and boots. "Excuse me," I say to the lady closing the tiny gift shop. "When does the last car arrive?"

"At 23:54."

"Thank you." *Grand, midnight. Come on, Jake, get here.* I move to the bench outside with my back to the station and sit hugging my pack thinking about the past three weeks meeting my new independent self here alone in Murren. The air is heavenly, and the stars are once again dazzling. I sit wondering what the remainder of the summer will bring. Will Jake and I travel together? Will Bolgheri still hold its charm? Will I run out of money? Will I master Italian? My peripheral vision picks up movement. Jake walks past with his oversized pack bowing his back. I jump to my feet dumping my pack on the ground and call, "Ja-kie." Jake holds a very special place in my heart. I remember melting when I first saw him. Of my three children, he is the only one born in a natural birthing setting, away from the sterile white and bright lights of a hospital delivery room. It was Easter Sunday morning in 1981. A bed, a rocking chair, and a desk all of dark-stained oak furnished the cozy room. The only light streamed through brightly colored pieces of glass in a large, stain-glass window of the Madonna and child. Then around eleven o'clock, as my labor reached the intense phase, a cool breeze blew, and soft rumbling thunder announced a storm, but no storm came, only soothing rain accompanying a gentle new soul to this world. When Jake was born, he wasn't swished away to be weighed and measured; in fact, he wasn't even cleaned, rather the nurse and doctor made a quick assessment and swaddled him in a white cloth, laid him beside me, and left. Undisturbed, with Jake at my breast, we two lay in that bed for the remainder of the day, his hand resting on my chest melting my heart. The light rain lulled us both as we went in and out of sleep, then at 7:00 p.m., my doctor returned asking if I was ready to go home. Carrying my bundle, I walked to the nursery where Jake was cleaned, weighed, measured, and given his first physical. Then we went home, and here he is twenty-four years later with me in Switzerland looking like a flower I forgot to water, wilted. "Oh, hi, Mom," he says casually, as I swing my arms around his neck gripping tightly. "I'm so glad to see you. My Jakie boy is here! I can hardly believe it. You look great."

"I haven't eaten in two days," he says.

"What? Why?"

He pulls a twenty-euro bill out of his pocket. "This is it," he says, with a hapless look. "I might have needed it for transportation."

"Well, you made the six hundred dollars last two months. You did good. Come on, we'll find something to eat," I say, slinging my pack over one shoulder. "So, how'd you get here?"

"Hitchhiking and trains. I'm not too good at the hitchhiking thing."

"I'm just glad you got here alive," I sigh. "You're going to love this place. It really is unbelievable. Yesterday was my last night in the hotel, but I found us a place to stay with an American girl. Maybe she'll let you take a shower. I just hope we can find some food for you. The grocery is closed. Oh, Jake, I'm so happy you're here." Jake is reminded why he left to travel alone—too much talking. I have trouble shutting up, but he looks so pitiful, and I know I am exhausting him more, so I walk quietly beside him hoping he'll talk. He doesn't.

We find Shannon sitting in a round booth with two women and a man, all drinking beer. "Shannon, he's here. This is Jake."

"Hi, Jake."

"Hello," he says with the first smile I've seen from him tonight.

"Shannon is letting us stay with her."

"Great."

"He very tire," one of the women says with a heavy accent.

"Yes," Jake says, loosening the pack's belt and letting it slide off his back onto the floor. "Ahhh," he says, adjusting the muscles in his back.

There were pretzels, nuts, and crackers sitting on the counter at the bar. *Great. A cracker can arm a gluten intolerant's intestines.*

"Do you know any place that has food this late? He hasn't eaten in two days," I say as Jake shoots me one of those 'I'm not a kid, Mom' looks. I'm anxious, watching Jake grab handfuls of pretzels. We could be in for an explosive night.

"I don't know, but we can ask Karl," Shannon offers, scooting off the bench. "Hey, Karl, is there any food left in the kitchen?"

"Uh, ve have bread and ... pasta."

"Cold pasta, Jake?" Shannon asks.

"Sounds great," Jake says. *A bowl of pasta, crackers, pretzels, and peanuts are sure to get his gut.*

At midnight, we three are walking through darkness to Shannon's place. "Would you guys stop? I have to get my flashlight. It's too dark for me." Jake and Shannon, now conversing about life as twenty-four-year-olds, stop and wait for me to get my flashlight out of my pack. "Okay." We continue down the steep path that sometimes has steps built into it and sometimes is just plain un-level earth. We follow Shannon upstairs where she acquaints Jake with her place. "Sweet," he says. "A teapot." Jake is a connoisseur of tea and carries at least ten different loose teas and the paraphernalia to steep them with him. A look into Shannon's small bathroom promises that a female who loves a generous variety of aromatic shower gels, shampoos, body lotions, and soaps lives here. A hot shower, a soft bed, and a heavenly breeze through the window take the three of us away at 1:30 a.m.

"Can we leave our packs here while we hike today?" I ask Shannon as she's walking out the door at 7:00 a.m.

"Sure. What's your plan?" she whispers.

"I want to take Jake up to the restaurant, and hike around a bit, just whatever."

"Okay, well, I'll be working. Not sure when I'll be off."

"Thanks for letting us stay."

"No problem."

"Keep in touch," I say.

"Okay, and I'd love to hear about the rest of your summer."

"I put you on my e-mail list, so you'll get the same updates everyone else gets."

"Great, later," she says, quietly closing the door. I lay, taking up as much of the bed as I can, enjoying the cool morning, and wondering when Jake will be willing to get up. I get dressed, write in my journal, re-organize my pack, and then it happens. "Oh good god, Jake. Okay, it's time to get up," I shout. "Jake, get up, you're polluting the room. Time to go."

"What?" he grogs.

"Good grief," I gasp. "Thank God Shannon's gone. Okay, I'm outta here," I say, making my bed. "Don't leave a mess, and don't forget to fold your blanket." He hates it when I talk like a mother, but I figure it's payback for blasting me out of the room.

After visiting the restaurant on the mountain, we hike through the velvety ski slopes that appear to sprout emeralds along the trail, moisture clinging to their surfaces. We stop to rest at farmhouses so sparsely scattered they look as if they were thoughtfully placed for hungry, thirsty hikers.

"People live in these houses and offer skiers and hikers a rest," I say as we look into one of them.

"*Willkommen guten morgan*," a stout man says, motioning us into the entry room that has been converted to a little dining area with three, small, round tables and chairs.

"Do you live here?" Jake asks.

"Yes, eez my home."

"Do you have rooms for rent?" I ask.

"Vrooms?"

"You know, rooms for travelers."

"Ah, no, no, no vroom, ve have food. You vant eat?"

"No, thank you, we just wanted to look. Thanks for letting us. It is very nice," I say as we turn to go and the cuckoo clock's bird darts out just above Jake's head surprising him as he instinctively ducks down. "Oh, the cuckoo," the man laughs. "Is hard verk the cuckoo. You must valk about look for the cuckoo," the man laughs, ducking his head looking around as he tip-toes along.

"Yeah, you gotta watch those cuckoos," Jake jokes.

"Well, thank you," I say, waving and barely able to hold my laughter at the man's antics.

Just about the time we get too far away from the house to take shelter, a single cloud surrounded by blue sky opens on us. Jake begins singing a song without words as he dances along the path in the downpour. "What are you singing?" I ask, running to catch up. He ignores me and continues entertaining us both. "Ja-kie."

"I don't know what it is. Something I heard in the train station," he shouts, lifting his arms to the sky. His feet leave the ground in fluid, rhythmical movement as he negotiates, with finesse, a rock in the path. "Jake, you're good," I say. "Don't quit. Dance all the way to Murren. I love it." The one time I tried simultaneously dancing and singing was the only community theater production for me. I was in the parents' chorus of *Bye Bye Birdie*. I spent weeks trying to get my feet to do particular steps while synchronizing my voice and the director wanted me to execute this in perfect harmony with the seven other adults in the chorus. I never was comfortable dancing and singing at the same time. It's harder than it looks.

"Jake, you're poetry in motion."

"Wasn't that a song back in your day?"

"Yeah."

"Who sang it?"

"Johnny Tillotson," I shout.

"Cool," he shouts, while executing some swift Lindy hop moves.

The rain shower came and went for fifteen minutes then the cloud drifted away. "Want to go to Gimmelwald?" I ask.

"What's Gimmelwald?"

"It's the next village over. We can hike there. Remember the book and movie about Heidi?"

"Uh, no."

"Well she lived in Gimmelwald, this very place."

"Okay, Mom." I hate it when my kids say that to me, like someone's pulled the wool over my naïve eyes. We walked through a herd of contented cows all looking for the perfect wildflower to eat so their cheese will be the finest. "Can you take my picture with a cow?" I ask.

"Pick one." I walk carefully down the slope toward the caramel-colored cow with white spots but can't keep my footing when my right shoe hits a rock, and down I go. I look up into the eyes of two indignant looking cows. "Jake, help me," I call, wondering if I'm going to meet my end right here. "Just get up slowly. They won't hurt you." I get up the hill as fast as I can. "I'll just stand near this one," I say, pointing to the cow now standing in the middle of the path. Jake aims the camera, I smile, and the cow looks disinterested. "Okay, now I want a picture of just my feet sticking up with flowers between my toes and the Alps behind them."

"Okay," Jake laughs. We spend the next thirty minutes finding the perfect wildflower patch with the right slope so we can stage the picture without my head or body in it and with the Alps as a background. Digital cameras are the greatest.

It is 6:05 p.m. when we get to Gimmelwald. The hostel is hopping, and dinner is ready. I order two beers and a pizza, hoping it's enough to fill Jake and give me a piece. "Great pizza," Jake says, taking a mouthful. "I met a guy who said we have to go to Naples. They have the best pizza in the world there. The place is called Trionon."

"Really?" I say, not sure I'm willing to go to Naples for pizza.

"Yeah, he says you can't describe it. You just have to go eat it."

"So tell me how France was. Did you like working on the organic farm?"

"I guess." (Jake makes me work for every bit of information he gives me.)

"What do you mean you guess? You either did or you didn't."

"It was boring. I picked raspberries all day, every day."

"For two weeks you picked raspberries? That's all?"

"Sometimes I planted lettuces, but the food was good, and I had a place to stay."

"So is it a day-to-day deal?"

"No, you sign up for two weeks."

"How many others were there?"

"I was the only one. The guy had to get local help because there weren't any volunteers.

"Would you do it again?"

"Probably not. I just kinda fell into it, and it was something cheap to do for two weeks. You'd like it."

"So did you see anything else?"

"The lavender fields. Pretty cool."

"How'd you get to the lavender fields?"

"This Couch Surfing lady took me."

"So how was the dancing?"

"Not much was going on."

"So what's your plan now?"

"I don't know. I don't have any money. I guess I'll go back to Bolgheri. Maybe I can get a job like Jenny, or maybe I'll just travel some more and put it on my credit card."

"Ooo," I wince. "You don't really want to do that, do you?"

"Yeah, I think I do." Not wanting to think about this, I get up and make my way through the tables of happy hikers to the counter. "Do you have any beds tonight?"

"No, no beds."

"How about the hay barn?"

"No, all full."

"Okay, thanks," I say, looking at Francine's ad for a nanny that is still on the wall to the left of the counter. Hope Shannon's up for another night.

"Do you still have the yellow card?" I ask Jake as I sit again.

"Yeah."

"Do you ever read it?"

"No, why?"

"Just wondered. Well, it's too late to leave tonight. Let's go find Shannon," I say.

We hike back up to Murren and go straight to Francine's where we find Shannon visiting with them. "You didn't make it out of town," she smiles.

"Yeah, we had fun wandering around in heaven all day. Can we stay again tonight?"

"Sure."

Tuesday morning, we dawdle around town and get off late. On our way to the train station, which is at the opposite end of town from the cable car, we stop at the Guesthouse hoping to see Bran and Elise. Bran greets us.

"Hi, Bran, this is my son, Jake."

"Nice to meet you," they exchange in unison.

"We're leaving today. Do you know anything yet?" I ask of the nanny pass.

"Yes, it is not so easy. I spoke with the government, and they say you are too old," he says in his Scottish-German-French accent.

"Too old?" I blurt. "In the U.S. we call that discrimination."

"Yes, they say the nanny pass is for seventeen to thirty years old. I tell them I want a mature nanny, and they say sorry. Then they say if I want an English-speaking nanny, I must advertise, then if none answers the ad, I can ask an American from seventeen to thirty years. I tell them you have raised three children, and you are a teacher, and this is what I want for my children. It is the government. Then if the English-speaking nanny does not know German, I must provide lessons in German for her while she is here. It is not so easy."

"Darn," I say, feeling like someone just let the air out of me.

"I say to the government, 'You mean you want me to trust a seventeen-year-old with my young children when I can have an experienced mother?' They say, 'Yes, is the law.' It is disappointing, but I will continue to see what we can do."

"Well, thank you for considering me," I say, trying to keep my spirits up.

"You can e-mail anytime or call," he says, giving me his card. "We will see."

"Well, thank you, anyway. You are welcome at my house in Texas anytime. Is Elise here? I'd like to say good-bye to her."

"No, she and the girls are in Interlaken today."

"Please tell them good-bye for me."

"I will. Be in touch."

"Okay," I say, walking out the door.

"What's that about?" Jake asks. "A nanny?"

"Yeah, doesn't it sound fun? I would be here during ski season."

"What about Grandma?"

"Well, I'm not sure, but someone is keeping her now. I guess I could do that again." Unlike Jenny, Jake isn't interested in discussing the possibilities to death, so that was the end of that conversation.

We take a train that winds us down to a funicular, which drops us into Lauterbrunnen, at 1:15 p.m. We emerge from the funicular station and walk into the bus station that is nothing more than a crowded ticket counter. "Hey, look, Mom," Jake says, pointing to a colorful ad for underground waterfalls.

"Oooo, pretty," I say, glancing that way while asking about tickets.

"Wanna go?"

"Uh, not really. We need to get to Italy."

"Train is more fast," the clerk says, pointing toward the station. "Bus make many stops."

"Okay, thank you," I say, deciding fast is what I want since I know it will take six or seven hours to get us anywhere near Bolgheri, Italy.

"Are you sure you don't want to go?" Jake looks at me with the same eyes I saw that Easter morning.

"You want to see underground waterfalls?" I ask.

"It looks interesting ... for seven francs. It's early. We can still get to Italy." 1:30 is early in the day unless you are facing waits in train stations and a seven-hour train ride that will get you no closer than twenty minutes from where you really need to be. I guess I haven't entirely embraced the concept of drifting from place to place. I keep saying I won't mind sleeping on a park bench while all the time trying to avoid it.

"Okay. You might as well spend your money today as tomorrow," I shrug. I'll just walk around town.

"You're not coming?" Jake asks as he turns to leave.

"No," I say, feeling a little guilty that Jake wants me to go, and I'm not. "I think I'd rather be outside than underground, so I'll just blend with the tourists here. Meet me at the train station."

"Okay," he says. Well, that was easy. Jenny would have challenged me making sure I understood that I'd probably be sorry if I didn't go, that I'd probably never get another chance to see several underground waterfalls, or that it wouldn't be fun without me, but Jake simply says okay.

While Jake boards a shuttle that will take him to the underground entrance, I walk the people-happy street of this touristy town, where a plush, green mountain shoots straight up from the sidewalk on one side, and on the other side a giant waterfall thrusts its wet power into a watery snake that winds in, out, and under tourist traps and everything else in town. I buy a new wash cloth to use as my sweat rag, then I visit the hostel that has no available rooms but whose desk attendant is able to transfer the pictures on my camera's memory card to a CD, and then I sit breathing the last of this air. Jake returns at 2:45; we buy tickets to Interlaken and sit—waiting. "Sooo, tell me about it." Jenny would be giving me all the details whether I asked or not, but not Jake.

"It was good."

If I could think like a man, I would probably be thinking, 'you didn't want to go see it, why would you want to hear about it' but I don't think like a man, so I prod.

"Good? Jake, a little more please."

"Well, the tonal quality was different from outdoor waterfalls.

It was lower. I took a bunch of pictures and recorded the sound. "Here," he says, handing me his camera. *Tonal quality?* I think.

We board a train with BOB (Berner Oberland Bahn) written across its side. There are only three cars pulled by this engine. It's a narrow gauge that connects the smaller towns of the Berner Oberland district to Interlaken. The train slowly pulls away from the station and keeps a constant speed, approximately that of a ninety-year-old running along beside, when suddenly it jerks to a stop in the middle of a wildflower-strewn meadow. We start again, lurch forward, pick up speed, then jerk to a stop. This time we passengers smell an undeniable odor of something electrical burning. A third time the train jumps forward, but can't build speed around the smoke rising from the tracks. I wait for panic to ensue, which is inevitable in these situations in Italy, but no one runs screaming down the aisle, and we all remain in our seats peering out the windows. Unlike the drama that is part of everything in Italy, here everyone knows the Swiss authorities are in control— all is organized, and all will be executed precisely. Sure enough, we nineteen passengers are systematically (car by car) brought to stand in the field beside the smoking tracks. The Swiss, in their perfection and stern work ethic, are not happy with themselves when something goes wrong. The BOB personnel apologize profusely for any inconvenience to those of us standing amid the wildflowers enjoying the alpine breeze on our faces. During the twenty minutes we stand by the tracks waiting for a replacement train, calm rules, and by the time we board the new BOB train, we hope to soon have another such experience.

In less than thirty minutes we are in Interlaken where we make a quick trip to the counter for tickets back to Italy. We are told that TrenItalia employees are on strike. Trains haven't been running for the past six hours, but we can get as far as Milan on the Swiss train. "Who can say," the clerk begins. "In Italy the trains go for an hour and not go for an hour then go again. Who knows?" It'll be fun getting back to good old Italy where food and wine are more important than whether or not the trains are running. "Okay, Jake, we have an hour," I say, looking at the huge Swiss clock on the wall. "What do you want to do?"

"Can we eat?" he asks.

"Yeah. What do you want?"

"I don't know."

"Well, ask your stomach what sounds good," I say as we face the traffic in an attempt to cross a busy street.

"I don't care," he says.

"Are you sure?" I ask, knowing Jake will say he doesn't care, but when I walk into the nearest café, he'll ask (with a tone of 'you've got to be kidding'), "Pizza?" or "A sandwich?" The closest option is a sit down restaurant, so we whip in and sit down. Then comes the task of Jake getting through the menu. Everything sounds good to him, and he has trouble choosing. It's almost as if he's afraid he'll never get to eat again, so this is an important decision and cannot be taken lightly. I suggest, "Since we only have an hour and we have no idea how long it will take them to cook something, let's share a sandwich or—"

"A sandwich?" he interrupts.

"Well, something quick."

"Why are you worried about time?"

"The train leaves at 5:50; it's 5:00 now, and we're not at the station, nor have we ordered."

"It's just over there," he says, pointing down the street. I consider myself a pretty laid-back person, but next to Jake, I appear tight as a drum. He will live forever. He simply doesn't get his blood pressure up over anything.

"So what'll it be?" I ask, prompting him. (Jenny by now would have narrowed the menu including appetizers to two things, pointing out their merit or unworthiness as possible options.)

"Okay. How about spaghetti and meatballs," he suggests.

"Sure. I'll just take a couple bites."

"*Haf vu decihh?*" The waitress says quickly running her French-accented English words together. "So, how are the spaghetti and meatballs?" Jake inquires.

"Dey goot," she answers. "Sah-lat?"

"???"

"Sah-lat," she says again. "Dee kar-rote, let-toos, ohn-yone," she says slowly.

"Oh, salad," Jake says. "Yes. I'd like a salad." Luckily, Jake eats fast. When she brings our food, we have exactly twenty minutes to get on the train.

Chapter Twenty-two

Italy Again

The Swiss train snakes us down and around the Alps into that mystical region where Italy kisses Switzerland. Deeper into Italy, the wealth of northern Italy with its high fashion and serious business is obvious. It hardly looks like the Italy we have come to love. We arrive at Milan's Centrale Stazione at 12:05 a.m. with no place to stay. "Okay, Jake, we have to decide whether to get on the Metro and go to the city center where the cathedral is or stay in this area. Do you want to see the cathedral?"

"I saw it when I came through on my way to France, but I could see it again."

"It's pretty cool, and a little scary the first time I saw it. It's so Gothic, or should I say Goth." Jake smiles at my attempt to be cool, but doesn't say anything.

"If you don't care, I'd rather get a room near the station so we can hop a train in the morning to Cinque Terre."

"Okay." We exit the station and are met by the hot, sticky, smelly, night air—a shock to my system after three weeks in cool, clean Murren. "Ohhh, I can't wait to take a cool shower and go to bed," I say. "When I'm dirty and sweaty, I feel ten pounds heavier."

"Yeah, but don't you want to walk around awhile?" Jake asks.

"Walk around? At this hour? No, I don't want to walk around. I'm hot and tired. I need a shower," I sigh.

"Okay," he says. We walk through the exit and start across the parking area toward the street. Coming toward us is a middle-aged woman, very thin, a cigarette dangling from her mouth. She is wearing a short black skirt (much too short for her age), a shimmering, gold, silky, sleeveless blouse, five-inch, black-patent, stiletto sandals, and slung over her left shoulder is a huge black-patent bag. Her black hair is done up in a fancy doo held together by gold clips and hairpins. Her lips are bright red. She sports three-inch-diameter gold hoop earrings, and her eyes are covered with black, rectangular, Italian-sized glasses. Prancing at her feet is a black miniature poodle with a rhinestone collar and red bows in its hair. Both pooch and mistress have painted red nails. "They must be going to a posh-pooch-pageant," I say.

"That's not your standard dog handler's uniform," Jake answers.

"Really. Have you noticed how many dogs over here are off leash?"

"Yeah, and they never run off."

At the edge of the parking lot, we pass what appears to be a couple of fifty-plus-year-old prostitutes. "You've got to be kidding," I laugh, shaking my head. "Somehow I thought menopausal women would be doing anything at this hour but hookin' it, wow. Okay, which way should we go?"

"That way," Jake chooses randomly, and we both veer to the right.

"Jake, we're the blind leading the blind—in the dark," I laugh. We end up strolling two city blocks before walking into a hotel.

"Are you sure you don't want to look around?" he asks.

"It's nearly 1:00 a.m. No, I don't want to look around," I say. *You've got to be kidding, Jake.*

"Okay. Just thought we could see Milan at night. I've seen several cities after midnight. When I arrive late and don't have a place to stay, I just walk around until daylight. It's a good time to see the statues, fountains, and outdoor stuff. No one is around and the sites are lit."

"You've been walking around foreign cities after midnight? Alone? Jake, I didn't need to know that. For the life of me, I don't remember saying things that I knew would shock my parents."

"I kinda enjoy it. I mean no crowds and no money, so it works for me," he says as we enter a hotel.

"*Mamma mia*, Jake," I say, rhythmically moving my hand like the Italians do.

"This looks nice," Jake says, noticing the clean, florally decorated lobby. Approaching the desk, I say to the man behind it, "*Una notte per due per favore.*"

"*Tre cento euro,*" comes the reply.

"*Quanto?*"

"*Tre cento,*" he repeats.

"Three hundred?" I gasp. "*Grazie,*" I say turning on my heel and walking back outside. That's four hundred dollars! Okay, let's keep trying. I have to have a cool shower tonight."

"You can cool off in a fountain and it doesn't cost anything," Jake suggests.

"Maybe next time. I'd love to write home that I played in a thousand-year-old fountain. They'd have fun with that one," I muse.

"Since it's nearly one o'clock, maybe they would give you a discount if you ask," Jake says.

"Good idea." We enter the next hotel that doesn't opulently greet us. At the desk a man sits with his head on his hand dozing. "*Scusi, signore.*" With a start, the dark-haired man jumps to his feet and waltzes to the counter. In a sing-song voice he says, "*Buona notte, signora e signore.*"

"*Buona notte,*" we answer.

"*Una camera?*"

"*Si,*" we nod.

"*Cento novanta euro,*" he says with a smile. We whisper to each other about the amount, 190 euros. The man takes a white card from under the counter and asks, "*Si, una notte?*"

Jake and I both look at our watches and make an attempt in

Italian to get our point across about the late hour. Then Jake says in English, "Hey, man, the night's almost over."

"*Che?*" is the man's response. Once again, we point to our watches and say, "*A ... la ... una.*"

"*Si, si, alla una,*" the man responds with an even broader smile. *I think he's playing with us.*

"*Si, a la una e io ... non ... pago ... cento ... novanta ... euro ... per ... sei ... ore, non possible,*" I say, extremely proud of myself for formulating a whole sentence even though my delivery of it was less worthy. He watches Jake and me working on our next sentence, which focused on the word, *sconto*, then he says, "Ah, you want discount, *sconto.*"

"You speak English," I say surprised.

"*Un po,*" he says.

"Look, we'll be getting up in six hours." He turns the registration card to face me and says, "Ok, discount *per la signora, novant'nove euro.*" I think about this number and say, "Ninety-nine euros?"

"*Si,* okay, you sign and leave pass-a-port." I pay the ninety-nine euros, leave my passport, and we take the elevator to the third floor. "It makes me nervous to leave my passport with a total stranger. At home, they just ask to see your driver's license. What if I go to leave in the morning and they can't find it?"

"It's just different here. Don't worry." To the right of the elevator, we enter Room 301, a small, clean room where two double beds, covered with heavy dark green spreads to match the heavy floor to ceiling drapes greet us. The bathroom is a clean black and white tile with fresh, white, terrycloth towels hanging. I drop my pack on the floor and fly through the shower. What happens next is a new experience for me. I leap into the bed and fall asleep before my head hits the pillow. I don't even hear Jake as he showers, but somewhere between galloping my horse on the beach in southern France and becoming a sculptor in Italy, my dreams are interrupted by Italian spewing from the television. "Jake!" I say with a start.

"Sorry, I didn't know it was turned up. Thought I'd watch TV. I haven't seen one all summer. Thought you were asleep."

"I was, oh, Jake, I was," I despair.

"Sorry, Mom." His comment 'I thought you were asleep' says it all. Once Jake is asleep, nothing wakes him. One spring he slept through a tornado taking everything out of the backyard. Just today, he slept through the starting and stopping of the train with all the noise of people getting on and off. He doesn't comprehend that some of us don't sleep all night just because we *go* to sleep. He'll get it in twenty years. He promptly mutes the TV, and I hide my head under my pillow.

We sleep till 9:00 a.m., pick up my passport on our way out, and grab a piece of focaccia at the station. "I think this is good timing. If we leave on the next train, we'll get to Cinque Terre by noon," I say, looking at the departure schedule hanging on the station wall, as Jake eyes three mini-skirted girls talking so fast they create a breeze as they pass. "So that'll give us time to get a room."

"Any Hospitality Club or Couch Surfers there?" Jake asks, bringing himself back from his mini vacation.

"One in Monterrosso, and if I remember what Piero said, he's out of town until sometime next month. Have you enjoyed the HC and CS people you've stayed with?" I ask.

"Yeah."

"Uh, can you elaborate on that?"

"Yeah, I enjoyed them."

"Great elaboration, Jake. I love staying with people. It makes me feel like I'm a part of Italy and not just visiting."

"Yeah, it's … didactic."

"Yeah," I smile.

We board a crowded train and walk through three cars before we find empty seats. Thirty minutes into our ride down the tracks, the smell of smoke wafts through the open windows. Five minutes later, we are stalled in the middle of nowhere. On our right is another set of tracks, and on our left is a weedy earthen wall climbing up and up. With the breeze blowing our way, smoke spills into the car, choking us, and we all scramble to close the windows.

The two Italian women facing me begin chattering intermittently tossing their heads and arms in typical Italian gesticulations. I smile at them. *You've got to learn Italian better so you can actually carry on a conversation.* Jake gets up and disappears. I think he is going to look out the door, but he doesn't return, and when I look around, he is nowhere to be seen. There's no telling what he's up to. Across the aisle from me is an older man from Boston. Six seats away is a young man from the San Francisco area. Our language melts us together, and we begin exchanging travel tales. The three of us are not as concerned with what's going on as our Italian counterparts. "This is good," the young man from San Francisco says, pulling a worn, brown, leather journal from his pack and beginning to write. "It makes good journal writing." Beads of sweat form on my forehead and quickly arrange themselves into streams that promptly flow down my face, stinging my eyes. I assume an announcement will be made, informing the passengers, but the evidence around me insists that such an assumption would be foolishly optimistic, for all hell has broken loose. The commotion escalates, and the expected messenger runs through our car shouting, "*fuoco, fuoco.*" He is followed by three uniformed TrenItalia personnel taking turns running back and forth through the cars like chickens that have lost their heads. This unseemly behavior by authorities offers no comfort to the travelers. Many of us attempt asking the authorities pertinent questions as they race past totally ignoring the patrons, but this is Italy, and it will all end as abruptly as it begins.

The heat quickly overcomes everyone, and we open windows and look in the direction of the smoke to see billowing, black clouds barreling from the train's engine. Twenty minutes later, the fire department arrives and dispatches four strapping young firemen, dressed in gray uniforms, with red canisters strapped to their backs. They form a line and run toward the engine heroically extinguishing the fire. I walk to the train's door that has been opened to see if I can get a look at the firemen but am told no one can exit. A train speeds past on the tracks parallel to us rocking our car for seconds and taking my breath away. I'll remember not to stick my head out on that side! We sit in the heat as our bodies become more aromatic with each passing minute. I count eighteen people in this car. An ambulance arrives and parks on top of the earthen wall, poised to take any who may have expired in the stifling heat. Still no sign of Jake. In the meantime, the three train personnel continue running through the cars in panicked theatrics shouting Italian into their walkie-talkies. We are stuck on the tracks for two hours when the Green Cross finally arrives (same as the American Red Cross). Green Cross workers, carrying cases of bottled water, enter the next train car. There is hope that we won't die, although heat stroke remains a possibility. The Green Cross official carries a case of bottled water into our car and sets it on the floor. In a heavy Italian accent he says something to the effect that only the weak or sick can have the few bottles of water. All of us rush to him with arms outstretched to receive our bottle of one hundred degree water.

I wonder where Jake is. What could he be doing? My fellow victims and I become acquainted with each other while we wait. There are a dozen Italians, two of whom speak some English; three Americans, two of whom know enough Italian to be dangerous; and teenage triplets from Brazil. We have an entertaining conversation focused on the fun e-mails we can write home about this adventure. We engage the Italians in what conversation we can, and soon half of them join in and are having a good time, attempting their English. The other five or six Italians are pestering their watches, wiping their brows, and repeating *"Oh mio Dio"* or *"mamma mia"* as a mantra while moving about in their seats. I learn that TrenItalia is privately owned and the Italians are sure that is why it is inefficient. They think the government could do a better job! Ha! I want to ask them if they have visited their post office lately. *Oh, mio Dio.* On this particular week, there has been a two-day train strike and a couple of two-hour strikes as well. The explanation the Italians give is that TrenItalia has few employees to do much work. I guess everyone wants to work for the government, which leaves few for private industry. I think the Italians in our car were favorably impressed with us as Americans since they constantly made comments about how happy we were in spite of the heat and delay. Jake returned just before the replacement engine pushed us to the nearest station. He had found someone to loan him a book to read, and that's how he was passing the time. The whole ordeal complete with pictures of the firemen spraying the engine made the papers the next day.

We finally reach our destination, Manarola, at 4:00 p.m. Good luck finding a room this late. The summer's heat is taking its toll on me, and I am happy to shell out a couple hundred euros for two nights' stay high on a hill in an efficiency that overlooks the Ligurian Sea. For two days I nap, sit on the porch sipping cold beer, watch Jake swimming below, write in my journal, and daydream. On our second day, Jake decides to rent a mountain bike and tackle the mountain trails between the five towns of the Cinque Terre. As a child, Jake never cared much for bike riding, and he is not your average tri-athlete or exercise guru, except on the dance floor. Mountain biking may require a finesse his dance moves may not have given him. "Have you ever gone mountain biking?" I ask.

"No, but it sounds fun."

"Yeah, I guess it would be fun, if you like extreme exertion in ninety-eight percent humidity and one hundred degree temps," I say, handing him a twenty-euro bill.

I am sitting on the porch enjoying the salty breezes on my face and watching the activity in the tiny harbor, when someone climbs the steps and walks through the wrought-iron gate that leads to a second flight of stairs ending at our rental. Who could it be? Jake's only been gone four hours. I look to my left. "Jake?" I ask, staring in disbelief at the shirtless being before me.

"Yeah."

"What happened?" His shorts are torn, and dried blood covers his body. "Oh my god, what happened to you?" I cry. The flesh on his arms, chest, and legs is sliced like he has been whipped with a razor strap. Then he turns around to expose hundreds of bloody stripes crossing his back. Thorns and slivers open the skin, even on his face. "Jake, what happened?" I whisper trying to control my desire to scream.

"I fell off the bike."

"It looks like someone's beat the crap out of you."

"Yeah, a bush."

"A what?"

"I fell in a thorny bush, and together we rolled down the mountain."

"Oooo," I flinch. "Are you okay?" I grimace as I begin picking out slivers and thorns.

"Well, I guess," he answers.

"There's so much dried blood. I could see better if you'd shower and clean it off."

"Okay," he says. He emerges from the shower looking cleaner but no better. I spend the next hour hovered over him removing foreign objects from his back then soaking his wounds in the lavender oil I have carried all summer. For two more days, pieces of thorns work their way to the surface and present themselves for plucking.

"Jake, you need a good meal." A bright look crosses his face. "Yeah, you need a good meal. Do you feel like going to Vernazza?"

"Sure." We walk through town to the station and hop the train for the mile ride down the tracks to Vernazza. We arrive just before sunset and sit at a charming sidewalk café on the main plaza. Huge colorful umbrellas shade us from the setting sun. "Anything you want, Jake."

"Anything?" he says, looking fascinated with the menu. In Italy, you are encouraged to spend an hour pondering the choices. Everything on the menu is in Italian, so Jake asks for an English translation. What followed was an elegant description in not so elegant English of the most mouthwatering entrees on the menu. "*Signore*, you make accident?"

"Yes, and the mountain won," Jake replies.

"You make accident with mountain?"

"Yes, well it was a bush."

"*Signore*, I no understand the boosh."

"Yeah, I made an accident with the mountain," Jake says, making it easy.

"Oh, is no good." We both smile at the man's concern, and Jake says, "But I think this will make me feel better." He chose a plate of *fruiti di mare* or fruits of the sea.

"Is *perfetto*. You like it," the waiter assures, kissing his fingers and closing his eyes in bliss. I ordered a green salad, bread, and a glass of local white wine.

An eternity passes before the waiter brings the entrée. Textures, colors, aromas, and flavors possess this plate of pasta topped with five different sea critters, a red herbal sauce, and, of course, a generous amount of *olio di virgine* (virgin olive oil). While I munch my salad and sip my wine, I thoroughly enjoy watching Jake savor every bite. "You want a taste?"

"No, thanks. I'm not fond of critters and things in the middle of pasta al dente."

"Mmm, it's harmony," he says.

"I guess it takes a cuisine hound to enjoy digging in shells for a tiny bite of meat."

"Mmm, ambrosial," he says, entertaining me with single word descriptions of each bite and its unique flavor.

Jake moves rather slowly on the way home. The impact of rolling down the mountain and his now-compromised skin have created stiffness in his young body. We stand a minute gazing over the watery abyss illuminated by the waxing moon. I rub more lavender oil into his wounds, and we retire to be swayed to sleep by the hypnotic sounds of the sea. At 1:00 a.m., I bolt straight up in bed, awakened by loud rock music blasting over a PA system. I bound out of bed, open the door, and step out on the porch that overlooks a section of concrete big enough for fifteen or twenty people to stand gazing out over the sea. But, tonight on the concrete are a drummer, a guitarist, a bass player, a spotlight, two large speakers, and twenty-five or so teenagers dancing, shouting, and cavorting.

I check my watch to make sure I haven't done the impossible, like oversleep, and sure enough it says 1:00, and the moon is out, so it's a.m., right? For the next two hours, I vacillate between sitting on the porch, with my earplugs in place, watching this early morning party, and shutting the door and lying on the bed listening to Jake snore against the music. What is it about paying for a room to sleep in and not being able to sleep that is so annoying? Am I missing something here? *You can sleep tomorrow. No, I can't.* By the time the band has packed up and left, it is 3:45 a.m.

We leave the Cinque Terre with a ticket to Lucca. On the way, we pass Carrara, where Michelangelo walked into the mines and handpicked the marble for his masterpieces. Hunks and slabs of various-sized, white marble lay in stacks and piles along the road for miles around this mining town. Looking at the setting around Carrara and imagining Michelangelo walking in the mine and thoughtfully choosing the perfect piece of marble for the David helps me feel connected to it all. It's an awesome feeling.

Lucca, a charming and equally beautiful town, is our next stop for a few hours. Lucca is surrounded by a two thousand-year-old, well-maintained, fortified wall. It is Italy's only city that is still completely surrounded by a wall. The history of Lucca dates back to biblical times, with the claim that Lucca's first bishop was St. Peter's disciple. Back in its day, Lucca was known for its fine silk, and then Napoleon came through this prosperous town and decided to give it to his dear sister as a gift. Later the gift was passed to Marie Louise, Napoleon's wife, who is given credit for turning the fortified wall into a lovely city park, one of Lucca's main attractions. The number and size of Lucca's beautiful trees is extraordinary and shade abounds. The plazas and streets are clean, and I would love to return when I have money to stay. "Let's walk around the wall," Jake says in answer to my suggestion that we get to the station.

"Our train leaves at 4:59. Is that enough time to stroll around two and a half miles?"

"Why is there always a time schedule? If we miss this train, we can take the next. I thought we were on vacation," a frustrated Jake says.

"I just want to get back to Bolgheri where I won't have to keep spending money. I'm running out! You go ahead. I'm dragged out. I can't face a two-and-a-half-mile walk in this heat. I'll go on to the station."

"Okay."

"Jake, please don't miss the train."

I stroll back across the street from Lucca's center and look in a couple of stores on the way. Maps, books on dusty shelves, pocketknives, and key chains hanging on racks clutter one store, and men's clothing, in an equally uninviting setting, the other. I plant myself on a bench just outside the station next to the tracks to sit and watch people. A tall, blond woman, nearing fifty, with a cased guitar slung over her shoulder walks up to me and asks if I know whether she has missed the train to San Gimignano. I did not know about that train but told her the one to Pisa was to leave in twenty-five minutes. "Where are you from?" I ask.

"Bakersfield, California," she says smiling. "And you?"

"Texas, Lubbock, Texas."

"Are you traveling alone?"

"No, my son is with me. And you?"

"I'm alone. I came to visit a friend in Milan. I stayed a week with her, and then I went to Sweden to visit another friend then decided I wanted to explore Italy more. I love it here."

"Yeah, I know. I'd love to be able to see it all. Here, sit down," I say, moving over. "I came with my daughter and son. We've been staying in people's homes. It's a great way to travel."

"I've been sleeping on benches and in a church or two," she says.

"By yourself?"

"Yes."

"You're brave. You aren't afraid?"

"No. So far I've felt pretty safe. Last night I slept on a bench in

320

that park out front. At two in the morning, a man tapped me on the shoulder and asked me if I was okay and did I need any help. When I told him I was okay, he left."

"Wow, I probably would have run away screaming," I admit.

"This trip has been an eye opener. I'm stretching myself, trying to get outside the box and learning to do things just for the delight of it. I think I could sleep on a bench if I had to, but not by myself. Have you been singing and playing to people in parks or train stations?" I ask, pointing to the guitar. At this moment, a voice comes over the loud speaker announcing, in Italian, the train to Pisa is delayed twenty minutes. We smile at each other. "Did you understand that to say *ritardo* twenty minutes?" I ask.

"Yeah, that's it."

"You gotta love Italy. There's no place in the world where romance is gauged by decay, age, disrepair, and lack of schedules."

"Yeah, they say, 'Hurry? What's that?'" she laughs. "You asked about the guitar. I wish I didn't have it, but my friend in Sweden asked me to bring it. I thought I was going home after visiting Sweden, but now I have to carry it around, and I'm sorta just staying day by day. I guess when I get tired, I'll go home."

"I admire you for being able to go it alone. I'm not that brave, yet. Although I did stay in Switzerland alone, but I was in one town and had a room. I have learned how little I can live with though. It's been two months, and I haven't even wished for anymore than what I have in this pack." We spend the next twenty minutes talking about what we've learned of Italian culture. How the relaxed atmosphere extends to morals, too. How freeing no judgment is. How only in Italy does a man's mistress accompany his wife to his funeral. How Italy has produced great art and science minds but has never become a major power. How Italians think the world is corrupt because they have lived for centuries in their own world of disorder, disaster, and fraud where monks and priests conspire with the Mafia. "Yeah, I guess they figure they can't trust anyone or anything," I say.

"But their senses," she laughs. "Italians are the perfect example of how to enjoy the moment," she adds.

"And … here is my son," I say. "Good thing the train was delayed twenty minutes."

"Hello," a breathless Jake says.

"We never introduced ourselves. My name is Sue Ellen."

"I'm Kath."

"This is my son, Jake. Kath is from California."

"Nice to meet you, Jake. And your daughter?"

"Oh, she got a job and is working in Bolgheri."

"Bolgheri?"

"It's tiny, but worth the trip. It's near Cecina, which is on the Tuscan coast not far from here. Bolgheri is mystical," I say dreamily. "She got a job ten days after we arrived. Luckily her boss let her travel some, but he told her she had to be on the job by July 15 when things get really busy."

"She came for vacation and got a job? Wow," Kath exclaims. At this moment, our train pulls up. "Why don't you come to Pisa with us?"

"I've been there and want to see a few specific places, then I better get back home," she says. We say good-bye without exchanging contact information, which I have always regretted.

We arrive in three-thousand-year-old Pisa at 6:00 p.m. and board Bus Number Three to make our way to Pisa's main attraction, the Field of Miracles. "Look, Jake, it's exactly like the pictures," I say, marveling at the leaning tower. "Let's walk through these streets close to the sights and see what we can find." Knowing that landing a cheap place to stay is a roll of the dice, we begin by walking past the main sights and into the back streets. Tonight we're in luck. We find a place three blocks from the leaning tower for forty-eight euros (approximately sixty-five dollars), and after climbing three flights of stairs and tossing our packs into the tiny hotbox room, we set off to find a pizza. "How do they figure that a ceiling fan on a twenty-foot ceiling is going to help any?" I laugh.

"Power of suggestion," Jake answers.

"I love the way you think, Jake." We wander around, stopping to look over street vendors' wares and end up sitting at a sidewalk café on a delightfully cobbled street with the leaning tower in perfect view. Being in the presence of the tower is fascinating to me. I don't know what I thought it would look like, but it looks exactly like the pictures I've seen all my life. Except in the pictures there aren't any people climbing it and right now people are swarming it like ants. "I want to climb it," Jake says. I put my hand on my money pouch, which has dwindled to the point it is flat. "What's it cost?"

"I don't know."

"Fifteen euros," the man on our left says.

"Really? That's twenty bucks," I say. "Forget it, Jake."

"It's actually pretty fun," the man adds, "because it's leaning."

We get back to our room at 11:00 p.m. Jake has trouble going to sleep so early, but he manages. Thank God, he doesn't insist on staying out late. I don't think we are the best travel partners. Since leaving Switzerland, I have been low on energy. The heat saps my life force, and I think the demand on my body that the three weeks in Murren made keeps reminding me that I am fifty-six. Jake is often reticent, and I like to talk about everything—more than once. I remember last Christmas when we were all together, Jake was lively and talkative, and he entertained us all. He was so happy and open, but I'm seeing a different Jake now. Maybe the heat bothers him and he doesn't know it, or maybe he's reached the age that he's embarrassed that his mother is paying for everything. No, that's not it.

The next morning we take our time getting around since we don't have far to go to reach Cecina. After posing for pictures staged to look like we are holding up the leaning tower, we tour the cathedral, baptistery, and Jake climbs the tower. I've seen so many cathedrals that they are blurring together. They are all beautiful works of art, but one doesn't stand out from another anymore. For me, the most fascinating thing about Pisa's cathedral was the bronze incense burner that hung from the ceiling, a replica of the original. A young Galileo, sitting in Mass, watched the burner swinging as a breeze moved it. Instead of listening to the priest's homily, Galileo was studying this pendulum's movement. He timed the swings and discovered that the burner swung back and forth in the same time in spite of the arc's width. What he learned in church that day, he put into theory and paid dearly for it. The Catholic church did not appreciate Galileo espousing science that contradicted the church's view. Unfortunately, the tasteless kiosks of junk that line the street thirty yards from the buildings cheapen the Field of Miracles' experience. There is no way to get in or out of the field but to walk past them. We board a bus, get back to the train station, and buy tickets to Cecina. "I hope we can get there before Goffredo goes to Bolgheri for the evening. Otherwise we won't have a ride and nowhere to stay," I say as we board.

"Can't we walk?"

"It's twenty miles. I guess we could walk, but I'm not sure I'd make it."

"We can hitchhike," Jake suggests.

"Yeah, maybe, but I thought you said you weren't too good at the hitchhiking thing, and I've never done it except when we left Bolgheri to travel last month. We had to get a ride from Bolgheri to Cecina to catch the train. Jenny stood in the middle of the road under the arch while I stood off to the side. I figured they'd come nearer stopping for her than me."

"Don't short yourself, Mom."

"Well, thank you, Jake."

Chapter Twenty-three

Bolgheri

Why did we plan this trip for the three hottest months of the Mediterranean calendar? I think to myself as I pull my sweat rag out of my pack. *Oh, yeah … Jenny, the fountain of youth, planned this trip. I can't wait to see her.* Jenny's energy always rubs off on me like a shot of adrenaline. This respite comes at just the right time, and as Goffredo drives us through the cypress-lined way and under the arch into tiny Bolgheri, my muscles relax and my lungs fill with sweet air. Bolgheri is now home, and it's good to be home. Candles shimmer amid flowers and vines crawling up stone walls. Ambience, Italian-style, cascades down the street trickling into every nook and sidewalk cafe. "Thank you, Goffredo," I say as I open the car door, get out, and pull the seat forward to let Jake out of the back. "I can't wait to see Jenny."

"Yes, she work," he answers.

Jake and I find the apartment key in the stone urn just outside the door. "This is where we live. Can you believe they leave the key outside?"

"Wow, it's big," Jake remarks as we enter.

"Yep, Jenny lives here," I say, looking around to see a purse spilling its contents on the heavy oak table, two lip liners and a tube of mascara lounging on the antique china cabinet, and a pile of clothes in the only easy chair. "Bedrooms are upstairs."

"Cool," Jake says, looking around.

"Your room is at the top on the left," I say, dropping my pack as Jake starts up the brick steps to the second floor. "I'm going around this corner where Jenny works," I say, pointing. I climb the street's incline that levels as I round the corner. Two of Bolgheri's grandmas sit under the sprawling three-hundred-year-old *quercia* (oak) as they do each night at this time. "*Buona notte*," I say, waving to them. They respond in kind and nod.

"Mom, you're back," Jenny says, running to me.

"Oh, it's sooo good to see you," I say, wrapping her in an octopus hug. "How are you? Are you having fun here?" I ask, even though the answer is written across her smiling face.

"We'll talk later. I have to work now. Where's Jake? Can you help me take down later?"

"Sure. Jake's checking out the apartment. What time later?"

"You know. Ten or so."

"Okay, later." Her delicious energy makes me giggle. She couldn't keep her delight in adventure or her love of life off her face if she tried. She sees sunshine, rainbows, and pots of gold in everything.

I wander around, re-acquainting myself with the shopkeepers who greet me with less enthusiasm than when I first came to town. Maybe summer is bearing down on them, too. Then I see Lina. Lina Serini, Bolgheri's matron, scurrying up the hill in her pale blue shirtwaist dress and white apron tied at her waist. "*Buona notte, Lina.*"

"*Hai retornato,*" she smiles, marking my return. I begin to shrink, realizing an obligatory conversation in Italian is closing in on me. I have been listening to German for three weeks, and I'm having to work hard to wrap my head around Italian again. "*Si, va bene,*" I say smiling, making every attempt to converse, but her desire is much greater than mine, and for the next sixty seconds, I stand before her vocal machine gun as she hoses me with her story of the day. "*Oh, Lina, no capito,*" I reply, terribly frustrated that I cannot converse with this eighty-four-year-old fireball, but this doesn't stop Lina from trying, so I talk in spontaneous blurts, then I think about 'computer,' a universal word, that technological necessity that keeps us connected to friends back home and ask if she might have one, "*Hai il computer?*"

"*Computer? No, pero domando un computer di Carlo.*" *Oh no,* domando *sounds like she's going to demand a computer from someone.* We part with a *ciao,* both smiling as we walk in different directions, me piecing a story from a few familiar words, and Lina thinking about helping me find a computer.

"Mom, these two guys came in tonight and invited us to lunch tomorrow," Jenny says as she hands me a tray of candles she's gathered off tables. "Would you carry these in? Goffredo will tell you where they go, and then we've got to carry in the tables and chairs. We stack them in the back room."

"Okay, but who invited us to lunch?"

"I'll tell you when you come back out." I walk inside, focused on Goffredo. "*No, no,*" he says, hurrying to take the tray of candles from me.

"The mamma no work," he says in English with Italian sing-song rhythm.

"I want to help," I insist.

"Please," I say, knowing he would never understand my desire to, in some way, repay his family for helping us.

"Okay," he motions me to a table butted against one wall. "Make new," he instructs, taking a short butter-colored taper from its silver holder and replacing it with a long, slender new candle. He then holds up a half-used votive and says, "Is good."

"We're talking in English," I say, smiling at him. He looks at me with a smile that could melt a glacier. "You make the English for teach me."

"I'd love to teach you English." Looking into Goffredo's eyes is an ethereal experience. They're not brown, they're not blue, but an unusual combination of both. They are introspective and melancholy, giving them the ability to stir an onlooker's soul.

I stand with the candles, preparing them for tomorrow

night's diners, then return outside. "So, tell me about the lunch invitation."

"Mario and Andrea. Mario is seventy-two and Andrea is thirty-ish. Anyway, they work with volunteers to restore local landmarks," Jenny says, handing me a stack of folded linen cloths in an array of colors.

"What do I do with these?"

"They have to go into the laundry bag. If you'll put them on that table by the door, Luci (lu-chee) will get them to the bag. I guess the volunteers commit for a couple weeks at a time like Jake did in France and in trade for three meals a day and a place to stay, they work—. Hey, Jake, can you help?" Jenny interrupts as Jake strolls by.

"Sure." At this moment five-foot six-inch Luciano (Lu-chah-no) enters, moving like he's on rollers. He is in his 50s, round, bald, bulging eyes, always laughing and smiling, an artist, and a committed employee who speaks Italian and German. "Mom, you should see his art. It's wild. I love it. He paints on bottles, stones, pieces of wood, canvas, everything," Jenny says. "I hope he'll paint a bottle or something for me to take home. In that room you can see two of his framed paintings," she says, pointing into one of the two small dining rooms.

"I'll look later," I promise.

"Watch him sometime. Setting the table is art for him. He's very intent. The atmosphere is more important to him than the food." At this very moment, he calls Jenny and Renato to him, admonishing them for speaking English while at work. Renato, the handsome young Albanian, begins each evening standing shirtless in the kitchen delighting the middle-aged cooks with his carved abs and bulging muscles as he cuts bread for the evening. Luciano, who speaks no English, declares, "*No.*" With the typical Italian gesture of his cupped hand bouncing up and down in front of them he continues in Italian that they should go elsewhere if they want to speak English. The people come to Bolgheri for the Italian experience. "No the English."

"*Ah Luci,*" Renato answers. "Everyone, they love the English."

"*Basta!*" Luciano exclaims as his face reddens. At this moment Goffredo enters, and the color drains from Luci's face as quickly as it appeared. Cool, collected Goffredo must not know his right hand man has shown his temper. Jenny and Renato leave, whispering to each other. "He hates that he doesn't understand what we're saying," Jenny says.

"Yes, is jealous," Renato says proud of his English.

"So, Jenny, what are the volunteers repairing around here?" I ask, getting back to our invitation for lunch.

"I think he said some historic place where women used to gather to wash clothes, but we can get the lowdown at lunch tomorrow. Did I tell you Marco is coming tomorrow night?"

"Who?"

"Marco from Venice."

"Coming here?"

"Yeah. He called me and said he wanted to come visit. He's staying two nights."

"Where will he sleep?"

"There are two beds in Jake's room," she says, with a grin only the Cheshire cat would recognize. "Don't worry."

"You're kidding, right?"

"No, he called today. He's got a couple days off work."

"Is there something between you two?" I ask, feeling uncomfortable.

"No, Mom," she bursts out laughing. "The way you say things is a hoot."

"Well?"

"He's definitely interested, but I'm not." A separation anxiety grips me as I think of the possibility of her marrying an Italian and staying here forever. We've learned that it happens often. How I loved growing up a mile from my grandmother. Seeing her every week and spending the night with her was dear to me. I've always prayed that I would be fortunate enough to live near my grandchildren. "Don't worry, Mom, we're just friends," she interrupts.

"Friends? Now look who's naïve. Italian men don't do friends."

"Mom," Jenny laughs, hardly getting the word out.

"What?"

"You," she laughs. "Hey, Jake, you hungry? We can eat after we stack these tables."

"Eat? Sweet," Jake chimes.

"Yeah. The kitchen lets me eat the leftovers. Sometimes Goffredo will even sit and have a glass of wine with me."

"Sue Ellen," Goffredo motions to me with two wine glasses in one hand. "Please," he says, pulling a chair from the table closest to the door. "Jenny, Renato, and Luciano they work," he says, shaking his head with a stressed look on his face.

"Thank you, Goffredo," I say, sounding a bit like a schoolgirl in spite of my efforts. He uncorks the half-used bottle of local wine. Its luscious fruit entices me as he pours two glasses. "Mmmm," I say, inhaling deeply with my nose inside the glass. "How to say," Goffredo says, making a sweeping motion with his arm.

"It's the most famous of all Italian wines," Jenny fills in, as she sits with us.

"Sergio," Jenny enthusiastically greets the burly figure lumbering around the corner of the building. I look up to see a slightly smaller version of Hagrid, the loveable animal keeper from the *Harry Potter* series. "*Buona notte,*" he greets in a bold, raspy voice as he kisses Goffredo on both cheeks. Goffredo jumps to grab another chair so Sergio can join us.

"*Mi mamma,*" Jenny says, as I nod to this creature whose unnaturally thick, long, black, curly hair (cut in a mullet) spills over his massive biceps that erupt from beneath a black tee shirt with amputated sleeves. Sergio's deep, scratchy voice and thick accent hide the melody of his native Italian. He is the first large Italian I have seen. Stefi, from the kitchen, scurries out spilling Italian over him. "They're married," Jenny leans in and whispers in my ear. Stefi, whose short, black hair is hidden by her kitchen hat, keeps her lit cigarette's two-inch long ash intact as she rattles at her husband. She is all of five feet tall, and from what I see, a firecracker.

"*Mi angela*," Sergio croons into Stefi's eyes. "*Mi angela*." But his crooning did not change Stefi's tone of voice. I have no idea what she said to him, but it was fierce for a five-footer. Luciano continues his racing in and out, tending to everything that has already been tended to and hands Goffredo a wad of receipts from this evening's dinners. "*Mangio?*" Jenny says, asking Stefi if she can eat.

"*Si, si*," Stefi responds, never missing a word with Sergio. Jenny rushes into the kitchen and returns in a minute with two bowls. "Pure, unadulterated vegetables," she says. "These zucchini, onions, and yellow squash have never seen a pesticide (although they may have been sprinkled with Stefi's cigarette ash) and are seasoned only with fresh garlic and olive oil," Jenny announces, as she sets the white bowl on the table. Her left hand holds a larger, blue bowl of *cinghale* (wild boar), decorated with bay leaves and small berries. Jenny has piled three, square pieces of hard bread on top. "This is the finest food and wine in the world," she boasts as she sits next to me. Then, jumping back up, she adds, "Guess I better get you a plate."

"Where's Jake?" I ask of Jenny, as Sergio, Stefi, and Goffredo talk.

"He's over there talking to Oliver."

"Oliver, that cute guy who's always smiling?"

"Yeah."

"He has the prettiest smile I've seen on a guy, well except for ... "Josh" we both say thinking of our handsome friend back home. Stefi returns to the kitchen as Goffredo and Sergio exchange looks. Sergio leans his enormous frame back against the chair, stretches his four-foot-long legs out in front of him, and rests his head in his interlocked hands that are at the base of his skull. Between our bites of *cinghale* and sips of wine, Goffredo tells us that Sergio writes children's books. Sergio begins the story of his two books that have been published. Goffredo makes every attempt at translating for me, but soon asks for Jenny's help. "Sounds like one of his books is poetry for children, and the other one is about a forest that children go into," Jenny says. "That's what I understand. It's probably about the cypress-lined road. Mom, you should get out the children's books you've written. Maybe you and Sergio could corroborate on one. Take it international."

"Yeah," I smile, still absorbing the news that this mammoth before me writes children's poetry.

At 11:30 p.m., a tired Goffredo leaves. Luciano continues his busy-ness for another fifteen minutes, then locks the door. Jake, Jenny, and I sit alone on the porch under the heavenly scent of the overhanging orange tree. It is midnight and the Tuscan air casts a thin haze softening the twinkling palette overhead. "Do you eat this late every night?"

"Yeah," Jenny says.

"No wonder you can't lose any weight."

"No wonder I'm gaining."

"That's some good meat," Jake says, looking at the empty plate. "Beats tomatoes and bread."

"Look," I whisper, pointing in front of us.

"Fireflies," Jenny breathes, with the fascination of a child.

"When I was a kid, we called them lightning bugs. I loved catching them in jars, watching them flash, and then letting them escape. My Aunt Claudia told me she used to catch them, pull their wings off, put their lighted bodies on her fingers, and pretend they were diamond rings."

"Well, that was mean," Jenny blurts.

"Yeah, you should have seen me when she told me. I was a little kid probably six or seven. I looked at her a bit differently after that. I was shocked that she could be so cruel."

"Well, it doesn't take much to shock you, Mom," Jenny laughs.

"So what do we do now?" Jake asks.

"Go to bed," Jenny answers.

"Sounds good to me," I say.

"You mean you just eat, drink, and sleep here?" Jake asks, feeling a bit claustrophobic.

"Yeah, this is it. No transportation out of here or back in. I wish I had a scooter," Jenny muses.

"Don't you love the peace?" I say, closing my eyes and breathing deeply.

"Is there anything on TV?"

"Yeah, old 70s and 80s sitcoms, all in Italian."

"Maybe I'll go to Rome," Jake says.

"What do we do with these?" I ask, stacking the dishes.

"Take them home, rinse them, and return them tomorrow," Jenny answers.

"Okay, well let's go."

In Bolgheri, everything lies close together inside the protective wall, and noise reverberates off the buildings and into our open windows. Some nights punks ride through town on their mufflerless motorbikes at two and three a.m., then the day begins at sun up for the locals whom I hear talking on the street below. My bed sinks in the middle like a hammock, and it's easy to stay dozing until mid morning.

I leave Jake and Jenny sleeping and stroll into the countryside, thanking God for this opportunity. Along the path, butterflies flit through flowered vines and skinny lizards scurry under leaves. I stop on a five-foot-long bridge that crosses a creek bed and take a deep breath, filling my senses with nearby honeysuckle, moist woodsy smells, and the swirling dust created by a passing car. Place is powerful and setting seductive. Walking through this countryside, I realize that being in a different culture and land has unchained and loosed my perceptions. This summer I have come to understand my insignificance in the grand scheme of things. I've always seen myself as vital, necessary, meaningful. I now know that I'm no more than a speck of dust in the earth of humanity. It has been a humbling experience. As I recall the spectacular sights in nature I've seen this summer, the biblical story of Job comes to mind. Job's life was going along just fine. He was a good man. He was a rich man. Then *boom*, it all fell apart. His friends told him the turbulence that had rained down on him was because he had sinned and, in their opinion, God had actually been easy on him. Job can't accept his friends' feedback, so he goes to God asking for an explanation to why bad things happen to good people. God tells Job to consider the power and magnificence of nature, and that even though he may not understand, there is a divine plan. God tells Job that he may think things are out of step, but in the gargantuan scope of the universe, they are not. In 1739, Thomas Gray said of nature, "There are certain scenes that would awe an atheist into belief without the help of any other argument." Nature's grandeur is easy to forget when all we see daily are man-made towers and seas of concrete splashed with restaurants and gas stations. Now I understand why I once hiked two days carrying a forty-pound pack to get to a remote mountain lake in Idaho to experience the sublime, or why sitting at the sea, gazing over acres of sunflowers, or standing in awe of the Alps, helps me accept what sometimes my mind cannot organize. Nature is so much greater than I am, and I can rest knowing I'll someday return to dust and be a part of it. As I sit in the gnarled, twisted opening of my favorite olive tree, thinking about poor Job, I can enjoy my insignificance. What I've seen and experienced this summer, and the time I've spent reflecting, have given me a greater respect and honor for humankind.

Jenny wakes in time to spend her normal hour primping. "I'm sooo glad I'm naturally beautiful and don't have to spend hours each week painting my face," I tease. Jake wakes thirty minutes before our lunch date and shouts from the hall, "Jenny, I need the bathroom."

"Okay, Jake, five more minutes," she promises.

"Mah-ahm, Jenny won't share the bathroom."

"He had it last," comes from inside the bathroom.

"She's been in there all morning. Mah-ahm, I need to pee."

"I said, just a minute," Jenny giggles.

"Mah-ahm, it's not fair. Jenny gets the bathroom more than I do." And on it went. Music to my ears just like the good ole days when they were kids.

We walk together along the same path I walked this morning, except we take a left and continue toward a large house in the distance. We pass a small stone house covered in vines where white laundry hangs stretching across the front from one window to the next. Yellow, white, and red rose bushes, blue morning glories, and creamy white coreopsis cover this yard. The humidity in the air carries the soft fragrance of white roses that have taken charge of the iron arch over the front gate. "That's it," Jenny says, pointing up the hill to a large, dilapidated, salmon-colored, Tuscan stucco with two imposing plaques hanging on the side above a crack that meanders from the faded and chipped red tile roof to the foundation. Chunks of pale stucco have fallen away. "What do those plaques say?" I ask, walking closer. We three rest our heads on our shoulders in an effort to read the dripping words high above us. "It says something about the Duke giving this house to the community of Bolgheri, maybe," Jenny says. "We'll ask Mario." As we round the corner of the house, voices are hiding among the menagerie of clothes that hang on the makeshift line strung from a sprawling oak tree to a nail in the stucco just outside the door. Two girls jump from behind the clothes to greet us. Blond, blue-eyed, Skiaste (Sky-stee) greets us first and introduces us to Rose. I can't take my eyes off Skiaste, whose fair skin and rosy, round cheeks are irresistible. I'd love to jiggle those cheeks with a pinch like my daddy's cousin in Hope, Arkansas, used to do to me while saying, "Just love it, love it, love it." I was never quite sure if she loved my cheeks or just pinching them, but it made visits to her a bit painful.

"I'm Jake. Where do you live?" Jake asks, looking directly at angelic Skiaste.

"Lithuania," she says cheerfully.

"And you?" he asks of Rose.

"Croatia."

"Hi, I'm Jenny, and this is my mom, Sue Ellen."

"Come. Mario in here," Rose says, opening the weathered, screen door and inviting us in. My eyes survey the enormous room with its vast ceiling. The room limps forth and greets us with an eclectic array of items that are long overdue for retirement. An off-white refrigerator that has no door and stores non-perishable items stands immediately to our right. Next, and smaller in size, is a refrigerator from the 1960s covered with stickers in different languages. A wooden chair is wedged between the handle and the floor to keep the door closed. On the adjacent wall is a large, stone fireplace someone ruined with black paint. Its bare hearth spills onto the stained and peeling gray linoleum floor. A dark brown wood cabinet, with doors concealing its contents, stands to the right of the fireplace. Two closed doors are on the adjacent wall, and between the doors is a white metal sideboard stacked with a collector's dream spanning at least four generations of various flatware, dishes, glasses, and cups. The third wall shows blue and white rose wallpaper with remnants of gold outlining. A banana-shaped tear runs diagonally for eight feet. A white, rubber dish rack and three stained dishtowels rest on a five-foot-long, rectangular, wooden table that has at times been gray, green, and brown. Between this table and the white, 50s apartment-sized, gas stove, is a white, Formica-topped round table holding various cooking utensils. A long-handled spoon, one large cast-iron skillet, and a yellow fly swatter hang from a rack nailed to the wall. Beneath the rack on the stove are a large covered aluminum pot and a skillet leaking appetizing aromas. This wall ends and the porcelain sink begins. In its prime, it was white, but stains and streaks, nicks and dings sketch a picture of untold numbers of dishes, pots and pans, and who knows what else that have passed its way. A long narrow waterspout extends a foot from the back of the sink. To the left of the sink and connected to it is a grooved extension of porcelain just long enough to stack half a dozen plates. In the middle of the room sits the room's heart, a heavy wood dining table, large enough to easily seat fourteen. It has been thoughtfully set with eleven vinyl placemats of varying colors and patterns and a paper napkin and fork at each place. A stack of plates sits at the end of the table nearest the stove. Two bottles each of red and white wines grace the head of the table.

"*Buon giorno.* We are happy you come to eat. Welcome to our home," Mario says, motioning around the room. "Now we make introductions," he says. "So sorry, I forget your name."

"Sue Ellen, Jake, and Jenny," Jenny says, pointing to each of us.

"Yes, yes," he begins. "It is Sue Ellen, the mamma; Jacob, the brother; and Jenny of Texas. We begin with Peter," Mario says, looking at Peter standing next to him. "Peter is of Bolivia. He speak no English, yet, but his Italian is quite good. Skiaste. We name her Sky, of Lithuania. Rose, of Croatia; Andrea, my assistant, of Italy; Esteban, of Spain; Marta, of Poland; and uh, uh," he says, stumbling over the dark-skinned, Greek god of a young man.

"Art," the kids help.

"Yes," Mario says, walking to Art to make his amends by patting him on the back and giving him a hug around the shoulders. "Sorry, so sorry," he says, pointing to his forehead. "I am now old and forget," then pointing to himself, he announces, "I am Mario, of Umbria. Okay," he sighs, relieved of the introductions. "We introduce. Now we eat." We all exchange smiles and greetings as Mario takes a plate and proceeds to the stove to uncover the delights that have been prepared. We follow suit and find a place at the table. "A feast for the poor," Mario announces as he opens a bottle of red and one of white wine. On the table are a bowl of black olives, a bowl of cucumbers, tomatoes, and fresh basil, and a bowl of fruits including red grapes, tangerines, and apples. For the next hour, we sit answering questions about life in Texas, J. R. Ewing, and Dallas, both the TV version and the city. Mario tells us he is a retired history teacher who became involved in an international volunteer organization whose sole purpose is to restore historical sites around the world. "All money for our work is donation. We have large American donation from a man in Boston. You know of Boston?"

"Yes," we nod. As we ingest culinary art prepared by willing hands from around the world, Mario tells us of the fountains, monuments, and other sites in the region they have restored. "Go down the hill below the town and you see our work. It is five wash pits for women washing the clothes. These young ones," he says, sweeping his hand before him, "they are good workers."

"Uh, excuse me, but what is this?" Jake asks, pointing to the piece of food at the end of his fork.

"*Gnocchi* from potato," Sky answers.

"Potato. Hmmm. That's the difference. It's really good. It's like dumplings … sort of."

"It's divine," Jenny adds.

"Mmm," is all I can say enjoying the *gnocchi*. "The girls," Mario says, "are chefs."

"No, no," the girls protest and promptly announce that it was Mario who prepared the *gnocchi*. The language shifts to Italian as the girls insist he must not give them the credit. Switching back to English, Mario continues explaining that everyone takes a turn making meals and each usually prepares a traditional dish from his or her native land.

The eleven of us finish off the four bottles of vino, and Mario offers to pull another one, but more than satisfied, we all pass. "Now we need to cook for you," Jenny volunteers. "Some Texas food."

"Yes, yes," Mario says to a backup chorus of "yeses."

"Let's set the date," she says. Mario looks at his schedule and chooses August 12.

"Can we use your stove?" Jenny asks.

"*Si, si,* anything you use, *si.*"

"Have you ever had tacos? refried beans? tostados?" Jenny asks, explaining they need to experience Tex-Mex cuisine.

"Tex-Mex?" comes the reply from Sky.

"Yes. It's either steak grilled outside or Tex-Mex. Those are the foods of Texas."

"Okay, is good, the twelfth?" Mario asks, marking on his calendar.

"Yes, the twelfth is fine," we agree.

"Sky," Mario says, with a twinkle in his eyes. "Skiaste, you make tiramisu for us all?" he asks imploringly.

"Yes," they all chime.

"Sky's tiramisu is the best I ever eat," Mario continues, "and I live in Italy all my life."

"You will?" he asks her again.

"Yes," she answers, her turquoise eyes sparkling against her blushing face.

"But today we have chocolate," Mario announces as he motions to Peter to bring the chocolate bites to the table.

Marta and Skiaste begin clearing the table. Jenny and I rise to help and are practically beaten back by the guys at the table. "You are guest. You do not work," Mario says.

"We want to help. You prepared for us, so we help clean," Jenny objects. I hang back not wanting to show disrespect yet feeling the need to give these kids a break. "It seems unfair," I say.

"No, you are guest," Mario says again as he leads Jenny and me to a chart on the opposite wall. "Today is Marta and Skiaste. The next day is Peter and Art, then Andrea and Rose. It is here." I obediently sit down and listen to the two young girls who have joined Mario in assuring us it is not good for guests to work.

We stay until 3:00 p.m., when Mario decides the kids need to get back to work. "Can I go with you?" Jake asks.

"Yes, you go to watch, but you have no documents for insurance. *Si, si,* you come watch us," he says, motioning to Jake.

"I'll come see it soon," I promise.

"Yes, is good. The kids, they do good work. Hard work," he praises.

"Thank you all for inviting us. It was wonderful, and we look forward to the twelfth when we can cook for you."

"You'll love Tex-Mex," Jenny says.

"Texxx-Mexxx," they all say, tasting the words.

The next week we spend rounding up the necessary items for our Tex-Mex dinner. Italy has ground beef but no taco shells, tostadas, or tortillas to be found, so we make adjustments to the menu. We have to forget guacamole since we can't find an avocado and ... no sour cream. "So what will it be?"

"How can we have Mexican food without sour cream or guacamole? There's gotta be avocados in Italy," Jenny laments, unwilling to accept total defeat.

"Let's just do Mexican stack-up. We can surely find corn chips that will suffice, rice, beans, lettuce, onions, raisins, coconut, some kind of nuts, tomatoes, olives, and the ground beef. Italian cheese will be great on Mexican stack-ups. We just won't have taco seasoning for the meat. What's in that stuff anyway? Maybe we could make it."

"Make powdered taco seasoning?" I laugh. "I'd just mix garlic, salt and pepper, and if we knew what cumin was in Italian, we could add that."

"Maybe we should just do steak and potatoes," I suggest, noting Jenny's mounting frustration over the growing list of necessary but missing items.

"Tex-Mex will be much more fun. They've all had steak and potatoes. Let's buy paper plates, so we won't fight over who's to clean the dishes. What should we drink? Beer goes better with stack-ups than wine."

"Iced tea is easy."

"They don't sell bags of ice in Italy, remember? They only recently began refrigerating their beer."

"Okay, wine. Everyone likes wine. It just seems funny with Mexican food. We'll buy six bottles of La Taverna's house wine."

The morning of August 12th, we carry our sacks of ingredients to the big house on the hill. We make ourselves at home and begin our preparations. So enthused are we about introducing our new friends to Tex-Mex cuisine, that we chatter incessantly about how they will love the meal; it will be so different from anything they have ever had, that we will likely be asked to share more of our unique Texas dishes with them. I chop the tomato, onion, and pepper while Jenny stirs the meat and steams the rice. We neglected to search for pitted olives so find ourselves pitting them by hand. We use every bowl we can find, filling them each with a different ingredient and lining the center of the table with the bowls. At noon, the hungry workers walk through the door and note the aroma. "Oh, is good," Mario comments with a smile. The volunteers peer into the line of bowls on the table and comment to each other as the boys walk to the bathroom to wash their hands and Skiaste, Rose, and Marta wash up at the kitchen sink. They arrive at the table one by one and stand behind their respective chairs waiting until all are present. "Where is Jake?" Marta asks.

"He left a few days ago to travel," I say as I spoon the meat into a bowl and set it on the table. "Not enough to do here. Jake is looking for dancing."

"I will dance with Jake," Sky says. "I like the dance. And Marta," she says, pointing to Marta across the table, "she like the dance."

"I'm sure if Jake had known you girls like dancing, he would have stayed in Bolgheri," I say.

"Is the disco in Cecina every week," Rose adds.

"Do you know the Lindy hop or West Coast Swing? Those are Jake's dances."

"The … hope?" Sky hesitates, with a confused look on her face.

"Lindy hop."

"No," Sky says as all three girls shake their heads in bewilderment.

"Well, I'm not sure that 70s disco music would be the right background for Jake. Are we ready?" I ask.

"Yes," Mario answers, then adding, "You tell us what we eat?"

"Well, we had to make a few changes since we couldn't find sour cream, avocados, or tostadas, but we call this Mexican stack-ups," Jenny explains, amid several people attempting to pronounce "tostadas."

"What is the sor crem?" Sky hesitatingly asks.

341

"Do you know what cream is? The cream from milk?" Jenny asks, looking at me for help.

"It's heavy cream with a bacteria added to sour it, I think," I answer.

"Bock-tee-ree-a?" The boys chime, with disapproval on their faces.

"Well, we couldn't find it, so there is no sour cream," I say. "Anyway, you just put a little of everything on your plate and mix it all up like this," I say, loading my plate. "Help yourself. It's lots of fun." Jenny and I lead the way glowing like jack-o-lanterns over our creation as the others fall in behind us.

"Is all for antipasti?" Esteban asks, with a confused look on his face. "Mexican stack-up is antipasti, primo piatto, secondo piatto, si tutti," I announce that all courses are in one dish today. I scan the plates around the table and of the ten plates present, only Jenny and I had dared heap chips, rice, beans, meat, coconut, walnuts, onions, tomatoes, lettuce, black olives, cheese, and a spoonful of pico de gallo delighting our dull, over-stimulated American palates. Suddenly I experienced a sensation of malevolence. All these kids are innocent of our way of eating with its poor food combining and complicated recipes gastronomically confusing to the body. At this moment, I understand what enlightened, sophisticated, savoir-faire palates are represented, and we have taken them hostage; no, what we are doing to these poor unsuspecting yet trusting people is nothing short of raping their European gastronomie. Each person has chosen carefully and spooned just three items onto their plates. "All the flavors need to be mixed for Mexican stack-up. Just pile a little of everything on," Jenny says, encouraging our victims who have already shared unobtrusive glances of disbelief with each other. Mario was the only one brave enough to mix more than three ingredients. He was also the only one willing to comment. "Is very, very interesting. *Oliva con frutto di cocco* ... in English?" he asks, pointing to the white, flaky coconut he is chewing.

"Coconut," I answer.

"Yes, the olive and the coconut is interesting, very interesting. So many things in this recipe. Is of Mexico?" he asks.

I have to admit, "Well, parts of it may have originated in Mexico, but once it crossed the border into Texas, we Americanized it." The polite but unvoiced responses obliterate any hope we may have entertained that we might be invited to prepare another Texas meal. We have failed. The only bowls that are completely emptied held the tomatoes, cheese, and olives, and of course, all six wine bottles are dry. While Jenny attempts to explain how the avocado and sour cream would have tied this all together, I know her words have fallen on deaf ears. I'm not sure they have any idea what to do or say, so out of respect for us, they all thank us and make attempts at expressing how 'different' the meal was. Then Mario asks Skiaste to bring her homemade tiramisu to the table. The sagging faces lift like they have been made new by a plastic surgeon. Indeed, Sky saves the day, and to date, I've not eaten tiramisu that could delight my taste buds and satisfy my sweet tooth like hers did. When we asked for her recipe, she flashs those Slavic cheeks at us and says, "I just make. No recipe." Eat your heart out, Martha Stewart.

Chapter Twenty-four
A New Friend

Our outing in the sticky afternoon heat is interrupted by a brief shower forcing us to take shelter in a restaurant at the end of Bolgheri's single street. This *enoteca* has a wine tasting bar where ten dollars buys a taste of the famous local wines in pre-measured two-ounce shots that you serve yourself. We have ten dollars between us, so we share the shots and pretend we are wine critics boasting wine lingo we have learned while attending a monthly wine tasting group back home. "It's woody and acidic," Jenny says of the first taste.

"I think it's round."

"Round? We'll have to throw that one out at the next meeting."

"I don't know what it is. I'd like to create my own terms. Words that express how the wine feels and tastes to me. In spite of the expense, these don't tickle my tongue."

"How about catastrophic?"

"Claustrophobic."

"Claustrophobic? Mom!"

"Well, think about it. It could make you feel tight. If it's not huggy-wuggy, which is warm and free and happy, it could be claustrophobic."

"My mom, the wine linguist."

"Taste this one," I say, passing the glass to her. "It's diagonal."
She giggles and replies, "It's obstinate."

"Only in Italy could you find obstinate wine. Let's go."

As quickly as it came, the shower is chased away by the Tuscan sun in its golden splendor, and we continue wandering in luxurious idleness breathing in the post-rain scents. As we approach Nicole's jewelry store, familiar words float our direction. "American," Jenny whispers as we both turn toward the store whose door is propped open. An attractive woman in a blue, halter-top sundress stands before the mirror admiring a necklace of orbicular jasper that she holds around her neck. The woman turns toward us as she returns the necklace to its display. "Americans! Texans, I bet," she says as her face lights.

"Yes, how'd you know?" I ask.

"I grew up right next door in Louisiana. I can hear a Texan in a room full of people. Stephanie Zwack," she says, extending her hand to shake.

"Sue Ellen Haning, and my daughter Jenny," I say, smiling.

"What a beautiful daughter you have!" She exclaims, smiling at Jenny.

"Thank you," we both answer. Once again, I find myself embarrassed meeting a well-dressed, fellow American. Jenny's youth and beauty draw the attention away from the clothes she has washed by hand in sinks around Italy for the past two and a half months, but I, well, what youth and beauty I may have had flew the coop thirty years ago, and here I stand looking worn in more ways than one. "Why don't you two come sit and visit while I set up?" Jenny suggests. "It's five o'clock. I gotta get to work."

"Work? Where are you working?" Stephanie asks in surprise.

"At La Taverna."

"How?"

"Mom, will you tell her? I really need to go. It is nice meeting you," Jenny says with a wave as she skips up the street.

"The story is pretty amazing," I say with a grin. "Do you want to?"

"Sure. Let's go."

Stephanie is open and friendly, and being with someone from my culture and language is cozy. Both of us, happy to converse in our native tongue, waste no time in getting acquainted as we walk to La Taverna and settle ourselves comfortably under the orange tree and watch Jenny setting up for the evening's diners. "*Ah signora Zwack,*" Luciano says bowing to Stephanie, "*Buona notte. Lei piacere il vino?*" Luci's attention is securely on Stephanie.

"*Si, Luciano, vorremmo il vino,*" Stephanie says, informing him that we both would like a glass.

"*Con piacere,*" he replies with a slight bow, scurrying inside and returning with two stemmed glasses of house wine atop a serving tray. Either Luci is enamored, or Stephanie is a celebrity. We sit sipping wine and talking about every mother's delight, our children, amid the interruptions of locals spotting Stephanie and greeting her. "So how is it you come to Bolgheri each year?" I ask, responding to her comment that her family spends a week in Bolgheri every summer.

"Ah, my husband's family. Now that's a story," she says with a grin. "How much time do you have?" Eager to hear, I say, "As long as you have."

"Well, it all began two or three hundred years ago during a period of the Hapsburg dynasty. The Zwacks were physicians to the ruling class and—"

"Ma-ahm, Marco is here," Jenny calls from a distance. "Would you take him to the apartment so he can put his things away?" *Damn. Jenny's working, so I get to entertain muscle man.*

"Hi, Marco," I call as he and Jenny release from their embrace. "Stephanie, please stay here. I just need to show Marco where to put his things."

"Who is this hunk?" she whispers.

"I'll tell you later."

"You know, my kids are probably getting hungry. I'd better get back. It takes me fifteen minutes to walk home. Why don't you come up tomorrow afternoon and we'll visit some more?"

"Come where?"

"Follow the road to the right. It's at the top. You can't miss it. Peter and the kids are going to the beach. We'll sit in the shade and sip wine."

"Thanks, Stephanie. It's great to talk with you. I look forward to meeting the rest of your family. I'll be up first thing tomorrow afternoon. *Grazie, Luci,*" I say, waving to him as I walk toward Marco. "Okay, Marco, the apartment is around here. How are you?"

"I am well."

"I can't believe you came all the way across Italy."

"I have never visit Bolgheri," he says. "In the e-mail, Jenny write to me, she make me want to come to Bolgheri. It is ..." he hesitates, "do you say quaint?"

"Yes, Bolgheri is quaint," I agree as we climb the steps to the second floor.

"This is your room. Sorry you have to share with my son. Looks like that's the unused bed," I say, pointing across Jake's unmade bed to the bed nearest the window. As we walk to the bathroom, I break the news to him, "We have three towels, and we each use our towel for a week, then Goffredo takes them and brings us clean ones. Sorry, we have no extras."

"*Va bene,*" he says.

"So, have you eaten?"

"No."

"We can eat where Jenny works if you'd like." His entire face smiles as he says, "*Si, si* is good."

"I'll go find Jenny's brother. I'm sure he would love to join us. I'll meet you back at La Taverna. I guess we'd better ask Goffredo if he can spare a table."

"Is good," he says.

I find Jake in the last place I look. He is sitting outside at Enoteca di Elena practicing his Italian with a table of giggling girls. "Hey, Jake, wanna eat? We have company, and we're going to eat at La Taverna," I call.

"Okay, Mom." As I walk back up the street, happy chatter from every direction heralds the essence of Bolgheri—gaiety mingled with bliss. Lovers gaze into each other's eyes ensconced in a candle's glow. Children's laughter ripples through the street as families stroll or enjoy gelato while lounging on a park bench. Overhead, and not to be outdone, are the swallows engaged in their daily ritual of dancing into the sunset as they welcome evening's first stars and the glow in the atmosphere that the rays of the setting sun cast.

Goffredo has two unreserved tables tonight and Marco, Jake, and I sit sipping wine that Jenny brings us. Marco positions his chair so he is facing out and can keep his eye on Jenny as she floats from table to table serving this evening's diners. The stallionoid shows little interest in conversation with us, his dinner companions; rather his preferred activity is studying Jenny's every move with a dreamy look in his eyes and a delectatious smile on his face. When he is not in this dreamy state, he is hyper-vigilant. The first time we met Marco in Venice, his guardedness caught my attention. I inquire about his work and he wiggles uneasily. "I sell art by appointment." This is the exact answer he gave Jenny when they met that day in Venice, and as he did then, he stopped to look around.

"What kind of art?" I ask.

"Fine art," he answers, following Jenny with his eyes. *I know he's a Mafioso.* Luciano comes to our table and greets us with the complimentary sip of water he knows I'll ask for. It continues to amaze me how little water the Italians consume. If you want more than four ounces of water, you're out of luck unless you want to buy a bottle of the pure stuff.

We decide on crostini misti for antipasti ... a mixture of bite-sized pieces of toasted bread covered with either caramelized onions, bruschetta, or sautéed yellow squash. Twenty minutes later when it is served, we sit enjoying it—well, at least Jake and I do. I'm not sure Marco is in touch with his taste buds this evening. "Yum, this is great," Jake says.

"Mmm the onions are sweet enough to be dessert," I answer.

Marco stares, smiling at Jenny. He catches her eye and nods to her. She comes over and they exchange a few Italian sentences, then I hear Marco order *insalata caprese*. "Is good for you?" he asks. "You like?"

"Sure, I mean, yes, I like it." Red tomatoes, green basil, and white buffalo mozzarella balls. "The Italian flag!" I exclaim when Jenny sets the plate before us. "Guess what, Mom."

"What?"

"Goffredo asked me to sing at his wedding."

"Really! What an honor! When is it?"

"October 22."

"Are you staying for it?"

"Well, I want to, but I don't know. We'll talk later," she says, returning to work. I glance at my watch. It is 9:15. It has taken us an hour and fifteen minutes to order and eat *crostini misti* and *insalata caprese*, basically two appetizers! Americans are often frustrated with the lack of customer service in Italy, but what they do not understand is that Italians are not concerned with service as we know it. Here no one will bring the ticket in an effort to free your table. Their concern is their patrons' happiness, relaxation, and digestion—how long they linger with friends, how relaxed they are, and how many hours they take to eat. I love it.

After the *insalata caprese*, Jake requests *pappardella cinghiale* (wild boar with wide strips of pasta), and as if that isn't enough, Marco orders *fiorentina*, a thick, juicy steak that we all share. "Wish I could store this. I haven't seen this much food all summer," Jake muses. All evening, our conversation is staccato, and only the two bottles of red wine we consume provide melody to the evening. I find no subject that can hold Marco's attention more than a few sentences until we hit politics, which he brings to the table, and now he won't shut up. "Politicians, they are all bad," he emphasizes with a sweep of his hand. "Jenny, she is so beautiful," he adds. I am amazed that this macho man whose muscles bulge from his tee shirt and tight pants can vacillate between his helpless, dreamy look and his serious, business-like expression like the on and off of a light switch.

"I don't think we can say all politicians are bad," I say, not wanting to lump the bad and good together.

"Yes," Marco emphasizes. "All, they are crooked," he says with another sweep of his arm. "Not just in America, but in all the world."

"In Italy?" I question.

"Yes, in Italy, of course." Jake and I sit listening to this Italian rant about American politicians, amazed at how much he says and how little he actually knows. Our three-hour meal ends when, at 11:00 p.m., Jenny asks if we will help carry furniture in and put things away. The difference in Italian dining and American dining is as vast as the ocean that separates them. The dollar rules in America. Turn the tables as quickly as possible. Feed as many people as you can herd through the doors. Here reservations are expected. Goffredo knows he can feed only as many people as he can seat once, since they will, to his delight, linger all evening, and he will sleep well knowing his diners' experiences at La Taverna made them happy.

Jake and I walk home, leaving Jenny and Marco sitting on the park bench. "I'm not sure how much more peace and quiet I can take," Jake says as we climb the stairs.

"Yeah, I know what you mean. This would be the perfect place to write or paint or compose, but you definitely have to rely on yourself for entertainment."

"Can I leave some things here?"

"What do you mean?"

"I'm sure Jenny and Marco will go somewhere tomorrow, so I'm going to ride into Cecina with them. I'll catch the train to Rome. Everyone says I can't go home without seeing Rome."

"You don't have any money, Jake."

"I know."

"Oh, Jake, don't do this to yourself."

"Ma--ahm."

350

"Sure, leave what you want. When will you be back?"

"I don't know. When do we go home?"

"My ticket is for August 31, but I don't know about yours."

"It's probably the same."

"You'd better check. You bought your ticket after Jenny and I did."

"Okay."

"Jake, please keep in touch, and come back so I'll have someone to go with to Venice. Why don't you look at your ticket now, so you'll know the departure date."

"I don't know where it is."

"Okay, whatever."

The three of them leave at noon, and I begin walking to Stephanie's house. The winding, rocky, dirt road keeps its steady incline through nothing but olive trees. I see only one other house, then the ground levels, and ten-foot-tall brick posts mark the entrance to the property. I stop to survey my surroundings. The red-tiled roof and Tuscan-peach villa sit peaceful and stoic on the hill to my right. Fifty feet away on my left, a massive oak towers over a large wooden deck with built-in benches around its perimeter. I decide to visit the deck first. I've never been in the presence of a sprawling oak the size of this one. What I don't see until I step upon the deck are the miles of vineyards in perfectly straight rows emptying into the sea, which sparkle like acres of diamonds under the Tuscan sun. I stand in the midst of picture perfectness with a gentle breeze as my companion, and I have a sudden desire to paint this scene. Moved by what I see, I believe I can put it on paper as well as any artist.

My moment with nature is interrupted by animal sounds and turning I see Stephanie walking through a gate at the side of the house. I jump from the deck and walk in that direction to see a donkey and two sheep, and hear the honking of a goose. "Hi, Stephanie," I call, picking up my pace. "Steph-a-nie."

"Sue Ellen," she answers.

"Is this your farm yard?" I ask as my senses come in contact with the muck. "Good golly, what a pig! That's the biggest pig I've ever seen."

"Come here, Millie, and meet Sue Ellen," Stephanie says as the pig saunters over to her.

"Gee, she gives new meaning to the word pig. Is she a special breed?"

"Just a pig. Lucy is the goose, Arturo, the donkey, and the sheep are Daisy and Snowball," she says, pointing to two hefty sheep. "You'd never know at one time they were a light cream color."

"How fun. Your own petting zoo."

"Where are you Tse-Tsa?" she calls. "Tse-Tsa. Oh, there you are," Stephanie says extending her left arm to the blue and gold macaw that climbs up to sit on her shoulder. "My youngest named her."

"Do they like strangers?" I ask, extending my hand to touch Arturo's fur.

"They like most people. They're animals, they know when danger is present."

"This is all so beautiful," I say, looking around.

"It's home. Come on. I'll show you the house." I follow her under the vine-covered pergola that shades a fourteen-foot pine table. Two metal folding chairs, six lawn chairs, and at the head of the table, a massive, wood, high-backed, thick-armed chair fit for a king surround the table. A tremendous, tarnished, silver candelabra with cream-colored taper candles of various lengths rises from the table. "This house was built somewhere in the early 1800s, so it's not old by European standards," Stephanie begins as she opens the screen door and invites me into the entry. "Really, it's nothing grand. Everyone in Peter's family including the 'steps' and other extensions of the family and friends come and go all year, so there's a little of everything in here."

"It looks grand to me," I say, eyeing the spacious downstairs furnished with well-used sofas and chairs. The rooms open into each other gracefully and generously, and then we enter the kitchen. Another long, rectangular table, seemingly custom made for the space, sits just under multi-paned windows that command one wall. "Where do you get such long tables?" I ask.

"I think Ann had these made in Florence."

"Ann?"

"She is Peter's mother, well, stepmother." The room's perimeter displays spacious countertops (covered in tiny blood-red tiles) and long, hung cabinets whose surfaces are well worn. The room is grand for sure, but it is the contents of the ceiling that most fascinate me. "Wow," I say admiring the enormous metal rack positioned in the ceiling's center. A dozen or so cooking utensils hang from it. I walk in a circle admiring the pots, pans, baskets, ladles, tongs, whisks, and other kitchen paraphernalia. "There have been some fun times here," I say, smiling as I imagine the entertainment a large family of cooks has had in this room. Positioned diagonally and closer to the windows hangs a dark cradle. "What is the significance of the cradle?" I ask, thinking most cradles are stuck in a corner with a doll in them or packed away in the attic, not hung from the kitchen ceiling.

"It came from Kosovo. Peter was stationed there for a time and thought it would be a great gift for his sister's new baby. Yeah, many batches of pasta have been hand-rolled, cut, and cooked here," she says, changing the subject.

"I am so deprived," I comment with a sigh.

"What?" Stephanie asks, half laughing.

"I've always dreamed of being in a big family that gathers regularly. I mean really big like fifty people at once."

"Fifty? If fifty is all that showed up, we'd feel deprived," she laughs.

"Really? Wow. My mother's family all lived in different states, and I think everyone was too poor to make trips across the country regularly. I have no idea where the cousins on my mother's side are now or if they are still living. I keep in touch with the two on my dad's side, but we don't see each other much."

"Gee," Stephanie says with a distant look that tells me she is trying to imagine this scenario as I try to imagine cooking for a hundred people.

"Let's go up, but let me warn you it's a mess." We climb the sinking stone steps that carve a path through a maze of art hanging among photographs on either side of the stairs. "Can you tell me about these pictures? Who are these people?"

"Well, the art work has collected over the years. Nothing famous, just what someone wanted at the time, and here is the Peter Zwack who began the liquor business and," her voice drops off as she thinks, then she adds, "heck, I can't remember everyone's name. There are too many, but here's my family."

"You have a handsome family. Peter is a good looking guy," I comment, looking at the picture of her husband in his military uniform. The artwork and photos continue across the walls upstairs and into the bathroom. "God, this is embarrassing," Stephanie says, eyeing the clothes on the floor.

"Looks lived in to me."

"Karina keeps the downstairs picked up, but she's too busy socializing to clean the entire house."

"Who's Karina?"

"The Zwack's Hungarian maid who goes everywhere with them. She's like another daughter. She really doesn't do much, but we all love her. She's probably in town now. Speaking of in town, who is that hunk who came to visit your daughter?"

"Oh, he's some guy we met in Venice the day after we arrived."

"Well, I'd say he is sure interested in Jenny."

"Yeah, but she says she's not much interested in him."

"Sure," Stephanie's voice trails off.

"Let's go outside and sit in the shade," she says, starting back down the stairs and heading to the kitchen. "Do you like red or white?"

"Red."

"Okay," and she hands me two wine glasses. "I like white, so we'll get two bottles."

For the next three hours we sit at one end of the massive outdoor table enjoying the shady overhang exchanging stories. Hers are by far the more interesting, about how the drink Zwack Unicum was born via the Zwack physicians mixing together forty herbs and concocting the famous brew that magically cured the ills of the Hapsburg kings and queens making them healthy and happy—so much so that they asked for their medicine every day. Stephanie is quite animated, and my laughter must have fueled her storytelling, for she entertained me with anecdotes all afternoon.

"Unicum is very popular here, but I don't know how anyone drinks it. Goffredo gave me a taste one night. No offense, but it's like drinking Valvoline!" I say as we erupt into laughter both feeling our wine.

"It's a man's drink."

"I was shocked at how thick it was or at least that's how it felt in my mouth," I confess.

"It's very popular in Europe, and Peter says after he retires from the Army, he's going to get it going in North America." At this moment, a Volvo station wagon swerves up the road and onto the grass as "faster, Daddy, faster," spills out the windows.

"Next time, next time," a tall, blond man says, jumping out and opening the back door. Four children emerge from the car and the three youngest grab an arm or leg, insisting on keeping their father engaged in play. He tosses, tickles, or wrestles them for another minute then as surely as they knew he would, he says, "No more, *finito*, go play," and without a challenge, they pull their plastic water guns from the back of the car and run to the hose lying in the yard.

"Whew," he sighs, putting his hands on Stephanie's shoulders and giving her a little squeeze.

"Sue Ellen, this is my husband, Peter. Sue Ellen and her daughter are backpacking through Italy and have settled in Bolgheri a while."

"Welcome, it's nice to meet you. Please excuse me. I have to hit the shower."

"How was it?" Stephanie asks.

"Great. The water is perfect today. The kids ... well they're like their mother ... creative ... always into something," he says with a wink, as he opens the front door. "See you ladies in a minute."

I stay longer than I think polite, enjoying their company, then beg their forgiveness for taking the entire afternoon. "No problem. Bring Jenny up sometime. We'll be here until Friday, right dear?" Stephanie asks of a nodding Peter.

"Ok. I'd love for her to see everything, and the view is spectacular from that deck. Wow. What a place to sit and think, or write, or meditate—"

"Or nap," Peter adds.

"Well, I better go," I say, rising to leave. "Thanks for everything. It is great to meet you and to see this wonderful vacation spot."

"Come again, and bring Jenny."

"Okay, see you soon," I say, waving as I cross the yard.

"Later," Stephanie says as she turns to Peter. I look back again to see them in a lock-down kiss that any sixteen-year-old would envy.

Chapter Twenty-five

Reality

We three make a trip into Cecina to thank the D'Andrea family for their kindness and generosity toward us. Each responds as if this generosity were nothing special, and they humbly accept our thanks. This family is the epitome of beneficence and brotherly love, and we are blessed to have met them.

Leaving my youngest to live on another continent is something I never considered having to do, and all the internal adjustments I thought I had made this summer do not prepare me for this moment. Jenny and I wipe the tears from our eyes, and I hold her so tightly I don't even realize I am cutting off circulation. "Mom, I can't breathe," she says, forcing me to release my grip.

"I can't either, but it's not from hugging," I say. "I'd better go before 'mother mode' kicks in and I can't."

"Oh, Mom."

"Will you come home after you sing in Goffredo's wedding?" I plead.

"I don't know, Mom, you know I want to stay if I can. We'll see." I look into her smile for the last time, choking on my tears and trying to breathe again, as she hugs her brother good-bye. We step into the train. "This is so hard, Jake," I say as we toss our packs overhead. "Do you remember when you moved out and went to Austin?" I ask feeling the need to keep myself busy talking. "That was hard enough. At least Jarrod just moved across town when he left, but Jenny is staying in Italy," I say fighting the tears. "I may never see her again."

"You'll see her again."

"You don't un...," I stop, realizing that of course he doesn't understand. He's not a mother. My mind races, like a car's engine whose accelerator is stuck, keeping me occupied with devastating thoughts while I attempt to pull myself together.

Jake and I spend the last ten days of our summer as tourists visiting Rome, Naples, Pompeii, Ischia, and Assisi. Travel with Jake is much quieter than travel with Jenny, and this is an adjustment for me. Jake doesn't want to talk about everything we see, what we are about to see, or what we missed seeing, as Jenny and I do, but neither is he opposed to sleeping in a hotel like she is. It isn't an adventure. We are simply sightseeing.

From Assisi we make our way back to Venice for our return flight. Our first hosts when we arrived in May, Nic and Christina, are also our last. The summer did not dampen Nic's passion for English, and he keeps us laughing all night making me wish I had the gusto for learning Italian that he has for English. Not wanting to arrive at their house hungry, we eat before we get there at 7:00 p.m., but Nic will not hear of our having already eaten. "Mi mamma, she want eat with you," he says. "She come here to dinner. Is good? My English?"

"Your English is wonderful," I assure him as he displays a smile the length of the Nile. His mother arrives at 9:00, and after introductions, we sit to a delicious dinner of pasta with cooked zucchini, hard bread, a green salad of fresh cucumbers, tomatoes, and arugula, and for dessert, Christina's tiramisu. With a sigh and an inward twinge, my heart sags, sad that we probably will never see them again. We say good-bye to Nic as he drops us at the airport on his way to work the following morning, August 31.

Once again, we give kudos to British Airways. My return flight was August 31. Jake's was August 30, but British Air gives him a seat on my flight with no extra charge for his mistake of arriving a day late. I stand looking in disbelief at the BA clerk. Jake has an e-ticket that is non-transferable, non-refundable, and whatever other restrictions are placed on those types of tickets, and the British Air clerk quickly and easily changes him to my flight. We can't grumble when our flight from Venice to London is three hours late due to mechanical problems thus assuring that we will miss our connecting British Air flight to Houston. With non-stop apologies for the inconveniences, British Airways accommodates us all in a hotel (attached to Gatwick Airport), complete with dinner and breakfast. Since we miss our connecting flight, we are re-routed via American Airlines to Dallas.

While gazing out the window at the clouds below, I sit contemplating what I have experienced these three months in Italy. The choice of American reality shows or the 1988 Auburn vs. LSU football game could not hold my attention after three months of not knowing where I would be sleeping; of learning to let go; of experiencing life outside my comfort zone; of practicing slowing down; of discovering the gift of travel; of enjoying the company of strangers; and of realizing I have reached the time in my life when I must reinvent myself. Reinventing me could prove to be the greatest of all adventures, but I don't dwell on this upcoming adventure due to the discomfort it causes me, so I lose myself reliving the summer's scenes as they float through my mind. I think about the importance the message, taken from Wayne Dyer's book, that I wrote on the little yellow card, has played in my ability to stretch myself for extended periods of time.

Good morning, this is God.
I will be handling ALL of your problems today.
I will not need your help, so have a
MIRACULOUS day!

"Mom."

"What?"

"Do you want to go home?"

"No."

"Me either." I look at Jake, and I can see my thoughts in his eyes, and we both wonder why we have boarded the plane. We are not ready to return to reality. Travel writer Bill Bryson says, "Coming back to your native land after an absence of many years is a surprising, unsettling business, a little like waking from a long coma. It is disconcerting to find yourself so simultaneously in your element and out of it." We experience this after only three months in another land. I can't imagine returning after "many years." We have been in an Italian coma...the best kind. When the plane touches the ground and taxies to the terminal, I have to laugh at the thought of again seeing my friends who, three months ago, thought I was nuts.

The scenery hits me first. The Dallas/Ft. Worth airport erupts in overweight, jean-clad Americans. The lights of chain restaurants blind us. The people around them are like horses pawing the ground, tense and anxious. Since May, I have not seen a retail chain or flashing lights. Standing here, I realize this is who I am. I am overweight, wear jeans, and am a slave to schedules and habits. My eyes soak in familiarity, but my spirit is violated. I stand trying to recapture my mind when I hear, "This is not what I ordered," barks a woman at the counter. These words and the tone behind them shock me. I recall the night a bird pooped on a freshly cleaned and pressed linen tablecloth while we were setting up tables, and Luciano whisked it away with a smile on his face, saying it was a sign the night would be a good one. When someone broke a wine glass, it was a sign of good fortune. I swallow the lump in my throat realizing what I just witnessed in my culture and the thought that instantly followed it.

I understand that different is not always better, but differences open eyes. I am seeing things differently. In Italy I came in contact with the far side of me. My spirit experienced a rebirth, and I learned to let it soar. I unearthed my passion and decided to let it live. I have spent three months in a country whose people see pasta, wine, and lovemaking as more important than money, time, and schedules. Getting directions from Italians is often a disaster. Who cares if you turn right or left? There's good wine in either direction. Hurry? What's that? Sure I can get somewhere fast, but what have I seen or experienced in my haste? What might I have experienced during my life if I had actually been present instead of pressed? The hustle and bustle and demands on time, the grasping at life, and the ocean of choices challenge the inner calm I have come to know. *Reality! No! Where's my fairy godmother to take me away?* My stomach drops to my knees, and a sour taste fills my mouth. The realization that I have left Jenny in Italy hits me. The yearning in me could move a wall, and I want to get back on the plane, but the gate is locked. Suddenly, everything tumbles down on me. My chest tightens and a panic swells in me. Jenny is across the Atlantic Ocean, and I stand here as a tsunami of flashbacks, fears, and facts floods me. I stand in the midst of who I was before May 25, and now I'm thinking, "Who are these people?" Can I reach out and accept others' differences? Can I be compassionately concerned about them? Curious? Interested? Can I break the barriers created by old prejudice, fear, doubt, and ignorance? Can I open my home to strangers? Or will I fall prey to the old habits and ways? Has this all been a dream and I'll wake to reality, like fairy tale characters, who live in a fantasy as the white knight sweeps them off their feet, but they soon wake up to his dirty socks on the floor and his day-to-day demands? We went with no idea what to expect. We were "nuts" with no plans, and because we had no plans, I moved so far away from my comfort zone that it's hard for me to believe. I spent nights with people, things, and in places I would have never before considered, even asking strangers to dine with me. In my country, I wouldn't ask a stranger if I could stay with them or walk into a hotel and ask for a job in trade for a room. Why is it easier to ask a total stranger for help? I stand trying to process what is whirling around me and realize my thinking has mutated several times this summer. Must it change again? While becoming more aware of the preciousness of each moment, my eyes were also opened to the larger scheme of things. I am a mere drop in the huge ocean of humanity, and instead of feeling lost, I feel more connected to my fellow man. Something touching my arm jerks me back to reality. "Come on, Mom. We're home," Jake says.

"Yeah, the real world," I say not moving.

"You okay, Mom?"

"I guess," I answer failing in my attempt to return to reality as my ruminations dominate. I've learned that if you seek involvement in another culture, the more money you spend, the farther away you get from the culture you are seeking to experience. Hotels, fine dining, and comfort separate a traveler from the day-to-day lives that comprise a culture. It's amazing to think that this trip was born of our 1998 two-week-trip to Germany, Austria, Switzerland, and Italy. In our haste to see four countries and as many sights as possible, we rushed from place to place, and our hurriedness left us not happier, wiser, or more receptive, just hurried; but as Italy breezed past us, Jenny knew she wanted more of it, and she hung on to her dream to return. How happy I am that she invited me to share a summer of nutty adventures that turned out to be life-changing experiences for me! Once I realized I could do things that at first made me very uncomfortable, a whole new world opened. It is true that travel to other cultures teaches us things we cannot learn any other way, and what we learn through travel continues enriching us for the rest of our lives.

I hope you have dreamed, if just for a moment, of chucking life's encumbrances and wandering free through the mystery and magic of something not just different but foreign, foreign to you in some way. It doesn't have to be visiting another country. It could be studying a different language, singing or speaking in public, volunteering, taking a job in a completely different field, or even inviting strangers into your home. I did not know how much more there was, until I experienced the sweet rush that life outside my day-to-day rut gave me. I challenge you to get outside your comfort zone, and I promise you'll love the experience of a new dimension to your life. I have recorded my experiences in this book, hoping to make you smile and encourage you to do something 'nuts' living at the heart of your life...delighting in every minute.

Epilogue

Fortunately a book doesn't always end with the final page. After a three-month stay at home, I returned to Italy for the three winter months to enjoy more spontaneous adventures with Jenny who stayed in Tuscany and worked for two years. Since my Italian experience, I'm a different person and continue exploring new endeavors that take me away from what I used to call comfort. I see opportunities now and open myself to them with a willingness to do things my pre-Italy self could not have done. I've learned to eat fire, ride a horse, and weld. At age sixty, I can't wait for the next sixty years! My next book could be: *One Nut's Journey Into Geriatrics!*

CPSIA information can be obtained at www.ICGtesting.com
Printed in the USA
267942BV00001B/26/P